PG 485

# TELEVISION
*in the lives of our*
## CHILDREN

# TELEVISION

*in the lives of our*

# CHILDREN

WILBUR SCHRAMM · JACK LYLE · EDWIN B. PARKER

*with a psychiatrist's comment on the effects of television*
*by* LAWRENCE Z. FREEDMAN, M.D.

*Stanford, California*
STANFORD UNIVERSITY PRESS
*1961*

STANFORD UNIVERSITY PRESS
STANFORD, CALIFORNIA
LONDON: OXFORD UNIVERSITY PRESS
TORONTO: UNIVERSITY OF TORONTO PRESS

LIBRARY OF CONGRESS CATALOG CARD NUMBER: 61-6533

PRINTED IN THE UNITED STATES OF AMERICA

First published, April 1961
Second printing, July 1961

# PREFACE

This book represents three years of research and analysis in ten communities in the United States and Canada.

Perhaps the study most nearly comparable to it is the excellent and important volume *Television and the Child* by Himmelweit, Oppenheim, and Vince, recently published in the United Kingdom. Their book is the first full-length study of the impact of television on English children; ours is the first full-length study of television and North American children.

This is not to imply that the studies are alike. Indeed, they are quite different, although there is an encouraging correspondence in results when they can be compared. But British television and English culture are not identical with American television or North American culture. Furthermore, the earlier study did not become available in time for the present study to repeat some of its questions so as to arrive at closer comparisons. Therefore, the studies are different in raw material, concept, and plan.

In one way especially this study was unlike the English study. Himmelweit, Oppenheim, and Vince knew in advance the amount of their support, and could therefore plan the entire study before they gathered any data. Our study, however, began as a study of the use of television by children in the first six grades of the San Francisco school system. The results there proved to be so interesting that we were able to get additional money to carry the investigation through the twelfth grade in San Francisco, and later into five Rocky Mountain communities where conditions contrasted considerably with any previous studies of this kind. From another source we got money to interview 188 entire families—as families—which was a very interesting experience for them and for us, and probably the first time that any researchers had ever explored in such detail the relation of television to family life and values. When it became apparent that we could not find a suitable control town in the United States where few or no children would have been exposed to television, we went to Canada and studied two very interesting communities in the same culture area, one of which did not yet have television whereas the other had a great deal of television. While this material was in the stage of analysis, we accepted the invitation of a metropolitan suburban city to come in and study in detail some of the television behavior of their young children. And finally we went to Denver to check one of our most important hypotheses on a sample of high school students.

This is not an uncommon history of research, especially when projects are not richly financed. As we went along, we improved our methods and our instruments, sharpened our hypotheses, checked our San Francisco metropolitan findings against our Rocky Mountain findings, our United States findings against our Canadian results, and so forth. But we should be less than honest if we did not admit that there were times when we wished, late in the study, that we had known from the first how far we were going to be able to carry it. If we had been able to plan from the first for the entire study, we should have made some plans differently. If this was sometimes a matter for regret, on the other hand it was highly satisfying to us that our first results should prove as useful as they did, and that the methods and hypotheses with which we began should stand up as well as they did. And we were pleased to be able to gather as much and as varied information as we did on an expenditure which, as research money goes, must be counted a shoestring.

We could not have done so without the generous, wholehearted, and interested cooperation of three groups of persons. One of these groups was the 6,000 children and the 2,000 parents, who gathered information and kept records for us and submitted to our tests and our questioning. A second group was the more than 300 teachers and school officials in ten communities who cooperated so fully with us. With the exception of San Francisco and Denver, we cannot name them here, because we have promised not to identify the communities. And it would be unfair to name the San Francisco and Denver people without naming the others. But if we could, we should print all their names and all their cities here in gold, because their cooperativeness, their quick understanding of what we were seeking, and their skill were all that made it possible for us to turn a few thousand dollars into many thousands of interviews.

In the third place, we are deeply grateful to the National Educational Television and Radio Center, which was the chief financer of this study, and which one year gave us a large fraction of its meager research budget so that we could go on with the study. The officials of this organization were generous not only with funds but also with their highly informed advice and counsel when we sought it. Moreover, they restricted in no way what we did, and sought to influence in not even the slightest way our conclusions.

Several donors to this study wish to remain anonymous, but we must mention the Institute for Communication Research, at Stanford, to which we belong, which supported us with money, facilities, personnel time, and advice. We should also mention the Center for Advanced Study in the Behavioral Sciences, which, by giving a Fellowship to the senior author, provided precious time for analysis and writing.

The people who have advised us are very many. Among them we must mention Hilde Himmelweit, of the University of London; Robert Silvey, of the British Broadcasting Corporation; Neil Morrison and Kenneth Adler, of the Canadian Broadcasting Corporation; Eleanor Maccoby, Nathan Maccoby, Robert R. Sears, and Richard F. Carter, of Stanford; Paul Lazarsfeld, of Columbia; Ithiel Pool, of the Massachusetts Institute of Technology; John and Matilda Riley, of Rutgers; William Kessen, of Yale; Lawrence Z. Freedman, formerly of Yale, now of the Center for Advanced Studies in the Behavioral Sciences, who contributed the excellent memorandum on a psychiatrist's view of television effect; William H. Sewell, of Wisconsin; Paul Deutschmann, of Michigan State; Fritz Redl, of Wayne; Theodore Newcomb, of Michigan; Robert B. Hudson, Ryland Crary, and President John White, of the National Educational Television and Radio Center; these and others, all of whom are blameless for the deficiencies of this work, but each of whom has talked over parts of it with us and contributed from his wisdom and experience.

We should also like to mention the names of the persons who, at various times during the study, served as editors, coders, IBM operators, data analysts, and typists. These are: Barbara Bachman, Stephen Baffrey, Jon Barker, Mimi Cutler, Margery Deutschmann, Douglas A. Fuchs, Edna Garfinkle, Jon Gilmore, Selma Greenberg, Ralph Haber, Joan Hoffman, Geraldine S. Jenkins, Gloria R. Jensen, Jonathan P. Lane, Suzanne Mason, Linda Miller, Ronald Rapaport, Galen Rarick, Dexter Roberts, Susan Roberts, Frederick Shoup, Christopher C. Smith, Carolyn Tucker, Robert J. Umphress, Thuan van Nguyen, and Jon W. Wilcox.

Finally, we owe a deep and special debt of gratitude to two of our colleagues at Stanford, Eleanor Maccoby and Richard F. Carter, who gave thoughtful and painstaking readings to this entire manuscript in its penultimate stage. Their penetrating criticisms and suggestions are reflected on many pages of this book.

WILBUR SCHRAMM
JACK LYLE
EDWIN B. PARKER

*Stanford, 1960*

# CONTENTS

TELEVISION
*in the lives of our*
CHILDREN

# CHAPTER 1

# INTRODUCTION

No informed person can say simply that television is bad or that it is good for children.

For *some* children, under *some* conditions, *some* television is harmful. For *other* children under the same conditions, or for the same children under *other* conditions, it may be beneficial. For *most* children, under *most* conditions, *most* television is probably neither particularly harmful nor particularly beneficial.

This may seem unduly cautious, or full of weasel words, or, perhaps, academic gobbledygook to cover up something inherently simple. But the topic we are dealing with in this book is not simple. We wish it were. We wish it were possible to say simply that television has such and such an effect on children, and therefore that this kind of television is bad, this kind is good. Unfortunately, it just does not work that way. Effects are not that simple.

When we say something about the effect of television on children, we are really making a double-edged statement. That is, we are saying something about television and something about children. For example, if we say that a television program is "interesting," we are saying that the program has a certain quality to which certain children respond in a certain way we call "interest." If we say that a program is "frightening," we are saying that the program has certain qualities to which children react in a certain other way.

In a sense the term "effect" is misleading because it suggests that television "does something" to children. The connotation is that television is the actor; the children are acted upon. Children are thus made to seem relatively inert; television, relatively active. Children are sitting victims; television bites them.

Nothing can be further from the fact.

It is the children who are most active in this relationship. It is they who use television, rather than television that uses them.

As between two favorite images of the situation—the image of children as helpless victims to be attacked by television, and the image of

television as a great and shiny cafeteria from which children select
what they want at the moment—the latter is the more nearly accurate.
It is true that the menu of this cafeteria is heavy in fantasy, that it contains a high proportion of violent dishes, and that there is less variety
available at any given time than some patrons might wish. But the cafeteria sets the food out; the children take what they want and eat it. The
very nature of television makes for a minimum of variety in the cafeteria; the nature of human beings makes for great variety on the side
of the children.

What television is bringing to children, as we shall show, is not
essentially different from what radio and movies brought them; but what
children bring to television and the other mass media is infinitely varied.

So when we talk about the effect of television, we are really talking
about how children use television. A child comes to television seeking
to satisfy some need. He finds something there, and uses it. The following pages of this book testify that children use the same television in
different ways. But some increment of this choice enters into their
funded experience, and ultimately into their understandings, values, and
behaviors. Under certain conditions the choice may thus contribute to
crime, violence, or lax morality; under others, to a better understanding
of adult life and democratic values; under still others, to none of these.
Therefore, in trying to understand the effect of television we have to
try to understand the conditions of effect.

To understand the conditions of effect, we have to understand a great
deal about the lives of children. Something in their lives makes them
reach out for a particular experience on television. This experience then
enters into their lives, and has to make its way amidst the stored experience, the codified values, the social relationships, and the immediately
urgent needs that are already a part of those lives. As a result, something happens to the original experience. Something is discarded, something is stored away, perhaps some overt behavior occurs. This is the
"effect of television." What we are really trying to understand, then, is
the part which the television experience plays in the lives of children.

### The critics and the scholars

In the last ten years, two groups of writers have addressed themselves to this problem.

One group—much the larger group—has written as critics. In many
cases they have written with extraordinary heat, for few things in our
culture generate as much difference of opinion as television, and nothing so exercises us as the thought that someone may be harming our
children. Because there has been an impressive lack of agreement in

this debate, and comparatively few facts to prove any of the points, the effect has been not so much to prove charges as to raise a series of disturbing questions.

*Does television deepen the ignorance or broaden the knowledge of children?* As Charles Siepmann puts the question [88, p. 2],* is it an "opiate of the masses, or a formative influence of high cultural importance"? On the one hand, there has been the hope that television would be an educator in every home, would open the far places of the world and carry great events, ideas, and men to children. On the other hand, it has been invariably reported that the poorest students in school are the heaviest users of television (this, of course, does not prove that television is the cause of their poor performance in school). Paul Witty reported [2, p. 256] in 1954 that television reduced children's reading, but was less sure of it in 1959 [45]. Remmers reported on the basis of a survey of teen-age opinion that two out of five teen-agers felt that television interferes with their schoolwork "somewhat" or "very much" [2, p. 258]. There is no doubt that children learn from television, but do they learn more from it than they would learn without it? Is it contributing to a more ignorant or a better informed generation? Or are there some kinds of children to whom it is an intellectual help, others to whom it is a hindrance?

*Does television debase the tastes of children?* Here the case has been stated mostly by intellectuals. Arthur Schlesinger, Jr., has written of television's "downward spiral of competitive debasement" [68, p. 394]. Louis II. Cohen says that many programs on television "encourage a degraded taste for a kind of knowledge which is unnecessary for healthy social life" [2, p. 259]. Thomas Griffith of *Time* writes of "The Waist-High Culture" and asks whether we haven't sold our souls "for a mess of pottage that goes snap, crackle, and pop." Television producer David Susskind told *Life*: "I'm an intellectual who cares about television. There are some good things in it, tiny atolls in the oceans of junk . . . I'm mad at TV because I really love it and it's lousy. It's a very beautiful woman who looks abominable. The only way to fix it is to clean out the pack who are running it . . ." [68, p. 379]. Against this intellectual attack there has been the silent reply of millions of television sets being turned on every day and every night in every part of the country.

*Does television distort children's values?* It has long been argued that television helps its viewers form accurate pictures of political candidates and public events. But questions have been raised as to the

* The numbers in brackets refer to articles and books listed in the Annotated Bibliography, pages 297–317.

picture of adult life which television shows children. In particular, some
critics have charged, like Arthur R. Timme, that thanks to television,
some children now grow up with a completely distorted sense of what
is right and wrong in human social behavior. Edward Podolsky wrote
to the Kefauver Committee: "The human mind in these [juvenile and
adolescent] age groups is quite impressionable and easily conditioned.
By constant and repeated presentation of undesirable and criminal activity in mass media, many children and adolescents in time accept these
as an attractive way of living." In slightly different tone, Charlotte
Buhler wrote: "It is a well-established fact that audiovisual learning
is one of our finest tools in education. To have television defeat this
purpose by presenting to the children assorted negativistic attitudes
some people have toward life and presenting this in dramatic form cannot help but have its repercussions . . ." [2, pp. 264–65].

*Does television teach children too much about life too early?* The
principal asker of this question has been Joseph Klapper. He points
out that children spend much of their television time on adult programs,
and says: "Adult fare deals almost exclusively with adults, and usually
with adults in conflict situations. Some psychologists and psychiatrists
feel that continued exposure to such fare might unnaturally accelerate
the impact of the adult environment on the child and force him into a
kind of premature maturity, marked by bewilderment, distrust of adults,
a superficial approach to adult problems, and even unwillingness to become an adult." He adds that "real adults in the child's primary group
are often found wanting by children who appeal to them in situations
which happen to be impelled by TV . . . Such inability on the part of
real adults may impress the child as much or more than does the inas-
surance of TV portrayed adults" [76, pp. 231–32]. Against this point of
view stands the argument that television speeds the intellectual development of children by bringing them earlier into contact with a wider
world and adult problems. Which viewpoint is right? And if both are
right, does the cognitive benefit overbalance the psychological harm?

But the most serious and frequent question raised about television is
this: *Does its violence teach children violence and crime?* The number of violent acts on television programs seen by children have been
counted and listed by observers like Smythe and Cousins. Of course,
there is violence in Shakespeare, too, but Edgar Dale argues that television violence should not be compared with the violence in a great
dramatist. He says: "I am not arguing that Shakespeare can get by with
something that Mickey Spillane cannot. I simply ask: 'does the violence
shown illuminate the wellsprings of conduct, help us better understand
why people act the way they do? Should bullets, guns, stabbing, kick-
ing, abduction be the daily imagery of childhood?" Walter Lippmann

says they should not: "There can be no real doubt," he writes, "that the movies and television and the comic books are purveying violence and lust to a vicious and intolerable degree. There can be no real doubt that public exhibitions of sadism tend to excite sadistic desires and to teach the audience how to gratify sadistic desires. Nor can there be any real doubt that there is a close connection between the suddenness in the increase in sadistic crimes and the new vogue of sadism among the mass media of entertainment." Arthur W. Wallander, the former police commissioner of New York City, says that crime programs on TV and radio glorify criminals and the "private eye" type of detective. They glory in having those characters "put it over on the cop . . . in making the policeman look dumb." Thus, he says, both children and parents tend to lose respect for "the very men they are supporting as their front line defender against crime" [2, pp. 262, 264].

The question of whether television actually causes crime turns into a colloquy of psychiatrists, with Ralph Banay saying that if "prison is college for crime, I believe for young disturbed adolescents, TV is a preparatory school for delinquency" [65, p. 83]; Otto Billig saying that television programs "have a very limited influence on the child"; and Frank Coburn concluding that, rather than causing delinquency, television provides a "direction for the delinquent's behavior to take" [quoted, 2, pp. 267–69].

Finally, the question is asked, *Does television cause withdrawn and addictive behavior?* On the one hand, it is argued that television keeps children at home and gets the family to do things together. On the other hand, psychiatrists like Joost Meerlo say that it has a "hypnotizing, seductive influence." It makes not for group behavior, but rather for private behavior. It encourages withdrawal from reality, and makes addicts. Robert Shayon says that it encourages in a child "a craving for violence and fantasy which drives him continuously to the mass media, particularly TV." There he finds unlimited fare but no wholesome satisfaction for an abnormal appetite" [52, p. 195]. What is the truth in this case? Does television make for happy home groups or for children who behave in its presence like schizoids? If it makes addicts, what are the conditions under which this occurs, and what kinds of children are vulnerable?

These are truly serious questions and charges. We have taken care to select the spokesmen, not from the lunatic fringe, not from the professional viewers of television with alarm, not from the amateurs. Siepmann, Witty, Remmers, Schlesinger, Dale, and Smythe are college professors, at New York University, Northwestern, Purdue, Harvard, Ohio State, and Illinois, respectively. Klapper is a researcher and executive of the General Electric Company. Wallander, as we have said, is a former police commissioner of New York City. Cohen, Timme, Podolsky, Meerlo, Banay, Billig, and Coburn are psychiatrists. Buhler is a psychologist. Lippman is the respected columnist; Cousins, the editor of the *Saturday Review*; Griffith, a staff member of *Time*. Susskind and Shayon are television producers and writers. The stature of these people dramatizes the importance of the unanswered questions about children and television.

For it is unfortunately the case that, not only have we been unable to answer the challenging final questions, such as, does television cause delinquency, and does it make for more knowledge or more ignorance; but also we have understood very little the process by which television had an effect, so that we could predict the part it would play in the lives of children. Whereas it was believed, as we said a few pages back, that *some* kinds of television, under *some* conditions, would have such effects on *some* children, we have been in no position to specify *what* kinds of television, conditions, or children.

Into this needy situation, a few research scholars have been moving. Their writings are a mere handful beside the outpouring represented by the other group of writers. Their conclusions tend to be more cautious. Yet, slowly, some progress has been made.

Eleanor Maccoby, a child psychologist, formerly of Harvard, now of Stanford, has made a series of illuminating studies on the relation between frustration and aggression in children, and aggression in television, trying to determine whether frustration in real life did not drive children to seek violent material in television, and to remember it longer.

John and Matilda Riley, sociologists of Rutgers University, made one exciting study in which they sought to find out whether a child who had good friends in his peer group made different use of fantasy from a child who had few friends and was much alone.

In 1955, Arthur Brodbeck presented a paper to the American Psychological Association which was full of insight in its hypotheses and descriptions of unpublished research concerning television's effect on children.

Lotte Bailyn, when a graduate student at Radcliffe, wrote a very interesting doctoral dissertation on what she called the "pictorial media" —meaning movies, television, and comics. She was able to make an index of use of pictorial media and to identify some of the variables that seemed to determine whether a child made much or little use of these media.

R. S. Albert and Robert Zajonc both studied the effect of the program ending. Albert obtained findings which seemed to mean that a "crime does not pay" ending does not necessarily reduce aggression in a child, and Zajonc found that children tended to remember behavior that was successful (or not punished) in a program, whether it was socially acceptable or not.

In addition to these, there have been a few other experimental studies on television and children published in American journals, and a number of surveys of television use, some private, some commercial, a few of them specializing in *children's* television behavior. The longest series of surveys of children's use of television has been Witty's annual series, made in the vicinity of Evanston, Illinois. Others are mentioned in the annotated biography in this volume.

The research on children's use of television in the United States, then, is not very extensive. We can say, in general, that neither the basic facts of how much a given kind of child uses television at a given age, or what his tastes are, or what he thinks of television, have been satisfactorily pinned down; nor are the dynamic questions of why he uses television as he does, and what happens as a result, well understood.

However, in 1958, the first full-length study of *Television and the Child* appeared in England, following several very useful short studies in the United Kingdom and other countries. The authors were Hilde Himmelweit, A. N. Oppenheim, and Pamela Vince, psychologists, of the University of London. This was a careful job of research, using large samples of two groups of English children, ten to eleven and thirteen to fourteen years of age. Although many of the results of this fine study apply only to England, and all the other results would have to be re-tested in North America, many of the conclusions are suggestive and probably applicable to all cultures. A number of the findings will be mentioned in the following pages.

## This book and the research behind it

This is where we came in. Beginning in 1957, a year and a half before the Himmelweit, Oppenheim, Vince volume and the Bailyn study became available, we planned and made a series of studies which we hoped would fill in some of the dark areas of our knowledge of children's use of television in the United States and Canada, and in our understanding of the part television plays in their lives. We had no hope of being able to answer all the great questions, but we did hope to be able to understand better the conditions under which children go to television and the conditions under which television has an effect on them.

The results of our studies are in this book.

Before describing the research we did, let us say a word about how the book is written.

We have done a great deal of new research. To present the results of it fully, we need tables and statistics. We realize, however, that many people who are concerned about television in the lives of our children do not enjoy reading tables and may not understand the statistics that accompany them. They are not much interested in research design, the nature and selection of samples, or questionnaire and test construction. We should prefer not to restrict the book to readers who have the concerns of scholars and understand the language of scholarship. Therefore, we have tried to present the text of the book —the following eight chapters—so far as possible without tables or statistics. In the Appendixes we have put full information about the samples, the research instruments, and the tables and statistics which scholars will want to read. For this purpose we have selected about 150 tables from the several thousands of tables the studies produced. In the Appendixes, also, we have treated certain other topics (for example, children's use of other mass media) which require tables but may still be of interest to nonscholars. Therefore, the text of this book may be read with as much or as little of the Appendixes as the reader wishes.

At this point, therefore, some readers will want to turn to Appendix I for full information on the nature of the research behind this book. For readers who do not need such a detailed picture and do not especially like to read scholar-talk, we are going to describe briefly here in a nontechnical way the research we conducted, on which many of our conclusions are based.

We made 11 studies between 1958 and 1960. These were:

*Study 1, San Francisco, 1958–59.*

Here we studied a total of 2,688 children, chosen so as to represent adequately the first six grades, and the eighth, tenth, and twelfth grades of the public school system. Some of these children we interviewed directly, many of them completed questionnaires and tests given in the classroom, several hundred kept diaries for us, and some of the younger children were represented through questionnaires completed by their parents. In the course of the study we collected questionnaires from 1,030 parents describing and reacting to their children's television behavior. The information we collected varied somewhat by the children's ages, but we usually tried to find out as much as possible about their mass media behavior; what they used the different media for and what the media meant to them; what they knew about public affairs, science, popular and fine art, and other parts of the world; something about their family lives and their relations with children their own age; some of their psychological characteristics; their mental ability and the use they were making of it in school; and so forth. We also talked to teachers, school officials, and other knowledgeable persons.

*Study 2, San Francisco, 1958.*

We interviewed 188 entire families *as families*—meaning that we talked to the parents and children together so that they could check up on one another and so that we could observe the interactions. We asked them chiefly about the use different members of the family made of the media, and what part the media played in family life. The total was 502 children, 188 mothers, and 187 fathers.

*Studies 3, 4, 5, 6, 7, Rocky Mountain communities, 1959.*

In five communities within the Rocky Mountain area of the United States we interviewed the entire sixth and tenth grades or an adequate sample of these, and in three of these communities we studied also the first grades. The information we sought was in most respects parallel to what we had sought in San Francisco, although the questionnaires were expanded and sharpened as the work went along. In the case of these first grades, for example, we gave the children vocabulary tests. In these five towns, our total sample was 1,708 children and 284 parents. As before, we talked to teachers and officials.

*Studies 8 and 9, Canada, 1959.*

We studied two communities in Canada, which were comparable in most respects except that one did and one did not have television. In each case we studied the first, sixth, and tenth grades, using the same materials as in the Rocky Mountain cities, although improved by use and somewhat expanded to take account of the characteristics of Canadian mass communication. We gave the first-graders a vocabulary test. The total was 913 children and 269 parents. As before, we talked to teachers and officials.

*Study 10, American suburb, 1960.*

In a metropolitan suburb of the United States we studied in detail the television behavior, program choice, and time allocations of all the elementary school children in one school. These totaled 474 children. We also talked to parents and teachers.

*Study 11, Denver, 1960.*

To test certain hypotheses developed in the previous studies, we studied 204 students in the tenth grade in Denver, Colorado. The information dealt with their media behavior in relation to mental ability and social norms.

In these eleven studies, then, we gathered information from 5,991 students, 1,958 parents, and several hundred teachers, officials, and other knowledgeable persons in ten communities in the United States and Canada, representing cities and towns, metropolitan areas and isolated areas, industrial, agricultural, and residential communities, and every major condition of television development now to be seen in North America including the condition of *no television*. It goes without saying that, in addition to our own data, we have made use of all the other research we have been able to find bearing on children's use of television.

These are the bases for the statements to be found in the following pages.

*What follows:*

In the chapter immediately following, we have tried to describe some of the changes television has made in the child's world. In Chapter 3, we have set down the essential facts and figures on the amount and kind of television children make use of at different ages and times, what it means to them, and how they compare it with other mass media. In Chapter 4 we have developed and tested some theory as to how and why children use television. Then follow three chapters that seek to analyze the chief elements in a child's life and personality that determine the use he makes of television. Chapter 8 considers in some detail the chief suppositions that have been made about television's effects. In that chapter we return to some of the questions we have just stated. Then there is a final chapter of summary, concluding with some pointed questions addressed to broadcasters, teachers, parents, and researchers.

Each of these chapters is keyed into the Appendix where the tabular and statistical evidence is to be found. "Table II-6" refers to Appendix II, Table 6.

# CHAPTER 2

# THE NEW WORLD OF TELEVISION

No mass medium has ever exploded over a continent as television exploded over North America in the 1950's.

At the beginning of 1948 there were barely 100,000 television receiving sets in use in the United States. In 1949, there were a million; at the end of 1959, 50 million. At the beginning of the 1950's, about one out of 15 U.S. homes had television. At the end of the 1950's, seven out of eight homes had it.

In Canada, which is larger in area and has more open country, television came into use a bit more slowly. But there, as in the United States, great prodigies of ingenuity and engineering were performed to jump the mountains and the wilderness and bring television to distant places. Cables were brought in from remote stations. Antennas were erected on mountains to feed the receivers in valleys. Stations, microwave carriers, receiver sales, and maintenance facilities, all spread at a fantastic pace. The familiar antennas began to appear first on the northeastern seaboard, first in the large cities, first in the high-income homes, and then spread like the common cold from one end of the continent to the other, from the metropolis to the town to the farm, and from the mansions to the shacks. (See Table II-1.)

More swiftly than anywhere else, television penetrated to homes where there were young children. Throughout the early years of American television, homes where there were children under twelve were almost twice as likely to have television as were childless homes. It was in homes with children where television was most eagerly awaited, and most intensively used.

Thus, as 150 million people rearranged their lives in the 1950's to accommodate the picture tube in the living room, the rearrangement was most striking in the homes with children. [Television became the greatest source of national entertainment, but most particularly it took over from movies, comic books, baby-sitters, and playmates a large part of the job of entertaining children.] It brought the world to every-

▶ For tables and other data applying to this chapter see Appendix II.

one's living room, but most particularly it gave children an earlier look at far places and adult behavior.) It became the greatest and loudest salesman of goods, and sent children clamoring to their parents for box tops. It created heroes and villains, fads, fashions, and stereotypes, and nowhere so successfully, apparently, as with the pliable minds of children. )

In the decade of the 1950's, television came to dominate the non-sleep, nonschool time of the North American child. One-sixth of all the child's waking hours, from the age of three on, is now typically given over to the magic picture tube. During the first sixteen years of life, the typical child now spends, in total, at least as much time with television as in school. Television is probably the greatest source of common experience in the lives of children, and, along with the home and the school, it has come to play a major part in socializing the child.

## The world of radio

If any of us were now compelled to find two or three hours every day for a new activity, we should probably resent that requirement as an intolerable intrusion on our scheduled lives. It would require us to make profound and far-reaching changes. And this is precisely what television has done. It has come as an interloper into lives which already seemed full. It has taken two or three hours daily from children who previously gave it no time at all.

Can you remember what a child's life was like before television? . Don't think nostalgically back to family evenings around the piano. Those were gone long before television. The age before television was the age of radio. Perhaps the best way to remind ourselves what it was like is to look at some of the research studies made in that time.

In 1950, Paul Lyness studied a large sample of Des Moines, Iowa, school children [55]. This was near the end of the radio age for Des Moines, just before television came in. At that time children were spending almost as much time on radio as they now spend on television. They listened about two hours a day when they were in the early school grades; a little over three hours a day in the middle school years; a little less in high school. From first through twelfth grades, then, the typical child gave radio two to three hours a day.

Des Moines children at that time were seeing an average of one movie a week (about three times as many as the average child sees in the movie theater today). They averaged more than four comic books a week (far above today's average). On the other hand, they were spending about as much time on newspapers, magazines, and books as children do today.

But it was radio that dominated their mass media time. They

scheduled their evenings, when they were old enough, around the feature shows of radio. Most of their music came from radio, and their drama about equally from movies and radio. They trusted radio news (as the polls showed) more than newspaper news. They drew their popular heroes, and much of their cosmogony of political heroes and villains, from radio.

Can you remember what was on radio at the end of the 1940's? Almost half of radio was music (now it is nearly three-fourths). A little over half of radio music was popular music, the rest of it about equally divided between classical music and a combination of Western songs, hill-billy ballads, and religious singing. About 16 per cent of radio was drama (now somewhat less). But much more than 16 per cent of audience time was spent on drama, for this included the popular crime shows and the daytime serials that followed one after another, day after day, week without end: "Stella Dallas," "Portia Faces Life," "When a Girl Marries," "The Romance of Helen Trent," and so on and so forth. About 12 per cent of radio was news; the five-minute newscast, featuring three commmercials, was uncommon, and the air was full of sober and respected news commentators like Edward R. Murrow, H. V. Kaltenborn, and Elmer Davis. There was a great deal of "audience participation" on the air, which means quiz shows, sidewalk interviews, breakfast clubs, and the like. But perhaps the feature that best indexed American radio for foreign visitors was the group of high-rating comedy and variety shows: Fred Allen, Jack Benny, Bob Hope, Arthur Godfrey, Charlie McCarthy, and the rest of them.

This was the world of entertainment to which American children used to be attached as they are now attached to television entertainment. So doing, they still had somewhat more playtime than children have today, and they got to bed a little earlier.

## The transition to television

In December of 1950 and January of 1951, Eleanor Maccoby interviewed 332 mothers of school children in Cambridge, Massachusetts [40, 1951]. This was at the time when television had only recently come to Boston and its surrounding communities like Cambridge, so that it was possible to compare children whose families did not have television with those whose families did.

She found, as everyone has in the early period of television, a great flurry of interest in the new medium. Children in television homes were spending two and a half hours weekdays, and three and a half hours Sundays, watching the shadows on the magic tube. Children without television were spending upwards of half an hour a day, on the average, watching someone else's receiver. This latter group waited impatiently for the time when their fathers and mothers would buy a set of their own.

In television homes, few children were listening much to radio any more. Movie-going and reading had considerably decreased. But even so, the total mass-media time per day for children in television homes was about one hour and a half greater than in homes without television.

Some of Mrs. Maccoby's more interesting observations, however, had to do with the way that children organized their nonmedia activities around television. For one thing, children in television homes went to bed, on the average, about 25 minutes later on weekdays, about 15 minutes later on Sundays, than children of their own age who did not have television in their homes. Children with television were less likely to do any homework. Carefully matching teen-age children for age, sex, and socioeconomic status, and matching also the day of the week for which the information was collected, Mrs. Maccoby came up with the following comparison:

| No Homework Done | Children with TV | Children without TV |
|---|---|---|
| On weekdays ................. | 54% | 43% |
| On Sundays ................. | 92% | 69%* |

And in television homes, children were sacrificing about an hour and a half of active playtime to the new medium. It is necessary, however, to add a word of caution to these comparisons: television was new, and behavior probably shows a novelty effect. Also, despite the matching, there may well have been a self-selection factor that distinguished the families who bought television early from the others.

When television came into a home, therefore, it meant a major re-arrangement in a child's living time. The question of interest to us is, of course, which of these changes persisted and which ones were only temporary?

So far as radio is concerned, it is the general experience that radio listening falls almost to zero in the early months of television. Then gradually it comes back. Now a child typically spends half to two-thirds as much time on radio as on television—somewhere from one to two hours a day. But it is a different order of attention. No longer is the family likely to gather around the radio, absorbed in the adventures of Mr. District Attorney or the barbed satire of Fred Allen. Rather, radio has become a *second* medium, to be listened to while one is doing something else. One hears the ball game while mowing the lawn, the music program while doing housework, the news while riding along in the car. Children use radio chiefly for popular music, which provides a pleasant and socially useful background while they read or study.

---

* These percentages were based on matched pairs chosen from among 622 children. *N*'s for this table were not given in Mrs. Maccoby's article.

Movie-going, however, has never recovered from the first shock of television. It may very well be that children today see more movies than they saw in the age of radio, but they see most of them on television rather than in the theater. It is an open question whether the old films that television replays, interspersed with frequent commercials, are likely to build any appetite for movie attendance.

Reading has retained its former time and prestige, with two exceptions. Books, newspapers, and most magazines are as much read as in the age of radio. But comic books, and the group of magazines which includes confessions, screen, detective, and pulp adventure types, are now read much less than in the days of radio.

Television viewing itself typically devours a tremendous amount of time in the first months of its availability, then decreases to a steady level. Mrs. Maccoby says that her figures are a "minimal estimate," and indeed they are about an hour less than the estimates of early television viewing we have been able to obtain elsewhere. That is, in the first weeks and months when a television set is introduced into the home, the typical viewing time of children is likely to be in the neighborhood of three and one-half hours on a weekday, four or four and a half on Sunday. Then the time settles down to about the levels Mrs. Maccoby found—two and a half hours on weekdays, an hour more on Sunday.

The total mass communication time remains an hour to an hour and one-half more than it used to be in the days of radio. A few minutes of this have been absorbed by postponing bedtime. A few more minutes have been gained by reducing the time for active play, especially play with other children. The major part of the additional time has been absorbed by combining radio with something else, so that one doesn't need more time for it. (See Table II-2.)

## The world of television

The two studies we have been talking about were made ten years ago, and therefore have certain disadvantages for our purposes. If we could find the two worlds of radio and television existing side by side today, we should find that situation very useful because then we could ask questions of live children, rather than dead studies, and find out many more things about them.

Therefore, we tried to find somewhere in the United States a pair of towns, at least 3,500 in population, which were similar in most important ways except that one has television and the other does not. The result of our search was a testimony to the remarkable attraction of television, and a failure to find the towns.

Even when we reduced the population requirements to 2,000, still we could find no such pair of towns. We reduced our television requirement. We assumed that if less than 20 per cent of the homes in a town had television, there would still be a large and representative group of children who did not see television. We went into some isolated towns, served with television only by a cable, to which less than 20 per cent of the families had so far subscribed. What we found was then, though no longer, mildly surprising to us. We found that in a town where 20 per cent of the homes had television, more than three-quarters of the children would see it regularly. How did they do so? Never underestimate the ingenuity of children, or the attraction of television. Television-less children went to a friend's house, or a relative's. Some found that by aiming their aerials toward nearby mountains they could get pictures that vaguely looked like television. Others found that there was sufficient leakage from the cable to put a snowy picture on their television screens without their paying for it. By one means or other, therefore, most of the children in town found a way to see television. It was a most impressive demonstration of the importance they attached to television, but it ruined the towns for research purposes.

But in western Canada, where the distances are greater and the population less, we found two communities that met our specifications. We shall call them Teletown and Radiotown, and we shall find them useful in checking the patterns of change that have been suggested by these earlier studies.

Teletown and Radiotown are communities of about 5,000 persons each. They are similar in industrial support, social structure, government, and school system. But Radiotown is 400 miles from any major metropolitan area, and 200 miles from the nearest open-circuit television station. Teletown, on the other hand, is within television distance of a metropolitan concentration, and not far from the United States border. Therefore, both Canadian and United States television pours into Teletown, whereas Radiotown received stray and undependable signals and those only a few nights a year.

In these two communities we studied the children who were at that time in the first, the sixth, and the tenth grades. We talked to their teachers and asked the parents of some of them to fill out questionnaires. We used tests and scales which we had tested elsewhere, and the results of which could therefore be compared with other parts of the study.

The first thing we found was that Radiotown residents, although they live without television, do not live in a pretelevision era. Both children and adults are very conscious of living in a world of television. Adult residents who have never seen television are very few; most of the adults have seen television either before moving to Radiotown or while visiting other communities. A number of them have brought their receiving sets to Radiotown, ready to install as soon as television becomes available. One family has connected its set to an antenna. This family reports that two or three nights a year they are able to receive some television. Stray signals bounce off the magnetic layer and give them either the sound or the picture of a television program—seldom both together. Two or three nights a year! And yet, practically every night they turn on the set, hoping that this is the night!

More than half of the school children in Radiotown have seen television. Through other media as well as the occasional sights of television itself, they have become conversant with a number of television programs and performers. One-third of the sixth- and tenth-grade children were able to name a "favorite" television program. They were most anxious to have television available to them. One of the recurring questions asked our interviewers was, "Will this study help to bring us television soon?" And the local drive-in theater capitalizes on their interest by means of a large billboard which boasts, "THE WORLD'S LARGEST TV SCREEN!"

While Radiotown yearns for television, Teletown is in the midst of the television era. Over 75 per cent of the children have receiving sets in their homes. Those who do not have sets view elsewhere as regularly as possible. There is a wide choice of programs, and television has been there long enough to become familiar and let viewing settle into patterns.

In Teletown, the first-graders view television, on the average, about 1 hour, 40 minutes, a day. The sixth-graders watch, on the average, 2 hours, 54 minutes, and the tenth-graders about 1 hour, 36 minutes, on a typical weekday. Counting Sunday listening, then, the first-graders have to make room for about 10.5 hours per week, the sixth-graders for 20.5 hours a week, and the tenth-graders for about 11.6 hours a week of television time, which their opposite numbers in Radiotown do not have to account for. Let us, therefore, see what kind of rearrangement of a child's life this brings about.

First let us compare the time allocations of first-grade children (who are five or six years old) in the two towns. In Radiotown, first-graders listen to radio on the average 56 minutes a day; in Teletown, about 21 minutes. Whereas 89 per cent of Radiotown first-graders had started going to movies by the time of our study, only 54 per cent of the Teletown first-graders had started. The average first-grade student in Radiotown already was in the habit of reading a little over four comic books a week; in Teletown, the figure was 1.5 per week. The Teletown first-grader was permitted to stay up an average of 13 minutes later at night, and in Teletown the average first-grade child played about 2 hours, 52 minutes, as compared with 3 hours, 25 minutes, in the case of Radiotown children.

In other words, the first-grade children in Teletown are making time for television by taking 35 minutes a day from radio, 33 minutes from play, 13 minutes from bedtime, and by seeing three fewer movies and reading four fewer comic books per month. The reduction in movie and comic book time averages out to about 20 minutes a day.

Now let us look at the sixth- and tenth-grade children.

Homework time for these two grades was only about 15 minutes higher in Radiotown than in Teletown. Most of the television time apparently had to be made up in Teletown through rearranging the time allocations for mass media.

In this rearrangement, three of the media suffered greatly. We have represented this in Figure 1.

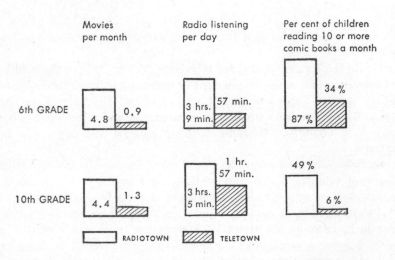

FIGURE 1    Three of the mass media before and after television.

These are rather spectacular differences, and a few notes are in order. The figures on radio listening point to a pattern we shall have occasion to notice again and again in this volume—the fact that radio has a special appeal and performs a special service in the television age for the teen-ager. It will be noticed that listening in Teletown doubles between sixth and tenth grade. And finally, it should be pointed out that the great differences in movie-going in the two communities are partly a cause and partly a consequence of something that has happened in Teletown. In that community, the movie theaters were early casualties of the television period. Two years before our study, the community had one regular and one drive-in movie theater, precisely as Radiotown has now. At the time of our study, both these theaters had closed down, and townspeople attributed the closure to lack of patronage because of the competition of television. Teletown people still had access to movies, of course, but only in neighboring communities.

In Teletown, then, children made time for television chiefly by taking it from radio, movies, and comic books (and, as we shall see shortly, a small amount of it from one type of magazine). But how about the other media—newspapers, books, magazines? Did they have to contribute time to television?

They did not. Newspaper reading was actually a bit higher in Teletown than in Radiotown, although the difference may be due to the fact that metropolitan daily papers were more readily available in Teletown. These were the percentages of children in the two towns who were reading the newspaper every day:

|  | N | Radiotown | N | Teletown |
|---|---|---|---|---|
| Sixth grade | 187 | 34% | 175 | 45% |
| Tenth grade | 109 | 44% | 113 | 57% |

There was no significant difference in the amount of book reading (in Radiotown 3.1 books per month; in Teletown 2.9) and only a very small, though statistically significant, difference in magazine reading (Radiotown 4 magazines per month, Teletown 3.7).

This is a very important fact to know when we try to understand the needs that television meets for children—the fact that television cuts into the time previously allocated for radio, movies, and comic books, but not the time for newspapers, books, and magazines. We shall want to return to this fact in Chapter 4, and assess its significance.

We have talked so far only about the *amount* of viewing, listening, and reading. What about the *content*? Are there important differences in the kind of mass media content that children receive in the television age?

For example, what kind of radio do they get now, under the shadow of television? In both Radiotown and Teletown, of course, popular music is the staple of radio listening, and in each town the children say they hear a considerable amount of radio news also. About half of the Radiotown children say they also hear a lot of other kinds of programs —chiefly, drama of some kind. But so far as the Teletown children are concerned, popular music and news are about all they get from radio. Only 14 per cent of the Teletown sixth-graders and 9 per cent of the tenth-graders said that they regularly hear anything except popular music and news on the radio.

This means that radio has become a much more specialized medium for children in the age of television. Another evidence of this specialization is in the answers to our questions about how often the children in the two communities "do something else" while they listen to radio. Apparently using radio as a "second" medium while studying, working, reading, or driving is a much more common behavior in Radiotown than in Teletown. In this respect, television has helped to specialize radio even further than we have indicated. Not only is it used by children mostly for popular music and news, but it is also used at times when they are doing something else more demanding with their eyes, sometimes with their limbs, and usually with a large part of their brains.

There is an important difference also in the kind of magazine content read by children in the two towns. Thirty-four per cent of Radiotown children, as compared with only 20 per cent of Teletown children, report that they often read confession, screen, detective, or adventure pulp magazines. On the other hand, only 52 per cent of Radiotown children, as compared to 65 per cent of Teletown children, reported frequent reading of general magazines—*Life, Saturday Evening Post,* and so forth. It appears, therefore, that television shifts the center of gravity in children's magazine reading from the pulps and the more violent and sensational magazines toward the general and the quality magazines. This would seem to imply in turn that television does a better job of meeting the needs formerly met by the pulps than by the general magazines. This, too, we shall want to talk about in Chapter 4.

### The child's mass communication input

It is clear that television has greatly rearranged the child's leisure time, particularly that portion of his leisure time spent receiving communication from the mass media. The child in this era of television spends less time reading comic books than did his counterpart in an earlier era. He gets less drama from radio and from theater movies, but he gets a large measure of drama from television. He still gets a lot of his popular music and news from radio, although he now gets some of these from television.

It is also apparent that there are changes in the content of the mass media which the child is now receiving, compared with what his counterpart received in the age before television.

New prestige figures are passing over the stage of television. But there would be new prestige figures even if television had never been developed. Just as Frank Sinatra succeeded Rudy Vallee, someone else would have followed Sinatra even if television had not helped popularize Pat Boone and Elvis Presley. There are different humorists, changes in style, but hardly any less laughter on the mass media.

The voice of the distinguished news commentator is now less heard in the land. But, on the other hand, there is the unequaled ability of television to *show* news. No news commentator could give children the living experience that television can give them, of seeing their President in India, the chief officer of the Soviet Union enunciating his doctrine in the United States, a Presidential candidate being nominated, or a political figure being quizzed at a lively press conference. There are changes in content, but we should be on very doubtful grounds if we were to claim that less news is now available to children.

Is there more violence on the mass media? There may be, if only because of the mass media pattern of imitating and repeating a successful formula. Violence and law-breaking have proved popular on television, and therefore have been endlessly repeated. On the other hand, it is apparent that television is replacing many of the crime comics that used to be thought so violent and some of the detective magazines that children read so avidly in radio times. There are certainly more Westerns on television than there used to be on radio, but television has replaced many of the Westerns children used to see in the movie theater. Without denying that more acts of violence may now occur on television, let us recall that some of the space shows on radio were accused of frightening young children; it may well be that for children what you can't see is more frightening than what you can see. There were also cases of phobias and hysterias ascribed to "brutal" movie content—for example, "The Hunchback of Notre Dame."

Granting all this, it is still an important and interesting question to ask how the total mass communication input of the child has changed as a result of television. Is there an increase in the total amount of mass media communication, apart from rearrangement of time spent on the various media? Is there any significant change in either the kind or the quality of content the child is receiving from the mass media that can be attributed to television? If the answer to either of these questions is affirmative, what implications does this have for our understanding of the child?

It is difficult to measure the total amount of mass communication input except in total number of hours spent on the mass media. Even an attempt to add up the number of hours per day presents problems, particularly if an effort is made to "balance the books." The total amount of time spent on the mass media is sometimes so much that it appears there is little time left for eating or sleeping or attending school. This is because children watch television or read a magazine or newspaper while eating lunch or dinner, listen to radio while doing homework or reading a book, read comic books hidden in notebooks during school hours. Voracious readers will read in bed, in the bath, while walking to school. Just as adults listen to radio while driving to work, children often engage in more than one activity at a time. The hours in the day often add up to more than 24.

In spite of these difficulties of measurement, the evidence points to an increase in the total amount of time spent on mass media. In the case of the preschool child and the child in his first years of school, there is a corresponding decrease in the amount of time spent playing, both alone and with other children. In the case of older children, there is little evidence of any decrease in non-mass media activities, except for aimless unorganized play time [4, p. 346]. Much of the increase found in total mass media time of older children may be the result of doing more things at once. There is clear evidence that radio listening is now largely an activity to be engaged in while doing something else.

Questions about changes in content of the mass media are even more difficult to answer. There are no studies of children's radio input, in the years before television, comparable to present studies of television. It can hardly be maintained that the radio now coming into Radiotown, Canada, is the same as pretelevision radio. Nor does it seem useful to compare the content of radio, when it was the dominant medium, with the content of television, now that it is the dominant medium. We know that television carries three times radio's pretelevision percentage of drama, half its percentage of news, and perhaps one-sixth its percentage of popular music. But so what? The important question hidden by most queries about changes in content is the question about what effect this content has on the children who receive it. Granting that there are changes in the content of the mass media with the advent of television, as there would have been even without television, are there any changes in the kind of content or in the proportions of different kinds of content, such that the effects on the children receiving the communication will be different?

We venture to say that, whatever changes may have occurred in emphasis or tone within the various content categories of the mass media, they are overshadowed by one change television has made in the content of the child's media input: television has given that world a visual dimension it never before had.

The outstanding power of television is its power to extend the vision of its viewers. To the ears of radio it adds eyes. Television is incomparably better than radio for showing an event, catching a classroom demonstration, reproducing a ballet, or showing how a distant land looks. It has much less advantage over radio in presenting a symphony orchestra, and in presenting a news commentator it may be positively distracting. Therefore, the kind of prestige figures it favors are those who can stand the test of the picture tube as well as the test of voice.

The kind of popular art it favors is the kind that one wants to see as well as to hear—and therefore, unfortunately, a very expensive kind of popular art. The kind of attention it invites is the absorbed kind that is loath to permit either eyes or ears to be used for another task. Television has therefore given a visual bias to the choice of content, and a new and unequaled absorbing quality to programs.

We are prepared to assume that children's needs are essentially the same in the age of television as they were in the age of radio, and that, over-all, media content is not essentially different except as television gives it a new visual dimension. Such changes in mass media content as we can observe seem to derive rather from changing times than from changing media, and the changes in children's mass media habits seem to derive rather from the vividness of television than from any change in children.

# CHAPTER 3

# HOW A CHILD USES TELEVISION

This chapter will be concerned with the facts and figures of a child's use of television. More details, and a large number of tables, will be found in the Appendix; here, we shall try to do mostly without tables.

## How Much and When Does a Child View Television?

Consider a typical child, born into the age of television. In his home the view through the picture tube is as much a part of the home setting as the view through the picture window. The sounds of television and radio blend into his surroundings like the wallpaper. Even so, television is probably not the first of the mass media with which he makes close contact. (See Tables IV-1, 2, 3.)

His first mass medium is books. He meets them when his mother or father reads him a bedtime story. Therefore, he comes to know books, not as print, but as the sound of a parent's voice telling a story. These are the two characteristics of his first years of mass media experience: they are audiovisual (or simply audio) experience, and their chief content is stories.

What are the first stories a child hears? We tried to collect a list of these from parents, and found a bewildering variety of titles. But they tend to be fantasy, rather than realism. They often have animal heroes. They very often are associated with pictures.

## When does a child begin to use television?

The first direct experience with television typically comes at age two. Chances are, the child will eavesdrop on a program someone else has tuned in. But he soon begin to explore the world of television and to develop tastes and preferences of his own. By the age of three he is able to shout for his favorite programs. The chances are, these are children's programs, by which we mean that they are billed as children's

▶ For tables and other data applying to pages 24–37 see Appendixes III and IV.

television, typically have animal heroes or animated cartoon figures, and all have a high proportion of fantasy and broad action. Thus we introduce children to television as fantasy. It is interesting to speculate what might be the influence on their later uses of television, if we let them see the medium very early as a window on the real rather than the fantasy world.

By the age of three, then, the average child is already making fairly regular use of television. He sees a number of "children's" programs, soon branches out into Westerns and similar entertainment.

Magazines have also become important for him. Most often, these are picture magazines. He does an impressive amount of "picture reading," hurrying over some pictures, staring a long while at the pictures that interest him. Until he is six or seven, he knows magazines only as pictures, as sources of the stories his parents read to him, or as vehicles for his own "pretend" reading. Yet the pictures he sees at an early age must have a considerable impact on him.

Somewhere between the ages of three and six, he usually becomes acquainted with radio. He hears it first as a program someone else in the family has tuned in. It may be popular music, chosen by a teen-age sister or brother; a day show, tuned in by his mother for entertainment while she does housework; or a news broadcast, perhaps tuned in by his father. The majority of his radio listening is likely to be eavesdropping, rather than his own choice, for some time. But he discovers some programs that please him and probably tries to return to them: lively music, or radio children's programs.

Some time before the years of going to school, he is probably taken to see movies. If he goes to the drive-in with his parents, the chances are that his first taste of movies is an adult show, and he dozes most of the evening in the back seat of the car. If he is taken to the theater, his first movie is probably a Western or an animated cartoon, or both of these on the same day. These tend to be his early favorites in movies; when he has a choice he tries to see a cartoon or a "cowboy" show.

By the age of six, then, the child ordinarily has been introduced to all the audiovisual media, has built up strong likings and preference for television programs, and has met printed media through pictures and through the stories people find in them to read to him.

His active use of printed media begins, of course, with school time. As he learns to read, he begins to sound out some of the stories for himself. He reads simple books, jumping back and forth from text to pictures. He discovers children's magazines, and begins to translate some of the captions in picture magazines. From some of his fellows, he has learned about comic books and has begun to look at them; now he reads them. And last of all, he begins to find the newspaper useful. Here, too, he typically begins with the comic strips (although a few children begin at once with news reading). He is ten or eleven before he reads any great variety of content in the newspaper.

This process of learning to use the mass media, from the time when broadcast sound first blends into the child's environment until he is able to look at a newspaper or magazine and decide, with some assurance and skill, what to read, requires for the average child about ten years. Let us point out some highlights on the map of this period.

For one thing, it is evident that the pattern by which a child is introduced to the media is one of increasing control over the content. At first, radio and television are merely background, entirely out of the child's control. The child does not even, for a long while, decide what bedtime story he will hear. Later, the child himself becomes able to choose favorite programs on television, and favorite stories to be read or told to him; but he is still in bondage to broadcast schedules and parental availability, and, of course, to someone else's sense of pace and emphasis. Looking at pictures gives the child a chance to repeat, to pace himself, to imagine his own stories, but he is still subject to the adult taste which provides the magazine in the first place. His first real control over the media occurs when he becomes able to read. As he becomes more skillful, he has more control over the conditions. He varies the timing, the speed, the repetitions to suit himself. Finally, he becomes master of the process of selection. He knows what can be found in the newspaper, what is available in different kinds of magazines, where to find the books he wants to read. It takes about ten years to win this freedom.

In the second place, it is worth noting that the child is introduced to the mass media almost wholly as fantasy and as audiovisual experiences. This is, of course, in the child's most pliable and impressionable years. The way he begins to use television may well help to explain why the idea that television is *for fantasy* is so deeply ingrained in a child that he often has the greatest difficulty in thinking of *educational* television, let us say, as a proper use of the medium. And similarly, this may help to explain why the printed media, associated with school as they are, seem the proper places to look for informational, as opposed to entertainment, material.

Third, the dominance of television in this first ten years is impressive.

In the Rocky Mountain city where television has been longest available, parents reported 2.8 as the median age at which children began to use television—meaning that half the children had begun to use it by about the age of two years and ten months. In San Francisco, where we made special efforts to distinguish between exploratory use and

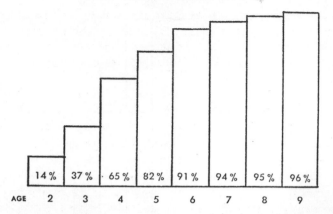

| 14% | 37% | 65% | 82% | 91% | 94% | 95% | 96% |

AGE    2      3      4      5      6      7      8      9

FIGURE 2   The beginnings of television use; percentage of children using it at different ages.

regular use of the medium, we found that 37 per cent of children were already making fairly regular use of the medium at age three; two-thirds, by age four; over 80 per cent, by age five (kindergarten); and over 90 per cent, by age six when they were in the first grade of elementary school.

When we compare this with their use of the other media, we find that television looms very large. Even at the age of three, when average viewing time is in the neighborhood of 45 minutes a day, the child spends more time on television than even on hearing stories. Throughout the preschool years, television time far exceeds other media time; in fact, it usually exceeds the total of other media time. Nine out of ten children are well acquainted with television (indeed, viewing it at least two hours a day) before they read their first newspaper copy. Eight out of ten are well acquainted with television before they begin to sound out the words of any print whatsoever. Two-thirds of them are already television viewers before they have much experience with movies. Even at the end of ten years, when they are making some use of all media, television is the only one they are using day after day. At age ten, three-fourths of all children, as we discovered, will be likely to be watching television *on any given day*. This is more than twice the percentage for any other medium at that age.

It is therefore television, more than any other medium, that furnishes a common body of information for the early socialization of children. It is television, more than any other channel, that builds the "set" with which a child approaches the mass media. All other media choices are judged against what he has come to expect of television.

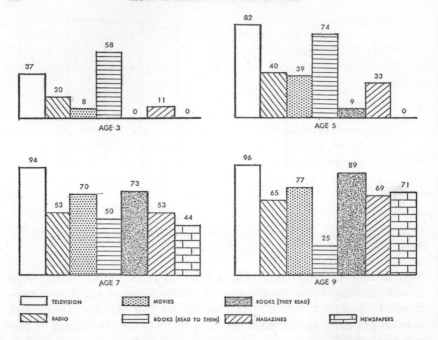

FIGURE 3    The beginnings of mass media use; percentage of children making regular use of each of the media at different ages.

There is considerable individual difference among children in the time of their beginning to use television and the other media. Let us therefore say a word about what children are likely to begin media use early. The phenomenally early users of television—for example, the cases, noted occasionally during this study, in which the baby's bassinet is pushed in front of the television set so the baby can watch—are likely to be in families where the parents have had little more than grade school education, hold blue-collar jobs, and can't afford baby-sitters. Over-all, however, children of better educated parents usually begin to use the media earlier.

In particular, they learn to use print earlier, probably because they have the example of their parents, and printed media are more likely to be available in the home. But they also typically start television earlier, and it is interesting that they are more likely to start with children's material in all the media. The children (relatively few) who begin with crime drama or Westerns are usually in families where their brothers and sisters or their parents see a great deal of such material. A large family is one condition that usually makes for an early beginning with television; in this case, the young child has the example of the older children, and the incentive to join them. Brighter children, other things being equal, usually begin media use earlier. But wherever television is available in the home, children are likely to do a phenomenal amount of viewing at what would have seemed, a few years ago, like an extraordinarily early age.

*How much time does a child spend on television?*

We should warn that this question is not as simple as it seems.

It would be prohibitively expensive to *observe* the television behavior of a large number of children over a long period of time; therefore a researcher must collect someone's *estimate* of time spent on television. But *whose* estimate? The child's or his mother's? And how is the estimate obtained? By memory, by diary, by checking a list of programs? Each of these things makes a difference in the size of the estimate one obtains.

In Appendix III we have discussed at some length the problem of arriving at an accurate estimate of television viewing time and have given a number of estimates obtained in different ways and by different researchers. In general, we are using figures which are in the middle of several estimates, and which we have reason to think are as accurate as we can obtain. But no reader of this book should think that estimates of a child's television time are as firm, let us say, as measurements of a child's height or weight.

Another warning: some researchers estimate a child's listening time per *average weekday*, others per *Sunday*, others per *average day* (which means weekday *or* Sunday). In comparing figures from book to book, or study to study, a reader must notice carefully what kind of day is being measured.

A final warning: There are very few average children. Therefore, averages must not be thought of as representing more than they do—a middle point. For example, in one large group of boys in a certain school grade we obtained an average weekday viewing time of just over two and one-half hours a day. But only one-sixth of all the viewing times actually were between two and one-quarter and two and three-quarter hours. Actually, 16 per cent of these boys viewed more than four hours a day; and 5 per cent viewed less than 15 minutes. Therefore, when you read about averages in the following pages, you should not think of the children all necessarily clustering closely around the average, but possibly large groups of them far under or far above the average. In this kind of situation, it is more important to find out why these large differences exist than what the average is, and in the latter part of this book we have given a great deal of consideration to the problem of why the television behavior of children of the same age is often so different.

Now, having warned you, let us proceed to answer the question.

A child who has begun to use television by age three typically uses it about 45 minutes a weekday (Monday through Friday). By age five, his viewing has increased until, on the average, it is a little over two hours a day. From age six until about the sixth grade, when the child is entering adolescence, viewing time is on a slowly rising plane between two and two and one-half hours. Then viewing time rises rather sharply to a high of a little over three hours a day. This hump usually occurs somewhere between the fifth and eighth grades. Then it enters upon a slowly falling slope until by the twelfth grade (about age seventeen) it is again between two and two and one-half hours.) (See Tables IV-4, 5, 6.)

These are weekday figures( Sunday viewing averages from one-half to one hour longer. )(Tables IV-6, 7, 8.)

These are conservative figures. They are less than some other studies have found, and, as we shall say in a minute, they are less than we found in some places. But, even so, they are spectacular. They mean that throughout the years of school, a child spends within 5 per cent as much time on television as on school. (From ages three through sixteen, he spends *more* total time on television than on school. In these years he devotes about one-sixth of all his waking hours to television.)(In fact, he is likely to devote more time to television than to any other activity except sleep and perhaps play, depending on how play is defined! ) (These figures will be found in Table IV-16.)

Does television time differ by place and time of year? Yes, it does. Viewing time is less during the summer months. (In the studies we made in isolated Rocky Mountain towns toward the end of winter, we found average viewing times about an hour more than for the relatively open climate of San Francisco.) The principle seems to be (that television is attractive in inverse proportion to the attractiveness of its competition.)

We are unable to prove that cultural differences have any effect on television viewing by children, independent of the effects of the relative availability of television and of the relative attractiveness of television's competition. For instance, the different estimates of viewing time obtained in the American Far West, the Mountain West, the Middle West, the East, and the South are all much more easily explained in terms of availability and competition, or of different methods of obtaining estimates, than in terms of the cultural differences between one region and another. The figures obtained by the Himmelweit, Oppenheim, and Vince study in England are slightly lower than ours, and were obtained, like ours, by taking a middle ground among several estimates. However, the differences are well within the limits of sampling or measurement error; and, in any case, television time available in England was at that time somewhat less than in this country, and children's programs were not precisely the same. In the Canadian community we call Teletown, we also obtained slightly lower viewing times than in the United States, but the differences are slight, and the one case is hardly basis for an intercultural comparison. Therefore, we are inclined to believe that what is available on television and what is available elsewhere are more likely to make these differences than are differences in the values the different cultures assign to television. (For example, see Table IV-15, which sums up a number of such measurements.)

We see no evidence to contradict the conclusion that television viewing in the years of childhood and youth everywhere follows the slope-mountain-slope pattern we have described, and that over-all the average time lies between two and three hours a weekday. In particular, we find no evidence to back up the nonscientific but vociferous statements that viewing averages four or five hours a day. Most children view that much occasionally, and some children average that much regularly; but they are far from the general average, and the reason for their unusual behavior will concern us later.

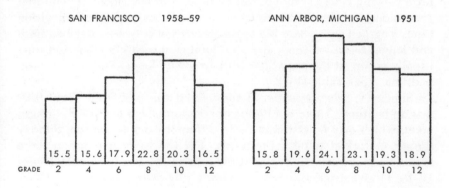

FIGURE 4    Average hours of television viewing per child per week in two cities, by grade in school.

*How about viewing time by day of the week and hours of the day?*

Sunday viewing, as we have noted, is usually longer than weekdays. Saturday viewing varies greatly by individuals, but is generally a little longer than other weekdays. We have some evidence that from Monday night through Friday there is a slight decrease in viewing time.

Mothers and teachers explain this by pointing out that the momentum of week-end homework doesn't carry the children much beyond Monday, and that tests, themes, and activities all tend to cluster late in the week. However, our observation is that a very popular program (for example, "Disneyland" among the elementary school children) can throw out this pattern. Viewing by day of the week is listed in Table IV-11.

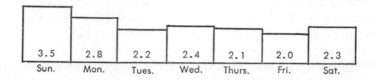

| 3.5 | 2.8 | 2.2 | 2.4 | 2.1 | 2.0 | 2.3 |
| Sun. | Mon. | Tues. | Wed. | Thurs. | Fri. | Sat. |

FIGURE 5   Typical viewing times, in hours, of children for different days of the week (San Francisco family study).

We obtained rather exceptionally detailed records on young children's viewing times by hours of the days. These tables will be found in the Appendix. However, the heavy viewing time for children begins about an hour after school ends and lasts until bedtime. There is a little viewing before school in the morning, but not much. As children grow older, and their bedtimes move to later hours, so do their television times lengthen out. There is a close correlation between later bedtimes and longer television time; and the "hump" in a child's television time usually occurs at the age when his parents no longer enforce an early bedtime. (See Table IV-12.)

Sunday viewing is scattered throughout the day, from about 9:00 A.M. to bedtime. There is a hiatus of about one hour and a half around noon, which may be attributable in different cases to church, Sunday dinner, or lack of suitable programs. For the younger children there is also a hiatus in viewing around the time of the evening meal. Tables IV-13, 14 give detailed figures on viewing by hour of the day.

## Who are the heavy viewers?

Throughout this book we shall be concerned with the explanation for heavy viewing, but here let us list some of the more obvious indices that might describe heavy viewers:

*Age.* We have already said that the heaviest period of a child's viewing comes in the neighborhood of the sixth, seventh, or eighth grade in school, ages eleven to thirteen, when he is entering adolescence and has won a new freedom to stay up late.

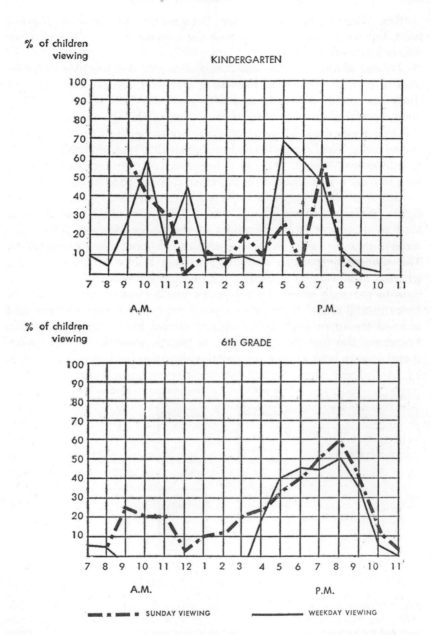

FIGURE 6  Typical patterns of children's viewing by hour of the day. (Source: Clifton sub-urban study.)

*Sex.* There are many differences between boys and girls in program taste, but we find no evidence that the amount of television viewing differs significantly by sex.

*Mental ability.* In the early school years, the brighter children tend to be high viewers of television. For example, we were able to study one group of fourth- and fifth-grade children who were being given special classes because of their very high IQ's. This group of children seemed to do more of everything—viewing, reading, radio, and so forth. They seemed to be burning an almost inexhaustible supply of intellectual energy. And to a lesser extent, this same behavior is seen in most bright children in the early grades. (See Table IV-17.)

But some time between the tenth and thirteenth year, fifth and eighth grade, a striking change occurs. The more intelligent children tend to disappear from the ranks of the heavy viewers. There are some impressive tables in the Appendix to support this generalization. The difference is quite dramatic. In our Rocky Mountain towns, whereas there was no particular relationship between IQ and viewing time in the sixth grade, by the tenth grade most of the children of lower mental ability had moved toward the ranks of high viewers, and most of the more intelligent children toward lower viewing. In San Francisco, the low third on IQ's, in eighth through twelfth grade, spend over an hour a day *more* on television than the high third on IQ's.

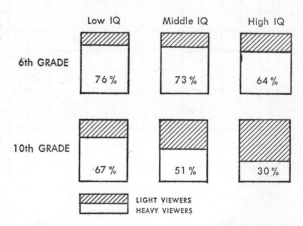

FIGURE 7   Percentage of children who are heavy viewers of television, by grade and mental ability. The chart shows that the percentage of light viewers increases generally between the sixth and the tenth grades, but that the chief increase is in the high IQ group.

Why should this occur? Why should the abler children leave the ranks of heavy viewers? Our talks with them indicate that television ceases to challenge them as it once did. Many of them are finding greater challenges and rewards in printed media and in social and school activities.

*Family.* Family example means a great deal, both in amount of viewing and in what is viewed. Children of highly educated parents tend to view less than other children, as their parents view less than less educated adults. Children of families which believe in the middle-class social norm of work, activity, and self-betterment tend to view less than families that do not hold to that norm. In general, a pattern of light or heavy viewing is likely to go through a family. These patterns will be seen in Tables IV-18, 19, 20, and 21.

But having pointed out these general patterns, now let us talk briefly about the exceptions to them. Whereas it is true that brighter children in high school are apt to view less than other children, that children of working-class parents are likely to view more, and so forth, still there are enough exceptions to these rules to lead us to believe that some of the most important factors must be missing from our list. Children who are highly intelligent, children in highly educated families, children whose families hold middle-class norms emphasizing work and self-improvement—children like these are found with far greater frequency than we should expect in the ranks of heavy viewers where, according to our predictors, they do not belong. Obviously there is something beyond age, intelligence, and family that is affecting their viewing patterns. The missing elements, we believe, are the child's social relationships, and some of his personal characteristics. We shall postpone discussion of these until later chapters, but here let us record them as important determinants of television behavior.

### A note on the other media

In Appendix VII will be found a number of tables and some comments on children's use of media other than television. Here we shall record only a few notes on children's use of the other media.

The following two tables give a bird's-eye view of the pattern of media use during the school years. The dominance of television is clearly evident. It fills nearly two-thirds of mass media time during the early grades, and until the very end of high school it occupies more time than all the other media together. But in addition to this extraordinary amount of television, there are two other patterns worth noticing. The tables in Appendix VII will make these patterns evident.

For one, the printed media are gaining steadily. Almost no one read the newspaper with any regularity in the early grades, but over half are reading it every day in the sixth grade, and two-thirds in grade twelve. The amount of magazine reading is rising steadily. The amount of book use rises between the second and sixth grade, and the fact that a twelfth-grader seems to read fewer books outside school than does a sixth-grader must not blind us to the fact that the twelfth-grade child is doing much more reading for his classes, and also that these figures are obtained during school months when homework in the twelfth grade fills a great deal of leisure time. Therefore, there is an increase throughout the twelve school years in the proportion of mass media time devoted to print.

MEDIA USE BY CHILDREN AT DIFFERENT AGES
DATA FROM SAN FRANCISCO SAMPLE, 1958–60

|  | Grade 2 | Grade 6 | Grade 12 |
|---|---|---|---|
| Average hours TV viewing per weekday | 2.2 | 2.9 | 2.3 |
| Average hours radio listening per weekday | 1.1 | 1.2 | 1.9 |
| Average number movies attended last month | 1.0 | 1.6 | 1.2 |
| Average number books read outside school during last month | 1.1 | 2.1 | 1.0 |
| Average number magazines read per month | 0.8 | 2.6 | 2.8 |
| Average number comic books read per month | .6 | 2.3 | .7 |
| Average percentage reading newspaper every day | 3.0% | 57.0% | 66.2% |

ESTIMATED DISTRIBUTION OF MASS MEDIA TIME AT DIFFERENT AGES*

|  | Grade 2 | Grade 6 | Grade 12 |
|---|---|---|---|
| Television | 62% | 60% | 46% |
| Radio | 27 | 20† | 37 |
| Movies | 2 | 2 | 2 |
| Books | 6 | 8 | 4 |
| Magazines | 2 | 2 | 2 |
| Comic books | —‡ | — | — |
| Newspapers | — | 5 | 7 |
| Total estimated time per week | 25.7 hours | 36.9 hours | 36.2 hours |

* This refers only to media read, seen, or heard outside school, and not for a class assignment.
† The over-all amount of radio listening is greater, but the percentage is smaller because the total mass media time greatly increases between second and sixth grades.
‡ Less than .5 per cent.

Another very interesting pattern is the "bulge" in mass communication use around the sixth grade. This is the time when television use is at its height, movie-going is high, book reading is near its maximum. There is a great increase in newspaper reading. Somewhere between the fifth and eighth grades, the exact point depending on the individual, mass communication time rises from under 30 hours a week, on the average, to between 35 and 40 hours. And thereafter there are certain significant changes. Television time decreases; television becomes less important to the child, as we shall see later. Radio time increases, and radio becomes more important. Comic book reading falls off almost to nothing, as adult behavior begins to set in. There is a general increase, especially among the brighter children, in proportion of reading time devoted to serious reading, and television choices become more selective.

The period of greatest mass media use comes at the time when the child finds himself relatively free of the restraints of early bedtimes. He has acquired sufficient skill in reading to permit him to explore widely in print. He has discovered the social utility of being informed about the new singers and their songs, the new programs and the other conversation pieces among teen-agers. His new sexual awareness leads him to the popular music on radio, which, he discovers, has both a courtship utility and a certain amount of wish-fulfillment. He discovers the social possibilities of going to movies. And so, while his homework is still not very demanding, when he is not yet engaged in the tense social activities of the teen years, and at the time when his energy is at a peak, he makes his most extensive use of the mass media.

Television is the great medium of a child's first ten years, and continues to dominate his time. But it is radio which has a peculiar appeal and utility to the teen-ager. Radio listening is never again as great as it is in the teen years. And throughout the teen years the patterns of adult media use are appearing: the newspaper and magazine reading, and the settling down of television taste after the time of exploration. Above all, one pattern appears in the teens that is of the greatest importance in predicting adult media use. Children are dividing into groups that differ in selection and use of the media. One emphasizes the use of print, another emphasizes the audiovisual media. The print group, as we shall see later, is in general trying to use the media to meet more serious and realistic needs. This group uses television for that purpose also; they tend to be the viewers of "educational" television and of public affairs programs and documentaries. The other group tends to look to the mass media largely for entertainment, fantasy, and escape from reality. These two groups are not readily identifiable before the increase in media use at the beginning of adolescence. But the fact that they do exist, and that they can be identified in the early teens, is one of the most interesting findings we have made. In Chapter 6 we shall return to it.

## What Children View

The first television programs that become a child's favorites, as we have suggested, are in most cases what the broadcasters call "children's" programs. These usually have animals, animated characters, or puppets as their chief characters (Donald Duck, Huckleberry Hound, Howdy

▶ For tables and other data applying to pages 37–48 see Appendix V.

Doody, Rin Tin Tin) although sometimes children themselves play the sympathetic parts. They are in story form, are full of action (often slapstick), and often have a heavy component of laughter. The traditional time for these programs is late afternoon or Saturday morning.

Programs of this type monopolize preschool viewing, and persist (often in slightly more adult form, as in the case of "Lassie") well into the elementary school years. But by the time the child is well settled in school, a new line-up of favorite programs establishes itself. These we can describe as follows:

1. *Children's variety shows.* The phenomenally successful "Walt Disney Presents," usually called simply "Disneyland," is an example of this type. It varies its offerings from cartoon to adventure to legend to history to nature studies, all filmed with superb showmanship.

2. *Children's adventure programs.* "Zorro" is an example of this type. Such a program usually tells the story of a simple, strong, "good" hero, who is always master of his fate despite a variety of adventures and perils that would daunt a less simple man.

3. *Children's science fiction.* This is another form of adventure program, but usually set in future time and dressed up with space travel, rocket guns, and other trappings of the Buck Rogers set. "Superman" and "Captain Video" are other examples.

4. *Children's Westerns.* These are the simpler Westerns, in which the characters are uncomplicated, the ritual is closely observed, the hero kisses the horse rather than the girl, and excitement and adventure get the full treatment.

This is the line-up that dominates the early school years. But very soon two other forms appear:

5. *The crime program.* It is only a short step from the adventure hero who rights a wrong by his own skill, strength, and daring to the detective who solves a crime by his own skill, strength, and daring. Therefore, many children, even in the early grades, begin to watch these programs which are usually scheduled in "adult" viewing hours. The crime programs, however, have their largest juvenile viewing audience in the teens. There is also another form of program which begins to be watched in the early school years and becomes very important by the teens. This is:

6. *Situation comedy.* Beginning with serials like "Leave It to Beaver," which has a boy hero with whom children can identify, the child moves to more adult serials like "Father Knows Best," "The Real McCoys," or to comedies like "I Love Lucy."

As the child approaches the years of adolescence, still another program type becomes important to him. This is:

7. *Popular music variety shows.* This program type features croon-

ers, dance tunes, and glamor. Dick Clark's "American Bandstand," "Perry Como," and "Dinah Shore" are examples of this kind. The girls find these programs first and view them more faithfully than do the boys; but they come to be a part of most teen-agers' viewing.

We have, then, almost the entire line-up for the teen years. Crime mysteries become more absorbing. Children's Westerns tend to be replaced by "adult" Westerns like "Gunsmoke" and "Maverick." Programs like "Disneyland," "Zorro," and "Superman" fade in popularity. Much of their time now goes to crime dramas and popular music. By this time there is very little of a child's viewing that is given any longer to "children's" programs. And as the child's tastes become more and more adult, a tiny flame of interest in public affairs programs begins to appear.

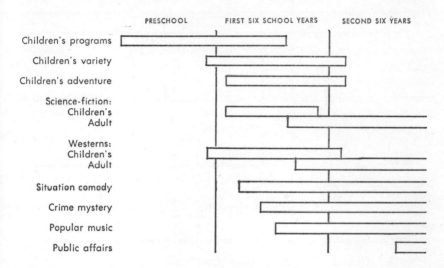

FIGURE 8    Periods in childhood and youth when different program types are most important.

Public affairs is an interest learned late. For that matter, any media use centering on something other than entertainment is learned late. Why this should be, and what conditions fan the little flame of serious public affairs interest so that it burns higher, are problems we shall take up in a later chapter.

In the list of favorite programs, as named by San Francisco children, you will notice the general pattern we have been describing. The full list is in Tables V-1 and 2. The accompanying chart summarizes them.

How representative are these San Francisco choices? Fortunately, we have reports from elsewhere in the country to compare with them. You will find in Appendix V a number of tables on the program preferences of children. These are not strictly comparable with San Francisco

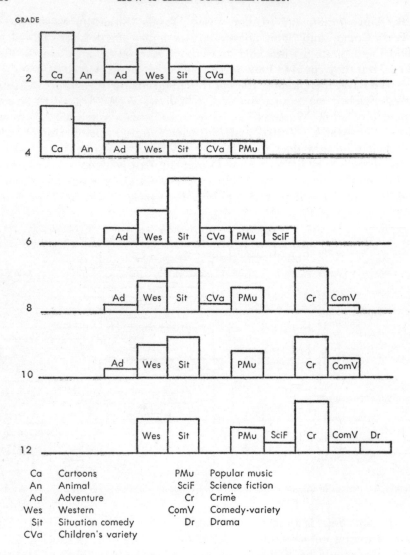

| Ca | Cartoons | PMu | Popular music |
|----|----------|-----|---------------|
| An | Animal | SciF | Science fiction |
| Ad | Adventure | Cr | Crime |
| Wes | Western | ComV | Comedy-variety |
| Sit | Situation comedy | Dr | Drama |
| CVa | Children's variety | | |

FIGURE 9   Percentage of different kinds of programs in first ten of favorites among school children in different grades.

—for the reasons that the same programs are not in every case available, and also that the studies were not made at precisely the same time—yet there is a very great similarity. It may be that the boys' tastes are more alike, from place to place, than are the girls' tastes.

There is another question worth asking about the San Francisco program list. Remember that this is a list of program "preferences." That is, these are the "favorite" programs of the children, not necessarily the most viewed programs. Do the children *actually view* programs they say they like? By examining the diaries kept for us by children, by questioning closely, by a detailed study of viewing patterns in the suburb we have called Clifton, and by examination of some of the tables you will find in the Appendix, we have concluded that their television behavior does indeed mirror their program preferences, so far as these programs are available to them. For example, commercial diary studies (to take some data which we ourselves did not gather) show that children's programs lose their audiences about half-way through elementary school; that children's science fiction lasts a little longer, then also loses most of its viewers; that Westerns are popular over a broad span of time; that situation comedy and comedy variety build up steadily. This particular study was made before the advent of popular programs like "Disneyland" and before the adult Westerns were fully developed.

Have we any evidence that television taste changes over time? Ten

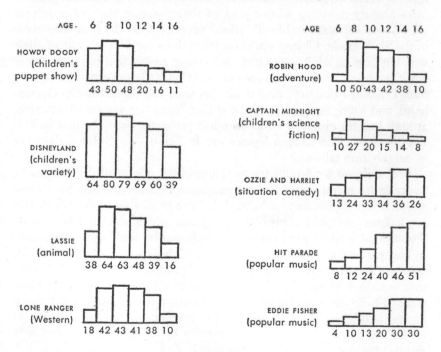

FIGURE 10 Profiles of children's interest in certain programs at different ages. (Information from Batten, Barton, Durstine, and Osborne, 1956, and American Research Bureau, 1952. Figures are percentages of children of a given age who try to view regularly.)

years of television is a very short time in which to separate the changes in television's programming (at the convenience of the program makers) from the changing preferences of children. New programs like "Disneyland" have appeared because someone had a brilliant idea, and these have become "favorite" programs. Some program types, like Fred Allen's satiric comedy, have tended to die out of television because they were too demanding on the performers and writers. Other types, like quiz shows, have declined because the public lost confidence in them. Westerns have proliferated because they proved popular. There are a number of such changes in programming, as one might expect from an entertainment industry so young. But in only ten years it is extremely hard to point to any evidence of a fundamental change. There may have been such a change, but we have not seen it.

## How much do children watch adult programs?

Children learn very quickly to watch adult programs. In the Clifton suburb where we studied children's viewing in great detail, first-graders were already devoting 40 per cent of their viewing time to programs which most viewers would call "adult" programs. By the time they were in the sixth grade, Clifton children were devoting 79 per cent of their viewing time to adult programs and seeing nearly five times as many adult programs as children's programs. This is almost exactly what we found in San Francisco, and it checks with the Himmelweit, Oppenheim, and Vince finding in England that "from the age of 10 onwards, at least half the children watched adult programmes in the first half of the evening." The Clifton figures are in Table V-6. Related data are in neighboring tables.

But suppose we do not try to define children's or adults' programs. Suppose we merely examine the programs that are viewed by a clear majority of children or of adults. We have been able to do this in two large American cities. Out of 80 programs which, during a test week, attracted at least 21 per cent of the audience from children (meaning, in that particular researcher's terminology, boys and girls under eighteen) we found the following division: 7 programs attracted audiences that were over 80 per cent children; 6 programs attracted audiences that were 61 to 80 per cent children; 15 programs were shared in fairly equal proportions by children and adults, the percentage of children being 41 to 60; and 53 programs were seen mostly by adults but attracted substantial percentages (21 to 40 per cent) of children.

The remaining, and rather larger, number of programs were seen by no more than 20 per cent of children.

Now, what kinds of programs were in these several groups?

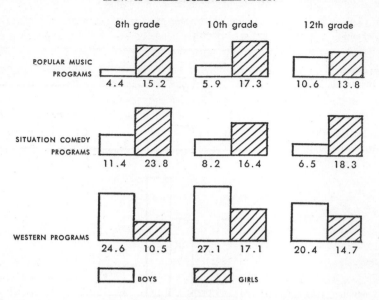

FIGURE 11 Are girls' and boys' tastes in television similar? Favorite programs named by boys and girls in San Francisco. Figures are percentages of children.

Figure 12 breaks them down by types of program. The programs with 81 per cent or more of their audience children were cartoons, general children's programs, children's science fiction, and children's adventure programs. "Ruff 'n Reddy," "Popeye," "Captain Kangaroo," "Porky Pig and His Pals," are examples.

The programs that had 61 to 80 per cent of the children had audiences of these same types but also included very popular animal programs (like "Lassie"), adventure programs (like "Zorro"), elementary situation comedy (like "This Is Alice"), and some audience participation.

The programs that were shared almost equally between children and adults were dominated by movies on television and by situation comedy (for example, "Leave It to Beaver" and "Father Knows Best"). "Walt Disney Presents" is in this group, and so are "American Bandstand" and "Shirley Temple's Storybook." A somewhat surprising name on this list is the animal program "Rin Tin Tin," which seems to attract about 45 per cent of its audience from among adults.

The programs that have only 21 to 40 per cent of their audiences children are chiefly crime programs, situation comedies, and Westerns—for example, "Cheyenne," "Maverick," "77 Sunset Strip," "Peter Gunn," and "I Love Lucy."

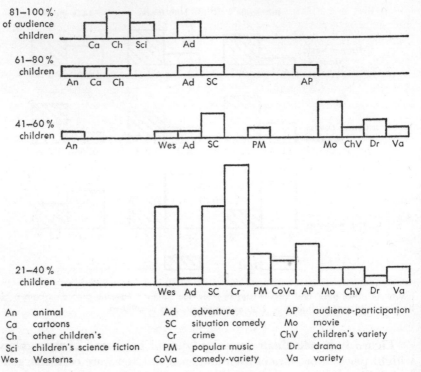

| | | |
|---|---|---|
| An | animal | |
| Ca | cartoons | |
| Ch | other children's | |
| Sci | children's science fiction | |
| Wes | Westerns | |

| | | |
|---|---|---|
| Ad | adventure | |
| SC | situation comedy | |
| Cr | crime | |
| PM | popular music | |
| CoVa | comedy-variety | |

| | | |
|---|---|---|
| AP | audience-participation | |
| Mo | movie | |
| ChV | children's variety | |
| Dr | drama | |
| Va | variety | |

FIGURE 12    Programs attracting different percentages of children. (Source: commercial station ratings.)

What kinds of programs, then, are the ones that attract less than 20 per cent of the children? Most of the public affairs programs; most of the drama—except for crime drama; special interest programs, or programs that appeal chiefly to adults of one sex—professional football and boxing, for example; and a variety of other programs, many of which come at an hour inconvenient for children's viewing.

So far as these figures tell us what is a "child" program and what is an "adult" program, they seem to say that at one end of a continuum we have the serious dramas and the sophisticated analyses of public affairs, in which the view of life is too complicated and subtle for most children. At the other end of the continuum we have cartoons, animal and puppet shows, and adventure programs in which the behavior is mostly ritual, the emotions are uncomplicated, and the interpretation is simple and direct. Between them is a world of adventure, Westerns, crime mysteries, and popular music programs which are attractive, in almost equal measure, to children and adults. It is clear that there is no distinct boundary between adult and children's programs, except at the extreme ends of the continuum, and networks which believe that they are producing programs for adults might do well to take another look at the age of their audiences.

In the larger of the two cities from which these data on adult and children's audiences have come, the thirteen programs which attracted over 60 per cent of their audience from among children were seen during a test week by audiences that included a total of 1.4 million children (not necessarily 1.4 million *different* children). During that same week, almost exactly the same number of children saw twelve Westerns, all of which had chiefly adult audiences. About 850,000 children saw eleven adult crime shows, 640,000 saw seven adult domestic dramas, and 250,000 saw three televised movies. Only a little over half a million saw the eight programs that were openly billed as "children's."

*What are some of the predictors of a child's television taste?*

We have already talked about the developing patterns of taste by age. Age is one of the predictors just referred to; if we know that one child is nine and the other fourteen, we can predict that, other things being equal, there will be certain differences in television taste between them; age is a signpost of those differences. Some of the other signposts are those we are going to list now.

*Sex.* One of the astonishing things about sex differences in taste is how early they appear to begin. Even in the first grade, a significantly larger proportion of girls like popular music programs, and significantly larger proportions of boys like Westerns and adventure programs.

This pattern continues throughout most of the school years—the girls preferring programs built around romance (popular music) or the family role (situation comedy), the boys preferring "masculine" programs of excitement and adventure. In general it seems that girls develop earlier than do boys their interest in adolescent and adult roles. The boys are still viewing cartoons and other juvenile programs when the girls are already buying current song hits and squealing over Dick Clark's featured singers. The boys develop their interest in popular music two years or so later than do the girls. For details, see Tables V-2, 3, 4.

We find approximately this same pattern in all the United States and Canadian areas we studied, but interesting differences from it seem to exist in England. Himmelweit, Oppenheim, and Vince found that Westerns, which are distinctly boys' programs in North America, are girls' favorites in England. The British Westerns correspond more closely to our children's than to our adult Westerns, but in the United

States both children's and adult Westerns are favorites of more boys than girls. Family or situation comedy, popular music and variety programs tend to be girls' favorites on both continents. But crime programs are very much more likely to be boys' programs in England, whereas here there is good reason to think that American girls are at least as interested as boys in crime and mystery.

In general, then, the pattern seems to be that girls early turn toward programs which relate to the responsibilities they will assume in adolescence and adult life. Boys, on the other hand, maintain "boy tastes" for adventure, excitement, and physical combat well into adolescence, pick up the taste for popular music several years later than the girls do, and only in the teens begin to assume the interest, expected of the male, in public affairs.

*Mental ability.* Brighter children tend to try things earlier. In particular, they take the hard steps earlier—the serious programs, the solid reading, and so forth.

You will see in the Appendix Table V-8, which demonstrates that almost twice as large a percentage of the brighter eighth-graders as of the lower intelligence groups were looking at television coverage of the 1958 congressional election. Furthermore, of those who viewed this program it was the brighter group who most enjoyed it. We found also that brighter children were the ones chiefly able to identify faces that had appeared on television for public affairs reasons as opposed to entertainment reasons. The patterns of public affairs news, public affairs commentary, and so forth begins earlier with these children, and it is they who first turn away from the whodunits, the Westerns, the situation comedies, and the like.

Furthermore, the brighter children are more selective in their tastes, and generally more critical than the others. In this connection, it will be interesting to examine Tables VI-10 and V-7 and 8.

In general, what is happening is that brighter children in their teens are being attracted away from television. They are also discovering that radio is a useful way to keep up with popular music while they study. They are being kept busier by homework and social life, and therefore have less time for television. Within the time they have, they are becoming more critical and turning away from some of the programs that seem to have less durable value for them.

Both the high and low groups, in mental ability, are therefore settling into adult patterns. The high group will use television less, and more selectively, and will turn to other media for much of its serious information needs. The low group will use television more, and printed media less. As their teen-age behavior suggests, they will use television heavily for crime mysteries, situation comedies, Westerns, variety and popular music.

*Family.* During a child's first ten years, the family is the chief influence on the shaping of the child's taste. His parents choose what they read to him. He has their example, and that of any older brothers and sisters. The reading material he finds most conveniently available is what the family brings into the home. And he speedily internalizes the family social norm. As we have already suggested, the work ethic norm of the middle class makes for less television and for a larger proportion of realistic, nonentertaining, self-betterment programs; whereas the pleasure ethic of the working class makes for more television and for a larger proportion of fantasy and entertainment. (See Tables V-9, 10, and 11.)

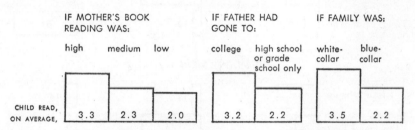

FIGURE 13   Amount of book reading (books per month) by children six to ten years old, related to parents' reading, education, and occupation.

Figure 13 illustrates the family's influence on mass media behavior in general.

There is some reason to think that the family's influence on taste is more noticeable between than within media. For example, a family of readers is likely to have a child who does a lot of reading; a family that reads little and sees a lot of television is likely to bring up a child in that same pattern. There is reason to believe, also, that family influence on taste is greater before adolescence. When a child becomes an adolescent, he is more likely to rebel against parental counsel, to experiment, to try to discover his own identity and personality. At the same time he comes to a greater extent under the influence of his peer group, and his media habits are likely to resemble those of other teen-agers he admires, or the general role of the teen-agers as he understands it.

Where family influence makes really spectacular differences, however, is in some of the fringe behavior such as viewing educational television. The following chart illustrates this relationship. Viewing educational television is a type of behavior which is relatively rare, which has little peer group utility to recommend it, and which runs directly counter to the popular idea that television is for entertainment. Therefore, the children who view it, as we have occasion to observe later in this volume, are usually the ones who have family example and encouragement.

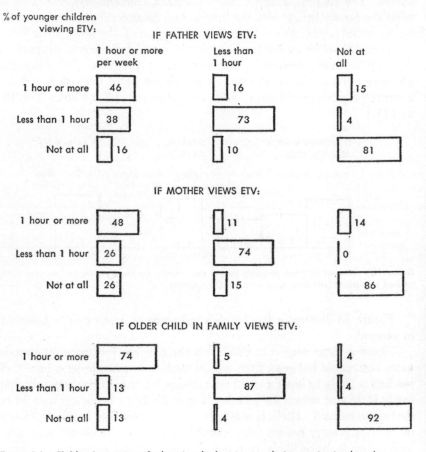

FIGURE 14    Children's viewing of educational television in relation to viewing by other members of family.

## What Children Think of Television

It goes without saying that most children hold television in affection and respect.

Indeed, so do most parents. When we interviewed 188 entire families

▶ For tables and other data applying to pages 48–56 see Appendix VI.

in San Francisco, we asked, along with other questions, which of the mass media each member of the family thought he would miss most if he had to do without it. We found that television was the medium most likely to be missed by the *whole family*; television was the medium most likely to be missed by the children; over-all, from parents and children alike, television was far more often mentioned as "most missed" than any other medium. (See Table VI-3.)

Let us note, in passing, that when radio was "most missed" it was usually by the mother (occasionally by a teen-age daughter). When the newspaper was "most missed," it was usually by the father. And a negative sort of testimony to the impact of television is the fact that when the people were asked, "Is there any medium that you wouldn't particularly miss at all, if you had to do without it?" 43 per cent of these families said that *no one* in the family would particularly miss theater movies.

Figure 15, based on data gathered by Dr. Reuben Mehling [84, 1959], indicates the general pattern of perceived importance of four media at different ages. He asked each person which medium that person would keep if he could keep only one. For every age level, more persons would want to keep television than anything else. Yet its relative importance falls sharply as children grow up. Whereas 91 per cent of younger children would want to keep television rather than any other medium, only 56 per cent of high school age children would prefer to keep TV, and only 38 per cent of college youth rank it first.

In Tables VI-1 and 2 you will find summaries of children's answers

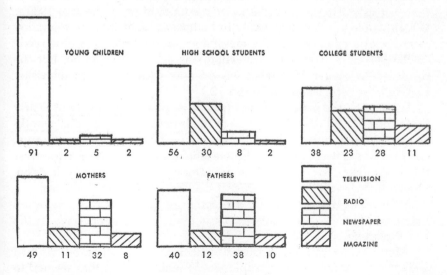

FIGURE 15  Which medium would you keep if you could keep only one? Answers, in per cent, from a sample in Indiana.

as to how much they would miss television in comparison to the other media. If you analyze these answers you will see that television looms much less large and important as a child grows older. In the teens, radio rises in importance to challenge television, and the newspaper begins to become important enough to be compared with television. But do not be misled by this falling curve of importance. Television is still, over-all, the medium that would be missed most, and this is true from the first grade to the twelfth.

If you look at Tables VI-2 and 6, in which "missing the media" is analyzed according to mental ability of the children, you will see that the brighter children are ahead of the others in their opinions; for example, television falls in importance, and the newspaper becomes important, earlier with the bright group than with the others. In general, the higher a child's IQ, after the age of ten or so, the less likely television is to be his most important medium. But the great swing away from television in the teen years is notably on the part of the middle and lower intelligence groups. The brightest children have made up their minds about television earlier, and already have begun using radio and newspaper more. Therefore television tends to depreciate with them less than with the others.

### Do they trust television?

How much do children trust television? Here we have two pieces of evidence. For one thing, in most of our studies we repeated a question first asked in some of the news media studies of the late 1930's: Which would you be more likely to believe—a news item on television or radio, or a news item in the newspaper—if the two items disagreed? In the 1930's, of course, this question was asked about radio, but the results were not far from what we get now with respect to television and radio. (See Tables VI-11 and 12.)

In general, the pattern we get from this question is a vote of nearly two to one, by children, in support of the broadcast media. Their mothers are typically ambivalent on the question; they would as readily trust one medium as the other. The fathers would, in a majority of cases, trust the newspaper. But the children are strongly on the side of television, although their willingness to trust it declines slightly in the teens.

What does this mean? Is it a function of age, or is this generation being brought up with a greater trust than their parents have in the broadcast media?

After these questions on trust had been framed and asked, we had a chance to see how young people would react to news that seemed to cast doubt on some of the trustworthiness of broadcasting. But we managed to talk to a number of children and parents about these developments, and can present their opinions.

The news of the quiz show "scandals" seemed relatively little to affect the teen-agers to whom we talked. It seemed more to affect their mothers, and it may well be that the mother of the flock was the chief worshiper at the feet of Charles Van Doren. But the teen-agers reacted sharply to the news and rumors about "payola." The most common reaction was angry denial: the "top 40" couldn't have been faked; their favorite disc jockeys wouldn't have taken money; and so forth. Others said that even if money had passed, it wouldn't have made any difference: the best tunes come to the top anyway. But there was sufficient talk about it, and a sufficient number of statements to the effect that "I wondered how that tune got into the top ten anyway," to suggest that the news made a deep impression. It is too bad that we were unable to test the effect, let us say, of Dick Clark's trouble on a large sample of teen-agers.

The teen-age girls to whom we talked appeared to be more disturbed about the payola news than were the boys. It may well be that the girls were the real hard core of the rock 'n' roll movement, and the shrieks and swoonings may be a peculiarly feminine ritual of worship for idols that have had less fervent worshipers among the boys.

### The prestige of television

We have been talking about how much television would be missed, and how much it is trusted. Now let us turn to the matter of its *prestige* with children. It is very hard to frame a question on prestige that can be answered reliably by very young children. For fifth-graders and beyond, however, we found it worked satisfactorily to use this approach.

> Some people are proud of one thing, some of another. For example, some would be prouder to have their friends see them watching television than to see them reading a book. Some would feel just the opposite about it. How about you? Suppose your best friend came along. Would you be prouder if this friend saw you reading a book or watching television? [And so forth with the other media.]

The comparisons that came out of this question appeared to be valid in view of longer and more searching talks we had with a smaller number of children.

In Tables VI-7 and 8 and in Figure 16 you will find results of this question. In general, here is the pattern that emerged:

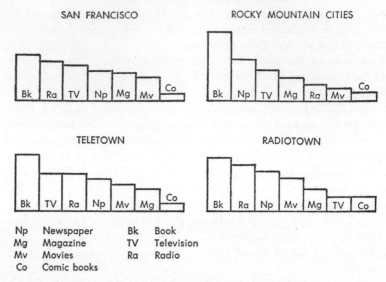

Np  Newspaper    Bk  Book
Mg  Magazine     TV  Television
Mv  Movies       Ra  Radio
Co  Comic books

FIGURE 16a  Relative prestige of the media by place.

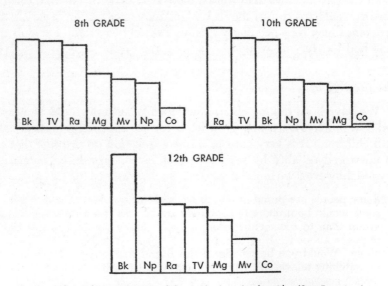

FIGURE 16b  Relative prestige of the media by school grades (San Francisco).

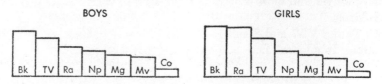

FIGURE 16c  Relative prestige of the media by sex.

The prestige of television declines considerably in the high school
years.
The prestige of the newspaper rises in those years. It is generally
higher with boys than with girls.
The prestige of movie-going falls in those years.
The prestige of comic-book reading falls from very little to still less.
The prestige of radio rises to a peak about the tenth grade, and then
falls off. It is generally higher with girls than with boys.
Above all, reading a book is still, even in this age of television, the
mass media activity with the most prestige among teen-agers.

When we look at the results more closely to see how the media stand
with different groups of students, we observe several trends of great
interest.

In the first place, and not entirely to our surprise, we find that the
prestige of television is higher with children who view a great deal of it.
The prestige of movies, and to some extent of radio, also seems to be
higher with the children who view a lot of television. But with these
children, the prestige of books and the other printed media seems to be
lower.

In the second place, high prestige ratings for books go with higher
mental ability; higher prestige ratings for television go with lower mental
ability. These correlations are very high. And in general, high mental
ability seems to go with high prestige ratings for the printed media, and
lower mental ability to go with high prestige ratings for television and
movies.

Thus we observe children's opinions dividing the media into two
groups, the printed media and the audiovisual media, and different
groups of children attaching themselves to each of these two groups of
media. This is an obviously important pattern.

The third trend we see in the prestige responses is one we have noted
before: the brighter children seem to make up their minds earlier. These
children, who do other things earlier and more quickly, seem also to
establish their estimates of the media earlier. By the beginning of high
school, they have a fairly firm idea of the prestige of books, television,
movies, and so on. The changes in their media use throughout the teen
years come about because of redistribution of their time and the availability of new and challenging activities, rather than because of any
noteworthy changes in their opinions with respect to the prestige of the
media. On the other hand, some real opinion changes and use changes
are taking place in the middle and lower intelligence groups.

### Do children marvel at it?

To some of us in the older generation, television is still rather wonderful. That is, it seems extraordinary to have in the house a box through
which one can look at a coronation in Westminster Abbey, a football

game on the other side of the continent, a great man being interviewed, or a national political convention.

Does it seem marvelous to children? It does not. One of the most interesting aspects of children's reaction to the magic tube is that it does not seem to them in any sense a magic tube. They take it for granted. If they do not have television in their homes, then it is exceedingly desirable. But once past the first excitement of exploring on their own television receiver, they settle down to use it just as though it were no more unusual than breakfast in the morning or a newspaper at the front door. It is fun; they would hate to do without it; but it isn't wonderful, or magical, or marvelous. It is simply something that people have and use today.

Lest we accuse them of being insensitive, let us recall that a most remarkable device within our own lifetimes has shrunk distances, made possible suburbia, made necessary thousands of miles of concrete ribbon across the landscape of the world, and, in fact, pretty well remade the map. But does any one of us take time to marvel when we get into an automobile?

*What would children like to see changed in television?*

Perhaps the most significant thing to be found out in asking children what changes they would like to see on television is how inarticulate they are on such a topic.

In general, they want more of the kinds of material they already see a great deal of. As they approach the teens, the girls want more popular music, more family situations. The boys want more sports, more war and police, more comedy. It is not until the later high school years, and then for the most part among the brighter children, that one finds any significant strain of "criticism" of television. At these ages, a few children think there are too many commercials; a few think that some of the personalities are unpleasant; a few think that television is "too much the same."

It is, of course, very difficult to decide that you would want something you have never experienced, yet it is interesting that children should be so unable to suggest any real *changes* in television. For example, it is a very small minority who seem to feel they want a higher type of programming—more classical music, more serious drama, more solid talks, debates, discussions, more science, and so forth. Almost nobody said he wanted more educational television, although when a child did say so, he wanted it very much indeed. For example, one Canadian boy lamented that the Seattle educational station laid down such an unreliable signal in British Columbia. He found its programs challenging and worth while, he said, in contrast to most commercial programs, and he tried frequently to pick it up. This was a lad who, in the 10th grade, was studying Arabic at home for his own amusement!

We do not think that children are wholly satisfied with television. As they go through the high school years, it falls in prestige and interest for them, and they find it less and less satisfying. But most of them are wholly unable to envisage any real alternatives. Partly this is due to the difficulty of imagining a medium one has never seen. Partly it is due to the general absence of a tradition in our culture for continuing and serious criticism of the mass media, except for books and to a lesser extent movies. Partly it is due to the great impact, the relatively recent impact, of television.

## What would their parents like to see changed?

In talking to the parents of grade school children, we asked what they do not like, or would want changed, in the mass media. We got answers from a little over 50 per cent, and almost 90 per cent of their answers concerned television. Only 10 per cent were about all the other media. It was a convincing demonstration of the dominance of television in their thinking. Twelve years ago, motion pictures and comic books would have monopolized their answers; now, those get very little attention in comparison to television.

Many parents of younger children are clearly concerned about the amount of violence and crime on television. The more highly educated the parents, the more worried they are about it. Blue-collar families tend to be more concerned about sexiness in programs; white-collar families, about the violence and law breaking. But above all, the objection is to the number of crimes and the extent of the violence which can be seen at hours when children view. "If you could prevent certain TV programs from being seen by your children, what kinds would you try to prevent?" parents were asked, and 65 per cent of their answers were that they would try to cut out programs of crime, violence, and horror.

"Why do you object to those?" these parents were asked. Because they frighten young children. Because children tend to keep them in their heads, remember them and dream about them. Because (a few of them said) they see children playing out some of these games. Because it gives children a wrong idea of what life is like. Because it might make for delinquency.

This is the general trend of the answers. It is a viewpoint more usually heard from college-educated parents and from middle-class rather than lower-class families. But it is unmistakably there, and must be reckoned with.

Among the more highly educated families, there was an occasional complaint that television was "cheap"; that it didn't challenge youngsters; that it was a waste of their time. This was seldom heard from noncollege parents or blue-collar families. In these latter cases, there was more likely to be gratitude that television kept their children "out of mischief" or "off the streets," and unspoken gratitude for its service as a baby-sitter.

There was some talk of commercials. Twelve years ago, Paul Lazarsfeld and Patricia Kendall wrote some observations on attitudes toward radio that might be repeated verbatim today with reference to television [78, p. 69]:

> First of all, people dislike what is known to the trade as "hard selling." It may be that such techniques lead to increased sales, but there can be little doubt that they also create hostility in the audience . . . We know also that commercials need not be "boring or repetitious." . . . Finally, listeners dislike interruptions in radio programs.

Although we were not trying to find out adult attitudes toward television in general, we heard these same complaints. They came usually from more highly educated listeners, they came in no great numbers (nor were they sought), but still, they came in sufficient quantity to indicate that there is dissatisfaction that goes far beyond a few cranks.

# CHAPTER 4

# WHAT A CHILD USES TELEVISION *FOR*

If you ask a child why he views television, he is unlikely to give you a good answer. He watches television because he likes it, of course. Because it is interesting. Why should you ask him such a question?

But as a result of asking children indirect questions and relating the answers to behavior, we have come to the conclusion that there are at least three great classes of reasons why children watch television. The first of these bulks many times the size of the second, and the second is larger than the third, but there are still three distinguishable ones.

## Why they view television

There is, first, the obvious reason: the passive pleasure of being entertained, living a fantasy, taking part vicariously in thrill play, identifying with exciting and attractive people, getting away from real-life problems and escaping real-life boredom—in other words, all the gratifications that come from having a superlative means of entertainment in one's living room, at one's command.

This is the reason that children find easiest to talk about. Yet it is hardly necessary for them to talk about it; the evidence is there. By the time they are three years old, they already are committed to favorite programs. A little later they begin to sit with absorbed faces, lost in the events of the picture tube. They astonish their mothers by being on time for a favorite program, although completely unable to be on time for anything else. They set up idols and find leaders to imitate on television. As children of an earlier generation pretended to swing through trees and scream like Tarzan, so do today's children mark Z in the sand because Zorro did it, or mount make-believe cow ponies and gallop over the imaginary range.

When they get along toward the teens, they begin to talk about how television keeps them from being bored. Why this younger generation

▶ For tables and other data applying to this chapter, see Appendix VIII.

should have such a capacity for being bored is not entirely evident, although it has been suggested that television, by providing so much excitement on the screen, makes the rest of life seem pallid. But whatever the reason, a mother now has a pat answer to that frequent question of childhood, "Mom, what shall I do?" And the child himself more and more comes to use the medium to bridge the gap between things that have to be done or things that he really wants to do, and to substitute for behavior that requires activity, initiative, and effort.

This is the schizoid side of television. It leads not toward human interaction, but rather toward withdrawal into private communion with the picture tube and the private life of fantasy. It is aimed less often at solving the problems of life than escaping from them. It is essentially a passive behavior—something a child surrenders himself to, something that is done to and for him, something that he doesn't have to work for or think about or pay for.

When children talk about this aspect of television, they tend to rate the entertainment or classify the performers. They judge the excitement or the magnetism of the entertainment. And they leave no doubt that these entertainment values are the chief reason, or at least the chief conscious reason, why they watch television.

But there is, nevertheless, a significant component of information which children also get, usually without seeking, from television. This represents the second great class of reasons for viewing.

Most children will acknowledge that they learn something from television. The girls say they learn something about how to wear their hair, how to walk and speak, how to choose garments for a tall or a short or a plump girl, by observing the well-groomed creatures on TV. They learn some details of manners and customs—for example, whether you tip the stewardess on an airplane. Some of the boys say they learn how young men dress in California or New York. Some of them say they learn a lot by watching the good athletes. More than one parent tells of a child who learned to swing a bat by watching Ted Williams or Stan Musial do it, and as a result was a playground sensation until he began to imitate his young friends rather than television. Children will say of television: "It helps me know how other kinds of people live," or "The news is more real when you have seen where it happens." Many of them say that television helps them in school, by giving them ideas for themes or topics to talk about.

Children are perfectly willing to admit that television pays this dividend of information. They are often irritated, however, when a program is all or mostly this kind of material. Apparently, they prefer incidental learning from television to purposeful and intentional learning. This is the heart of their objection to educational television. They can't go to educational television primarily for entertainment and expect to derive an incidental benefit by learning something useful. Instead, they have to go to it with the main purpose of learning something useful, and any entertainment they derive is incidental. So educational television tends to be classified as "square." It is something they are expected to take because "it is good for them." It suggests that the parental generation may be working on them, trying to teach them, trying to extend school into the play hours, keeping them from enjoying television in their own way.

This is not to say that children do not sometimes intentionally go to television to learn something from it, or that some children do not seek out and appreciate educational television. But the majority regard such behavior as an incursion on the chief function and the chief reward of television.

There is still another dimension of television's attractiveness. This is its social utility apart from what one learns from it. For example, teen-agers find that television is a useful tool in providing an excuse for boys and girls to enjoy each other's company, or furnishing something to do on dates, and especially in providing an excuse for young men and women to sit close together. The previous evening's television programs provide an excellent common ground of shared experience for conversation at school. If you can't talk about the new programs or the new stars, you simply aren't up to date with your peer group; thus television has a direct social utility. Some children appear to be quite compulsive about television. They feel vaguely ill at ease when they miss a favorite program, sometimes even when the television set is out of commission for a few days, when one of their favorite performers is off the air for a time, or when they go away from television for a summer vacation. Asked to explain this, one girl said, "It's just as if they were your friends or your family. You miss them when you don't see them." Other children give vague explanations about feeling "out of things," "not doing what the gang's doing," or "missing what you're used to doing." But there is little doubt that television is functional beyond specific entertainment or specific learning.

This social use of television is not essentially different from social use of an automobile or any other instrument that bulks large in a child's world. Therefore, we are going to talk about the other two uses which are directly related to television content.

It is clear that any television program is likely to be attractive in some measure on both of these information dimensions. The deadliest crime program may teach some skills and also convey information on "what the world is like." It may also contribute to the child's sense of community (his friends are probably watching it, too) and give him something to talk about the next day. Most teaching programs will have an entertainment bonus (even a lecturer tells stories and shows pictures or demonstrations). A sports program, which most people will see as entertainment, may be directly informative for a boy who is trying to play that sport. An orchestra, which is on the air for entertainment, may teach some skills to a young musician in the audience. Different programs thus offer different gratifications to different people. A domestic comedy may seem uproariously funny to a boy, but may set a girl thinking about how a tall woman should dress, or how a wife keeps her husband loving her. A news story about a murder trial may be a whodunit to one child; a commentary on conditions in the real world, to another; and to a third, a way of learning to commit a murder.

There is little doubt that learning to use television for useful information is a later, and a relatively more sophisticated, type of behavior than learning to use it for entertainment. Television is first, and always predominantly, a magic doorway into a world of fantasy, glamor, and excitement. It is an invitation to relax, to disregard one's real-life problems, to surrender oneself to the charming and handsome people, the absorbing events, that flicker on the picture tube. A child learns that not all entertainment is pure pleasure, and that there are different kinds of entertainment to be sought. After a while he learns that there are certain incidentally useful dividends from entertainment programs. All this he learns with time. He may or may not discover that there are sometimes sufficient reasons to seek out a program that is not immediately pleasant or entertaining, simply because it offers information that may in the future be useful to him. And if he does learn that, it comes later.

### The functions of television

Let us now try to put these uses of television into a broader framework.

As A. J. Brodbeck pointed out [8], in the classical theories of aesthetics there have always been two fundamentally opposed types of theory concerning the function of art in people's lives. On the one hand are the theories of emotion in which art appears as "a producer of relief, pleasure and indulgence for frustrated human wish and desire," and, on the other hand, theories "which have stressed the cognitive functions of art, in which art appears as a producer of insight, knowledge, and learning." In modern writings on the mass media, theories of the former type take the "psychoanalytical and voluntaristic view that art is, like the dream, a form of wish-fulfillment under the sway of the pleasure principle." Theories of the second type are likely to picture art as "an agency of socialization and social learning—an agency which, in other words, inculcates values, reinforces habits, and creates expectations much as parents and other real-life socializers do." We used to talk about these two kinds of theory in terms of *emotion* and *cognition*. Now we are more likely to use the terms *wish-fulfillment* and *socialization*. Criticism drawn from the first type of theory is much more likely to be negative (in the belief that art acts as a soporific, an opiate of the masses, which is more likely to prevent than to aid maturity) than criticism drawn from the second type (which is more likely to discuss art as "teacher of the masses"). Or if they are both used negatively, they are negative in different ways. The first leads us to worry that the mass media may delay maturation; the second, to worry that the teaching powers of the media are being used for the wrong thing.

It seems to us that a theory adequate for the present day, and for the mass media, must include both these points of view. It must concede that the two theoretical traditions do indeed reflect two kinds of content, two kinds of behavior, and two possible outcomes associated with mass media art.

From the beginning, let us avoid the trap of making value judgments about children's use of television—the trap of calling informational uses "good" and entertainment uses "bad." Such judgments about the consequences of television viewing can only hinder the answering of questions about *why* children view television. It is helpful to assume that viewing of television is behavior that is engaged in because it has met needs in the past, or that is being tried because it is expected to meet present needs. This general assumption justifies the search for the particular needs which can be used to account for why children view television.

In a real sense, every item of a culture exists because it is useful. Malinowski speaks for anthropologists when he says that "in every type of civilization, every custom, material object, idea and belief fulfills some vital function, has some task to accomplish, represents an indispensable part within a working whole." Even an apparently obsolescent and functionless artifact like the buttons on a sleeves of a man's jacket, Kluckhohn points out, is still useful in that it preserves the familiar and maintains a sense of tradition.

Why do we have mass media? In the passing of traditional society from the Western world, at the time of the Renaissance, men worked up such a storm of need and activity that the old system of communication was no longer adequate to human needs. That is to say, the generally speeded-up tempo of the world, the new needs to pass information over great distances, the new attention to ideas and science, the increasing interlocking of economics from place to place, the rise of the middle class to economic and political importance, the generally heightened mobility of society—all this upswing of action and interaction called for something more than hand-written books, minstrels, and town criers.

We need not say what was cause and what was consequence. There is a great deal of circularity within all culture change. Certain needs call for a change in behavior or the development of a new instrument, and the new development in turn encourages new needs. But, cause or consequence, the new institutions of the printed word were a great aid in meeting needs of human beings at that time with faster, wider, more flexible communication. It is worth remembering that in Asia men knew how to print with movable types, paper, and ink two hundred years before Gutenberg, and nothing happened to create mass media until in Western Europe the process and the needs came together.

Mass communication, then, came into use at that time because it was the best device available to meet certain important needs.

We are not meaning to imply that all men are rational at all times about doing what must be done to meet their needs, or that they are omniscient about the outcomes of their choices of behavior. We are merely contending that, in the process of cultural change, the behaviors that are finally adopted (whether by trial and error, or by rational planning, or by whatever means) are more rewarding for the individuals who adopt them than are the known alternates which were not adopted.

Similarly, we are not contending that behavior which is rewarding for one individual may not have unfavorable consequences for other individuals or for the society as a whole. Society tries, by coercion, social pressure, laws, and other means, to adjust the consequences of differential behavior. The resulting pattern of behavior may or may not be the "best" pattern, as viewed by philosophers or historians. It seems to us now that bread and circuses may not have been the best pattern for Roman society, but they seem to have been perceived at the time as more rewarding for the individual Romans of the time than any other available alternatives. By the same token, the verdict of tomorrow may be that television was not the "best" way in which American children of the 1950's and the 1960's might have spent time. We are saying only that television has come into use, and children have given it the great amount of time they have given it, because it is seen to be a way of meeting certain important needs, and the *best* way of meeting them among known and available alternatives.

What are the special needs of children that television meets?

Physically, a child is maturing. Socially, he is in process of preparing and being prepared to take part as an adult in society—or, as we say, being socialized. That is, he is learning the skills, such as reading and counting and getting along with people, which he will need for adult life. He is mastering the norms, the values, the customs of his society. He is acquainting himself with the more important laws and history of the culture, and the rituals which he will be expected to follow. He is being brought to the point where he can be "turned loose," without parental supervision, in the society of his elders and his fellows. At the same time, psychologically, he is in the process of discovery and goal-seeking. He is trying to form a picture of his environment, and trying to separate himself from that environment so as to form an image of his own identity. He is in quest of goals: where does he belong in the world? what work should he do? where should he stand on religion, politics, and ethics? what kind of friends should he cultivate? what kind of life partner should he and can he get?

For a child, these are difficult experiences, often productive of hard blows, fears, and frustrations. He can turn to television to escape from the conflicts and frustrations of the real world or, perhaps, to seek aid and enlightenment on his problems. Alternatively, because of the social environment in which he finds himself, he may give up the search for goals and resign himself to drifting in an environment over which he feels he has no control. He may then turn to television merely as entertainment and escape from boredom.

When he tries to meet these needs in television he finds two kinds of materials, which offer two kinds of reward and stimulate two kinds of behavior. It is hard to talk about these without recalling the analogy of Freud's Pleasure Principle and Reality Principle. In Freud's concept of the human personality, as you will recall, the Pleasure Principle is operative very early in life, and results simply in the organism making responses which have been found to return pleasure. Thus, for example, the infant may make sucking motions even though no source of food is at hand. The Reality Principle, on the other hand, is something learned later—the ability to seek out the right time and place where drives can be rewarded, and to withhold the pleasure-seeking responses until such time as they can be used with expectation of reward. The Pleasure Principle is thus related to the primary processes and to the Id; the Reality Principle to the secondary processes and to the Ego. Thinking of this analogy, one of the present authors once wrote of mass media behavior as "immediate reward" and "delayed reward" seeking, because the second behavior requires delayed gratification of impulses.

It seems preferable to label these two strands of mass communication with the terms *fantasy* and *reality*. And by way of identifying them, we can say that

| *fantasy* content: | whereas *reality* content: |
|---|---|
| invites the viewer to take leave of his problems in the real world; | constantly refers the viewer to the problems of the real world; |
| invites surrender, relaxation, passivity; | invites alertness, effort, activity; |
| invites emotion; | invites cognition; |

| *fantasy* content: | whereas *reality* content: |
|---|---|
| works chiefly through abrogating the rules of the real world; | works chiefly through realistic materials and situations; |
| acts to remove, at least temporarily, threat and anxiety, and often offers wish-fulfillment; | tends to make viewer even more aware of threat, perhaps more anxious, in return for better view of problem; |
| offers pleasure. | offers enlightenment. |

Now let us be sure what we understand by these two strands of content and response. We do not mean that two members of the audience will necessarily respond in the same way to the same material; for example, a story about a man of great wealth could be wish-fulfillment to one viewer and a realistic revelation of social injustice to another. Nor do we mean that many television programs are "pure fantasy" or "pure reality." In fact, one characteristic of mass media art is its ability to dwell in both kingdoms at once. Reality suggestions may be gained from fantasy, and reality material may start the process of fantasy. But summing over a great deal of content and over many audiences, we can say that, in general, Westerns, crime drama, popular music, and variety shows belong chiefly with fantasy, whereas news, documentaries, interviews, public affairs programs, and educational television are chiefly in the domain of reality materials. In other media, we can be fairly confident that comic books and strips will usually evoke a fantasy response, and most nonfiction books will evoke a reality response; that screen, confession, adventure magazines will usually belong with fantasy, and quality magazines with reality materials; that a newspaper sports story will be more likely to be read as fantasy material than will a newspaper editorial or a story of foreign affairs; and that an evening of films will probably contain more fantasy materials than will an evening of educational television.

## Television as fantasy

Eleanor Maccoby has written with insight on some of the uses of fantasy for children [18, p. 239 f.]. She lists three possible functions:

> The first is that fantasy provides a child with experience which is free from real-life controls so that, in attempting to find solutions to a problem, he can try out various modes of action without risking the injury or punishment which might ensue if he experimented overtly. Another function of fantasy is as a distractor. Readers are doubtless all familiar with the impulse to pick up a detective story and thus temporarily escape from the pressures of real life. Similarly for children, if the environment imposes strain, we may assume that the child will be motivated to "get away from it all" by immersing himself in fantasy. A

third function of fantasy, which was emphasized by Freud in connection with his analysis of dreams, is wish-fulfillment. According to this point of view, fantasy provides an outlet for impulses which are not allowed free expression in real life. Supporting this view is the fact that young children take an especially great interest in stories depicting violence and sudden death (reflecting perhaps the inhibition of aggressive impulses in their daily life) while adolescents are more interested in themes of romantic love. The vicarious satisfactions provided by fantasy are presumably of a lower order than real-life satisfactions, so that fantasy outlets are chosen only as second-best solutions when real-life satisfactions are lacking.

It might be possible to list other functions, but these illustrate the point: that children do meet real needs through the fantasy derived from television.

The outcome of their seeking behavior is not always predictable in terms of the kind of material they reach. For most children, fantasy may help to drain off excess aggression, but for some it may actually build aggression and contribute to violent acts. This, we repeat, is not wholly predictable from the content; it is necessary also to know the children.

Furthermore, whether fantasy is, in the long view, "good for them" is something we are not fully ready to discuss at this point. For some children, as Mrs. Maccoby suggests, fantasy may make possible the testing of solutions to problems without the restrictions or the embarrassment of doing so in real life. For others it may merely result in postponing those problems or pretending that they do not exist.

This is one of the most troubling questions one can ask about television as purveyor of fantasy: does it get in the way of solving real-life problems? There are moments and situations when it is useful to anesthetize a person against pain and distress—for example, when surgery is being performed, or when a broken limb is in traction. In these situations, the anesthetic gains time for a long-range solution to a problem. This may sometimes also be the effect of television used as anesthetic. But there is a great difference between a surgeon prescribing an anesthetic while he operates and a patient's self-prescription of fantasy as a cure for frustrations and anxieties. The latter is more like the self-prescription of liquor or drugs. And while it is perfectly true that one can temporarily get rid of frustrations and anxieties by getting drunk or taking a shot of cocaine, still these are hardly to be recommended as long-range solutions to human problems. In how many cases does television meet children's needs in the same way as alcohol or drugs might do so? Does it encourage them to seek immediate (but vicarious and thus inferior) satisfactions, and decrease their ability to tolerate frustration long enough to seek and find more adequate solutions? Does it tend to leave the real problems untouched?

These are disturbing questions—all the more disturbing because television is a master at making fantasy. Its extraordinary vividness, its ability to absorb one's attention, its ability to focus on the tiniest of details or on a great scene, its extraordinary freedom to tell a story in whatever way its imagination dictates—these qualities and others all make it the great purveyor of fantasy in our time. It is not surprising that this is the chief quality that attracts children to television.

### Television as reality

Television has certain advantages and certain disadvantages as a conveyor of reality experiences.

One of its advantages is that it can convey information earlier than most media. It is not necessary to learn to read before learning from television. Even after one learns to read, television still has the quality of speeding up the conveying of adult information. Indeed, with television in the living room, it is all but impossible to keep to the old, measured schedules of releasing "the facts" slowly—telling the children only bit by bit, year by year, about "life." We shall be able to demonstrate a little later that television does indeed speed up the process of learning at an early age.

In the second place, television has all the advantages inherent in an audiovisual channel. It can present information which would be much harder to carry through pictures or sound or print alone. For example, think of television's advantage in describing what a surgical operation is really like, or how people live and work in Africa. Furthermore, the same quality often makes it possible for television to present information in such a way that it is absorbed more easily. For example, consider how effectively television can reproduce a natural science demonstration, or show how cricket is played.

In the third place, by virtue of its organization and sources and ability to exchange tapes, television is in a unique position to enlarge the environment of viewers. TV cameras can go where few of their viewers can. They can carry the young child out of his family circle and his immediate neighborhood. They can offer the older child countless new worlds to explore, from the depths of the sea to the far corners of the earth to the preparation for space travel.

But not all its characteristics are favorable.

One quality in particular leaves television at some disadvantage as compared to print. Watching television, the viewer cannot set his own pace. He cannot repeat when he feels the need to do so, unless the television producer also wants to repeat. He cannot check back over what has gone before, unless the program recapitulates. Inasmuch as the producer has very little contact with his viewers, he is unlikely to set a pace and include repeats and summaries which will please everybody. Further, the viewer is at the mercy of a schedule. If it is a particular kind of information program he wants, he cannot get it for the asking; he must often wait weeks or months.

This quality, of course, makes for good storytelling, good fantasy, because in those forms the storyteller *should* be in charge, and the viewer *should* surrender himself. But it makes learning harder. That is why the child, after he learns to read well and finds how to use libraries and reference sources, tends to seek information more often from print. With print he is in greater control.

Another quality of television which may make learning harder is, paradoxically, the very concreteness of the audiovisual mode of presentation. The higher level of abstraction in the print media may be more successful in forcing attention to the abstractions and generalizations which increase learning and retention and which aid the application of what is learned to new situations. The specificity and real-seeming nature of television may, by its very detailed audiovisual presentation, distract a viewer from such abstractions.

There is another reason why television may be less effective than we might expect it to be as a conveyor of information. Because it has been such a great success as a fantasy medium, a great part of the support, the talent, and, of course, the viewer interest has been diverted there. The act of seeking information on television has seemed almost like a perversion of the medium.

However, let us remind ourselves that very little of the information learned from television comes from seeking. Much of it is incidental learning, usually gained as a by-product of fantasy materials. Once again, let us not make any advance judgments about which of these incidental learnings are necessarily "good." Children may learn good manners or bad grammar, without ever seeking it, from television. They may learn how to decorate a room or how to burglarize a home. What they see, what they learn, and the use they make of it, depend on the child as well as on the program.

The point is that children do not typically go to television to learn. They more often go to television to escape boredom or forget their problems.

## The two worlds

It must have occurred to you, as you have read the preceding pages, that a child spending two to three hours a day on television has to do an extraordinary amount of jumping back and forth between a world of fantasy and a real world. This is true. And this fact is getting close to the heart of what television means to a child.

Consider some of the differences in those two worlds of a child. Fantasy faces ever away from reality. It refuses to be bound by the rules of life. The handsome hero of fantasy is much more likely to get the girl of his dreams than is the average high school student. Superman may look like an ordinary fellow in his street clothes, but he can fly. For one of us to take the chances that a TV crime-buster takes would quickly land us six feet underground. But the rules of fantasy protect the foolhardy hero. The rules protect the viewer, too. If he walked down some of the streets he sees on television, he would have his heart in his mouth, two guns in his hands, and a farewell letter in his pocket. But he can sit, relaxed and at ease, in front of the set, six feet from a shooting, and nothing can happen to him.

This bouncing back and forth is a difficult behavior to learn. A typical child, for a few years, probably considers one world about as real as another. We know that when a young child believes a program "really happened" the program has more impact on him. But what stride of development does it require before a student learns to sort out the make-believe from the real? What advance in psychological map-making has to occur before the child knows clearly where the border of fantasy lies and where the real world begins?

This is a very important part of growth. If a child carries some of the rules of fantasy over to real life, if he behaves in real life as though he were protected by the rules of fantasy, if he withdraws too often from the real world to the comfort and delights of fantasy, this is the predictor of trouble. We shall return to this point.

## The importance of fantasy

Although the child finds in television two types of materials which help to meet his needs by calling forth what we have designated fantasy and reality responses, it is clear that the primary function of television for children is its contribution to fantasy behavior. And whereas it contributes some information, it tends also to distract from the solution of real-life problems.

Not only do children chiefly seek the material on television most likely to arouse fantasy behavior, but they also learn to seek this kind of material much earlier than they learn to seek reality materials. It is not surprising that it should be so. It is relatively easy to sit down to be entertained. But to seek after information which requires you deliberately to defer any pleasure you may get from it, to accept the possibility of greater tension rather than tension reduction for a while, to work hard before the very picture tube that implores you to relax and enjoy it—this is altogether a more difficult and more sophisticated behavior. When the usefulness of reality seeking is learned, for the reasons we have suggested, children are more likely to seek reality material in print than on television.

*Testing the function*

How do we know that this is a correct statement of the case—that children use television overwhelmingly for fantasy; and that although there is considerable reality seeking from television, a much larger proportion of that takes place with printed materials?

We know, for one thing, that when children talk about the gratifications they get from television, the fantasy gratifications come out first and in much greater number. When they list favorite programs, fantasy types of program are likely to outnumber reality programs by a ratio of twenty to one.

This, too, is the general conclusion to be drawn from earlier research in the field. Mrs. Himmelweit, in England, found children seeking a great amount of fantasy. Mrs. Bailyn, studying fifth- and sixth-grade school children in New England, came to a carefully qualified conclusion that a chief goal children sought on television is "escape" [6]. Mrs. Maccoby, also studying children in New England, found that upper-middle-class children who were highly frustrated in their home lives (who did not get along with their parents, or faced a great deal of parental disciplining) spent considerably more time with television than did children of their own age who were not so frustrated [18]. What was apparently going on was that these frustrated children built up a great deal of aggression, which they could not get rid of overtly by running away or fighting their parents, and therefore went to television to get away from the real world and its strains. It is not surprising to find out, not only that they chose fantasy programs, but also that they tended to choose programs of violence in which they could work off the aggression vicariously.

We are also in position to test this idea from our own Radiotown and Teletown data, and at the same time to interpret some of the changes in children's living habits which we discussed in Chapter 2. You will recall that we studied a small city in western Canada which had television, and another small city much like the first except that television had not yet come to it. Therefore, we can compare, approximately at least, some of the behavior of children before and after television.

We know already that television, when it arrives, tremendously rearranges a child's habits and time allocations. In so doing, it replaces previous habits of living. What does it replace? If our theory, stated in this chapter, is correct, it replaces activities which were aimed at meeting the same needs it meets. It replaces them because it can do a better job at meeting the same needs. Therefore, if we know precisely what television replaces, we know something about what needs it is meeting.

Now if television were meeting what we call the fantasy need—that is, the need for escape, for reduction of threat and tension, for vicarious excitement, for wish-fulfillment, and so forth—what activities in a child's pretelevision life should we expect it to replace?

One of the clearest cases would seem to be the reading of comic books. Certainly the fantasy rewards named above are those usually associated with comics. We can test this because we inquired in both cities about children's comic book reading.*

|  | Radiotown | Teletown |
|---|---|---|
| Number of comic books read per month by average child: | | |
| In first grade | 4.32 | 1.86 |
| In sixth and tenth grades | 7.92 | 3.60 |

In other words, television reduces the comic book reading among children to less than half what it had been! We are going to spare you the statistics and other details on these comparisons (full tables and statistics are in Appendix VI), but it is worth noting that these differences are highly significant. They could not occur by chance one in a thousand times.

We should also expect that television might replace some movie-going. The movies, too, have traditionally catered to fantasy needs. Here is what we find when we compare the movie-going of children before and after television:

|  | Radiotown | Teletown |
|---|---|---|
| Percentage of first-grade children who attend at least one movie a month | 89.3% | 30.6% |
| Average number of movies seen per month by sixth- and tenth-grade children | 4.45 | 1.15 |

So television cuts movie-going by a factor of three. These differences are as highly significant statistically as the differences in the case of comics.

We should also expect television to cut into radio-listening. Recall that many of the radio entertainers reappeared on television, and that many programs were transformed and transferred. We recall, too, that radio used to be considered one of a child's great sources of escape and

* N's for the following tabulations in this chapter are as follows:

|  | Radiotown | Teletown |
|---|---|---|
| First grade | 137 | 172 |
| Sixth grade | 110 | 194 |
| Tenth grade | 115 | 185 |

Supporting figures on statistical results will be found in Tables VIII-1 through 7.

of vicarious excitement and wish-fulfillment. And we do indeed find that television replaces much of the previous radio-listening:

|  | Radiotown | Teletown |
|---|---|---|
| Average number of hours spent on average school day listening to radio: | | |
| By first-grade children | 1.29 | 0.69 |
| By sixth- and tenth-grade children | 3.07 | 1.68 |

These, too, are highly significant differences statistically. We see that television cuts radio-listening almost exactly in two.

If television is indeed filling mainly the fantasy need of children, we should expect that it would replace, to some extent, the reading of escape magazines (for example, confession, screen, adventure, detective magazines) but *not* the reading of other kinds of magazines. And we find that only 20 per cent of the sixth- and tenth-grade children in Teletown read escape magazines, as compared to 34 per cent in Radiotown. The total reading of magazines in Teletown is just enough lower (about half a magazine per child per month) to account for this difference in reading of escape magazines.

We can assume, then, that television is taking over many of the services previously performed for children by comic books, movies, radio, and escape magazines. If these services are, indeed, chiefly the providing of fantasy experiences, then we should expect that television would *not* replace, to any significant extent, the reading of newspapers, books, or general magazines. None of these media, of course, is exclusively fantasy- or exclusively reality-providing, but certainly the weight of newspaper-reading experience, let us say, is on the other side of the reality border from the experience of reading comics; the experience of reading books (especially nonfiction books) on the other side from the experience of radio or movies; and the experience of reading general, quality, and news magazines on the other side from that of escape magazines. If television is providing as much for reality needs as for fantasy needs, we should expect it to cut into books, newspapers, and magazine reading as much as into radio, movies, comic books, and escape magazines; if it is chiefly fantasy-providing, on the other hand, we should expect a real difference between what it does to the one group of media and what it does to the other.

We have already demonstrated that television cuts into the reading of escape magazines rather than general magazines. Here is what we find about books and newspapers:

|  | Radiotown | Teletown |
|---|---|---|
| Average number of books read per month by sixth- and tenth-grade children | 3.41 | 3.18 |
| Percentage of sixth- and tenth-grade students reading newspaper more than once a week | 72.3% | 74.4% |

In the case of newspapers, the amount of reading is almost exactly the same. The amount of book reading in Teletown is slightly less than in Radiotown, but the difference is not statistically significant.

We discover, also, that in the pretelevision community, radio, comic books, movies, and escape magazines tend to cluster together. That is, if a child is high in comic reading, he is likely to be high in movie-going too, and so forth. Similarly, book, newspaper, and magazine reading also cluster together in children's behavior. That is, it seems clear that the two groups of media are providing different experiences, and we can assume that one is providing chiefly what we call the fantasy experience, and the other chiefly the reality experience.

Testimony to the tremendous impact of television is what happens to these correlations in Teletown. Here, as we have shown, there has been a significant reduction in the use of the other fantasy media, and television has taken over a large part of the job. But there is no longer the same tight grouping among all these behaviors. Comic book reading still goes with high television viewing, but no longer is television use associated with either movie-going or radio-listening. We have to go behind the scenes to find what has happened. In the case of radio, it becomes clear that radio has been forced, for survival, to become a "second medium." Two-thirds of the sixth- and tenth-grade children in Teletown are using radio as background sound while they read or do homework, and therefore it tends to correspond in time more with reading behavior than with television behavior. As for movies, television has brought about the closing of both movie theaters in Teletown. Children are seeing most of their movies on television. In a later chapter we shall look at figures on this print-television behavior in other communities where the effect has not been quite so traumatic and where the relationships are easier to see.

We are in position to make at least three more predictions about expected differences between Teletown and Radiotown, on the basis of our theory that television replaces activities whose job of meeting needs it can do better. We can predict that television will cut into playtime, because it is meeting some of the same needs. We can predict also that it will not cut greatly into homework time, because the needs which lead to doing homework are not met to any great degree by television; and that it will cut slightly, if at all, into sleep because it clearly does not meet that need. In the case of the latter two, we have conflicting needs: the child feels he ought to do homework at the same hour he really wants to watch television; and he wants to stay up for a television program even though it leaves him sleepy the next morning. It is likely, therefore, that the school and the parent, and the child's own heaviness of eye, will defend against any great reduction of study and sleep time, regardless of the great attraction of the picture tube. Similarly, the social attractions of play, and the need to stretch muscles and get outside, will make sure that television does not completely oust play from a child's schedule. The competition between fantasy-providing mass media and other activities was present before TV.

What do we find?

| | Radiotown | Teletown |
|---|---|---|
| Average number of hours first-grade children spend playing | 3.51 | 2.92 |
| Average number of hours reported spent on homework by sixth- and tenth-grade children | 5.61 | 5.32 |
| Average bedtimes for first-grade children | 8:02 | 8:13 |

As expected, the playtime is cut a little over half an hour a day. Bedtime is pushed back about 11 minutes, on the average, and homework is reduced by the insignificant amount of about 15 minutes a week. These results give us considerable confidence that we are indeed getting a measure of the needs television is meeting and is not meeting.

### Finally

We have advanced the theory that the mass media exist because they are useful in meeting human needs, and that television has come into use and made such a change in the lives of children because it meets some of these needs better than any other known alternative. We have presented some evidence to indicate that the chief needs television meets for children are those we group under the head of fantasy, as opposed to those we call reality needs. In other words, the chief part television plays in the lives of children is that of stimulating fantasy seeking and fantasy behavior.

Now let us be careful not to say that fantasy or reality seeking is necessarily either good or bad, or that one contributes to socialization and the other does not. It is clear that either may contribute to, or slow up, socialization and adjustment.

For example, *fantasy* behavior may

(a) Drain off some of the discontent resulting from the hard blows of socialization;

(b) Provide insights and analogies that may help an alert viewer to see himself better;

or

(c) Lead a child into withdrawal from the real world, encourage the confusion of real situations with fantasy, and thereby cause him more trouble than he should have in learning the rules of the real world;

(d) Build up aggression, rather than draining it off, so that socially acceptable adjustment becomes more difficult.

*Reality-seeking* behavior may

(a) By clear interpretation, skill learning, and practical suggestions, help a child to make socially acceptable adjustments;

or

(b) Prove unadapted to the conditions the child faces, hence frustrating; or permit him to learn socially undesirable behavior.

Which outcomes occur will depend on the conditions of the experience. Let us repeat that we feel the outcome depends at least as much on what the child brings to television as on what television brings to the child. Therefore, the problems that will chiefly concern us in the remainder of this book will be the conditions under which a child selects what he selects—the fantasy, the reality materials, in whatever proportion—from television; and the conditions under which a favorable or unfavorable result, in terms of socialization and general well-being, is likely to result from either choice.

briefly the relation of mental ability to the learning experiences to which a child chooses to expose himself on television.

## Mental ability and television behavior

Mental ability* is one of the great building blocks (along with personal relationships and social norms, and, of course, age and sex) which go into the structure of a child's television patterns. When you examine the television behavior of children, in relation to their mental ability, you find a highly characteristic pattern.

The heart of this pattern is a quite remarkable turning point, usually between the ages of ten and thirteen, at which the bright and the less bright children to a certain extent exchange television roles.

Typically, the bright children are early starters. They usually begin earlier to watch television, to look at the picture magazines earlier, and to read earlier. In the early school years, these students of high mental ability are more likely than the others to be heavy viewers of television.

In one school system we had the opportunity to study a group of fourth- and fifth-grade children who had been brought together, because of their very high intelligence scores, for some special classes. These were most remarkable children. They were studying nuclear physics with great interest, specifying the different shells of the atom and considering the tables of periodic weights. They were handling mathematics in a way that would have done credit to most high school and some college students. They were voracious readers. We rather expected that their broad intellectual curiosity and their wide reading would eat into their television time. But quite the contrary! Their television time was proportionally nearly as high as their reading time. They seemed to have an almost inexhaustible fund of energy for mental activities. They did *more* of everything—more television, more movies, more reading, more discussing, more investigating on their own.

Theirs was an extreme example, but in general the pattern holds. During the first six or eight years of television viewing, the bright children tend to be heavy rather than light viewers.

Then an abrupt change occurs.

This generally comes about soon after the age of ten. Already, by the time of the sixth grade, as Figure 17 shows, some of the change has taken place. The bright children are a little less likely than the

---

* When we speak in the following pages of "high mental ability" or "high IQ" we usually mean an intelligence score of 115 or over. By "low mental ability" or "low IQ" we mean intelligence scores under 100. The "middle" group is therefore the children with scores from 100 to 114, inclusive.

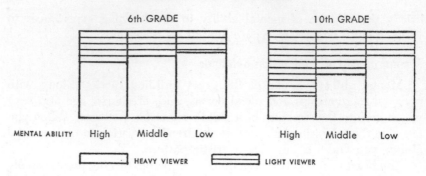

FIGURE 17 Proportion of Rocky Mountain children of different mental abilities above or below a given level of TV use.

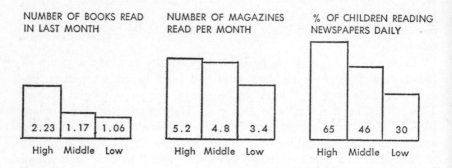

FIGURE 18 Reading of printed media by eighth-grade children of different mental abilities (high, middle, low).

others to be heavy viewers, although there is still relatively little difference among the three mental ability groups. But by the tenth grade, as this same figure shows, and even by the eighth grade (see Figure 18), the three groups are clearly differentiated, and low viewing goes with high mental ability. As a matter of fact, in two of the three grades shown in Figure 18, viewing time for the top intelligence group is less than half that of the low group.

Now, what is happening to bring about this change?

For one thing, of course, the change coincides with the beginning of adolescence, when the child discovers new social needs. Again, it comes at a time when the child discovers new intellectual challenges. School grows harder; the newspaper becomes more than a carrier of comic strips; the child's peers begin to talk about politics, religion, and other controversial questions that require taking a stand. The child is, therefore, led to a more purposeful use of the media; rather than merely absorbing content, he goes seeking specific content. And he tends to make proportionately greater use of the media that will "stand still" while he seeks what he needs—in other words, print.

Now, of course, there is a general decrease in amount of mass media use during the teens. Young people are seeking social, rather than solitary, experience. They are becoming busier. Therefore, their out-of-school reading decreases during the teens, although it decreases relatively less than does their television time. We are dealing, then, with *relative* distributions of time. Within a shrinking total allocation of time for the mass media during these years, the bright children are devoting an increasing *proportion* of that time to print and to reality experiences.

The middle and lower groups also undergo a change of this kind. It is quite clear from the tables in the Appendix and some of the charts in this part of the book that their television viewing and the importance of television for them do decrease during the teen years; and at the same time their use of print and their seeking of reality materials do increase. But in their case, the change comes more slowly.

Why should the bright children make this change more quickly and in a more extreme fashion? Because they seem to have the ability to take all the long mental steps earlier. They turn more quickly away from the fantasy materials because they have the ability to be challenged by and to make use of the more difficult reality materials.

This helps to explain why you will see, on the accompanying charts and in the tables in Appendix VII, that after the fifth or sixth grade the bright children make more use of print (except pulp magazines and comic books), less use of television, movies, comic books, and pulps. You will see that the figures on radio use are somewhat ambiguous; it is hard to tell whether radio belongs with the print or with the audiovisual group. This is simply because radio is used much of the time in the teens as background sound while a child reads. Because its time overlaps that of reading, therefore, it seems to correlate with the print media; but actually it is still used largely for popular music, and therefore for a fantasy, rather than a reality, purpose. You will notice, in the charts and the tables, that the picture is quite consistent. The bright children are first to turn to reality materials in all the media. They are the first to read foreign news, news of the national government, and editorials in newspapers. They are the ones most likely at an early age to view public affairs programs on television. They are the most frequent viewers of educational television stations. Whenever a bright child does not follow this pattern, a good guess is that he has troubles in his home or with his peer group, and is being driven to seek fantasy as an escape.

What do the bright children think of the mass media? They are more critical, more selective. They give higher prestige to books and newspapers, lower prestige to television and movies. In general, they give prestige to reality as opposed to fantasy materials. But Figure 20 is a useful corrective to possible misconceptions of what has just been said. This figure is a summary of children's judgments as to which media they would miss most. Even though there is a general movement away from television in the teens, still television is the medium which a majority of *all* mental ability groups would miss most. Even though the bright children give television little prestige, they would still miss it—though the middle and low groups would miss it more. The middle and lower groups, in the eighth grade at least, have not yet learned to miss books or newspapers; the children who would miss these media come chiefly from the top mental ability group. The percentage who would miss movies increases somewhat after this time, and the percentage who would miss comic books fades almost to zero.

## What learning should we expect?

On the basis of what we have been saying, a reasonable hypothesis would be that television contributes to a fast start in learning, but that the advantage does not last.

We should expect, for example, that children would come to school with larger vocabularies than children the same age commanded before the time of television. We should expect them to be familiar with wider worlds, and to be able to relate their school work more broadly. We should expect them at an early age to know more about adult life, sex, crime, and social problems.

This is because the young child in the television era is being exposed to much more information about the world beyond his immediate neighborhood than was the young child in a pretelevision era. A child without television who cannot read must depend on his own direct observations of the world around him and on other people who may take time to read or tell stories to him. For the young child who has access to television, an entire new world is opened up. The television set is always, parents willing, available to tell a story or show the child pictures of people and places strange to him. Once he learns to tune the TV set himself, he has a ready gateway to a world of knowledge and excitement. Consequently, the young child with television spends more time in a situation where he is likely to gain incidental information than the child who depends on parents to read or tell stories to him.

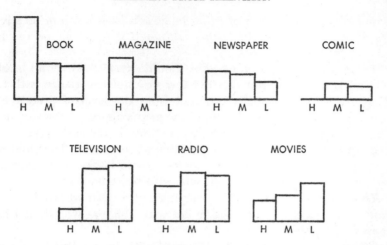

FIGURE 19   Prestige of media with eighth-grade children of different mental abilities (high, middle, low).

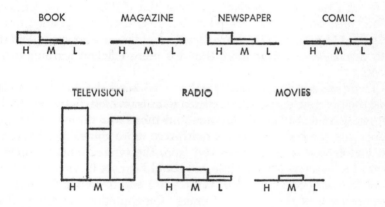

FIGURE 20   Percentages of eighth-grade children who would most miss each of the media, by mental ability (high, middle, low).

However, we should expect that this increase in general knowledge resulting from television would not last beyond a few grades. That is, we should expect a six-year-old in the television age to come to school with more knowledge than a six-year-old in the pretelevision age, but we should expect to find very little difference in ten- or twelve-year-olds.

After the child has learned to read and has access to the world around him through doors of print, television loses much of its advantage as a doorway to information, although it may still be the best doorway to fantasy.

There is another reason why we should expect the over-all level of a child's knowledge, after the first few years of experience with television, not to be essentially different from the level of pretelevision years. This is because the content of the media appears to be very much of a piece. The extra learning from television in the early years comes from the extra time that television is able to command. The child who learns incidentally from radio, movies, comic books, and magazines tends to catch up with the child who also has television.

This early advantage and later equalizing is what we would expect, comparing children in a television era with children who do not have access to television.

Comparing heavy television viewers with light television viewers in the same community is a different kind of comparison. For young children who have only limited access to other media, i.e., six-year-olds who have not yet learned to read well, the heavy viewers should learn more than the light viewers. However, the children who continue to spend considerable time with television after they have learned to read well would be expected to learn less than children who spend less time with television and have more time for more efficient learning experiences.

There are certain differences in knowledge we should expect to find, after the first few years of experience with television, between children who view a great deal of television and those who do not. We should expect that the heavy viewers would have more knowledge about subject matter that is directly derived from the typical fantasy entertainment of television. For example, we should expect them to know more about ranches (because of the "Westerns") and be better able to recognize the faces of popular entertainers. On the other hand, we should expect these heavy viewers to know less about subject matter that is more directly derivable from other media than from the fantasy content of television. For example, we should expect them to know less about literature and public affairs. In the case of subject matter which is learned in school, rather than being easily derived from any of the mass media, we should expect very little difference—other things being equal—between heavy and light viewers.

We should also expect some differences by mental ability. For one thing, we should expect the bright children to learn more of every kind of subject matter, from whatever source, than the other children. We should also expect that the bright children would learn *proportionally* more than the average children from any *new* experience with television. For example, in the early childhood years when television is new, we should expect the bright children to come to school showing proportionally more vocabulary gain over pretelevision children than the less bright children show. This is because the bright children have more ability to learn, and are more likely to be "achievers"—that is, to have strong motivation to learn.

By the same token, we should expect the slower children to show proportionally more gain from a new experience with television than the average children. This is because television absorbs them and therefore leads them to expose themselves to incidental learning for much longer than they would were it not for television. In a sense, television thus makes up for their lack of motivation.

But we should expect to find that these phenomena would ordinarily occur only as a result of *new* experiences with television. As the newness fades and the material becomes more and more familiar, continual viewing would bring no additional advantage over children without television. Further, as children without access to television expose themselves to similar content in movies, radio, and print, they should catch up with children who view television.

To sum up, we are hypothesizing that television probably gives children a faster start in learning vocabulary and general knowledge about their environment than they were able to get in pretelevision times, but that this advantage vanishes after a few years. Also, at first (and with every *new* experience with television) the brightest and the slowest children make proportionally more gain in knowledge than the average children, although for different reasons. And finally, in these days of television, heavy viewing will make for more knowledge about subject matter directly related to the fantasy content of television, for less knowledge about reality subject matter more easily learned from other media than from the predominantly fantasy-producing content of television, and for neither more nor less knowledge of subject matter usually learned in school rather than from the media.

These hypotheses are not easy to test. But let us try them against such knowledge as we have.

*Television vs. pretelevision*

Let us start with Radiotown and Teletown. The latter of these, as you will recall, has television; the former has not. Here, if our assumptions are correct, we should find that television makes it possible for the children of Teletown to get a faster start in learning. And we should find that it gives a special advantage to the children of above-average and below-average intelligence.

The best means we have for testing this is with vocabulary. We gave a standard test of oral vocabulary to first-grade children in both communities, in the same week of the school year.

We found, as expected, that the children of high intelligence in Teletown scored higher in vocabulary than the corresponding children of Radiotown. And so did the children of below-average intelligence. In each case, the vocabulary level was about one year more advanced in Teletown. As between children of average intelligence in the two towns, however, there was no significant difference.

These results in detail will be found in Tables IX-1, 2, 5, 6.

In addition to this standard vocabulary test, which has been given all over North America and for which norms have been established from the performance of many thousands of children, we also gave children in these two communities a special vocabulary test composed of timely and topical words like *satellite, war,* and *cancer.* Here we found that all three intelligence groups in Teletown scored higher than their corresponding groups in Radiotown, but only one difference was statistically significant—the below-average intelligence group. (See Tables IX-3, 4, 7, 8.)*

Trying to check the contribution of television to these differences, we divided the Teletown children into two groups in terms of how much time they spent on television. In the special "timely" vocabulary test, we found in each intelligence group that the heavy viewers scored higher than the light viewers, although only the difference in the above-average and below-average intelligence groups were significant. In the general vocabulary test, heavy viewers in both high- and average-intelligence groups scored significantly higher than their corresponding groups of

* There is some evidence in the literature of *instructional* television and films to support the idea that high- and low-intelligence groups may under some conditions learn more than average intelligence groups from a film or program. Hoban and Van Ormer [63(1951)], reviewing 12 film studies, report: "It appears that . . . there is a fairly high positive correlation between intelligence and learning from . . . a pictorial-verbal medium of communication." J. H. Kanner, R. P. Runyon, and O. Desiderato (*Television in Army Training: Evaluation of Television in Army Basic Training,* Washington, D.C., Human Resources Research Office, George Washington University, Technical Report No. 14, (1954) found that among army recruits taught by television, in ten achievement tests out of seventeen (seven showed no significant difference), low-aptitude trainees scored significantly higher than comparable trainees taught by conventional methods; but that there was no significant difference in groups of high-aptitude trainees taught by the two methods. They suggest, however, that the lack of difference in the high groups might have been due to the fact that these trainees scored so near the ceiling of the tests that there was little room to show improvement. Barrow and Westley [66(1959)], studying a series of news background programs taught simultaneously by radio and television to sixth-grade students, found that television was significantly superior to radio among high- and low-intelligence groups, but not in middle groups.

light viewers, but there was no difference between heavy and light viewers in the below-average intelligence group. Our tentative explanation for these results in the low group is that television had brought these slower children close to the upper limit of their ability on the more difficult general vocabulary test, and therefore that additional practice made little difference beyond the difference already achieved. In any case, the results give us good reason to think that it is really the presence of television, rather than something else, that is making the difference in vocabulary scores in the two towns.

Let us now sum up these findings among first-grade children of high, average, and low intelligence:

*General vocabulary:*

| | Comparison of Two Towns | Teletown Only |
|---|---|---|
| High | Teletown children scored higher | Heavy television viewers scored significantly higher |
| Average | There was no significant difference | Heavy viewers scored significantly higher |
| Low | Teletown children scored significantly higher | Very little difference |

*Special vocabulary:*

| | Comparison of Two Towns | Teletown Only |
|---|---|---|
| High | Teletown scored higher but not significantly so | Heavy viewers scored significantly higher than light ones |
| Average | Teletown scored higher but not significantly so | Heavy viewers scored higher but not significantly so |
| Low | Teletown children scored significantly higher | Heavy viewers scored significantly higher |

So far as vocabulary represents general knowledge, then, we can say with some confidence that television appears to help children get off to a faster start.

But does the advantage continue, or does it—as we predicted—fade out? Here we are on less firm ground. We gave a number of tests and scales to sixth- and tenth-grade children in Teletown and Radiotown, trying to measure their knowledge in a variety of areas: science, ability to name band leaders and popular singers, knowledge of literature, faraway place names, and statesmen and rulers. We found no over-all significant differences between the children of the two communities in either the sixth or the tenth grade, and very few significant differences even when we divided the children into smaller groups by intelligence and by amount of viewing. This is precisely the experience of the Himmelweit-Oppenheim-Vince team in England, who were "not able to find a sufficiently large number of information items . . . which, without being trivial or abstruse, were not only known equally well to the controls—a further indication of the essential similarity of the material put over by the different mass media" [4, p. 291].

But when one looks at trends, there is a clear difference.

When the children are divided into groups by school grade and intelligence, and each of these groups is compared on each of the seven tests mentioned with its corresponding group in the other town, we have a possibility of 21 comparisons in each grade, a total of 42 in all. *All* the comparisons in the *sixth* grade are in favor of Radiotown; 60 per cent of the comparisons in the *tenth* grade are in favor of Teletown. All the comparisons in the science test, where there is a difference, are in favor of Radiotown. To be sure, very few of these comparisons are themselves statistically significant. However, by sign test, the performance of the Radiotown children is significantly superior in the sixth grade, and there is no significant difference in the tenth grade (see Table IX-9 for details). Therefore, we can say at least that there is no evidence in these tests that children in the upper grades in a television town are superior in general knowledge to children in a comparable nontelevision town.

The evidence at hand, then, seems to support our hypothesis that whereas television contributes to a fast start in learning of general knowledge, the advantage does not last; and that the advantage is greater to the children above and below the middle intelligence group.

### Heavy vs. light viewing

We predicted that heavy viewers of television would know more about subjects closely connected to the principal content of television, that light viewers would know more about subject matter closer to the content of other media, and that there would be no difference between them on their knowledge of subjects more easily learned elsewhere than from the mass media.

These predictions can be tested by dividing three of our samples—San Francisco, the Rocky Mountain communities, and Teletown—into heavy and light viewers, by grade in school and by intelligence, and in each case comparing the two groups of viewers on each of the knowledge tests. We have to use sixth and tenth grades in Rocky Mountain and Teletown samples, and eighth, tenth, and twelfth grades in San Francisco. For this reason, and because there are a few differences in items between samples (for example, Canadian children were not asked to name U.S. Senators, as the Rocky Mountain children were), it seems preferable to use comparisons within the samples, rather than combining them.

Four of the tests were given throughout the three samples. These tests, and the results of the comparisons, are as follows:

| Test | Result |
|------|--------|
| Ability to name writers | 11 out of 12 comparisons, where there was a difference, were in favor of LIGHT viewers; 1 was even |
| Ability to name statesmen | 10 out of 11 comparisons, where there was a difference, were in favor of LIGHT viewers; 2 were even |
| Ability to name singers | 11 out of 12 comparisons, where there was a difference, were in favor of HEAVY viewers; 1 was even |
| Ability to name band leaders | 8 out of 11 comparisons, where there was a difference, were in favor of HEAVY viewers; 2 were even |

These are statistically significant. (See Table IX-10.)

The remaining tests were not given in all places, and we therefore have fewer comparisons. We also have more ambiguous results. On the science test, for example, three comparisons were in favor of light viewers, two in favor of heavy viewers, and two even. On the test of ability to name faraway places, the results in seven comparisons were two in favor of heavy viewing, three in favor of light viewing, and one even. Obviously we have no grounds on which to believe that there is any real difference between heavy and light viewers on these tests.

The results as a whole follow our predictions. The ability to name singers and band leaders is closely related to the entertainment content of television, and therefore heavy viewers ought to know more about those subjects—and they do. The ability to name writers and statesmen is more closely connected to book, magazine, and newspaper reading than to television, and we should therefore expect heavy viewers to know *less* about these subjects—and they do. A topic like science is perhaps more closely related to school than to the mass media, and we should therefore expect the amount of viewing not to make much difference—and it seems not to. Place names we should expect to be learned from all the media, by the time a child is in sixth grade or more, and therefore we should expect little difference as between light and heavy viewers—which is what we find.

Therefore, so far as this evidence goes, we can say that heavy viewing of television by children seems to make for more knowledge of topics related to the fantasy content of television, which is what children chiefly watch. On the other hand, heavy viewing seems to make for *less* knowledge of subject matter which is more closely related to reality materials than to the fantasy content of television. This happens, we assume, because heavy television viewing pre-empts time which otherwise might be put on the printed media.

*Television in school*

So far we have been talking about incidental learning from television, which, in the case of children, means mostly incidental learning from the entertainment and fantasy-producing parts of television. There is, of course, another side to television, although it is much the smaller side. This is the side that brings master teachers into school classrooms, that furnishes public affairs, fine arts, and science programs to supplement school studies, and that maintains a network of serious-minded and non-commercial television stations over the country. Let us now consider this side of television.

The effectiveness of television as a tool for classroom teaching has been well demonstrated. In general, if motivation can be kept up, a child can learn as much from a television as from a face-to-face lesson. The more interaction the topic calls for, the more advantage to face-to-face teaching; the more the topic depends on good lectures, demonstrations, and in particular on demonstrations of complex or small things, hard to organize or hard to see in a classroom, the more television has the advantage. But Chicago has demonstrated that an entire junior college curriculum can be taught efficiently on television. Elementary and high schools have now shown, many times over, that courses as unlike as foreign language, mathematics, natural science, social science, English, and even driver education can be taught in large part by television. When teaching machine programs become widely available so that the student can supplement television teaching with his self-controlled drill and practice, education will have a truly impressive new set of tools by which to extend and enrich the learning experience of students.

The number of American school children who have had classroom teaching by television must now be in the millions. Thirty per cent of our eighth-grade sample in San Francisco, for example, said that they had been taught all or part of at least one class by television (Table IX-13). Students have mixed feelings about it: in general, favorable, but with articulate reservations. In general, elementary school children like it. High school and college students like it less. (It is worth noting that they probably did not experience television teaching until the time of high school or college; their attitudes might be different if they had experienced it earlier.) Adults who study at home like television teaching very much.

Seventy per cent of the elementary school children we studied in San Francisco said they thought home television sometimes helps them in school. How does it help them? The largest number said it is an aid in studying current events. A considerable number said that it helps them with science, and another group that it helps them learn new words and read new material. Some said it helps in class discussions, and others that it teaches them about foreign countries. One or two said it helped them in drawing. Some said they thought it helped, but didn't know just how. (Details are in Tables IX-11, 12.)

As might be expected, the percentage of children who think television helps them in school decreases as they grow older. The elementary school percentage is 70. Less than 50 per cent of eighth-graders are sure television helps them, and the percentage is below 40 per cent in the twelfth grade. These are the years in which many of the children are discovering other and often greater intellectual challenges, and when the subject matter of school classes is moving beyond the level at which most of television is much help.

What mass medium is most helpful in school? Among elementary students, television wins easily. Half the children name it. Newspapers get a little less than a quarter of the votes. No other medium gets even 10 per cent. But by the time of high school, this, too, is changed. Television no longer rates at the top. Books, newspapers, magazines all get a few more votes than television, and radio gets almost as many as television. Clearly, television has come, by that time, to play a different part in the lives of its young viewers.

What do the teachers think? Those to whom we talked believed that television is indeed helpful, especially to elementary school children, and that it has many programs which are worth being assigned as outside work. On the other hand, many of them mentioned cases of drowsy children the morning after late and popular programs, of daydreaming that might well be connected to the fantasy of television programs, of what some of them felt was a tendency on the part of some pupils to expect to be entertained passively in class, as they are before the television set. Some of the teachers said laughingly that they had a pretty stiff standard of entertainment and production to compete with.

What do the parents think? Almost invariably, they think television helps. In general the higher their own education, the less enthusiastic they are about television's aid to their children.

After watching TV, is school dull? A very large number of students say that it is (Tables IX-14, 15). This number seems to increase between the sixth and the eighth grades, and decrease a bit thereafter. In San Francisco, at least, a significantly larger number of boys than girls report that school is sometimes dull after the excitement of television. But the importance of these responses should not be exaggerated. As one sixth-grade boy said to us, "Aw, nuts! School is dull anyway!"

A majority of parents admitted to having to face, at some time, the problem of television cutting into study time. Methods for solving this problem were as varied as the parents. Many of them simply turned off the set, or put the children in another room, and required them to finish their homework first. Quite a number had enforced a schedule, putting homework in first priority. Some had used TV as a reward for studying or for good grades. Despite such restrictions, there was little doubt in

either the parents' or the interviewers' minds that the children in question were still seeing a lot of television.

This much, at least, is clear: the school has a real resource and aid
in television, if children can be directed to some of the fine reality programs in place of some of the fantasy which they now see. There are
excellent public affairs, fine arts, and science programs on television,
among others, but they are not the big audience programs, and they do
not have very large audiences among children. Yet some children find
them, enjoy them, and profit by them; and many others could do likewise, to their own and their generation's profit.

It is significant that the bright children should be the ones who are
most sure that television helps them in school. These are the children
who typically view television least, but yet are most likely to view
reality programs rather than fantasy.

## Educational television at home

Forty-three communities in the United States, at the time of this
writing, have educational television stations. These are noncommercial
stations, supported by community donations, by school systems, or by
universities. They carry a relatively "high-brow" type of program; or
at least they seem high-brow in comparison with commercial stations,
for they carry no Westerns, no crime drama, no family situation comedy,
and very little fantasy entertainment of any kind. They tend to program
classical music rather than popular; ballet and folk dance, rather than
popular dance; discussions of the news, rather than reports of it; and a
whole series of programs (for example, on what the Soviet press is saying, or how to do Japanese brush painting) which would be very unlikely to appear on commercial stations. They offer home study courses
by television. They discuss books, art, ideas, history, science, and social
problems in a thoughtful way. They carry children's programs without
violence and with only a minimum of slapstick. In other words—a different sort of television than we have become used to.

From the beginning of these stations, it was hoped that they would
be attractive to children and provide an alternative to the diet of fantasy
and violence offered by commercial television. Has this hope been
realized?

Two of these stations came within the territory of our samples. These
were KQED, the San Francisco community station, and KRMA, which
is operated, for community service and in-school instruction, by the
Denver public schools. The samples were not entirely comparable, in
that we had a large school-age sample in San Francisco itself, whereas
our KRMA sample was in a smaller town near Denver, but within
the primary coverage area of the station. In each case, the educational
stations have to compete with a full set of commercial network stations.

Figure 21 shows children's viewing of educational stations in these two communities. In the sixth and eighth grades, from 15 to 20 per cent of the children view the stations at least once a week. In the tenth grade viewing falls off to around 10 per cent. In the twelfth grade it seems to pick up a few per cent. About 65 per cent of the San Francisco sample and 69 per cent of the Rocky Mountain sample able to receive educational television say they do not view the educational stations at all. Tables IX-16, 17, 18 illustrate these results.

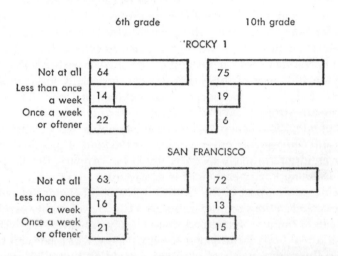

FIGURE 21    Percentage of children in two cities viewing educational television stations.

Is this encouraging or discouraging? It is less than the architects of educational television had hoped for. It is much less than children's viewing of commercial stations. But on the other hand, it is almost exactly as much as the parents view these same stations. Four separate studies of KQED have returned estimates of weekly audiences between 15 and 20 per cent, total audience around 40 per cent, of the potential audience in the area. Two studies of KRMA have also estimated weekly viewing at 15 per cent or a little more.

Nor is the correspondence between parents' and children's amount of listening at all strange, in view of the high correlation between children's and parents' viewing of educational television in the same family, as shown earlier. Viewing of educational television tends to be learned in the family.

As the child grows toward the teens, the influence of the peer group tends to compete with the influence of his family. The family norm may teach that self-betterment is to be preferred to enjoyment, purposeful activity to being entertained, and "nice" programs to "shooting" programs. The peer group is likely to say that education is for school hours. Our observation is that teen-agers feel very keenly the contrast between the (commercial) use of television as entertainment, and its (noncommercial) use as education. Their lives are already full of education; they are a bit rebellious about it. They are attracted more to experiences that promise a relaxation from school work than to experiences that promise more school. That is why some teen-agers say that educational television is for the "squares." From their point of view, the use of television other than as entertainment is an unnatural use of the medium.

The increasing influence of the peer group and the increasing competition for time are probably the reasons why children's use of educational television, or ETV, seems to decrease after the sixth grade.

It is interesting to note that bright children are more likely than others to be in the audiences of these two stations, especially in view of what we know of the adult audiences of educational stations. These adult audiences are strongly skewed toward better-educated persons, light viewers of television, heavy readers of print, active participants in civic and cultural activities—in other words, just the kind of people that these brighter children are likely to grow up to be. Apparently the pattern of ETV listening begins early and is consistent.

Considered as a part of the over-all television behavior of children, the educational stations represent merely a tiny bay of reality experience in an ocean of fantasy. Examined more closely, however, these stations represent a real hope for utilizing the great power of television to contribute to the reality needs of children, providing that ETV programs can be made attractive to children or that a taste for ETV can be encouraged in the years of children's taste building.

### How do children learn taste?

This raises the question of how a child learns his television tastes. Clearly they are learned, not born in him, and are developed out of a

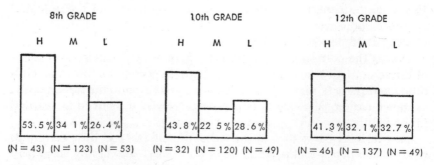

FIGURE 22  Percentage of children of different mental ability (high, middle, low) who view educational television stations.

complex interaction of individual needs, trial and error at meeting those needs, and the effect of example.

Himmelweit, Oppenheim, and Vince noted an interesting phenomenon in the formation of television taste among English children. When educational programs like "Science Review," "From Tropical Forests," or "Have You a Camera?" appeared on BBC, children who had access to both BBC and the commercial channel would almost invariably turn to the commercial one, where they would find usually a choice of cartoons, Westerns, and the like, much like American commercial television. But if the child had access only to BBC—that is, if the commercial service had not yet reached his community—then there was a choice only of turning off the set or of watching the educational program. Under those circumstances, the English investigators report, "quite a number of children chose to see such programmes *and in fact enjoyed them*" [4, p. 14].

A choice of programs, therefore, paradoxically may make for less variety in program taste. Himmelweit, Oppenheim, and Vince continue: "Children with access to one channel only get the chance to discover such programmes, but those with two channels hardly ever. The more the child can follow his favourite choices by switching from channel to channel, the less likely he is to come in contact with programmes which, from an educational viewpoint, would prove more worth-while and which would enable him to experience new things and so broaden his taste" [4, p. 14].

In this country, of course, every large city has three or four commercial channels, as compared to England's one. But they are all alike in emphasizing fantasy, almost to the exclusion of reality materials for children. Therefore, if a child does not find his light entertainment on one station, he can usually find it on another. His taste fails to broaden, and concentrates on fantasy of a particularly stereotyped nature. By the time the child is old enough to develop a sense of his reality needs, as opposed to his fantasy needs, his concept of television, and his taste for its programs, has hardened; and in any case he finds it easier to seek reality experiences in print.

Ithiel Pool discussed the same Himmelweit finding before the Federal Communications Commission. Although the evidence suggests that a wide variety of offerings at the same time will not necessarily raise public taste, Pool contended that the presence of "poor" programs amidst such variety does not necessarily *lower* taste, either. "If the situation is reciprocal," he said, "then we may guess that at times when *only* poor programming is available on the air people will watch it for lack of something better to do, and in so doing they may develop bad taste habits. If the Himmelweit finding can be generalized, then when there is a choice of program levels people will pick programs at their own level, and the presence of a poor program among those available will do little or no harm, for it will not be chosen by viewers whom it would change" [51, p. 21]. Nevertheless, the failure of television to raise children's program tastes can still be used to account for the fact that only a minority find television's excellent serious programs.

## A comparison

In summing up this chapter, it may be interesting to recall what the Himmelweit, Oppenheim, and Vince study in England reported about learning from television.

Comparing children with and children without television, in years when television service was being expanded in the United Kingdom, these investigators concluded that television mainly benefits "the younger and duller viewers." They found that children who had television at home did a little less well in school than children in the same classroom who did not have television at home, but decided that television "appears to be neither a distinct advantage nor a severe handicap as far as the child's performance at school is concerned." They surmised that television might be more hindrance than help to brighter children. They decided that TV does not markedly stimulate a child's cultural, intellectual, or creative interests, nor is it more effective than other media in broadening his horizon. Their over-all conclusion, therefore, was that television really doesn't make much difference, but they asked the question whether what children learn from it "can compensate the child for the time viewing takes from reading, radio listening, and other sources of information."

What we have found in general agrees with these English findings, although it expands upon them at some points. It seems very important to us that most of children's learning from television is incidental learning from fantasy programs. On the basis of assumptions about the nature of this kind of learning, we made some predictions about children's learning, with and without television, among heavy viewers and among light viewers, and on different levels of mental ability. When we tested these against such evidence as we had, the results gave us a good deal of encouragement that our predictions were well based.

We conclude, as did the English investigators, that television is of most help, as a source to knowledge, to young children. In fact, we should put the years rather earlier than any of those measured in the English study. It seems to us that the period of greatest learning from television comes probably before the child learns to read well enough to read on his own. The child, in this television age, probably brings to school a larger vocabulary and doubtless a larger supply of other kinds of knowledge than a child who lived in the years before television.

We believe, therefore, that children today get a faster start in learning of the world around them, but that the gain is temporary only.

For example, we find no evidence of any over-all advantage to children-with-television over children-without-television in the sixth through twelfth grades. If there is an advantage that comes with television in the early grades, it is apparently gone by the time the child is in the sixth grade. Rather, we found that television children in these upper grades tend to know more than nontelevision children about subjects closely related to the fantasy content of television, and less about subjects related more closely to reality topics and to other media—for example, literature and public affairs. This, indeed, raised the question of whether the amount and kind of thing children learn from their typical television viewing is worth what they miss by taking television time from other learning experiences.

We found that television does seem to benefit the duller viewers (at least at an early age) more than it benefits the average viewer. But we found also that it benefits the bright child relatively more than the average child. In fact, we have come to believe that the bright children are always the greater beneficiaries from any new learning experiences with television.

We found no more evidence than the English investigators did that television improves school performance. Many children think it helps them. Teachers are ambivalent about it. And we found nothing to controvert the conclusion that (after the early years, at least) television does not markedly broaden a child's horizon or stimulate him intellectually or culturally. This is not to say that television does *not* stimulate or broaden a child; our observation is merely that it probably does not do those things to a greater degree than would be done without television.

So far, most of the learning we have been talking about has been incidental learning from entertainment programs. However, television has made two attempts to serve as a direct and purposeful learning source, with serious reality programs. These are instructional television delivered to the classroom, and noncommercial educational television delivered to the home. The former of these has proved its ability to teach, and the latter is one of the best reasons to hope that television may yet be a major source of reality experiences for children, as it has been a source of fantasy experiences.

# CHAPTER 6

# REALITY SEEKING AND
# SOCIAL NORMS

A principle of television behavior seems to emerge from the two preceding chapters. We might call it the "Principle of Maturation." It says, in effect, that when children mature to a certain point, television becomes less attractive and rewarding to them and they increase their attention to reality-oriented media material. By "reality-oriented" we mean material which is at least as useful for its information content as for its entertainment content—if not more so.

This principle holds for most children. But while the majority of children decrease their television viewing time considerably during the high school years, others decrease their viewing little or not at all. While most lay aside their comic books at the start of adolescence, not all do so. Most children give the mass media a large amount of attention in the elementary school years, but, even then, some children are moderate or abstemious users of these media.

Are these merely random groupings, or are there identifiable influences at work which control the different behaviors? Trying to answer this question led us into the analysis which we are about to report.

## The TV-print difference*

We had seen signs that among adolescent children those who read more than average (and whom we called high print users) tended to use the media more for seeking information than did the other children.

▶ For tables and other data applying to this chapter see Appendix X.

* Let us hasten to point out that many different kinds of experiences are obtainable from print or from television, or from any medium, or even from a type of program. For example, there are numerous kinds of crime drama on television, each one offering an experience potentially somewhat unlike the experiences obtainable from the other. Even within the same variant of the same type, no two programs are completely alike. Therefore, when we talk about the behavior of viewing television or reading print we are talking about a relationship between a particular kind of child and countless kinds of mass media content. It is possible, of course, to find out something about the behavior of viewing or reading or hearing any individual

Conversely, those children who watched more than average television tended to use the media largely for entertainment, to be fantasy seekers.

Trying to understand this better, we constructed an index of television-print behavior. First, we divided the children in our sample, by grade, into high and low television users. The dividing point was arbitrarily picked as two hours and fifteen minutes daily spent on watching television.* Next we divided each of these groups into high and low users of print. To determine high and low use of print we tested only book and magazine reading because the number who do not read the newspaper, particularly in the tenth grade, was very small. To qualify as a high user of print, the child had to have read three or more books, or more than four magazines exclusive of pulps, during the preceding month. This division, then, gave us four groups of children:

1. Children who are high users of television and low users of print (called hereafter the "fantasy group").
2. Children who are high users of print and low users of television (called hereafter the "reality group").
3. Children who are high users of both television and print (called hereafter the "high users group").
4. Children who are low users of both television and print (called hereafter the "low users group").

You will find more details on these groups in Table X-1.

The first thing we notice about these groupings is that they occur in each of our samples, and in about the same relative size. Furthermore, in all our samples they change in the same direction as the children grow older. Between the sixth and the tenth grades in our Rocky Mountain and Canadian samples, and between the eighth and twelfth grades in our San Francisco sample, the direction of change is consistently the same: the fantasy group decreases in size; the reality group increases;

---

bit of media content by studying that experience in isolation. We feel, however, that there is something to be gained at this point by talking about the media and their content at a higher level of abstraction, so that we can deal with sums of experiences, rather than individual experiences. Therefore, throughout much of this book we have talked about "television" or "print," in complete awareness that television and print each offer diverse experiences; and similarly we have talked about "fantasy" and "reality" experiences and content, fully aware that there is more than one kind of fantasy and more than one kind of reality experience. In this way we are trying to deal with certain large relationships, into which more precise relationships may be fitted as we learn more about them.

* This was approximately the mean watching time for the tenth-graders. It was considerably below the mean for sixth-graders, since children in that grade generally watch much more television than those in the older group.

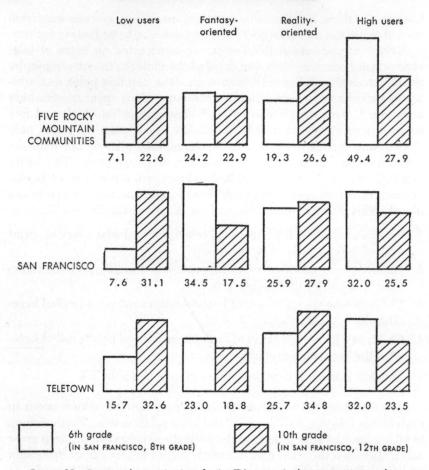

FIGURE 23    Per cent changes in size of print-TV groups in three separate samples.

the high users group decreases; the low users group increases. These changes are considerable in size, and are highly significant by statistical test.

Now, the question is whether these groups really distinguish between fantasy and reality seekers. We proceeded to test that in a number of ways.

## The Radiotown test

If we are really dealing with a basic difference between fantasy and reality seeking, we should find the same groupings and changes in Radio-town, the Canadian community where television is not yet available.

Recalling that the major decreases in media behavior between Radio-town and Teletown were found in comic book reading and movie-going, we substituted attention to these media in place of television as our fantasy group criterion. If a child had seen more than three movies during the previous month, or read more than nine comic books, he was considered to belong in the high movie-comic group; if not, in the low group. Dividing these two groups by the high and low print usage criterion, we came up with four groups in much the same proportions as the groups in the television communities. Although the number of cases in some of the groups was too small for statistical testing, the same changes in proportions were evident between grades. In other words, before television, presumably, many children went through the same type of change as today from fantasy-seeking media behavior toward reality-seeking media behavior. (See Table X-2.)

*The test in other media*

Another possible test of whether these groupings distinguish to some extent between reality and fantasy seeking is in the media behavior that goes along with high television or high print usage. We find that high television use is associated with high movie attendance and reading of comic books, as we should expect. The high-print groups are significantly higher than the others in newspaper reading. More important, the high-print group reads more "hard" news: 88 per cent of them read local news, as compared to 56 per cent in the high-television group; 43 per cent of them read foreign news, as compared to 18 per cent in the television group; 40 per cent of them read news of our national government, as compared to 16 per cent in the television group; and 22 per cent read editorials as compared to 9 per cent. Further, the differences were far more marked when the students were asked which part of the newspaper they would miss most. There was practically no difference between the groups in reading of comic strips. But the proportion saying they would miss the comics most differed greatly. In the sixth grade 54 per cent of the fantasy group said comics were what they would miss most, compared to 45 per cent in the reality group. In the tenth grade 42 per cent of the fantasy group still said comics, but only 23 per cent of the reality group selected comics at this age. (See Table X-3.)

Pulp magazine reading is considerably higher in the high-television group. Conversely, reading of general magazines, news magazines, and quality magazines is *lower* in the high-television group. In order to examine magazine reading without the bias inherent in having used magazine behavior as one element in the original distinction between high and low users of print, we devised a new index by giving arbitrary

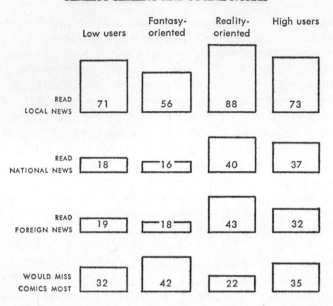

FIGURE 24    Per cent of tenth-grade children (Rocky Mountain sample) who read different kinds of newspaper news in tenth grade by different print-TV groups.

values to different classes of magazines. We gave a value of *1* to pulp magazines; *2*, to hobby and sports; *3*, to general magazines; *4*, to news; and *5*, to quality magazines. Using these values, we computed the average rating for all magazines read by each individual. This eliminated the influence of *how many* magazines were read, and therefore gave us a comparison of high- and low-print groups in terms of the probable proportion of fantasy and reality they were seeking in magazines. The differences were small, showing that most of the distinctions in magazine reading reported above resulted from the *amount* of reading done by the high-print group. But these differences are all in the direction predicted: the high-print group read magazines that were more likely to supply reality needs. Details are in Table X-4.

Another thing we observed is that, despite the much greater use of television made by the high-television group, this group did not see any more news and public affairs programs than the reality group, and by the tenth grade was actually seeing fewer of those programs (Table X-5).

### The test of media dependency

If these groups are operating on the basis of such norms as we have described, we should expect the reality-oriented group to consider the

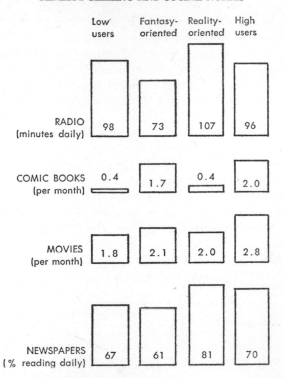

Fiqure 25   Use of radio, movies, comic books, and newspapers in tenth grade by different print-TV groups.

fantasy media less important and to remember more of the reality content of the media.

As a measure of importance, we asked all children which of the major mass media—books, magazines, newspapers, comic books, television, radio, and movies—they would miss most if they had to do without them. Among sixth-graders, a majority of all children named television as the medium they would miss most; but 81 per cent of the fantasy-oriented group named it, in contrast to 54 per cent of the reality-oriented group. In the tenth, only *2 per cent* of the reality group named television, as compared to 69 per cent of the fantasy group. As would be expected, books and newspapers are much more highly rated by the reality children than by the fantasy group (Table X-6).

## The test of remembered knowledge

Equally impressive differences are found between these groups in their performance on tests of what they remember from the mass media. The average member of the reality group was able to name three times as many American writers and nearly three times as many senators as the average member of the fantasy-oriented group; he could identify nearly twice as many faraway place names; he could identify more pictures of persons in the news, and, as we might expect, he identified as many as or more public affairs than entertainment personalities, whereas the fantasy-oriented child could identify mostly entertainment personalities. (For details, see Table X-8.)

It must be remembered, of course, that the average IQ is higher in the reality-oriented group than in the fantasy group, and brighter children remember more facts than slower children. And it is true that in many tests of popular knowledge (naming popular singers, for example) the reality-oriented children did as well as the fantasy-oriented children. But the differences in the retention of reality materials are large, and all in favor of the reality-oriented children; the differences in retention of fantasy materials, when in favor of the reality-oriented groups, are small. There seems to be no doubt that the group we have described as being "reality-oriented" does give much attention to reality materials in the media.

### The test of educational television

In previous pages we have said that the viewing of educational television is a very different kind of behavior than watching commercial entertainment television. Going to ETV, we decided, is chiefly reality-seeking and is a break with the tradition of going to television for entertainment and escape. Therefore, when we studied the behavior of our four groups, we observed with interest what the high-print and high-television groups did in the parts of our sample where an educational television station could be received. The percentage of *high-print* children who viewed ETV was two and one-half times as large as the percentage of *high-television* children who viewed it—despite the much greater amount of television seen by the high-TV group! (See Table X-7.)

On this evidence we concluded that these groups do exist in substantial proportions, that they promise to be helpful in understanding children's media behavior, and that they are related to fantasy and reality seeking. We next proceeded to find out all we could about the children who fell under these different classifications.

### Differences by sex

One of the things we found was that there is a significantly greater number of girls than boys in the reality group in the sixth grade. By the tenth grade, this difference has disappeared. This is as we should expect. Consistently we have observed that girls change media tastes earlier than boys. In this case, we suggest that they are starting the change to reality seeking a bit earlier. (See Table X-9.)

## Differences by intelligence

We found a large and dramatic difference between the groups in intelligence. Consistently, a much larger proportion of the bright children are found in the reality group.* This is true to a much greater degree in the tenth than in the sixth grade, indicating that it is the bright children who lead the shift to reality seeking during the intervening years. In the sixth grade, 23 per cent of the children of above-average intelligence are in the reality group, and only 14 per cent in the fantasy group; but in the tenth grade, 44 per cent are in the reality group and but 9 per cent in the fantasy group. That is the measure of the change that takes place during the teens. Contrast this with the distribution of below-average-intelligence children. In the sixth grade, 16 per cent of these are in the reality group, 34 per cent in the fantasy group. In the tenth grade, the percentages are almost the same: 15 per cent in the reality group, and 37 per cent in the fantasy group. Over-all, in the tenth grade, only 30 per cent of the bright children are fantasy-oriented, as compared to 67 per cent of the slower children.

This same relationship between intelligence and reality seeking is found in all our samples, including the Canadian town without television. (See Table X-10.)

## Socioeconomic differences

There was also an interesting relationship with socioeconomic status. We developed an index of socioeconomic status based upon the occupation and education of the child's father. Past studies† have shown the importance of occupation as an index of social stratification position. By coupling occupation with education, our index was given some additional refinement. Our index worked so as to place the professional, managerial, skilled, and other generally white-collar occupations, and the more highly educated persons high on the index. Com-

---

* Lazarsfeld and Kendall [78, p. 139] found signs of what is probably this same phenomenon in a national survey of radio listening. Here, for example, is their finding about preference for "serious" or "entertainment" programs in the 30- to 49-year-old group:

| | Education | | |
| --- | --- | --- | --- |
| | College | High School | Grammar School |
| Prefer entertainment ................. | 17% | 29% | 31% |
| Prefer serious programs ............... | 33 | 16 | 16 |

† See Joseph A. Kahl and James A. Davis, "A Comparison of Indexes of Socioeconomic Status," *Amer. Sociol. Rev.*, 20 (1955), 317–25.

binations of "high" occupation and "high" education were ranked highest.*

Dividing our samples at the middle of this index, we had in the upper group almost all the children from what would be called middle-class families, along with the few upper-class children who appeared in the samples; and in the lower index-score group were most of the children who came from what would be working class or blue-collar families.

When we set this index against the four groups of children whom we had identified on the basis of their TV-print behavior, we found sharp and very interesting differences. In the sixth grade there was little difference in the proportion of each socioeconomic group which fell into the reality category, but the proportion of the low socioeconomic group which fell in the fantasy group was twice that of the highest socioeconomic group. Looking at these children in another way, 75 per cent of the highest socioeconomic group were high users of print, contrasted to 55 per cent of the lowest. In high use of television, there was little difference between our highest and lowest socioeconomic groups—69 per cent against 73 per cent. The difference is that high socioeconomic children who were high users of television were also high users of print, whereas the lowest socioeconomic children were more likely to depend on television, and television alone.

In the tenth grade, the differences are even more striking. Reality users of the media for the highest socioeconomic group constituted almost half the total group, 44 per cent, contrasted to only 15 per cent in the lowest socioeconomic group. Conversely, only 8 per cent of the highest socioeconomic group were fantasy media users, but 32 per cent of the lowest socioeconomic group fell into this category.

Figure 26 shows the relationship between socioeconomic status and TV-print behavior for sixth- and tenth-grade students in the Rocky Mountain sample. Table X-11 presents this relationship in more detail.

You will notice that there are large differences not only within the grades but also between the grades. The differences shown in this table are significant by statistical test. In other words, there are some large and possibly important changes taking place here.

---

* More specifically, we dichotomized the Centers occupational categories, so as to put professional, managerial, proprietal, sales, clerical, and skilled mechanical categories in the upper part; semiskilled, unskilled, service, and farm categories in the lower part. Then we divided education into three categories—elementary, high school, and college—and combined the education and occupation scores into an index of four levels, thus: (1) high occupation, college education; (2) low occupation, college education, or high occupation, high school education; (3) low occupation, high school education, or high occupation, elementary school education; (4) low occupation, elementary school education.

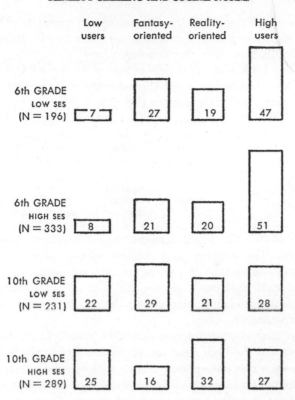

FIGURE 26   Percentage of sixth- and tenth-grade students in different media-use groups, by socioeconomic status.

Notice that the size of the groups changes considerably. If we look at all the children together, this is the picture we get:

|  | Low Users | Fantasy | Reality | High Users |
|---|---|---|---|---|
| Sixth grade | Very small group | About average in size | Below average in size | Very large group |
| Tenth grade | Average in size | Below average in size | Slightly above average in size | Slightly above average in size |

The trend, then, is *from* the groups of high users and fantasy seekers, and *to* the groups of low users and reality seekers. But what most interests us is *who* changes? If you will look again at the table we have just given, you will see that there are about as many of the lower socioeconomic group in the reality group in the tenth grade as in the sixth grade. Almost the entire growth of the reality group between sixth and tenth grades comes from the high socioeconomic strata. In other words, children of higher socioeconomic status are the ones who chiefly change to become reality seekers in the teen years.

Taking the high socioeconomic category to represent the middle class and the lower to represent the working class, we can plot the changes between grades six and ten like this:

| | Low Users | Fantasy | Reality | High Users |
|---|---|---|---|---|
| Middle class | Many more low users | Fewer fantasy-oriented | Many more reality-oriented | Many fewer high users |
| Working class | More low users | Oriented about the same | Oriented about the same | Fewer high users |

Thus it is clear that the larger changes are taking place in the middle-class children. The working-class children change less; most of those who do change move toward low use of both television and print. But between the sixth and tenth grades, children of white-collar families are making a major change, decreasing their use of television, turning to reality experiences.

One more item of great interest should be noted. In the tenth grade, the low users and the high users are fairly evenly distributed by socioeconomic level. The only places where socioeconomic level makes a difference are the fantasy-oriented group and the reality-oriented group. In both of these, it makes a very great difference. The higher the social level, the more likely children are to be in the reality group, the less likely they are to be in the fantasy group.

Therefore, it is clear that what happens to children's television patterns during what we called the "turning point" at the beginning of the teens is related fundamentally in some manner to class patterns and class norms. Our next task is to try to puzzle out this relationship.

The work of such men as W. Lloyd Warner and A. B. Hollingshead leaves little doubt that American people are placed in a stratified social structure within their communities, which they themselves generally recognize. They chiefly associate with others whom they feel to be at or near their own level, although there is a great deal of upward mobility in the social structure. They recognize the difference in levels by the outward signs of prosperity or affluence, by customs and behaviors, and by norms or beliefs.

Between the individuals who score on different levels of our socioeconomic index, we have found striking differences in behavior and belief. This gives us considerable confidence that we are really distinguishing different social groups, whether we call them classes or not. However, our observation has been that most of the people in the upper two levels of our scale—that is, the people who have some combination of above-average education and white-collar jobs—have the characteristics which Warner and Hollingshead would ascribe to the middle class; and that most of the people who score on the lower two levels of our scale have the characteristics which would be ascribed to the so-called working class. Therefore, we are going to continue to speak of the upper two levels as middle class, and of the lower two levels as working class.

But especially for readers of this book who come from another culture, let us add the warning that social classes in North America are not precisely what they are in certain other nations of the world. There are very few persons who would be clearly distinguished as upper class, and few who would, in less fluid cultures, clearly be recognized as lower class. The boundaries between classes are extremely easy to pass, and a large percentage of the people are in process of moving upward educationally, economically, and socially. So far as worldly goods are concerned, there is much less sign of class difference in North America than in most other places. It is entirely possible for a member of the lower class to have a Cadillac, while a man driving an old-model car to work may belong to the middle class.

Therefore, when we talk of social class in the following pages, we shall not be using the word in any pejorative sense, or implying any such distinctions as would exist in some countries, for example, between the middle class and the peasant class, or between the tenant class and the nobility or landowner class. The groups we distinguish here under the names middle and working class are really two social groups characterized less by outward signs than by the amount of education they have had, by the work they do, and, as we shall see, by some of their beliefs and behaviors.

## Class norms and fantasy seeking

There is a considerable amount of theory and research in the literature which suggests a relation of media behavior to class norms.

Ten years ago, the senior author of this volume advanced a theory of what he called "immediate and delayed reward" as a way of explaining selection of news stories. He found that people with more education and higher on the occupational scale were more likely to select the kind of newspaper material that offered a realistic reward, rather than only an escape from realistic problems. Although he called these two kinds of behavior delayed and immediate reward seeking, the relationship to our terms, reality and fantasy seeking, is obvious.

A few years later, Schneider and Lysgaard* related these distinctions

* "The Deferred Gratification Pattern," *Amer. Sociol. Rev.*, 18 (1953), 142–49.

directly to social class. Middle-class people, they said, typically follow a pattern of behavior that might be called "deferred gratification." They "feel it their moral obligation to save, to plan ahead, and to postpone or renounce a wide variety of gratifications and impulses." Working-class people, on the other hand, are characterized by behavior that might be called "impulse-following." They are readier than are middle-class people to engage in physical violence, to express themselves freely in sex; their educational aims are to get by with as little as they can; they have little drive toward upward mobility, and prefer to enjoy life rather than to prepare for tomorrow, to spend freely rather than to save. In short, they tend to follow their impulses, whereas middle-class people engage in a great deal of "impulse renunciation."

Geiger and Sokol, in a report to the National Educational Television and Radio Center, related these ideas to television. They said that "television clashes with the traditional commitment of 'middle class America' to activity, sociability, and productive, goal-directed concerns" [14, p. 12]. They saw television as "a symbol of passive entertainment, of withdrawal from social activity, of escape from responsibilities, and of unproductive behavior." In their study they found that watching television was an activity regarded more highly by the working class than by the middle class. They were able to demonstrate that these attitudes toward television had a normative quality—that is, they were broadly held social group standards.

Meanwhile, several researchers had been relating social class to children's television behavior. In England, Himmelweit, Oppenheim, and Vince found that working-class children in the 10–11 year bracket viewed more television than middle-class children of the same age. Between middle- and working-class children 13–14 years of age, however, they found no difference in amount of television viewing. They explained this in the following terms. Middle-class parents, they said, maintain tighter control over their children than do working-class parents. Left to their own devices, the 10- to 11-year-old middle-class children would probably have watched as much television as working-class children of the same age; and when they grow a little older, and more independent of their parents, they do actually watch as much. But when 10 or 11, they are still under more control from their parents, and the implication is that middle-class parents have a reason for wanting to restrict the television viewing of their children.

Eleanor Maccoby discovered that middle-class children who were brought up in such a way as to feel a great deal of frustration in their home lives behaved differently in regard to television than did working-class children who were similarly frustrated. The "frustrated" middle-class children considerably increased their television viewing; the "frustrated" working-class children did not.

A reasonable explanation is that the middle-class children were using the additional television as an escape mechanism—to drain off the discontents of their home lives. But why should working-class children not do the same thing? Mrs. Maccoby pointed out that if a middle-class child has a warm and permissive relationship with his parents, he will want to be with them as much as possible; and because they place a rather low value on viewing television, he too will tend to draw away from television. But if he has "parent trouble," then he is likely to retreat to television, which will have the dual advantage of helping him escape his parents and get a back-handed revenge on them by doing something they don't approve. A working-class child who has a warm and permissive relationship with his parents will likewise try to be much with them, but in this case will be drawn toward television, because his parents already view a great deal of it. If he, then, has "parent trouble" he can't so well escape it by turning to television. Therefore, his amount of television viewing does not increase with home frustration.

The implication here, of course, is that the two classes look differently on television and they apply different standards to television viewing.

Geiger and Sokol, whom we have already mentioned, tested their class theory on the viewing of educational television in Boston and one of its suburbs. They found, as we have elsewhere, that educational television viewing is much more likely to be engaged in by middle-class, more highly educated, socially and culturally active people than by working-class people. The viewing of commercial, entertainment television was just the reverse; lower-class people were likely to do more of it. They concluded, in terms much like Schneider and Lysgaard, "We can describe TV-watching as predominantly entertainment and compare it with the general social-class values. It seems more congruous with the present orientation and the value given to *immediate* gratification in the lower or working class than with the time orientation and ideal of *deferred* gratification of the middle class."

This chain of theory and findings has a relationship to the kind of theory developed in Chapter 4 to explain the behaviors of reality seeking and fantasy seeking. What we are now preparing to test is the hypothesis that reality seeking is related to a middle-class norm, and that fantasy seeking is related to a working-class norm.

## The two social norms

But first let us try to describe these two sets of social class norms as social investigators have seen them.

Suppose that we could find two individuals who were thoroughly typical of the two groups and norms we have been talking about. Let us call them A and B, and describe certain things about them:

| A | B |
|---|---|
| Works with his muscles all day; when evening comes, likes to relax at home. | Sits at a desk all day; when evening comes, often glad to go out. |
| Has had two years of high school; finds it rather hard to read thoughtful articles and books, and gets bored quickly when the subject is too abstract. | Has had a college education; reads easily, and knows something about modern science, foreign relations, and so forth; accustomed to deal with abstractions. |
| Income is somewhat smaller than B's; when the big new car is bought every two years, the payments don't leave so much free money for tickets; therefore, glad to have entertainment in living room. | Has a bit more money in the budget than A has for tickets; not so dependent on home entertainment. |
| Has a "present time orientation": believes in enjoying today while he can. | Has a "future time orientation": believes in planning and preparing for tomorrow. |
| Feels relatively little need to work toward "bettering" himself in job or status. | Feels tremendous drive to "better himself" and move upward on economic and social ladder. |
| Believes in getting by with as little education as possible and going to work in order to have *things*. | Values education highly, and wants his children to have as much of it as possible. |
| Believes in spending freely. | Believes in saving. |
| Believes in yielding freely to impulses. | Believes in self-restraint; thinks a person should renounce large number of impulses and make rational, rather than impulsive, decisions. |
| Believes it is good to relax and be entertained. | Believes that it is good to be active; suspicious of what people "may do to you" when you are passive. |
| Tests activity by whether it is "fun." | Tests activity by what it accomplishes. |
| Sees nothing wrong with trying to escape from his problems; feels he has more than his share of problems anyway. | Thinks it wrong to try to evade problems; feels they should be faced. |
| Feels modern problems, and even many of his own personal problems, are too big for him to solve. | Feels responsible for trying to solve his own problems, and at least trying to understand world problems. |

Now, of course, there may be no two people exactly like this. Most individuals will be some combination of these two imaginary people. But in general, these are some of the norms and normative behaviors, as we understand them, that characterize the two largest groups in our society. A person who belongs to the working class will tend to be more like *A*; a person who belongs to the middle class will tend to be more like *B*.

## Do children really hold these norms?

There is little doubt that adults hold social class norms of these kinds. But do children really internalize them so that they could affect communication behavior?

We can test this, in part, from our data. For example, we know something about a child's aspirations as related to his background. We find a strong relationship between the socioeconomic status of a child's family and how far the child thinks he will go in school. In the highest of our four socioeconomic levels, over 80 per cent of the children say they plan to finish college, and 90 per cent say they will at least enter college. On the lowest of the four levels, only 36 per cent plan to finish college, and no more than 49 per cent think they will go to college at all. (See Table X-12.) We checked the relation between educational aspiration and television behavior. In middle-class children, the relationship was sharp and clear; those with high aspirations were below average in their television time; those with low aspirations were above average. There was no such clear relationship in the case of the working-class children, as we should expect from the Maccoby study.

So far as we could rely on the children's own statements of their occupational goals, it was apparent that high achievers in this respect also tended to come from higher socioeconomic strata and to be lighter users of television. We got another measure of the value placed on education by asking children whether they found school dull. Although a majority of all children answered affirmatively, the low-television, high socioeconomic children were much less likely to do so. Between the sixth and the tenth grades, the percentage of high-television children answering yes to this question increased greatly. (Table X-14.)

Another indirect indication as to whether children are actively interested in realistic problems—as we should expect them to be if they follow middle-class norms—comes from their answers to questions on how often they discuss news with other people. The proportion of the reality group (whose members also represent in greater numbers the middle class) who said that they did discuss the news with other people was very much larger than the proportion of the fantasy group who discuss news. (Table X-13.)

But these are merely indirect evidence. We wanted to find out with greater surety whether children really hold such norms as we have been describing, and whether these are related in a significant way to their television behavior. Therefore, we conducted a special study in Denver, Colorado.

## The Denver Study

Using 198 tenth-grade pupils, whose IQs were known to us, we secured answers to a number of questions on some of their beliefs and preferences, their media behavior, and their family background.

Between their socioeconomic positions and their television behavior, we found the same relationships as in the other studies. But in the Denver Study we asked quite directly for their opinions on their acceptance of the central norms we were examining. These we considered to be the present vs. the future time orientation, the choice of yielding to impulses or deferring them, the question of whether one should be content to enjoy today or work and plan for possible greater enjoyment tomorrow. We framed three statements along this line:

*The best way to live is to enjoy today and not think about tomorrow.*
*The best way to be happy is to plan ahead.*
*It's a good idea to work harder today so you can enjoy tomorrow more.*

In each case we asked the children the extent of their agreement or disagreement with the statement. Here are the results, set against the TV-print behavior of the children:

|  | The Best Way to Live Is to Enjoy Today and Not Think about Tomorrow | The Best Way to Be Happy Is to Plan Ahead | It's a Good Idea to Work Harder Today So You Can Enjoy Tomorrow More |
|---|---|---|---|
|  | Per Cent Disagreeing | Per Cent Agreeing | Per Cent Agreeing |
| Low users (low TV, low print) | 57 | 43 | 39 |
| Fantasy-oriented (high TV, low print) | 43 | 36 | 40 |
| Reality-oriented (low TV, high print) | 83 | 58 | 56 |
| High users (high TV, high print) | 59 | 59 | 50 |

Over all three questions, it is the reality group which is most in favor of deferred gratification, and the high fantasy group is much less in favor of it. In general, high use of TV goes with "present" orientation, low use of TV with "future" orientation. Combining these three questions into an index, we get a result which is shown in Figure 27. These differences

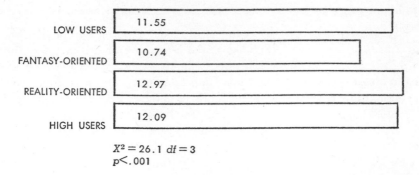

$X^2 = 26.1$  $df = 3$
$p < .001$

FIGURE 27    Average scores of different groups on social norms questions: the higher the score, the more in favor of deferred gratification, "middle-class" norms.

are highly significant by statistical test. They demonstrate quite clearly that future orientation goes with low use of TV, and in general with high use of print. For results in greater detail, see Tables X-15, 16, 17.

We asked one more question which we expected to reveal differences of this kind: Would you rather have a plain monaural record player today, or wait six months and get a stereo set? Unfortunately for our purposes, all but 20 students said they would prefer to wait: apparently stereo is highly valued at this age in Denver. Some of the groups on this question are too small to justify significance tests. Nevertheless, the pattern was the same. The children who preferred to get a plain record player now rather than to wait were overwhelmingly high-TV viewers.

Furthermore, we asked the children how many of their friends they felt agreed with their answers to the opinion questions cited. Those who believed most strongly in either of the positions were also those who felt that all or almost all their friends felt the same way—indicating that a social norm was felt.

Therefore, we conclude that children really do internalize these norms, and that social norms are an active element in determining the extent to which they become fantasy seekers or reality seekers from the mass media.

Is the holding of these norms related, as expected, to social class? The higher socioeconomic children (as measured by father's occupation and education) do indeed score higher than the lower socioeconomic children on the index of "future" orientation (see Table X-15). For these higher socioeconomic children, the relationship between "future" orientation and the four media use categories is statistically significant (Table X-16). Thus, the Denver results encourage us to believe that we are really dealing with a *class* norm.

*The four groups*

So far we have been spending most of our time on two of the four groups of children we identified at the beginning of this chapter. But we have said relatively little about the two other groups, which we called high users (high print *and* high television) and low users (low print *and* low television). What kinds of children are in these groups?

The high users change greatly between the sixth and the tenth grades. In grade six, you will recall, the high users group contained the majority of children. The average IQ for this group was highest of all groups, as were also job aspirations. These children also had very high average educational aspirations, were typically consistent readers of hard news, and tended to give lower-than-average ratings to fantasy media like comics. This description may remind you of a group of students we described in the preceding chapter. This was a group of children with very high IQs, who had been gathered together for some special classes. We noted about them that all their media behavior was very high. They seemed to have insatiable energy for mental activity, and so they read a lot, viewed a lot, listened a lot, talked a lot.

Now, the number of children with intelligence of that order is very small in the population, and we are not implying that all the members of the high users in the sixth grade are extremely high in mental ability. But the group certainly contains many children who are highly intelligent, intellectually curious, alert, and active. Perhaps the best way to characterize this group is to say that it is a *prechange* group. It is a group of children who stand on the threshold of the teens, with the new freedom of later bedtimes and greater independence, but without the burdens of high school classes and without yet having learned to act consistently in their social class norms.

When we look at the high users group in the tenth grade, we see quite a different picture. The group is half as large. Its members are evenly distributed on the socioeconomic scale. As a whole, its membership is below average in intelligence. They have high job and educational aspirations, but are probably never going to realize these aspirations because of their mental ability. As one might expect, they do not find school very interesting. They give very high prestige ratings to TV, and make more use of the comic strips than do their peers. Looking at this group from the outside, it seems more like the fantasy-oriented group than any of the others. There is a suggestion that these children feel, consciously or unconsciously, some degree of conflict between their future hopes and their ability to realize such hopes. If this is the case, they may be turning to the mass media in large part for escape. Our expectation is that this group, too, may be a temporary group, and that when the members make peace between their aspirations and their abilities they may turn to one of the other groups—most likely, the fantasy group—for the adult years.

What about the low users group? These children, like the high users, are almost evenly distributed socioeconomically. The group is above average in intelligence, and its members do not find school dull. But they seem to have low aspirations for both career and education. In a sense, they are just the opposite of the high users in the tenth grade. The high users aspire further than their mental ability is likely to carry them; the low users have more mental ability than their aspirations need. These children may have other absorbing interests and activities—hobbies, jobs, athletics, radio-building. Or they may simply be lazy. The nature of both the low and the high users group, and their relation to the groups of adult viewers which they will join in a few years, is an enticing problem for future research.

*Finally*

We are now in better position to explain what happens at the "turning point," the time near the beginning of the teens when adult patterns begin to replace childish ones and spectacular changes in media behavior occur. We have observed that most of the change at that time takes place among children in the higher socioeconomic levels. In general, they are changing from the fairly universal childhood pattern of impulse gratification to the pattern of deferred gratification which is the adult behavior sanctioned by their class norm. In the case of the lower socioeconomic levels, less change is necessary to go from childhood to adult pattern. But in the case of the middle-class children, the norm of self-betterment, activity, and future time orientation becomes demanding. If their mental ability is equal to the ambitions encouraged by the norm, they tend toward high-print, low-TV behavior; if not, toward high use of the media generally.

# CHAPTER 7

# TELEVISION AND SOCIAL RELATIONSHIPS

We have now identified two of the key elements (in addition to age and sex) that help to determine how a child uses television. They are mental ability and social norms. But these are clearly not *all* the important elements. They leave too much unexplained. For example, they do not say why some teen-age children who have high mental ability and live under strong middle-class norms nevertheless watch an abnormally large amount of television. It is evident that at least one important element is missing, and we can profitably look for it in the area of a child's social relationships and problems.

We have already noted that childhood in general, and adolescence in particular, are times of intense social problems. The child has to learn to live in a family, ruled by parents who sometimes seem to him inconsistent or unfair. He goes through periods when he feels insecure and rejected. He has to learn to play the role expected of a child, and to bend his behavior to the patterns taught him as part of his socialization. He has to learn to get along with people his own age. He has to learn to get along in a school group and a play group. When he goes into adolescence all these peer group relationships become doubly important because of his greater independence, and because he can no longer retreat so readily into the protective security of home and family. He learns new roles that point toward marriage and jobs. Competition becomes more important in the peer group.

Problems of interpersonal relationships, problems of relating oneself to the patterns of society, are therefore many and difficult in the growing years, and it would be strange if they were not in some way related to the way children use the mass media.

## Interpersonal problems and television viewing

There are several studies in the research literature which bear on the relation of a child's social problems to his television viewing.

▶ For tables and other data applying to this chapter see Appendix XI.

One of these is a thoughtful and ingenious study by Lotte Bailyn, who found that intelligence, class, and religion were all related to the amount of television viewing by a group of fifth- and sixth-grade New England children. Personal problems such as worries over being too fat, having a poor complexion, having too few friends, and so forth, were found to be related to the kind of television content preferred. These problems, involving as they do the acceptance and success of a young person in his peer group, are social problems. Mrs. Bailyn found that a child who has these problems tends to spend more time on what she calls the "aggressive hero" type of television content.

Studying the upper third in viewing time among their sample of English children, Himmelweit, Oppenheim, and Vince reported as follows [4, p. 388]: "We found, contrary to expectations, that it was not the only child, or the child whose mother goes out to work, who was a heavy viewer, but the insecure child, in particular the child who had difficulties in making friends with other children." They found also that the heavy viewers were more likely to include children who felt rejected by their peer groups, who expressed more worries and more fears, and more anxiety about growing up. The children who had these qualities and viewed more than the average child also went to movies oftener than the average child. Therefore, their study suggests that peer group problems are clearly related to fantasy seeking.

Eleanor Maccoby found, in a series of interviews with the mothers of kindergarten children in New England, that middle-class children who are frustrated in their home life—in the sense of being subjected to many parental restrictions and not treated warmly or permissively—tended to spend more time than other children of the same age in watching television. This relationship was by no means so clear, however, in the case of working-class children. Whereas severe physical punishment and strictness regarding sexual behavior tend to make for more viewing by middle-class children, most of the home frustrations which send middle-class children to television do not have this effect on working-class children. For example, the working-class children who are frustrated by strictly enforced bedtimes, by being required to be neat, quiet, and mannerly, actually view *less* television than do the children who are given more freedom in these respects. The great majority of Mrs. Maccoby's measures of frustration show no relation to TV viewing in working-class families. We have already discussed the reason for these class differences. The important point is that certain problems of family relationships seem to be related to the amount of television a child tries to see, at least in middle-class families.

In a later study, Mrs. Maccoby deliberately frustrated a group of children just before showing them a movie. The children were given a spelling test more difficult than they were prepared to handle. She found some evidence that this group remembered more of the violence from the movie than did a comparable group who had been given an easy spelling test, and therefore were supposedly less frustrated. A replication failed to produce similar results [20]. However, the question raised here is whether a child frustrated by family relationships does not seek to work out vicariously through television some of the aggression which he is prohibited from employing against his parents; whether he does not try to win some of the satifactions through television which he is unable to obtain in real life.

Finally, an interesting study by John and Matilda Riley [25] has demonstrated that children appear to make different use of mass media experience according to their peer group relationships. Those who have unsatisfactory relationships with other children their own age are the ones who seem to retain the fantasy, play it, and daydream it. In other words, the fantasy experience is apparently prolonged and continues to substitute for satisfactory social relationships long after the actual experience of viewing.

It seems clear, then, that a child's social relationships are closely involved with his television viewing. A child tends to go to television to escape from pressing social problems, to leave the field of frustration, and to obtain vicariously some of the satisfactions he is unable to obtain from real interpersonal relationships. However, this behavior is complicated by its relation to class norms, intelligence, and the nature of the problems a child has. In the remainder of this chapter we shall look at some new evidence and try to understand the relationship somewhat more clearly.

### Aggression in children

Since frustration with interpersonal relationships seems to be behind most of the behavior we have been describing, and since frustration usually is taken out in the form of aggression, let us begin with some evidence on levels and kinds of aggression in children.

To our entire sixth and tenth grade Rocky Mountain sample we gave a series of abbreviated scales developed by Robert R. Sears to measure six different kinds of aggression in children.* The types of aggression, and examples of statements on which the children were asked to indicate the extent of their agreement or disagreement, follow:

Aggression anxiety (for example, "It makes me uncomfortable to see two of my friends fighting.")

---

* Validation of these scales was not complete at the time of our use, but results look promising, and the results of our use of the scales furnish a great deal of face validity.

*Projective aggression* ("I have to be careful what I say to people, because they get mad so easily.")

*Attenuated aggression* ("A good cleanly fought football game is about the best sport there is.")

*Self-aggression* ("There have been times when I was so angry I felt like practically killing myself.")

*Prosocial aggression* ("Every club should have a set of definite rules for its members, and someone should be chosen to enforce the rules.")

*Antisocial aggression* ("I don't see anything especially wrong about a fight between two gangs of teen-agers; it's their business, and adults should stay out of it.")

After administering these scales, we divided the Rocky Mountain children into the TV-print groups which we described in the preceding chapter, and computed aggression scores for each of the groups. Thus we had scores on each of six kinds of aggression for eight large groups of children, four in each of two grades:

| *Kinds of Aggression* | *Kinds of Group* |
| --- | --- |
| Aggression anxiety | High users (high TV, high print) |
| Projective aggression | Fantasy-oriented (high TV, low print) |
| Attenuated aggression | Reality-oriented (low TV, high print) |
| Self-aggression | Low users (low TV, low print) |
| Prosocial aggression | |
| Antisocial aggression | |

The results were quite interesting. There were no significant differences whatsoever, on any kind of aggression, between the four groups in the sixth grade. There were trends, but nothing statistically significant. However, in the tenth grade there were two significant differences. The fantasy-oriented group is significantly higher than the other groups in antisocial aggression. The reality-oriented group is not only the lowest in antisocial aggression, but also significantly higher than the other groups in aggression anxiety. When socioeconomic status is held constant, these differences are still significant in the higher social group, as would be expected. The differences on antisocial aggression approach .05 in the lower SES group also. (See Figure 28.)

What do these findings mean? The fact that higher antisocial aggression is related to fantasy seeking fits with the studies we have just examined; the frustrated children tend to try to work out some of their aggression vicariously through television fantasy. The finding about aggression anxiety is not surprising either. Anxiety over, and disapproval of, aggressive conduct is one of the intended products of socialization. Our culture tries to inhibit violence and teach its members to place a low value on many kinds of aggressive conduct. The reality-oriented group might be expected to accept socialization more readily than others.

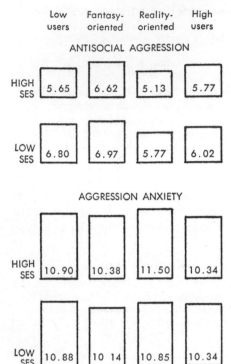

FIGURE 28 Two aggression measures in different media-use groups of children, tenth grade; socioeconomic status held constant. (Differences between reality and fantasy groups are significant beyond the .05 level on both measures, in the high SES groups. Differences between those in the low SES groups are not significant, although the difference in the antisocial aggression (low SES) groups closely approximates the .05 level.)

Then what is the meaning of the fact that there are no significant differences in the sixth grade, whereas there are significant ones in the tenth? As we have seen in previous chapters, children's television behavior tends to differentiate after the sixth grade. We saw, for example, that many children of high intelligence were still heavy viewers of television in the sixth grade, but comparatively few of them were still heavy viewers in the tenth grade; and also that the middle-class norm was much less effective on television behavior in the sixth than in the tenth grade, as was shown by the size of the reality-oriented group. Consequently, we should expect more differences of this kind in the tenth grade. Furthermore, it is quite probable that social problems, and resultant frustrations, are more intense in the tenth grade than in the sixth. It is at this time that courtship roles, academic and social competition, and preparation for adult roles begin to be highly demanding. (See Table XI-1.)

The failure to find any significant difference between Teletown and Radiotown on aggression scores in the tenth grade rules out the possible alternate explanation that aggression scores might be an effect of television viewing. (See Table XI-12.)

We can learn a little more about these aggressions in children by looking at one of the groups which we have already found in the preceding chapter to be deviant. You will recall that, of the children who fell into our highest socioeconomic stratum, only 17 per cent in the sixth grade and 8 per cent in the tenth grade fell into the fantasy-oriented group in their television behavior. These groups were so small, we assumed, because fantasy seeking is somewhat at variance with the social norm of work, self-improvement, and deferred gratification under which children of this socioeconomic level operate. These children were, therefore, flouting the norm, and we should expect something else in their experience to be affecting their needs in such a way as to bring this about. (See Table XI-2.)

When we look at the aggression scores of this deviant group we find that they are much higher than the nondeviants on antisocial aggression (Figure 29). They also have less aggression anxiety, more projective aggression, and less prosocial aggression, although the small number of children in the tenth-grade group makes it difficult to claim statistical significance for these differences. Therefore, whatever it is that drives these children so hard to disregard the social norm and seek fantasy is probably related to aggression; and the studies we have cited would seem to indicate that their aggression may well result from social frustration of some sort. (Relevant data will be found in Tables X-3, 4, 5.)

Now, we do not have the data to search out all possible kinds of frustrations in these children, but we have been able to construct an index which would help to identify some conflict between them and their parents or their peer groups. We asked all children a set of questions about their occupational and educational aspirations and their feeling about how much time should be given to homework. We asked also whether they considered that their parents and "most people their own age" were in agreement with them on these matters or were higher or lower in their standards. Thus we obtained scores for the child's opinion concerning the parent's aspiration for the child being higher than the child's own aspirations; for the parent's aspirations being lower; for the peer group aspirations being higher than the child's; and for the peer group aspirations being lower than the child's; and, in each case, for no difference.

In the sixth grade, there were relatively small differences on any of these scores between the deviants we have been looking at and the remaining children. In other words, if there was a real conflict between these children's aspirations and those of their parents or their peer groups, it was not clearly perceived by any large proportion of the children at that time. This is what we should expect on the basis of our frustration-aggression hypothesis, inasmuch as the aggression scores in

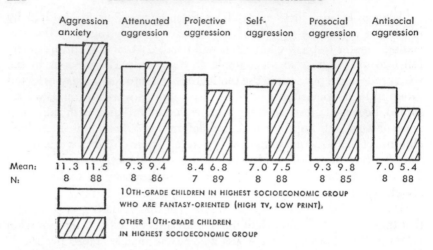

FIGURE 29    Aggression levels in a group of children who are deviant on television behavior, compared to levels of other children.

that grade were not much different as between the deviant group and the others. Most of the high socioeconomic children in the sixth grade who were fantasy-oriented were apparently not being driven to escape social problems, but rather were children who had not yet internalized the social norm and had not yet passed the "turning point" in television behavior.

In the tenth grade, however, there are large differences (Figure 30). The deviants are much more likely than the other children to have lower aspirations for themselves than they think their parents have; and also to differ from the aspirations of their peer groups. Only in the cases

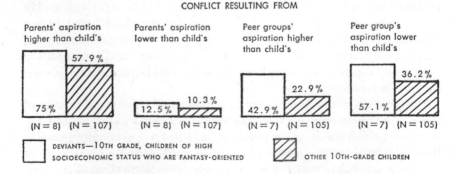

FIGURE 30    Relative amounts of different kinds of conflict perceived by deviants and others.

where the child sees his parents' aspirations as *lower* than his own is there no marked difference between the deviants and the others.

We can be fairly confident, then, that fantasy seeking in the teen years is related to the kind of parental and peer group conflict which we have identified in terms of differences in aspiration. Since the small number in one of our deviant groups (only 8 cases in the highest socioeconomic group in the tenth grade) handicaps us in going on with this analysis, let us take one of these kinds of conflict and examine it in the whole Rocky Mountain sample, where numbers are more nearly adequate.

### Parent-child conflict and mass media behavior

The particular type of conflict which we propose to study at greater length is that in which the child perceives his parents' aspirations for himself (as measured by our index) as higher than his own. This is apparently the most widely prevalent of the types, and for the readers of this book, many of whom are parents, it may be the most directly interesting. Therefore, let us look more closely at the characteristics and behaviors of the children who have "parent trouble."

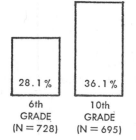

28.1 %  36.1 %

6th GRADE (N = 728)  10th GRADE (N = 695)

FIGURE 31   Per cent of sixth- and tenth-grade children in five Rocky Mountain communities perceiving moderate or heavy conflict because of parents having higher aspirations for them than they themselves.

As Figure 31 illustrates, there is considerably more of this conflict among tenth-grade than sixth-grade children. The tenth-graders are closer to the time when they face decisions about occupation and higher education; therefore, the problems are more salient and the parents are likely to be exerting more pressure.

Boys (Figure 32) are more likely to have this kind of parental conflict than are girls. This is to be expected because boys' occupational and educational decisions are more closely related to "success" and to breadwinning, and therefore more likely to come under parental scrutiny.

Intelligence also is related to the amount of this kind of conflict. Conflict occurs much more frequently in the case of children with lower

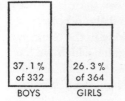

FIGURE 32    Per cent of tenth-grade boys and girls in five Rocky Mountain communities perceiving moderate or heavy conflict because of parents having higher aspirations for them than they themselves.

mental ability. These are the children who have most difficulty in living up to parental aspirations for them.

Then let us see how this type of conflict relates to media behavior. Figure 33 summarizes this for five media and Table XI-7 for six. It will be seen that the greater the degree of parent-child conflict,

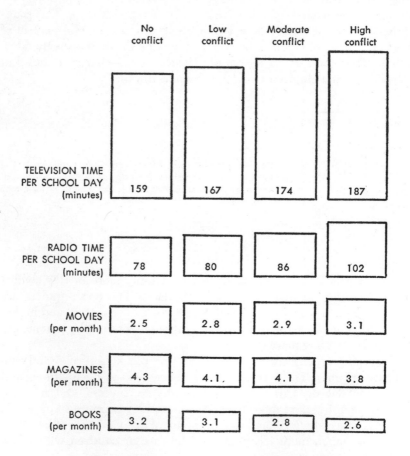

FIGURE 33    Effect of different amounts of parent-child conflict on media use.

the more television a child watches,
the more radio he hears,
the more movies he sees,
the fewer magazines he reads,
the fewer books he reads.

In other words, this kind of conflict apparently helps to distinguish children on the TV-print continuum. It helps send them to fantasy rather than to reality. All the differences represented in Figure 34 are statistically significant.

The differences in number of comics read and frequency of newspaper reading, related to degree of parent-child conflict, were not significant. However, when we analyze the reading of different kinds of magazines in terms of degrees of conflict (Figure 34) we see that it is

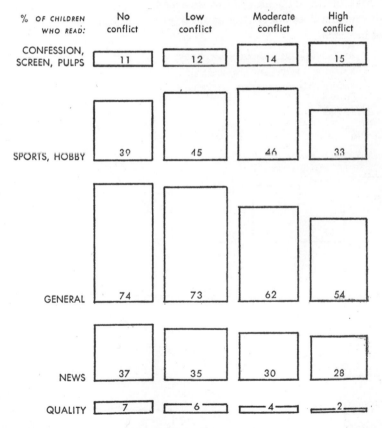

FIGURE 34    Per cent of tenth-grade children who read different types of magazines under different degrees of parent-child conflict.

only the use of pulps, confession, and screen magazines which increases as conflict increases. The use of newsmagazines, quality magazines, general magazines, and even hobby magazines invariably decreases as conflict grows more severe. There is little doubt that it is fantasy which the children with conflict are seeking.

The more a child has a "parent problem," then, the more he tends to "leave the field," to seek his satisfactions and work out his aggressions with fantasy, to select the audiovisual, entertainment media rather than the printed ones.

### Parent-child conflict and aggression scores

Let us now return to our six aggression measures and see how they are affected by a conflict between parental and child aspirations. Figure 35 and Table XI-8 give us this information.

Five of the six scales show statistically significant differences; the only one that does not is attenuated aggression. But as parent-child conflict increases,

> antisocial aggression increases,
> self-aggression increases,
> projective aggression increases,

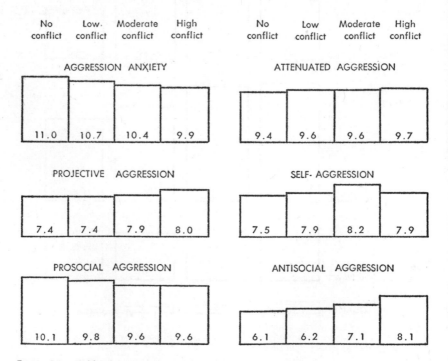

FIGURE 35   Children's average aggression scores related to degrees of parent-child conflict.

prosocial aggression decreases,
aggression anxiety decreases.

The most impressive difference is in antisocial aggression, in which the mean scores increase 30 per cent from low to high conflict. This gives us some idea what difference with a parent must mean to a child. As his sense of conflict increases, he drops his anxiety about aggression and his wish to use aggression for defending the mores. His feeling of aggression against society rises in a great wave. He turns some of his aggression against himself and projects some of it on others. If he finds no better way to cope with this great charge of aggressive impulses, he turns to fantasy.

## Different types and amounts of conflict

We are not going to follow the different types of conflict in any detail, but let us at least look at some of the combinations of parent and peer group conflict.

For one thing, as Figure 36 shows, when kinds of conflict pile up on a child he becomes increasingly likely to seek fantasy. If he has high parent or high peer group conflict *only,* he is somewhat more likely to be in the fantasy-oriented group on media behavior than if he had no high conflict. But if he has *both* high parent and high peer group conflict, he is *twice* as likely to be in the fantasy-oriented group.

DEGREE AND KIND OF CONFLICT

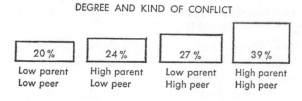

| 20 % | 24 % | 27 % | 39 % |
| Low parent | High parent | Low parent | High parent |
| Low peer | Low peer | High peer | High peer |

FIGURE 36    Percentage of children in fantasy-oriented group, under different kinds of perceived social conflict.

Similarly, as conflict piles up, so does his antisocial aggression (Figure 37 and Table XI-9). If he feels himself to be in conflict with both parents and peers, he is 40 per cent more likely to show high antisocial aggression than if he senses only one kind of conflict, 60 per cent more likely than if he perceived no significant conflict with either parents or peers.

We made a number of more sophisticated analyses, the results of which will be found in Appendix XI, holding various elements constant so as to identify the effect of others. Following are some of the conclusions.

Holding socioeconomic status constant, when the conflict increases the percentage of children showing high antisocial aggression also increases. The amount of increase is greater in the high social strata than in the low ones, but in the lower strata there is a much higher percentage of antisocial aggression, even without conflict. Therefore, there is very little difference between the percentage of children in the highest and in the lowest social levels who show high antisocial aggression if they have high parent and high peer group conflict. (See Table X-10.) The following simplified tabulation will illustrate this:

|  | Per Cent Who Show High Antisocial Aggression | |
| --- | --- | --- |
|  | Highest Social Level | Lowest Social Level |
| High parent, high peer group conflict .............. | 78% | 75% |
| Low parent, low peer group conflict ............... | 37% | 63% |

Holding intelligence constant, we get much the same kind of results. Increasing conflict increases the amount of antisocial aggression in every intelligence group. It increases slightly more in the highest intelligence group, but the low intelligence group shows nearly twice as much antisocial aggression *without* conflict, and therefore its level of aggression is higher with high conflict. This simplified tabulation shows what we mean:

|  | Per Cent Who Show High Antisocial Aggression | |
| --- | --- | --- |
|  | Highest Intelligence Group | Lowest Intelligence Group |
| High parent, high peer group conflict .............. | 56% | 76% |
| Low parent, low peer group conflict ............... | 31% | 59% |

Why should the children who are lowest on the socioeconomic scale and lowest on the scale of mental ability display so much more antisocial aggression even in the absence of parent or peer group conflict? Because they have other frustrations? We can guess that, in the case of the children who are low in mental ability, many of these frustrations may come from school. In the case of children who are low in socioeconomic status, the frustrations may be economic. In either case, frustration might arise from thwarted career plans. And it must be remembered that we have been dealing with only a few of the social relationships that may frustrate a child.

If that is the case, then we should expect high antisocial aggression to increase fantasy seeking (and especially television use) even when conflict is held steady. This is difficult to test because it requires us to break a table into so many divisions that some of them contain only a few children and therefore will hardly yield reliable results. But this is exactly what we find in the only groups which have large enough numbers to use: there is apparently an effect of the aggression level beyond the effect of the parent-child conflict level, indicating that some other frustrations are working.

By holding all other elements constant, we can roughly test Mrs. Maccoby's observation that home frustration tends to drive higher socioeconomic children to television, but has little effect on lower socioeconomic children. In making these breaks we come out again with very small numbers in some cells, and therefore cannot make satisfactory statistical tests. But the trend is exactly what we should expect. In the higher strata, with other elements held constant, television use increases with conflict; in the lower strata, there is a slight tendency for television use to *decrease* with conflict. For the higher strata, the greatest amount of television use is found in the children who show both high conflict and high aggression; in the lower strata, the greatest amount of television use is found in the low conflict, low aggression group. These results support Mrs. Maccoby's hypothesis.

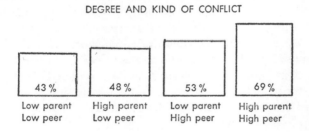

DEGREE AND KIND OF CONFLICT

| 43 % | 48 % | 53 % | 69 % |
|---|---|---|---|
| Low parent Low peer | High parent Low peer | Low parent High peer | High parent High peer |

FIGURE 37    Percentage of children who display high levels of antisocial aggression under different degrees of parent and peer conflict.

## When does television reduce aggression?

So far in this chapter we have been describing a fairly simple psychological pattern: a child going to television to escape from some of the pressures and frustrations of social problems. In particular we have been describing the television behavior of a child who is frustrated in his home or peer group relationships, builds up a heavy load of aggressive impulses which he cannot fully get rid of in real life, and therefore goes to television as an outlet. We have merely suggested the complications that enter into this problem when other things are *not* equal—that is, when other elements such as age, intelligence, and social norms are considered along with social relationships.

Most particularly, we have not yet raised the question of whether, and under what conditions, a child is likely to find that television does "drain off his discontents." This is the import of an experiment by Feshbach [13] in which half of a group of college students who had been severely frustrated by experimental conditions were presented four thematic apperception pictures and asked to respond to each by building a fantasy around it. Those who had this fantasy experience were found to have considerably lowered their level of aggression. The assumption is, therefore, that under at least some conditions a fantasy experience on television will reduce aggressive tendencies.

There is a slight indication in the data from Radiotown and Teletown that television might serve to reduce antisocial aggression. This indication is the finding that antisocial aggression scores of sixth-grade children are higher in Radiotown than in Teletown (See Table XI-12). This result, at least, provides no support for the contention that television serves to increase aggression.

On the other hand, an experiment by Siegel [29] indicates that a group of four-year-olds, after seeing a picture, were more likely to reproduce aggressive acts in their play. And the general conclusion of Emery [11], based on projective responses before and after seeing a Western picture, is that there is no definite pattern: sometimes aggression seems to be reduced, sometimes increased.

There is an important table in a study by Albert of 220 children, eight to ten years of age. His problem was the effect of different endings of a Western film. He was comparing the conventional Western ending with a doctored ending in which the villain wins, and comparing those with a third version in which there was no ending at all and the solution was left up to the viewer.

He found no significant difference between the before and after aggression scores in the conventional (hero wins) and the unconventional (villain wins) versions of the film. He did find, however, that there was a decrease in the amount of aggression shown by children who saw the version of the film which had no ending. The difference between the conventional-ending group and the no-ending group on changes in aggression scores was statistically significant with a greater increase in aggression shown in the group viewing the film with the conventional ending.

The film Albert used was a Hopalong Cassidy picture, of the same general type that is seen over and over again on television. There are a great many things we do not know about the effect which this experiment describes. We do not know, for example, how long a decrease or an increase in aggression will last. But we have no reason to think that the result of exposing these 220 children to a Hopalong Cassidy film is substantially unlike exposing them to the television Westerns of which they now see so many. In the absence of better evidence, we can assume that in some cases television fantasy is likely to reduce aggression and in some cases to increase it; in some cases to provide vicarious drive reduction, in others not; in some cases to provide at least a temporary solution to a problem, in others to make the problem less manageable.

The question is, under what conditions is television exposure likely to do one rather than the other?

It is clear, in the first place, that television is not likely to reduce a physiological drive. A picture of a roast of beef does not make a hungry man any less hungry. And a teen-ager who is sexually frustrated is unlikely to reduce any of that through television; if anything, television is likely to frustrate him more.

In the second place, it is unlikely that television will either reduce or increase tension unless it provides something with which the child can identify. To the extent that he stands aside and "observes" the program, to the extent that he employs what Dysinger and Ruckmick [54] called "adult discount," he is unlikely to get much emotional experience out of the program. Therefore, unless he can go through some of the aggressive experiences of his Western hero or his favorite character in the crime drama, there is not likely to be much change in his state of tension.

The tentative conclusion of the first of the series of Australian studies on the effect of types of television program [11, 31] is that a child who identifies with a strong villain is likely to arouse anxiety and guilt, if the villain is properly punished in the story, so that he will tend to inhibit the aggression that might otherwise result from the identification. This cannot yet be considered proved, and doubtless varies with the personality of the child and the kind and amount of aggression he is carrying. There is also at least a suggestion in these studies that under some conditions a child who identifies with a Western hero may get rid of some aggressive tendencies and improve his view of social justice. In any case, it is clear that the nature of the child's identification is going to make some difference in the effect on his aggression.

What happens to a child's state of frustration may depend, not only on whom he identifies with, but also on whether he has been taught at home to express or inhibit aggression. If the former, there is more hope that he will get rid of some of it vicariously through identifying with a television character. If the latter, he is more likely to build up further frustration.

Finally, there may be a "critical mass" of aggression, beyond which it becomes much harder to reduce the level vicariously. That is to say, a child with a relatively low level of aggression may find it easier to use fantasy as a harmless safety valve—to blow off steam, so to speak. A child with a very high level of aggression may be so wrapped up in his problems that he is unable to blow off steam.

We do not know precisely what are the conditions under which one or the other of these outcomes can be anticipated. They need to be researched. But we do know that television is by no means an auto-matic outlet for aggressive impulses, and it probably builds aggression and frustration as often as it reduces them.

## Leaving the field

At this point it is well to remember the Riley and Riley [25] find-ing that children with unsatisfactory social relationships tend to retain longer, and daydream longer about, the fantasy they get from the mass media.

The result of going to television fantasy, in a great proportion of the cases, may not be to reduce the level of tension in the real world, but only to *change worlds*. The child leaves the field where he finds frustration and discontent. He moves into a new field where he can temporarily fence out some of the discontent. He goes to the violence in the fantasy as thrill play rather than as a way to drain off aggression. In the same way he might ride a steep roller coaster, or dive from a high platform, or shoot off a long and dangerous firecracker. Each of these would build tension to a very high level, but reduce it quickly. And each of them would temporarily distract attention from a toothache, or a bad report card, or a snub from a pretty girl, or parent trouble. The longer he can make the fantasy world last—the longer he can watch television, or dream about it after he is through watching—the longer he can distract himself from the social conflict that is troubling him. But when he returns to the world of real problems, if his problems are severe they will still frustrate him.

Here, again, we may have a "critical mass" to think about. If the child's frustrations are slight, he may be able to distract his attention from them by thrill play, and the distraction may be permanent; or he may take out his aggressions on characters in the programs. Thus he may be able to forget his disappointments and turn his attention to other matters. But if these problems are serious and continuing, there is no reason to think that temporary thrill play will permanently reduce levels of tension when the child returns to the real world. Rather, he will be under temptation to continue the fantasy, to daydream it, and thus to put off the return to real problems. And this confusion of worlds is not recommended therapy.

# CHAPTER 8

# THE EFFECTS OF TELEVISION

The relationship between a picture tube and a child can be understood only in terms of the characteristics of the two. Therefore, let us say a little more about the nature of television and the nature of a child.

### The pattern of effect—the medium

One of the distinguishing characteristics of television is its absorbing quality. This is innate in the medium. It commands both eyes and ears. It focuses attention on movement within a small space. It puts this small space into one's living room, or beside the dining table, or wherever one finds it most convenient. A user does not have to go out, or buy tickets. Without rising from his chair, he can connect his vision and hearing to studios, stages, and news cameras in distant places. All the conditions for attention and absorption are therefore built into the medium.

But the medium is extraordinarily hungry for talent and material. Three networks, in the United States, must keep their wires full for a remarkable number of hours per week. A large number of stations must have programs for sixteen or more hours a day. Furthermore, these programs must be supported by commercial advertisers (except in the case of educational stations) who pay off in return for audiences to whom they can sell goods or services. Therefore, a successful program on commercial television is first and foremost a program that attracts a large audience. Consequently, it is dangerous for a station or a network to experiment with anything more than slight changes in tried and tested formulas for pleasing large audiences. Rather than trying new things, commercial television tends to do *more* of what has proved successful. When the "$64 Question" proved successful, it gradually became the "$64,000 Question," and then the "$64,000 Challenge," and speedily the quiz programs proliferated until a contestant could win a quarter of a million dollars. And, as we saw, it became necessary, in order to compete for audiences, to rig the quizzes and make actors of contestants.

We do not mean that commercial television is not able on many occasions to come up with experimental or special-audience programs. But the whole tendency of the medium, thanks to its advertising base, is not to take a chance, not to do something new; not to do anything except what promises to be attractive to large numbers of people; therefore to do more of what has proved workable.

This tendency is reinforced by the scarcity of talent. There simply is not enough new, fresh, and high-quality talent in the world to fill with fresh and original programs the number of hours that television has to fill. Before broadcasting, a vaudeville comedian could use the same routine for years. In radio, changes in the routine or setting were fairly easy, because much could be left to the visual imagination of listeners. But with television, a change of scene required not a new sound effect but a studio full of scenery and costumes. The comedian had no more secrets from the audience. In the vaudeville days he faced a new audience each night. In radio, he had about the same audience every night, but with the freedom to let his audience imagine many visual details. In television, he could use a routine but once, and he had to show the full setting. Some comedians have estimated that television demands of them 500 times as much material as did the old stage. That is why comedians have not in general prospered on television, and why television has concentrated on situation comedies, crime dramas, and Westerns which can use the same formula and scene over and over, with only slight changes.

So commercial television is a medium that is by its physical nature absorbing, but by its human organization doomed to be repetitious, predominantly shallow, and stereotyped. By its physical nature, it is bound to take up much of the leisure time of people; by its human organization it is bound to be cautious about newness and change. Indeed, the most likely social effect of television is no effect. There is a remarkable paper by Paul Lazarsfeld and Robert Merton [17] which most convincingly supports the thesis that the mass media, by their very nature, must work to maintain the status quo in society and taste. The media have great sums invested in them, and stand to lose by any great change in taste or standards. They are big business, therefore typically conservative. They face a demand for entertainment which is beyond their ability to meet; therefore, they tend to be extremely repetitive. They have inefficient feedback from their audiences, and so tend to oppose change from any pattern that has proved successful. They dare not do anything that might alienate large segments of their audience. Thus they dare small changes, but not fundamental ones; and their whole impact is to retain the status quo, not to encourage change.

Of course, an influence toward conservatism and against change is itself a directional influence of importance. It points to the fact that the chief effects of television are likely to be the long, slow effects on values, on awareness, on response patterns, and on culture and individual behavior, which are hard to identify with short-term research, indeed, hard to identify at all because they are always the result of a combination of forces and influences.

## What television brings to the child

In order to be specific and as nearly up to date as possible in speaking of the content of television, we monitored and analyzed a week of television in late October of 1960. Here let us summarize what appeared on the picture tubes during the period from 4:00 to 9:00 P.M., Monday through Friday, which is often called "the children's hour."*

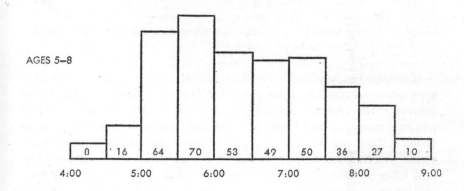

AGES 5–8

| 0 | 16 | 64 | 70 | 53 | 49 | 50 | 36 | 27 | 10 |

4:00    5:00    6:00    7:00    8:00    9:00

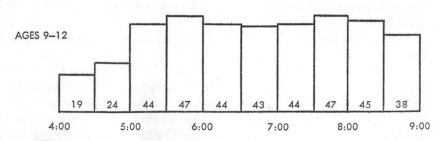

AGES 9–12

| 19 | 24 | 44 | 47 | 44 | 43 | 44 | 47 | 45 | 38 |

4:00    5:00    6:00    7:00    8:00    9:00

FIGURE 38  Percentages of children in a metropolitan area viewing television during the "children's hour": 4:00 to 9:00 P.M., Monday through Friday.

* There is also considerable viewing by children on parts of Saturday and Sunday. On Saturday some of them see more sports (football in season, pro basketball, golf, bowling), but otherwise programs are much the same as on weekdays. On Sundays

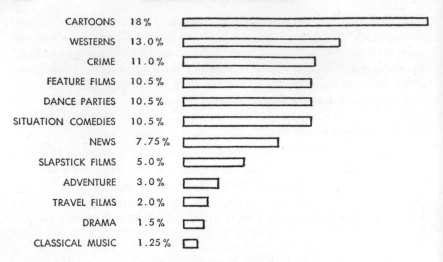

FIGURE 39  Content of commercial television (over 1.0 per cent) during "the children's hour" —4:00 to 9:00 P.M., Monday through Friday, late October, 1960.

Five stations furnish the major television service of the metropolitan area where we monitored the programs. Three of these carry the major networks, the fourth is an independent station carrying a number of package programs and films, and the fifth is a noncommercial educational station carrying the programs of the National Educational Television and Radio Center as well as its locally produced programs. Several other stations can be received in some homes within the metropolitan area, particularly if the antennas are aimed toward these more distant stations, but these latter stations contribute relatively few programs between 4:00 and 9:00 on weekdays not already available on the five metropolitan stations.

Let us first look at what is to be found on the four commercial stations.

An adult watching this kind of television can be forgiven for sometimes imagining that he is back in the years of his youth watching the movies he used to see. Animated cartoons of the familiar music-and-slapstick kind fill 18 per cent of the "children's hour." Another 5 per cent are filled by ancient slapstick movies, another 10.5 per cent by feature

---

they see more of the expensive variety shows, and in the less popular hours they have available to them a certain number of press conferences and other public affairs programs. However, the number of them who view these public affairs programs is not large, and the average Sunday choices include about as large a proportion of fantasy as on weekdays.

movies, 13 per cent by Westerns, 11 per cent by whodunits or other crime shows, and another 2 per cent by travel films. These represent nearly 60 per cent of all the programs. Many of them *did* first appear in the movie theater, and most of the others (for example, the Westerns) are direct descendants of movie types.

A generous estimate of the amount of reality programs in the 100 hours of commercial television we have called the children's hour would be 15 per cent. More than half of this is news, which gets low viewing from children; so that the effective reality offerings are about 7 per cent, seven hours out of 100. Even these seven hours, however, demonstrate that children can find some rewarding reality experiences on commercial television if they know where to look. For example, during the test week they could have heard the Beethoven Ninth Symphony performed by the Philadelphia Orchestra playing at the United Nations building. They could have heard a political debate between Senator Javits and Senator Church. They could have seen an explanation of human metabolism, and observed a brief sequence on measuring the heartbeat of a whale. They could have traveled by camera to Iceland, Peru, and the Canadian Rockies. They could have seen striking pictures of the early days of one of America's great cities, and a documentary report on the problem of money and government. They could have seen local political candidates and pictures of the Presidential campaign. To see these, of course, they would have had to pick and choose amidst a vastly greater number of fantasy programs, but still the opportunity was present.

For the most part, however, the children's hour on commercial television is a succession of fast-moving, exciting fantasy, leavened with broad humor and a considerable amount of romantic interest. It is extremely violent. Shootings and sluggings follow each other interminably. More than half the 100 hours are given over to programs in which violence plays an important part. Not all this violence is to be taken seriously; the cartoons and the ancient slapstick films are intended to be funny, rather than exciting. Therefore, let us disregard all the slapstick material, and look at the following inventory, which will give us some idea of the amount and kind of nonhumorous violence available to children at the hours of their intense viewing.

In the hundred hours we are describing, there were

12 *murders.*
16 *major gunfights.*
21 *persons shot* (apparently not fatally).
21 *other violent incidents with guns* (ranging from shooting at but missing persons, to shooting up a town).
37 *hand-to-hand fights* (15 fist fights, 15 incidents in which one person slugged another, an attempted murder with a pitchfork, 2 stran-

glings, a fight in the water, a case in which a woman was gagged and tied to a bed, and so forth).

*One stabbing in the back with a butcher knife.*
*Four attempted suicides, three successful.*
*Four people falling or pushed over cliffs.*
*Two cars running over cliffs.*
*Two attempts made in automobiles to run over persons on the sidewalk.*
*A psychotic loose and raving, in a flying airliner.*
*Two mob scenes, in one of which the mob hangs the wrong man.*
*A horse grinding a man under its hooves.*
*A great deal of miscellaneous violence, including a plane fight, a hired killer stalking his prey, 2 robberies, a pickpocket working, a woman killed by falling from a train, a tidal wave, an earthquake, and a guillotining.*

It was not this violence that seemed chiefly to frighten the children whom we had watching these programs. Rather it was the dark and the mysterious scenes—for example, a picture that was mostly in the dark, and a scene in which persons dug for a body in a cellar—or the scenes into which they could easily put themselves, such as a person uncovering tarantulas by turning over a rock. Yet for hour after hour this parade of violence passed, as it must pass before our children week after week—men packing guns, packing knives, shooting at each other, slugging each other—and the amount and intensity of it gives one pause.

The picture of the adult world presented on the children's hour is, therefore, heavy in physical violence, light in intellectual interchange, and deeply concerned with crime. About half the story characters are connected with enforcing or breaking the law. Sixteen different detectives, sixteen sheriffs, nine policemen, and an assorted group of other law enforcement officials appeared during the week. In general the detectives were more successful than the sheriffs, who were more successful than the policemen. But still a large part of law enforcement and crime detection had to be carried out by those amateurs with steely nerves and lightning draw. The crooks, for the most part, were not identified as to occupation; television has learned, like the movies, that trade associations protest when their occupation is connected with crime stories. Thus, there were "gunmen," "robbers," "crooks," "bandits," but comparatively few of them had any other business. A much larger proportion of them seemed to be blue-collar than white-collar. There were no particular race or nationality distinctions except that when the cowboys and Indians tangled, the red men were invariably the bad guys.

The picture of family life was mixed. Some of the situation comedies showed a tolerant, good-humored relationship within the family. Other programs showed people screaming at each other, distrust and faithlessness, and violence within the family. There was little attention to the business of earning a living, and the child who wanted career information would have got little from this week of commercial television unless he cared to be a private eye, a Western sheriff, or a crook. On the other hand, some of the programs, particularly the situation plays, went out of the way to implant homely little morals: don't undervalue your real friends; what comes easy, goes easy; don't always believe what you hear; and so on.

How much choice was there? About 22 per cent of the time, a child could have found a reality program, other than news, somewhere on one of the four commercial stations. Over half the time, the choice had to be exclusively among fantasy programs. Even at these times, the child usually had the choice of different types of fantasy—two crime programs vs. a Western vs. a cartoon, for example.

The real choice open to the child, however, was between the commercial and the educational channels. So far, we have been talking exclusively about the four commercial channels. The noncommercial station was far different from the others. It programmed about six hours of its twenty-four, during this time period, for young children. These were the only such programs other than slapstick cartoons available for young children. These noncommercial programs included one hour and a quarter of folk songs, while the child viewer was invited to sing along with the children on the picture tube; one hour of story telling, and fifteen minutes of poetry reading; an hour and a quarter of science for children; a half hour on Leif Ericson; and other imaginative programs directed at preschool and elementary school ages. In addition to this, the educational station programmed six and one-half hours of classical music (as compared to a total of seventy-five minutes on all four commercial stations during this time), including the Boston Symphony, the Philadelphia Woodwind Quintet, and the Salt Lake City Tabernacle organ. Beyond these programs the educational channel offered chiefly adult education. A few programs—one on the career of a famous psychiatrist, another on prospecting for uranium, another on the bakery business—might have interested children, but most of the programs were beyond the level of elementary school interests. The richness of the offering for older teen-agers and adults, however, can be judged from the following examples, all available during the "children's hour": Montgomery of Alamein on his battles; David Susskind, with "Open End"; Russian and French language lessons; lessons in Japanese brush painting; an hour and three-quarters of news analysis; nearly three hours of analysis of political campaign issues; a program on Zen Buddhism; programs on African nationalism, the history of printing, the nature of humor, interviews with authors, and analysis of a musical comedy.

In other words, then, the educational channel was strong on imaginative programs for very young children, and on reality programs for abler and more serious minded teen-agers and adults. The commercial stations offered slapstick cartoons for very young children, and mostly fantasy—Westerns, crime mysteries, old movies, and situation comedies—along with a very few but high-quality reality programs, for all except the very young ones.

The commercial stations were exciting, emotional, violent, and not very intellectual.* The educational station was thoughtful, aesthetically sensitive, not at all violent, and, in comparison, a bit dull.

This is what television was bringing to children at the end of October, 1960.

## The pattern of effect—the child

We have said something about television. Now, what is a child? A child is a young animal learning to be human. Then he is a young human, being socialized by his elders so that he may assume a place among them. The child is at first a relatively blank slate on which experience is written, and for a number of years he has an enormous capacity for learning (which is not always demonstrated by his school work). He is changing more rapidly than he ever will change again. He has barely learned the role of a child when he finds himself no longer a child and having to play the role of an adolescent, a courtship role, or a pre-occupational role. Today he is scornful of the opposite sex; tomorrow he is sighing and panting like a lover. In this process of change he is passing through severe social experiences. He has many moments of insecurity. By his family he is disciplined; by his peer group he is pressured. By some reference groups he may be rejected. From being the center of a family group in his early months of life, he grows into an almost exactly opposite situation which requires him to find a place in groups in which he is no longer the center and into which he must earn his way.

The child is by no means always easy to get along with. Recall Edgar Z. Friedenburg's description of the adolescent: "Adolescents, at their best, are not nice, either; not a bit. At their best, they are rough, randy and affectionate, mercurial, passionate, moody and difficult; infuriatingly honest; responsive as a souped-up Jaguar—and just as safe to fool around with, if you are counting more on your good intentions than on your skill, love, and empathy. Generally speaking, our culture is afraid of them."

The child is therefore a person who needs help in finding his way, but can't usually be shoved along the way. He needs much truth told to him, many chances to talk out fears, suspicions, and half-baked ideas.

---

* We should add that many of the late-afternoon programs rewarded viewers with opportunities to win prizes or earn premiums.

He needs to feel that he "belongs" and is appreciated. He needs a great deal of soothing and comforting for the bruises and disappointments he picks up.

But the child who goes to television to meet some of these needs is by no means naïve or untaught. He has been exposed to continuous and intensive influence and teaching in his home. If he is old enough to spend much time outside the home, he has learned an infinite amount of lore, values, and skills from his peers. He has learned both formally and informally from school, and perhaps from church. And all his living hours, although usually unknown to him, the norms of his culture have poured into him and shaped his habits and values.

Therefore, there are spectacular differences in the children who go to television. They are different not only in the values and standards they bring, but also in the years of experience they have behind them, the physiological bases of their needs, and their abilities. What they select from television, and what they do with it, will invariably reflect these differences.

Dr. Fritz Redl was for some years in charge of an experiment with disturbed and delinquent children, in whose dormitories television was available. He tells us that, whereas for ordinary children the late-evening programs to be avoided would be violent and frightening ones, it was the "nice" and "sweet" programs showing loving parents and warm family relationships that caused his particular group of "problem children" to lie awake or to have bad dreams. These family programs reminded the children of what was lacking in their lives. And thus what would have been soothing (or at least innocuous) for most children was traumatic for these particular children because of their particular needs and backgrounds.

In this case as in every other one, the background and needs of the children determined what use they would make of television, and therefore the "effect" it would have. It is not necessary to go to a group of disturbed children to find such differences. There is enormous difference between the uses that a child with IQ 135 and one with IQ 95 is able to make of television. There is an enormous difference between the approach to television made by a young person who has strongly internalized the middle-class self-betterment norm and one who has not. And, as we have seen, television fantasy will be used quite differently by a child who has good friends and playmates and by one who does not.

*The pattern of effect—interaction*

The effect of television, then, is an interaction between characteristics of television and characteristics of its users. The question now is what is the minimum number of television variables and user variables that will let us understand and predict this interaction.

In the case of television, we have suggested that the irreducible minimum is perhaps the two kinds of materials that make possible *fantasy* or *reality* experiences—or, in other words, immediate and deferred gratifications. We have also suggested that certain refinements of these categories, such as amount of violence, intellectual level of the programs, and the particular set of value cues offered, would further help us understand what is going on. But the great divisions within the medium are fantasy and reality.

In talking about these matters, we have tried not to confuse materials with experience; that is, not to imply that only one kind of experience can derive from a given piece of material. This is manifestly not the case. A televised football game which is pure entertainment and escape to most of its audience may be an important reality experience to the coach whose team has to meet the televised teams later in the season. Therefore, the effective content of television is what a viewer perceives in it.

And this, in turn, can be understood in terms of, and perhaps predicted from, certain elements in the life of the viewer. We have suggested a minimum list in the case of children and have tried to show how they interact with fantasy and reality materials on television. These basic variables are:

*Mental ability*—which governs in large part the child's ability to learn from the medium, his ability to discriminate within it, his eagerness to try new things, and his ability and willingness to use television at its most challenging rather than its lowest common level.

*Social norms*—meaning chiefly the degree to which a child has internalized the middle-class norm of activity, self-betterment, and deferred gratification, and reflected chiefly (other things being equal) in the extent to which he uses television for reality as opposed to fantasy experiences.

[*Social relationships*—the kind of relationships a child has with his parents and with his peer group, reflected chiefly in the extent to which he uses television as an escape from the problems of these relationships or as a substitute for satisfactions not obtained from these sources, and in the extent to which the fantasy of television becomes important to him in his daily living.

And, of course,

*Age*—using chronological age as an indication of the kinds of experience a child has had at a given time, where he stands on the scale of socialization, and the particular sex and social needs he has at the moment.

*Sex*—using sex as an indicator of the different roles children must prepare for, and the different interests they must feed.

In each case, the list is minimal. There are doubtless other variables and indicators which would sharpen prediction and deepen understanding. But we have found each of these present variables useful, and with them have been able to make reasonably accurate predictions of how children would use television.

These, then, are the bare bones of the interaction which we have been describing:

| Television contributes: | The child contributes: |
|---|---|
| Opportunities for fantasy experiences<br>Opportunities for reality experiences<br>(And different degrees of violence<br>    and sex, different intellectual levels,<br>    different value cues) | Mental ability<br>Social norms<br>Social relations<br>(And the needs and experien-<br>    ces of which age and sex are<br>    partial indicators) |

Out of this complicated interaction, something is selected, something is stored away, often some behavior occurs. These uses are cumulative over a long series of exposures to television. This is what we are talking about when we speak of the effect of television on children.

### Other characteristics of the interaction

Now, there are two further comments that should be made about this interaction. In the first place, it is obviously a second-level substitute for the kind of satisfactions possible to obtain by direct interpersonal relations.

It is unlikely that the level of gratification children can obtain from television will ever be as high as that they can obtain from life. Television is in large measure a substitute activity. When a child sucks his thumb and immerses himself in television, we can guess that television is substituting for the warmth of a mother-relationship. When a girl watches Dick Clark or a crooner, we can guess that she wouldn't be in front of the television set if at that moment she could be dating a handsome young man. When a frustrated child turns to television, he is seeking a substitute for the needs he was unable to meet in his real-life relationships.

There is probably a hierarchy among childhood needs in terms of how well they can be satisfied by television in comparison to real-life experience. For example, television can do some of the tasks of teaching (but not others) better than a classroom teacher. Television can tell a story at least as well as a student is likely to hear it told in real life. But television, despite its enormous prestige, is not likely to give advice as effectively as advice can be given in real life, because it does not have the feedback to enable it to adjust to the child's own problem. It is unlikely to give as much comfort as a child could obtain in real life. Certainly it will not satisfy the raging sex impulses of adolescents as well as they could be satisfied in life. Therefore, for the child who is not shut out from real-life satisfactions, television is always likely to be no more than a substitute for the real and deep gratifications to be found in successful interpersonal relationships. For the child who *is* shut out from interpersonal warmth and activity and support, we may suppose that the substitute will be more highly valued and more ardently sought than by the other kind of child, at least until such a time as he becomes more successful at meeting his needs among people rather than among programs.

There is another reason for expecting that the effects of television may not be so potent as they have sometimes been pictured. This is the fact that television always enters into a pattern of influences that already exist. Actually television may bulk rather small beside these other influences, for they come from the home, the peer group, the school, the church, and the culture generally.

In any case it is seldom that we can point to any behavior of a child and say that this is due *solely* to television. Television contributes to it, or catalyzes it, or gives it a particular shape. For example, a child commits a burglary and says that he learned to do it from television. Even without questioning the truth of his statement, we must then ask why did this particular child learn to commit a burglary when others did not; and why did he commit the burglary when other children did not? A little reflection will suggest that many other forces and influences were active in determining his particular behavior. The child who came to television and therefrom learned to commit and did commit a burglary was different in some important ways from other children who came to television. And these differences grew out of experiences and qualities other than television. It is seldom that the causes of any complex behavior in human beings are simple or single causes, and it is well to keep that in mind while reading through the following pages.

Now let us answer, as best we presently can, some of the chief questions that are being asked about television's effect upon children.

## Physical Effects

Questions of physical effect are easiest to answer. It is safe to say that few harmful results have been found in this area, and that the anxiety and heat have gradually melted out of the questioning. The two questions still most often asked are the following ones:

### Is television hard on children's eyesight?

Any sustained and concentrated use of the eyes on small figures or small movements may cause eyestrain. This is equally true of reading

and of television. Eyestrain is more likely to occur when the conditions
of viewing are not good. Too much or too little light, too much or too
little distance, or an awkward position will make for eyestrain in reading. (Eye specialists say that the child who sits very close to the television set, who looks *up* at the picture tube, who views in a dark room
and thus maximizes the glare, is also risking eyestrain.) There is little
doubt that many children violate these rules of viewing.

But on the other hand there is no evidence in the literature that television is any harder on children's eyes than other concentrated use of
them, such as reading. Himmelweit, Oppenheim, and Vince [4, pp.
367–68] found no more children in England wearing glasses or complaining of eye headaches among their viewing sample than among their
nonviewing sample, and no greater amount of these symptoms among
heavy viewers than light viewers. All the evidence we have supports
this finding. Given proper viewing conditions, there apparently is no
special reason to fear what television will do to a child's eyesight.

### Does television send children to school sleepy and tired?

Sometimes it does. Almost all the teachers we talked to could cite
some instance of children's inattention or sleepiness which they ascribed
to television. One teacher told us that on some days she had to open
the windows wide five minutes every hour and let the children exercise,
to keep them awake. Others told us that their worst mornings came
always after the nights on which very popular television programs came
on late.

On the other hand, there is no indication that the average bedtime
is much later as a result of television. We found that bedtime in Teletown was, on the average, only thirteen minutes later than in Radiotown, and a number of parents told us that their children, since television's coming, were more likely to go right to sleep instead of reading in
bed. In England, Himmelweit, Oppenheim, and Vince [4, pp. 369–71]
found that the average bedtime was postponed only ten to twenty minutes when television came. In New England, Maccoby [40, pp. 431]
found that, in homes which had recently installed television, weekday
bedtime was about twenty-five minutes later and Sunday bedtimes about
fifteen minutes later than in homes which did not yet have television.

If the average difference is fifteen minutes or so between bedtimes
in television and nontelevision homes, however, some children with television will then go to bed thirty minutes or an hour later than some
children of the same age without television. There is some evidence
in the English study that the children who stay up latest with television
are usually the ones least able to afford it—the children of lower intelligence who are doing less well in school. In other studies, evidence has

been cited (Clark [34]) that the late bedtimes tend to occur in homes where parental control is lax, where intelligence is not high, and where poor school performance is rather taken for granted. The implication is that the child might have come to school sleepy and inattentive even without television.

These problems point directly to the parent and the care he takes with his children's health.

## Emotional Effects

Less easily evaluated than physical effects, emotional effects are nevertheless more easily detectable by short-term studies than are some of the kinds of effect we are going to discuss later. Parents and intuitive critics of television have been most disturbed by the amount of frightening material and the high level of excitement on television. So far as the content of television is concerned, the case must be considered proved: there *is* a great deal of material on television that might frighten young children, and there is a high level of excitement. But the effects are not so clear. The effects of high excitement, in particular, must be, for the most part, long-term effects, and it is impossible to estimate their magnitude except by long-term studies. However, the parent can do much to shield a child from undue fright resulting from television, and both broadcasters and parents must consider their responsibilities in regard to excitement on television.

### Are children often frightened by television?

Ritual violence does not usually frighten children. For example, they are not ordinarily frightened when a cartoon figure like Donald Duck is in a fight or being chased, or when a puppet takes a clown-fall. Westerns are not usually frightening, because the behavior in them is of a ritual nature, and the children know how it is going to come out.

There are three situations on television which seem most likely to frighten children. One is the situation when harm threatens a character with whom they identify closely or to whom they feel specially attached. This is particularly true when the harm is physically more direct than by shooting. Perhaps because of the ritual quality of the Westerns or because a bullet cannot be seen on its way, gunfire is not usually very disturbing to any except a very young child. But being cut by a knife, or stepping into a bear trap—these are injuries a child can feel. And if they happen, let us say, to a character like Lassie the dog, concerning which the child feels both attached and protective—then, as one child said to us, "When I thought the dog was going to step in that old bear trap, I just about died!"

Another frightening situation is one which reminds the child of his own real-life fears, especially darkness and loneliness. Fear of the unknown and unseen is still one of the deepest human emotions, and this is the stock in trade of horror programs. The dark room, the stormy night, the ominous shadow (seen by a flash of lightning) of someone or something looking in the window—this is the kind of program that frightens many children. It reminds them of their own dark bedrooms and their own fears of night. They can imagine themselves in the situation.

A third situation is simply one in which a child comes too young to a stressful situation. There is a time, as we have said, in which all television is real to a child. He has not yet developed "adult discount." He has not had much experience with television, and doesn't know that "things will come out all right." He is unable to detach himself from the events of the silver tube. This kind of fear, in particular, can be handled by some control over what a young child views. It and the other kinds can be lessened by maintaining a warm, secure family atmosphere, by not encouraging a child to view television in a dark room, by giving him some older company as often as possible when he views, and, when necessary, by "talking out" what he has seen.

Most children, when they get well enough acquainted with you to be frank, will tell you that at some time they can remember being frightened by a television program. This is not, however, a property peculiar to television. Deep, unreasoning, unforgettable terror was roused in many children by such films as "The Hunchback of Notre Dame." Some books have been known to make the "hair stand up" or "gooseflesh" to crawl up one's back. The only difference between television and the other media is the fact that television is so vivid and that the child sees so much of it. All the more reason, then, to make the child feel secure, and to introduce him to the more frightening kinds of content only when he is old enough.

*Is television too exciting for children?*

The question really is, what is "too" exciting?

Children love excitement. They seek it, in thrill play on roller coasters, high diving boards, and drag races. As many writers on children's emotional development have observed, there is a fine line between excitement and fear. Fear may leave scars; excitement is relatively harmless unless it gets out of control.

There is a quality about television, as we have observed, that tends to keep piling up excitement. It is a by-product of the competition for audiences. Thus, the quiz shows had to become ever bigger and more exciting. A little violence had to grow into a great deal of violence. As a critic of television noted, the Lone Ranger was exciting enough to serve as a radio hero for ten years, but Davy Crockett, a hero "of almost mythic proportions" lasted on television only one year.

What is the end of all this? How high can excitement be raised? E. D. Glynn, a psychiatrist, has asked worried questions about this [47, p. 181]. He said: "It is too soon to know what children so massively exposed to sex on television will consider exciting and sex-stimulating as adults. A critical question is raised here: is television ultimately blunting and destructive of sensibility? This, too, one wonders: will reality match up to the television fantasies this generation has been nursed on? These children are in a peculiar position; experience is exhausted in advance. There is little they have not seen or done or lived through, and yet this is secondhand experience. When the experience itself comes, it is watered down, for it has already been half lived, but never truly felt."

He might also have asked what sorts of expectations children have about school as a result of their exciting experience on television. How exciting do they expect their teachers to be, and how much do they expect to learn passively, rather than by study and drill? He might further have inquired how often the abnormally high level of excitement on television makes addicts of children, makes them organize their activities at that level, and leaves them bored and ill-at-ease when the excitement drops.

These are serious questions, and no one now is in a position to answer them confidently. A large number of children of the television generation must be observed closely for a number of years before we can be sure what part the heightened excitement of television is playing in their lives.

However, in this case as in so many others the life situation of the child should have a controlling influence. If the child is well grounded in his reality experiences and secure in his personal relationships, he is more likely to be able to take the heightened excitement in stride. If he can relate to it as thrill play, he can probably put it into proper relationship with reality. If he can learn to view it with "adult discount," he is not likely to be deeply harmed by it. And there is a good chance that familiarity with TV excitement may build defenses against it (see Thompson [31]).

We are not trying to minimize the possible ill effects of reiterated excitement, especially on an insecure or withdrawn child. We feel that the problem should be under intense study. But without waiting for the result of long-term studies, we can do something about it. As parents, we can try to make our children secure in their interpersonal relationships, and maximize their reality experiences both on television and in real life, so that they will perceive alternatives to the hyperthyroid part of television. As broadcasters, we can apply ourselves seriously to the question of how we can make programs that will be attractive to the large numbers of children that commercial television requires, using appeals other than violence and keeping excitement within bounds.

## Cognitive Effects

This is an area in which observers held out most hope for beneficial effects from television, and an area in which very many such hopes have been disappointed. Television has ushered in no new age of enlightenment. It can teach, but in order to do so efficiently it must be linked with one of the teaching institutions of society. It is better at interesting people than in stimulating them. And serious questions have been asked about its effect on taste and children's information—questions like the following:

### Is television raising a better-informed generation?

The generation now growing to adulthood will probably be better informed, because so many aspects of science, economics, and foreign relations have become important for an American citizen to know, because we now talk more frankly and fully than we used to about mental and physical health and social problems, because Americans are traveling more, and, finally, because the average American will have more education. It is not at all certain, though, that television can be credited with much of the improvement.

We saw (Chapter 5) that the most and the least intelligent children in a television community now start school about one grade higher in vocabulary than do their fellow students in nontelevision communities; and furthermore that, at this stage, high vocabulary is related to heavy viewing. However, by the sixth grade, most or all of this fast start seems to have been lost, and thereafter children with television know more about the subject matter which is emphasized on television, less about what is not. That is not encouraging, because it implies that television would help bring up a generation better informed about the fantasy entertainment which is the major part of television, but not about matters of reality.

However, to children who select some of the reality experiences of television, unusual opportunities are offered. Here are chances to meet great men, to hear issues discussed and public figures quizzed, to see far places and great events, to hear some great teachers and see some great demonstrations of science and learning.

The first indicator of whether television is going to contribute a generally higher level of information, then, is whether a child selects from television experiences like these just mentioned. We know who are the children that chiefly select these things. They tend to be the most intelligent children, and the ones who operate under the deferred gratification norm.

A second indicator is whether the experiences a child gets from television teach him more than the experiences he might be having if he were not spending the time on television.

It is our observation, for example, that a very bright child who spends more than average time on television (probably because of social problems) is likely to deprive himself of highly useful learning experiences from print or personal contacts. On the other hand, a child of low intelligence is probably substituting television for time that would otherwise be given to other fantasy materials—comics, pulps, movies, and so forth. If this child spends more than average time on television, he is probably learning at least as much as, perhaps more than, he would otherwise get.

Therefore, our answer to the question is that television is probably helping some children more than others to grow into better-informed adults, and our prediction as to who is being helped would be about as follows:

| | Amount of Viewing of Television | |
|---|---|---|
| Intelligence | Above Average | Below Average |
| High | Probably *less* well informed than comparable children | Probably better informed if selects reality experiences |
| Middle | Probably not much difference | Probably not much difference |
| Low | Perhaps slightly better informed | Probably not much difference |

## Does television help in school?

Himmelweit, Oppenheim, and Vince, who made more of a study of this question than anyone else, concluded that television is neither "a distinct advantage nor a severe handicap" [4, p. 308] in school performance. This, of course, refers not to in-school television but to home television. They found that viewers in the same classroom tended, on the average, to do a little less well than nonviewers; and that television tended to be more a hindrance than a help to the brighter children. They found, as we did in Radiotown and Teletown, that television seems to have little effect on homework time.

We had no opportunity to make a controlled comparison of the influence of television on grades. However, we did not find many teachers who were prepared to say that television is responsible for either an over-all gain or an over-all loss in school performance. As against the cases of sleepiness or inattention, they also cited instances in which a play on television had caused a run on the library for the books of a first-class author; instances in which they had actually been able to make an assignment on television; and other instances in which the classroom discussion of such a process as national political conventions had obviously gained in realism and understanding from the fact that the conventions were on television.

Who profits most in school from television? The bright children are much more likely than the slow ones to say that television helps them in school. The teachers are more likely to cite examples of what the bright children bring from television into the class discussion. Therefore, the most likely conclusion is that the bright children who are selective about television find it of considerable help in school; that the bright children who are less selective and view a great deal of television find that it is somewhat of a handicap to them because they are missing some experiences that might teach them more than television does; and that for most other children it probably makes little difference except to add a new vividness and depth to their understanding of certain important events.

### Does television stimulate intellectual or creative activity?

Television is probably more effective in stimulating interest and contributing to already existing interests than in stimulating activity or creation. There are, of course, the cases where television has stimulated children to read books which have some relation to a TV program, and there have been a few occasions like the one in which a San Francisco educational station put a Japanese brush painter on the air and got several thousands of San Franciscans started painting. But Himmelweit et al. [4, p. 27] noted few occasions in which a child had actually made something after seeing it modeled on TV. And the kinds of activities we saw resulting from television were for the most part either fads (like the Davy Crockett hats) or adopted details which fit into already existing interests. For example, a boy changes his batting stance after seeing a major league game on television, or a young couple add to their house plans a fireplace like one they saw in a situation comedy.

Our opinion is that for television to be really effective in stimulating continuing intellectual or creative activity, or even continuing systematic learning, it must be geared into one or more of the organizations which are concerned with such activity in our society. We mean the schools, the adult education groups, the children's organizations, the libraries, the hobby groups, and so forth.* Selected television programs can be a tremendous stimulus to a discussion group; a series of television plays can stimulate the work of a women's drama club or a high school class; and a college course on television, as we now know, can

---

* This is also substantially the opinion of Lazarsfeld [77, p. 46] concerning the use of radio for "serious communication." He says: "Print did not raise the intellectual standard of living just because it was invented, but because it was used by educational institutions such as schools and promoted by cultural agencies such as libraries and publishers. In the same way, serious broadcasting will have to become

bring an individual back into the exciting experiences of higher education. But without some relationship of this kind, there tends to be no more than incidental later use of television experience.

### Does television "debase" children's tastes?

We are not on firm ground if we assume that the level of public taste has gone down in recent decades under the assault of popularized mass media. As Pool points out [51, p. 20], what has really happened has been a broadening of media use, rather than a lowering of high culture. He says:

> As Raymond and Alice Bauer show in a forthcoming publication, more people than ever have developed a taste for classical music, museums, and other similar cultural fare. The rise in circulation of inferior cultural materials has not been at the expense of higher culture. The consumption of higher culture is at similar levels to what it was in the past. It is just that there has been an increase in total consumption of entertainment and in that increase the main increment has been in pap consumed by people *who earlier had little access to any media at all.* The higher grade material shares a smaller part of the increase in media use.

So far as television builds a child's tastes at all, we have to assume that it operates to reinforce whatever tastes a child can satisfy from it. Now if it were sufficiently varied that a child could satisfy almost any level of taste and could experiment with widely different selections, this would not be worrisome. But the truth is that television is not greatly varied, and is mostly on the level that will appeal to a very broad audience.

In that situation, will television in time shape children's tastes to its own offering? We have already cited a finding of the Himmelweit team in England that when children had only one choice of program they came to like the programs, although if they had been offered a choice they would not have selected those particular programs at all. Supporting this is our own finding that children are almost wholly unable to suggest changes they would like made in television—only to suggest more of some kind of program they particularly like.

If it is indeed true that present-day television is perpetuating itself by shaping children's tastes, then this is rather sad news for people whose aspirations for television are considerably higher than the present level. What television might contribute to the reality and the fine arts experiences of a child is obviously much more than it is now doing. We are not blaming the network or station personnel, many of whom

linked with the whole plexus of educational and cultural institutions before it can contribute substantially to the enlightenment of the American community. Forces outside of radio will have to be brought into operation to provide vehicles and establish audiences for serious broadcasts."

hold very high aspirations for television. Rather, if anything is to be blamed, it is the medium's hunger for talent, its great cost, and its need of advertising support, which in turn needs large audiences. But this situation calls for research into the problem of how tastes are formed, and also for parents and schools and wise counselors generally to lead children to as great a variety as possible among the appropriate offerings of television.

*Does television convey an inaccurate picture of adult life?*

The child's-eye view of the adult world is curiously restricted. He sees his parents as mother and father, rather than husband and wife. He sees government and authority as a kind man in a blue suit. He sees little of criminality of any kind. He sees surprisingly little of the actual behavior of making a living.

There is no doubt in our minds, after talking to as many children as we have talked to in the last three years, that information on this little-known part of life (little-known by the child, that is) is one of the chief topics of incidental learning from television.

On television the child gets a picture of the sexual element in marriage and the problems of interpersonal relations between mother and father that he has little opportunity to get at home. He gets information about crooks, private eyes, violent crimes, and punishment that is quite a revelation to him. From a very early age he gets an insight into parts of adult life which are otherwise closed to him for some time. He drinks this information in. Now the question is, does he get an accurate and balanced picture?

There is no doubt that television's picture of the world includes an abnormally high proportion of sexy women, violent acts, and extra-legal solutions to legal problems. There is some reason to think that it contains also an overrepresentation of inadequate fathers, of get-rich-quick careers, and of crooked police and judges. We are not prepared to say whether or not these last statements are true; it would take a very large content analysis to decide, and in any case the problem lies rather with the child's selection and interpretation than in the actual number of seconds per day devoted, let us say, to the depiction of crooked policemen.

If this is the case—if a child is absorbing a markedly erroneous picture of adult life—then obviously this is no positive contribution to socializing him, and may require some very hard adjustments later.

The picture of adult life is something that should cause the broadcasters some concern. It also should cause parents and teachers to query whether they are doing enough to give the child some counterbalancing insight into adult life.

*mentally*

## Does television prematurely "age" children?

We have shown that a very large proportion of children's television viewing is of adult programs. The effect of this is that the old timetable for gradually exposing a child to adult ideas is gone forever. There is no use looking nostalgically back toward it—it is gone.

Klapper has written most about this. He points out that adult television fare "deals almost exclusively with adults, and usually with adults in conflict situations" [75, pp. 231–32]. He suggests that "continued exposure to such fare might unnaturally accelerate the impact of the adult environment on the child and force him into a kind of premature maturity, marked by bewilderment, distrust of adults, a superficial approach to adult problems, or even unwillingness to become an adult."

Himmelweit, Oppenheim, and Vince provide some corroboration for this hypothesis. They say that "adult television plays leave few of the comforting black and white philosophies of childhood intact" [4, p. 249]. Fewer of their viewers than their nonviewers, for example, believed that "good people always come out all right in the end." "Television," they write, "seemed to produce an earlier intellectual awareness of the complexity and essential unfairness of life." They found that adolescent viewers, especially girls, were more frightened than nonviewers about growing up, leaving school, leaving home, taking up their first jobs, and getting married.

Robert Shayon also has some observations on this topic. He says [52, p. 37]:

> Television is the shortest cut yet devised, the most accessible backdoor to the grownup world. Television is never too busy to talk to our children. It never shuts them off because it has to prepare dinner. Television plays with them, shares its work with them. Television wants their attention, goes to any length to get it.

This statement suggests an all-too-frequent weakness of busy parents in the process of helping their children to become adults. As Klapper says, all too often the parents are caught short when a child appeals to them as a result of some treatment of adult life he has seen on television. They are unprepared to help him understand, or they are caught in a white lie. Again, the behavior of these real adults may be considerably at variance with that of television adults, and this may confuse and bewilder the child.

## Behavioral Effects

At this point we suggest that the reader turn a few pages and read the commentary prepared for this volume by Dr. Freedman on "Daydream in a Vacuum Tube: A Psychiatrist's Comment on the Effects of

Television." Dr. Freedman is a distinguished research psychiatrist who has specialized in the study of delinquency and crime; and here he has written with commendable scientific caution and insight.

For those who prefer not to read the original just yet, let us sum up here some of Dr. Freedman's main points. He says frankly that "no competent psychiatric study . . . demonstrates that schizoid symptomatology [withdrawn behavior] in children has increased since television became widespread; nor has any careful investigation linked the rise in juvenile delinquency to the content of television programs or the act of watching them." Nevertheless, he argues, we have no reason to assume that we shall be pleased with the answers to those questions when we get them.

Then he points out that the child's task of developing into an adult human being is far too complex psychologically to make it likely that any single influence (such as television) will predictably produce a particular line of behavior. We have to understand an intricate meshing of influences and personal qualities before we can predict the child's behavior. It is necessary to know a great deal about the child's personality and environment before we can evaluate the effect of television on him.

In particular, he says, "The intensity and psychic significance of the child's response to television is the *reciprocal* of the satisfaction he gains in the milieu of his family, school, and friends. One would predict that the less intelligent, the most disturbed youngsters, and those having the poorest relationship with their family and peers would be most likely to immerse themselves in televiewing as escape and stimulus. Intelligent, relatively stable youngsters in reasonably harmonious homes would be comparatively unaffected by it."

Dr. Freedman wrote this without knowledge of our results, but what he says from his clinical experience is precisely parallel to our findings about the effect of a child's interpersonal relationships on his television behavior.

Children with satisfactory interpersonal relationships, then, are least likely to be harmed by any experience with television. But suppose there are flaws in the mental health and the social relationships of the child. Dr. Freedman constructs a sort of typology of mental health and illness, trying to predict how television might affect a child at each level.

Suppose the child has psychopathic tendencies. A psychopath's "self-censoring and self-governing mechanisms are defective." He doesn't feel the anxiety that a healthy person feels at acts of violence. He is "poised to rebel." This kind of child may use a television crime as a model for his own rebellion.

Suppose that a child is psychotic. His aggressive impulse may be out of control. Here the violence of television may be the "final stimulus" that brings on the eruption. In rare instances, the recommendations of television characters and advertisers may be mechanically responded to, as directions, by a schizophrenic child. More frequently, he may be passively and completely absorbed, reacting emotionally but physically immobile. But, as Dr. Freedman indicates, the response of a psychotic youngster, while important, is not representative.

As we have said, Dr. Freedman set down these comments quite independently of our research and our results, but everything we have been able to find supports his generalizations, and we find them a healthful antidote to some of the cries of "Wolf" that are now heard on all sides.

With this general introduction, let us now look at some of the questions that are asked about television's effect on passivity, violence, crime, and other undesirable behavior.

### Does television make children passive?

Dr. Glynn, whom we have previously quoted, makes the most impressive argument for the passivity effects of television. Among his examples of television's use in mental illness is this one [47, pp. 178–79]:

> The staff of a hospital for schizophrenic adolescent girls finds that these girls, insatiable in their demands, and yet themselves incapable of sustaining activity, want nothing so much as to be allowed endless hours of television. Without it they are soon noisy, unruly and frequently destructive. Significantly, the only other control of these girls is an adult who constantly directs them or organizes their entertainment for them.

Such examples, he says, could be multiplied endlessly:

> They all demonstrate quite clearly the special set of needs television satisfied, needs centering around the wish for someone to care, to nurse, to give comfort and solace. . . . These infantile longings can be satisfied only symbolically, and how readily the television set fills in. Warmth, sound, constancy, availability, a steady giving without ever a demand for return, the encouragement to complete passive surrender and development—all this and active fantasy besides. Watching these [viewers], one is deeply impressed by their acting out with the television set of their unconscious longings to be infants in their mothers' lap.
> These, then, are traits television can so easily satisfy in adults, or foster in children: traits of passivity, receptiveness, being fed, taking in and absorbing what is offered. Activity, self-reliance, and aggression are notably absent. A great deal of activity and aggression may be present, but they are deceptive, for the demands and even rages are not to be doing but to be getting. . . . Typical, too, of this character structure are the intensity with which needs are felt, the poor tolerance of frustration and delay, the demand for immediate satisfaction. The television set is easily and agreeably a mother to whom the child readily turns with the same expectations as to her.

These traits, of course, are inherent in all spectator participation, be it sport or art or reading. What is crucially important about television is its ubiquitousness: there is so much television, so early, so steadily; five-year-olds watch television as a matter of course, and, increasingly, so do three-year-olds and even two-year-olds. Television at this age can, in the limited experience of the child, only be seen as a mother-substitute or a mother-extension. These needs of the child should be outgrown, and his relationship to his mother changed. Basically, this growth depends in great part on the mother's attitude toward the child: her encouraging him to greater activity and self-reliance, the lessening of her feeding functions. It is of the greatest importance in character formation that the child can now have these infantile wishes and needs satisfied by the always available television set. Indeed, to continue enjoying television, it becomes necessary that these traits remain prominent. The danger is here: the passive dependent oral character traits become fixed. There are endless differences between children playing tag or cops and robbers and watching even the most action-filled Western; even between walking to the movies once a week and just switching on television by reaching out.

Hence, the chief effect of television is passivity and dependence in multiple shapes and forms.

This is a powerful and alarming argument, based, as it is, on a psychiatrist's clinical insights. All of us have seen the television set used as baby sitter, the child sucking his thumb as he watches, completely absorbed in the program. Many of us have seen a television addict, a child who is uncomfortable at home until he can turn on the set, and then buries himself in the program, shutting out all the outside world.

But we are inclined to believe this effect is less widespread than Dr. Glynn implies. Children, on the average, have given up a fairly small part of their active life in return for passive television. As we saw in Teletown, they seem to have replaced about half an hour of play (out of two or three hours), about an hour of radio (which is also passive), and a few minutes each from films, comics, pulps, and bed (activities which are passive in varying degrees). Except in the case of the addicts who watch television five or more hours a day, there has been no massive change in children's behavior in the direction of passivity.

We do not find the absence of aggression which Dr. Glynn notes. We find (Chapter 5) that aggression is rather higher in heavy viewers. Nor is all this aggression turned away from activity. The thing that impresses us is how deeply engrained in a child the love of activity is. Few children we have observed would trade an active experience for a passive television experience which would satisfy their needs no better. The vicarious satisfactions a child can get through television are almost invariably lower on his hierarchy than the satisfactions he can get directly—providing, of course, he *can* get the direct ones.

Himmelweit, Oppenheim, and Vince found in England that teachers rated viewers as high as nonviewers on initiative and imagination. They saw, as we did, little sign of children preferring the "edited" life on television to real life, if they had a true choice. As we did, they saw no sign of a "jaded palate" in children with television; if anything, these children tended to be interested in a wider spectrum of activities.

We do not argue with Dr. Glynn as to the effect of television on schizophrenic adolescent girls, which he cites; nor as to television's particular power in serving needs of comfort, solace, and escape. It seems clear to us that television would have a dangerous fascination for a schizoid child, who wants to withdraw anyway, and television might well so reinforce that behavior as to build up the habit of withdrawal and fantasy to a dangerous level. But we see no evidence whatsoever that television *makes* a child withdrawn, or *makes* passivity. Rather, it encourages and reinforces those tendencies *when they exist in dangerous amounts*.

It seems to us fair to assume, in the absence of evidence to the contrary, that a child with normally active personality, with a happy home and satisfactory peer group relationships, is not in danger of being made abnormally passive by television.

It seems to us also fair to assume that certain danger signs exist, which parents should be aware of. If a child starts spending an abnormally large amount of time on television, the parents might well review the child's interpersonal relationships. Are they providing a warm and secure home life for the child? Are they helping the child over his peer group frustration? Are they giving the child a chance to talk to them?

Or if a child shows withdrawal symptoms—overmuch daydreaming, a distaste for personal relationships, and so forth—once again they should review the child's interpersonal problems.

Some of their own behavior may be a danger sign. For example, any mother who uses television often as a baby sitter should be aware that she is taking a risk. Any parents who are neglectful can look for an unfavorable result.

These, then, seem to us the dimensions of the battleground. If a child is mentally healthy and has good home and peer group relationships, there is little to worry about so far as television and passivity are concerned. If the child has acute withdrawal symptoms, he may well need professional therapy. The field of battle lies in between: with the child who has *slight* withdrawal symptoms, or who daydreams or watches television a *little* too much, or who is having trouble with interpersonal relations. This is the kind of child whose passive behavior television might possibly reinforce to an undesirable degree, and perhaps make therapy necessary. But the strategy for this battle is to counterattack before therapy becomes necessary: to give the child a warm and loving home life, to make him feel wanted, to open up hobbies, books, family activities, and peer group activities to him. A child who has those surroundings, unless he has abnormal personality traits, is highly unlikely to develop any malignant and crippling passivity or dependence from watching television or from reading comics or from any other fantasy behavior.

## Does television violence teach violence?

There is another possible pattern of effect which is quite different from the one just described. We do not have to decide that one of these patterns is right and the other wrong; both may exist at the same time in different children.

The teaching of violent behavior is the most common charge levied against television. For example, recall what Norman Cousins wrote in the *Saturday Review* (December 24, 1949):

> In a Boston suburb, a nine-year-old boy reluctantly showed his father a report card heavily decorated with red marks, then proposed one way of getting at the heart of the matter: they could give the teacher a box of poisoned chocolates for Christmas. "It's easy, Dad, they did it on television last week. A man wanted to kill his wife, so he gave her candy with poison in it and she didn't know who did it."
>
> In Brooklyn, New York, a six-year-old son of a policeman asked his father for real bullets because his little sister "doesn't die for real when I shoot her like they do when Hopalong Cassidy kills 'em."
>
> In Los Angeles, a housemaid caught a seven-year-old boy in the act of sprinkling ground glass into the family's lamb stew. There was no malice behind the act. It was purely experimental, having been inspired by curiosity to learn whether it would really work as well as it did on television.

These cases could be many times multiplied. They all have a common pattern: the child applies to a real-life situation the kind of solution he has seen used on television. Now what are the conditions under which a child does that?

We pointed out, in Chapter 7, that television does not necessarily reduce aggression. It is just as likely to build aggression. The vicarious satisfactions of television will not for very long take care of real-life sexual frustrations or other social troubles. More likely, the sex on television will further frustrate an already frustrated child. The violence on television may stimulate the aggression in an already frustrated and aggressive child. Therefore, in some, though not all, of these cases, television may both suggest the tool of violence and help build up the aggression drive that needs such a tool. Then, when aggression in a real-life situation is at a sufficient height, the child remembers how aggressive acts were done on television.

This is one pattern, but not the only one. As a matter of fact, the latter two of Cousins' cases fit a quite different pattern. In those cases there was no apparent high level of aggression. Rather, there was a confusion between the rules of the real world and the rules of the television world. The child who wanted real bullets to use on his sister was merely carrying fantasy over to the real world, without considering the differences. The child who wanted to use ground glass in the stew was merely experimenting in the real world with the tools of the fantasy world. We have already noted that, to young children, television is terribly real.

Confusion between the real and the fantasy world will always exist to some extent in young children, and as long as violence is so prominent in the fantasy world of television and movies and comics, there will always be the possibility of confusion between fantasy violence and real-world violence.

There is the further problem of why an older child learns a violent act from television. Sometimes he, too, confuses the real with the fantasy world. Some of the boys' gang members who have been interrogated have talked as though they thought they were behaving like Robin Hood, rather than the Capone mob or the Syndicate. But in general these older boys' use of television violence has been fairly realistic. They have found on television an effective way to do something and they have adopted it.

One thing we can presume, in interpreting this pattern, is that the children who come to television with more frustrations and higher latent aggression are more likely to remember aggressive acts. This is the import of one of the Maccoby studies [82]. They identify with the character who is working out his aggressions on television and remember what he does.

Furthermore, whether this act is ethically "right" or not does not necessarily determine whether it is used. Brodbeck [8] reports some rather disturbing research in which children who were exposed to violence on films did not in the least change their beliefs that such behavior was wrong, but nevertheless were much more likely to recall the behavior in time of aggressive need and—we may presume—would be more likely to use it when they needed to be aggressive.

Suppose the violent act is not punished—is a child more likely to remember and adopt it? Zajonc [58] studied this, and found that when a fantasy sequence in comic books showed a villain relatively successful, children were more likely to identify with him and want "to be like him" than to identify with or want to be like a weak hero. In other words, the key question was whether a certain behavior worked. As Zajonc says, the children "would rather be like the characters who were successful, regardless of the specific mechanism they used in solving interpersonal problems."

Superficially this seems like an endorsement of the central article of the television, radio, and film codes—that crime should not be shown to pay. But it is a great deal more than that, for Albert's study [5] appears to mean that the "crime does not pay" ending does not inhibit aggression. The implication of Zajonc's study is that the child would rather be like a strong villain than a weak hero, and consequently an ethical ending will not necessarily counteract the influence of a strong, dynamic, attractive villain. This is one of the reasons why law enforcement officers have been concerned over the content of TV. They have said that policemen are typically shown as stupid and awkward, that most crimes are solved by extralegal methods, and that the crooks tend to be shown, not as police know them in real life, but as dynamic, exciting characters.

Let us sum up:

1. A certain number of young children (and a few older ones) will inevitably confuse the rules of the fantasy world with the rules of the real world and transfer violence from television to real life.

2. Children who come to television with aggression will be more likely to remember aggressive acts and be able to apply them when they are aggressive in real life.

3. Children may remember (and presumably be able to use) violence, even though it is in conflict with their ethics and values.

4. Children want to be like the "successful" characters they see in fantasy, and tend to imitate them, villainous or not.

These are partly questions of what television brings to children, partly what children bring to television. Although there is an abundance—most observers would say an overabundance—of opportunities to learn violence from television, on the other hand children who do not confuse the fantasy world with reality, who do not come to television with a great deal of aggression, who do not have psychopathic tendencies toward crime, will be much less likely than others to pick up this violence. In other words, satisfactory reality experiences, lack of undue frustration in social relationships, and mental health will insulate a child against this kind of harm. So will less violence!

## Does television cause juvenile delinquency?

You can find both figures and charges to support this relationship.*
In the ten years of television's great growth, the number of juvenile

* These figures were quoted in the U.S. Government *Social Security Bulletin* for May 1959 (p. 12): 1940, 200,000 juvenile court delinquency cases (10.5 per 1,000 children age 10–17); 1948, 254,000 cases (14.7 per 1,000); 1950, 280,000 cases (16.1 per 1,000); 1957, 603,000 cases (27.2 per 1,000).

crimes reported has more than doubled. Some of the charges we have quoted in Chapter 1. For example, Ralph Banay, a psychiatrist, said that "if the proverb is true that prison is a college for crime, I believe that for young disturbed adolescents, TV is a preparatory school for delinquency" [65, p. 83]. There are frequent newspaper items of the following kind (in which we have changed the place names):

JONESTOWN, N.D., March 10—A 10-year-old boy held here is accused of writing four bad checks to get money for candy and cookies. Sheriff Gerald Gutzwiller said the boy admitted getting the idea from a television show.

MELON PARK, ILL., July 19—Two 17-year-old Allerton youths were arrested yesterday for sniping at Melon Park pedestrians with a BB pistol from a car.

Inspectors William Moran and Rudolph Siemssen charged one boy with assault with a deadly weapon, the other with being an accessory.

One BB struck Mrs. Theresa Cromelin of 174 Watkins Avenue in the neck beneath her left ear. She required surgery.

The teen-agers continued cruising until they came to 1640 Oak Avenue, where 13-year-old Barry Morningstar was riding a bike.

The youth with the pistol fired again and a pellet lodged in Barry's left cheek.

The two snipers, students at Melon-Allerton High School, said they got the idea from a television program.

OAKVILLE, CALIF., Sept. 24—A 13-year-old Oakville boy, who said he received his inspiration from a television program, admitted to police last night that he sent threatening notes to a Hayman school teacher.

His inspiration for the first letter came while he was helping the pastor of his church write some letters. When the minister left the office for an hour, the boy wrote his first poison pen letter.

"I got the idea when I saw it happen on TV," he told Juvenile Sgt. George Rathouser. "I saw it on the 'Lineup' program."

However, when one looks at these items more closely, they seem less impressive. The increase in reported juvenile crime is quite closely parallel to, in fact a little behind, the increase in juvenile courts. Many states and cities have opened these courts in the last ten years; the result is that more juvenile offenses are being handled and reported. And in Banay's statement is a very important word which many readers pass over. He says that TV may be a preparatory school for delinquency "for young *disturbed* adolescents." In other words, the young people who are influenced by television toward crime seem to be different from others who are not so influenced, even before they are influenced by television.

We have followed up as many as we could of the items typified by the North Dakota story cited above. We have talked to a number of psychiatrists and judges about such cases. Almost invariably we learned that delinquent children who blame television for their crimes have something seriously wrong with their lives quite apart from television. For the most part, they have home trouble: a broken home, or parents that reject them or seem to reject them. Some of them appear to be psychopathic personalities, with their superegos disconnected, so to speak, from the rest of their behavior pattern. But with few exceptions these problem children had problems before they learned anything about crime from television.

We have been encouraged in this conclusion by statements from competent psychiatrists who have also studied this relationship. This is Dr. Otto Billig, of Vanderbilt University, speaking to the Kefauver Committee:

> My clinical experience has led me to believe that television programs, movies, etc., have a very limited influence on the child or juvenile. We have performed rather exhaustive psychiatric and psychological studies on juvenile delinquents. Most youngsters do not seem at all influenced by such outside factors. The well adjusted personality can resist them without difficulties. A very occasional case was triggered into some delinquent act and possibly received specific ideas on how to carry out a crime. But only the emotionally disturbed and insecure individual appears susceptible to such outside forces. Other outside pressures have probably greater significance, such as recognition by neighborhood gangs, inadequate or lack of group activities, etc.
>
> There is little question as to the disturbing educational or artistic value in the poor taste of the mentioned programs, but I would consider it as disadvantageous and even detrimental to the problem of juvenile delinquency to blame them as the actual cause. In so doing we would avoid the main issues. We need to focus our efforts on the principal causative forces rather than on surface appearances. Our clinical experience has shown us that insecurities in the individual family play a major part in juvenile delinquency. [2, pp. 267–68.]

Dr. Frank Coburn, of the University of Iowa, said to the same Committee: "The primary and most important factor in the production of juvenile delinquency in my opinion is a disturbed family relationship in the home of the child who is considered a delinquent." [2, p. 269.]

Therefore, our belief is that the kind of child we send to television, rather than television itself, is the chief element in delinquency. According to our best current understanding of delinquency, the delinquent child (unless he is psychopathic) is typically not different from other children in standards or knowledge or intelligence, but rather in the speed with which he can rouse his aggressive feelings, and the intensity and violence of his hostility. He has typically come from a home which has not given him the security and warmth children need. He often has had peer group trouble, too, and sometimes has felt he had to do extraordinary things to be recognized by his peers. We found out in Chapter 7 that conflict of this kind leads a middle-class child to seek more television; a lower-class child is already seeing a great deal of it. Television then interacts with the needs and emotions the child brings to it. It stimulates, rather than drains off, his aggressions. It gives him violence to watch, and he stores up information from it which he can perhaps later use. It is quite likely that if television were not available to him, he would be seeking the same kind of returns from other fantasy media.

The roots of delinquency are, therefore, much lower and broader than television. They grow from the home life, the neighborhood life, and the disturbed personality. The most that television can do is to feed the malignant impulses that already exist.

### Does television cause a child to "withdraw" from life?

This is clearly akin to the question on passivity. Television contributes to such behavior because of its high proportion of vivid fantasy. With most children, the result is no more than a temporary "escape," a brief surrender to fantasy and then a return to the responsibilities of reality. With a few children, however, the withdrawal symptoms are so severe that psychiatric help is necessary.

Dr. Joost A. M. Meerlo, a psychiatrist, reports the following case:

> A psychologist had made the diagnosis of schizophrenia, based on the increasing symptoms of apathy and a lack of mental contact. First, I tended to agree with this diagnosis. But gradually I found that she was more willing to relate to me when we started to talk about the television programs. Then the girl became vivid, showed interest, told about her wishes to take part in the programs, and so forth. It took several sessions of psychotherapy to make her better aware of the fact that she had completely surrendered to fantasy life. [2, p. 263.]

Dr. Glynn reported a somewhat similar case of a young adult:

> A twenty-five-year-old musician, daughter of an adoring, constantly present, constantly acting mother, quarrels with her parents and gives up her own quite busy professional life. She turns to the television set, and soon is spending ten or twelve hours a day watching it, constantly sitting before it, transfixed, drinking beer or eating ice cream, lost and desperate if the set is turned off. Making a joke one day, she said, "Boy, I don't know what I would do for a mother if that tube ever burned out." This girl, of real intellectual attainment, was completely indifferent as to what the programs actually were. [47, p. 178.]

The second of these young women (and the first one probably) had great lacks in her interpersonal life which she was trying to escape from in television. The programs meant nothing to her; the escape hatch was the important thing. So, too, we may suppose that Dr. Meerlo found some real-life troubles which the first girl was seeking to escape from. This is the general pattern: that abnormal addiction to television and withdrawal from reality do not occur if a child has a normal and reasonably satisfying interpersonal life away from television.

Everyone indulges in a certain amount of fantasy. Television merely makes a great deal of fantasy very easily available. By absorbing the attention, by offering a very high level of excitement, it invites children to it. If they have very dull lives, if they are frustrated in their interpersonal relations, then television has a very special appeal. But here our conclusion is about the same as to the threat of television-caused delinquency: If parents will but give their children a warm and secure home life, and try to see that they have interesting activities with their peer group, they need not fear that the children will make too much use of the television escape hatch. The two instances cited at the beginning of this section are highly abnormal behavior. They are not something to be blamed on television or to be expected in any normal home.

### Does television make addicts of children?

Television addiction may result when a child "becomes accustomed to a heightened level of excitement and organizes much of his learned excitement at that particular level of excitement," so that "his behavior will be disrupted if the level of excitement declines, and he will be restless, bored, ill-at-ease until he does something to restore the particular level of excitement around which his behavior has been organized" (Maccoby [40], pp. 441–42). It may also result when the child retreats from unpleasant problems of reality to soothing fantasy and finds the difference so great and his responses so pleasantly reinforced by television, in contrast to what happens to them in reality, that he retreats ever more deeply. In either of these cases, if the child has internalized the self-betterment norm, he will find himself doing a great deal of what he has learned he should not do. In that case the appeal of "forbidden fruit" may contribute to his addiction.

It is undoubtedly true that television addicts exist, and among children who are not psychologically disturbed in a serious way. However, there is no reason to think that television *of itself* makes addicts.

The child who becomes addicted to the excitement of television is usually one who is not well grounded in reality and not able to make a clear distinction between the real and the fantasy world. The child who becomes addicted to the dream world of television is usually either schizoid or suffering from very unsatisfactory personal relations, at home or with the peer group or both.

Therefore, what television does is to exploit the weakness—to seize on the impulse toward fantasy and reinforce it. It contributes, but it is very unlikely to originate.

Thus we return to a familiar theme. Some children have in them the seeds of addiction; others do not. Like most of the undesirable behavioral effects, addiction in a healthy child is what Dr. Freedman calls "the reciprocal of the satisfaction he gains in the milieu of his family, school, and friends."

# CHAPTER 9

# A SHORT SUMMARY AND
# A FEW QUESTIONS

It seems clear that in order to understand television's impact and effect on children we have first to get away from the unrealistic concept of what television "does to children" and substitute the concept of *what children do with television.*

This is what we have tried to do in this book. As we look back over the preceding pages and forward to the appendixes and tables, we can see that there is nothing simple about the relationship. As we tried to indicate in Chapters 4 and 8, it isn't scientifically justifiable to say that television is good or bad for children. The relationship is always between a *kind* of television and a *kind* of child in a *kind* of situation. And always behind the child there are other relationships of importance—notably with family and friends, school and church. Television enters into the *whole life* of the child, not merely the corner of it that happens to intersect a particular program.

Let us look back over the road we have come.

In Chapter 2 we tried to sketch in some of the surface changes that television has made in the world of the child. Comparing pretelevision with television communities, we saw that the new medium reorganizes leisure time and mass media use in a spectacular manner. It cuts deeply into movie-going, radio-listening, comic book and pulp magazine reading. It reduces the time for play. It postpones bedtime slightly. It dominates the child's leisure. To persons who have had this happen to them, it may not seem like a jarring change; but viewed from the vantage of distance or history, it is quite remarkable. Overnight a new box appears in the home, and thereafter all leisure is organized around *it!*

In Chapter 3, we tried to set down the basic facts and figures concerning the child's use of television. These certainly are spectacular. One out of three children is watching television at the age of three, four out of five at age five, nine out of ten by the time they are in the first grade. In the early grades the average time a child spends on television is about two hours a day. Thereafter it rises to a mountain peak of three to four hours about the sixth or seventh grade, and falls slowly throughout high school. There are great individual differences among children in their television. For example, the brighter children are usually heavy listeners until about the age of eleven, and then tend to turn away from television to the supposedly greater intellectual challenges of print. When the average is 2.5 hours, a considerable number of children will view more than four hours a day, and another considerable group less than one hour. But despite these differences, the average child spends on television in his first sixteen years as much time as he spends on school, more time than he spends on all the rest of the media.

In Chapter 3 we tried also to sketch in the patterns of children's taste for programs, which proceeds quickly from so-called "children's" programs to Westerns, adventure programs, crime shows, situation comedies, popular music and variety shows, and other chiefly adult program types. The greater part of children's television viewing is of programs for which the majority of viewers are adults. Most of it is fantasy and entertainment. The taste for public affairs programs is little and late.

Children have a high affection for television. It is the medium which the great majority feel they would miss most, if they had to do without the mass media. They are almost completely inarticulate when asked what changes they would like to see made in it. Chiefly they say they would want more of what they now select. This is not to say that television is completely satisfying, only that it is extremely difficult for children to visualize a substitute for its present content in the absence of a real and existing alternative. It is noteworthy that the prestige and importance of television declines during the teen years, especially with the brighter children. In these years the printed media come to be more highly valued, and radio (used chiefly as a second channel to provide a music background for reading and studying) develops a new importance.

In Chapters 4, 5, 6, and 7, we have been concerned with the process and the dynamics which determine what a child selects from television and the use he makes of it.

In Chapter 4 we developed some theory of television's usefulness to children. Children use television for entertainment and escape, for information, and as a social tool—for example, to entertain a date. The latter use is not unique to television or the mass media; it applies equally, for example, to the automobile. We defined the chief needs for which children go to television as the needs for *fantasy* and *reality experiences*. And by comparing pretelevision with television behavior we were able to show that it is overwhelmingly the *fantasy* needs of children which television is meeting.

In Chapter 5 we considered the nature and amount of children's learning from television. We noted the effectiveness of instructional television used as a part of school, and the presence of forty-seven non-commercial educational television stations devoted to providing reality experiences to their viewers. But we concentrated on the television services to which children give most of their viewing time: commercial television. Here it is apparent that most of the learning is an incidental increment from fantasy programs. In the preschool years, this is a very important learning source. It sends the bright children and the slow children to school with vocabularies about a grade higher than children have if they are without the benefit of television. Similarly, children of average intelligence who are heavy viewers come to school with significantly greater vocabularies than light viewers. Thereafter, however, incidental learning from fantasy programs becomes of less use to children, both because of the repetitiveness and the fairly low intellectual level of fantasy programming, and because, as the child grows older and becomes expert in using print, he increasingly uses the printed media for reality experiences and for serious learning.

This is especially noticeable in the case of children with high mental ability. If they are heavy users of television in the teen years, they tend to do less well on knowledge tests and in school than do their fellows who are light users of television. In general, however, television is a real aid to the learning of very young children, and thereafter contributes to the kind of knowledge which is closely connected to its fantasy programs (for example, the names of popular singers), and not especially to the kind of knowledge which is more closely related to reality experiences (for example, public affairs) or to the kind of knowledge which is chiefly learned in school (for example, science). We do not say that television does not or cannot stimulate a child or broaden horizons; merely that it seems not to do those things in any greater degree than takes place in the absence of television.

Mental ability, social norms, and social relationships, in addition to age and sex, we found to be the chief variables in a child's life that helped us predict what use he would make of television. Age and sex, of course, are merely indicators of some of the needs and experiences which a child will have at a given time. Age helps to give us an idea of the kinds of experiences a child has had by a given time, where he stands in the process of socialization, and the type of social needs he is likely to have at the moment. Sex, combined with age, tells us what roles a child must be preparing for, and what interests he must feed. But the other three are more than indicators; they are active elements. Mental ability is the most influential of these in determining how much and what a child is likely to learn from television. In Chapter 6, we took up the second of these powerful and active variables, social norms.

In that chapter we were trying to understand the patterns of fantasy seeking and reality seeking which, more than anything else, differentiate children's media behavior. We divided children into four groups according to the amount of their television use and their use of books and magazines. That gave us a group that was fantasy-oriented (high TV, low print), one that was reality-oriented (low TV, high print), a group of heavy users (high TV, high print), and a group of light users (low TV, low print). In the sixth grade the reality-oriented group is very small, but by the tenth grade it has grown a great deal. When we studied children in this group we found that they are different from others in that they have internalized the social norm of self-betterment, deferred gratification, and activity which is considered, in our culture, to be typical of the upward mobile middle class. There is a sort of turning point at the beginning of adolescence when a considerable number of children change from the fairly universal pleasure norm of childhood to the norm we have been talking about. It is these children who, if their mental ability is up to their normative requirements, become the chief serious users of print, viewers of educational television, and the viewers who more than others select reality programs from commercial television. Social norms, then, have a great deal to do with the kind of use a child makes of television.

In Chapter 7 we considered the relation of a child's social relationships to his use of television. The basic rule, we found, is that when a child has unsatisfactory relationships with his family or his peer group, he tends to retreat to television where he can for a time leave the field of real-life problems and possibly reduce his tension. More conflict, more television.

But when we crank in some of the other variables, this is no longer a simple relationship. For example, in the case of children of high intelligence and high social status, when social relations worsen, the amount of television use goes up, as we should expect. But take the case of children of low intelligence and low social status. These children, we know, will have more than average aggression and make more than average use of television. But what happens if they develop unsatisfying parent or peer group relationships? In this case, more conflict does not make for more television; if anything, it makes for less.

The quality of a child's home and peer group relationships thus helps to determine the *amount* of television he sees, but also much more. We saw that the child who comes to television full of aggression because of home or peer group frustration is likely to seek and remember the violent content of television. If his social relationships are not satisfactory, he is likely to daydream over the fantasy from television. If he seeks violence in answer to his own social needs, he is likely to remember and resurrect that violence when he has need in real life to be aggressive. In other words, parents, friends, schools have it in their power to make a significant contribution to the healthfulness of a child's use of television by giving him a warm and loving home, and helping him to normal and satisfying friendships with children his own age.)

So we came, in Chapter 8, to an inventory of the effects of television. By this time we were able to say something about the nature of effects because we knew more about how television enters into the life of the child.

The *physical* effects of television we were inclined to rate not very important. Television seems to cause no special amount of eyestrain if children view under proper conditions. There is little evidence of serious loss of sleep or energy as a result of television.

The *emotional* effects of television, however, are less innocuous. Almost all children, at some time or other, are frightened by a television program. Chiefly they are frightened when harm threatens some character or animal with whom they identiy or to whom they are closely attached, and particularly when the harm involves cutting, or stepping in a trap, or some nonritual violence. They are frightened when they come too early to violent and stressful programs, and again particularly when they view such programs in dark rooms or alone.

In general, children like and seek excitement, on television as in real life, so long as it doesn't spill over too far into fear. This is the reason they engage in "thrill play," which has its parallel in television. Serious questions have to be raised, however, about the possible effect of the high and still heightening level of excitement in television. What is the effect of this excitement on children's perceptions of reality? Does it take the edge off actual experience and lead children to demand of real life something it cannot give them? There are some signs of this, but the answer cannot really be given without long-term research.

Concerning the *cognitive* effects of television, the general conclusion is one of disappointment. This is not because television is doing any special harm in this respect, but rather because it isn't realizing its full potential as a carrier of ideas and information. In school work, commercial television is "neither a distinct advantage nor a severe handicap." In some ways it is doubtless raising up a better-informed generation, but its accomplishment in that respect is nothing compared to what it could do if more of its power were used for reality experiences. Commercial television, which is rich in talent and money, is supported chiefly for offering fantasy experiences. Noncommercial educational television, which is devoted to offering reality experiences, is starved for talent and money. The old dream of television as the supermedium for informing and teaching the people of a democracy has never been fully realized.

Television has proved itself better at stimulating interest than stimulating intellectual or creative activity. For this latter task, it apparently needs to be geared into an organizational framework. There is little sign that television is raising taste, and some fear has been expressed that it may be hardening in children a taste level based on its own common-denominator standards. The finding that children learn to like the programs available to them, although ordinarily they would not even select those programs, is a disturbing result. Some students of television are concerned about its effect on taste formation; others are equally worried because it gives children information about adult life much earlier than they have been accustomed to hear such things. Furthermore, much of its treatment of adult life shows adults in conflict, and many of its portraits are far from flattering. There is a real worry lest this "premature aging," these portraits of adult life made available before a child is really ready to discriminate among them, may mislead and perhaps discourage children, even to the extent of making them fear the process of growing up.

Then we come to the *behavioral* effects of television. These are the ones that have caused the most worry, and yet they seem to us in almost every case controllable through the nontelevision life of the child.

Does television make children too passive? It does in some cases, and only long-term studies can determine the magnitude and lasting quality of the effect. But the way to avoid an excessive passivity in our children is not to give them television as a mother substitute early in life; rather to make them feel loved and wanted at home, and so far as possible to surround them with friends and activities.

Does television teach violence and cause delinquency? We suggested a number of situations in which television might encourage violence. Some children will confuse the rules of the fantasy world with the rules of the real world. Children who bring aggression to television are more likely to remember the aggressive acts on television. Children want to be like the "successful" characters they see, whether those characters are good or bad. And so forth. But very little delinquency can be traced directly to television. Delinquency is complex behavior growing usually out of a number of roots, the chief one usually being some great lack in the child's life—often a broken home, or a feeling of rejection by parents or peer group. Television is at best a contributory cause.

Does television make children withdraw from life? In a few cases this happens to a serious degree, and the child needs therapy. In most cases, the child's withdrawal from life is no more than his withdrawal to any fantasy experience, and he has no difficulty in making the return trip to normal rules of behavior. Here, as elsewhere, if parents will but give their children a warm, secure, and interesting home life, they need have little fear of any abnormal withdrawal into fantasy life.

These behavioral effects of television, then, point as much to parents as to broadcasters. Parents can make sure that their children view television under proper optical conditions and do not stay up too late to view it; and so they can avoid what we called the physical bad effects of television. Broadcasters must assume the blame for the intellectual level of television, and for the amount of frightening material and the level of excitement and violence, but even here parents and schools and other nontelevision forces in the lives of children can help by cushioning the shock and directing some of their exploratory viewing. In short, although we are not trying to excuse the sins of television, whether of omission or commission, it seems to us quite a remarkable thing that if a child has security and love, interests, friendships, and healthful activities in his nontelevision hours, there is little chance that anything very bad is going to happen to him as a result of television.

Television, therefore, is not something either to be feared, or given a clean bill of health, but rather something that calls for understanding and for certain special responsibilities, on the part of parents, broadcasters, teachers, and other persons influential in a child's life. This circumstance has encouraged us to ask a few questions.

## Questions to Broadcasters

We have been careful in this volume not to push the panic button on television. We have pointed out that whenever television is connected with delinquency or other violent or asocial behavior on the part of children, there are causes in addition to, and more influential than, television. We have admitted that research has not gone far enough to understand completely the effects of television, particularly the long-range effects. We have duly noted that children *like* television as it is.

Yet, granted all these things, and granted that a secure and happy home life will insulate a child against many of the ills that might possibly result from television, still the charge that television harms otherwise undisturbed children must be considered *not* proved rather than *disproved*.

It is clear that, except for such cases as an already disturbed child learning a criminal technique or an insecure child having a bad fright from television, most of the potentially dangerous effects of television on children are long-range effects. We have pointed out some of the patterns by which a continuing input of violence and abnormally high excitement from television might adversely affect the lives of children. We have suggested some of the implications of exposing children, year after year for several hours a day, to material which, after the first few years, carries little intellectual stimulation for them. We have posed some of the possible results of retreating several hours a day for a number of years into a fantasy world where the rules are, to say the least, unlike those of the real world.

Now, effects like these take a long time to develop, and are very difficult to detect except over a long period. If it becomes clear, as a result of long-term research, that these results are indeed adverse, then it will be too late to do anything about television for a whole generation of children.

These circumstances, it seems to us, raise particularly bothersome and challenging questions for television broadcasters.

It is hard for us today to imagine television any different. And yet, it need not have developed in its present pattern. Most of the national television systems of the world *have* developed in quite different patterns. In the early days of American broadcasting, some of the founding fathers, like David Sarnoff, insisted that such a powerful instrument as broadcasting should be used only for the public service, never for the service of commerce. It is possible, even now, to imagine an American television service which, in place of covering an important session of the United Nations for a few minutes per day, would carry the whole session; which would cover the national government more directly and at length rather than devote a few minutes per day to a handsome announcer reading news bulletins; which would carry great plays and music as a matter of regular practice, not merely as "spectaculars"; which, instead of filling every waking hour on three networks and a number of independent stations with whatever can be found to fill them, and thus draining dry the pool of talent and repeating over and over again whatever proves attractive to viewers, would fill only a few hours a day, and as much as possible of that with fresh programs and offerings of high quality. It is possible, that is, to conceive of such a development if television had grown along another path. It is no longer possible to return to that path, but on the other hand it is not completely necessary to follow our present path to a lugubrious end.

It seems to us that the responsible men and women of television, both as fathers and mothers and as the custodians of one-sixth of children's waking lives, must ask themselves questions like these:

*Cannot programs be produced that will be attractive to children without such large doses of violence and excitement?*

The succession of violent and sadistic acts on evening television, the routine of repetitive but hyperglandular excitement in programs, is a shock not only to foreign visitors to the United States but also to many parents who look at television over their children's shoulders. We don't want to overemphasize the possible effects of television experience. We believe that most children will accept it and dispose of it routinely. And yet, is the risk worth taking?

Is it the best we can do? Is this the only way we can find to interest children and at the same time attract the large audiences that sponsors require? It seems to us that this might be a matter of pride as well as conscience for broadcasters. These are men of great skill and talent: is it really true that they find it necessary to appeal to large audiences of children with a stream of physical violence, abnormal excitement, and crime? This doesn't check with our knowledge of broadcasters and suggests that the top people may be delegating some of their responsibility to less able persons. It seems to be a confession of weakness or lack of ingenuity. It doesn't check with what we have seen of the high sense of public responsibility typical of the best broadcasters. Can these leaders in their profession not find a way to do the job of television without the succession of violent acts and frenzied excitement which now characterizes the programs children see?

We should like to see broadcasters look hard at those of today's programs which, without offering a diet of violence, still earn high ratings among children. These programs might suggest some new and promising avenues in programming. We should like to see the networks and the stations turn their most creative personnel loose for a while on any such roads that promise better programming for children, and, in particular, programs that look as though they might fill the gap between the animal, puppet, and cartoon stage of childhood and the years when the child is ready for adult programs.

As a matter of fact, we should like to see a major project in experimental production of television, using all we know about children and a good sample of the best talent in television; and with it a high-level program of research to find out and interpret children's responses to these experimental programs. It is entirely possible that a serious cooperative effort of this kind might provide an acceptable alternative to the private eyes, two-gun men, and clever crooks who now occupy so much of the spectrum.

Another question:

*Can television not offer more challenge to bright children?*

Scattered through the commercial television week is a great deal more intellectual stimulation than critics give the industry credit for. Chiefly this stimulation emanates from or is closely related to the news departments, and includes commentary, interviews and press conferences, occasional discussions and documentaries, and special events. We feel that the industry is to be complimented for what it has done in these respects, and that parents and schools have been remiss if they have not directed children to programs of this sort that are available.

But this is a tiny part of television, and an even tinier part of children's typical selection from television. It is safe to say that, compared to the effort that has been made to attract children with slapstick cartoons, gun-happy Westerns, junior situation comedies, loose-hipped crooners, and private eye heroics, only an infinitesimal part of the effort of commercial television has been put on the problem of how to attract children to stimulating reality experiences.

In community after community, during the course of this study, we have observed a disappointing pattern. In their early years, children have benefitted intellectually from television. They have picked up larger vocabularies, filled their minds with concepts, names, and behaviors which they would never have learned otherwise so early. But as they passed through the first years of school, their viewing patterns settled into the old repetitive pattern of entertainment television. As they approached adolescence we watched the bright children begin to devote larger proportions of their time to print, where they found more intellectual challenge. In fact, whenever we found a bright child who was an above-average viewer of television, we learned to look at once for some unsatisfactory social relationship that was driving him to seek escape in television. Whenever we found a bright child who was a heavy user of television, we learned to expect that he would score less well on knowledge tests; and other researchers found that this kind of viewer would do less well in school than an equally bright child who was a light viewer of television. We found that bright children in their teens considered that television was less important and had less prestige than did children who were not so bright.

It seems to us a disappointment, and a waste of potential, that television should thus have its influence with children so overwhelmingly as a fantasy medium rather than as a source of reality experiences. No one doubts that it can be a great reality medium. It seems to us that it might be a matter of pride with television people to do a little more toward making it a great reality medium. Is our skill only with fantasy? Do we consider our children so slight a resource that we can afford to bring them up on an intellectual diet of such a kind? Do we really believe that this is the way to make leaders and thinkers?

Again:

*Can the picture of adult life now offered on commercial television be made more adequate to the needs of children?*

Let us carefully qualify this question, as we have the preceding ones. We are not advocating the kind of realism which Zhdanov insisted on— that art be used consistently to show patterns for emulation. And we believe that if a child has healthy experiences with adults which let him compare reality with fantasy, he will probably get to the age of "adult discount" without any serious trouble from misconception of adult life. But we are impressed with the fact that television has done away with the old slow timetable for informing children about the adult world. And we are also impressed with certain aspects of the picture of the adult world which is offered children at an early age—the high percentage of adults involved in conflict, the high percentage of crimes that are settled extralegally, the general inadequacy of fathers and the sorrows of mothers, and the stupidity of law enforcement officers in comparison to crooks.

It is entirely possible, as we have said, that this kind of picture may introduce certain troubles and difficulties into the already troubled process of growing up, although this too will be a long-range effect probably not detectable without long-term study. We are not suggesting that the bright crooks, the inadequate fathers, the unhappy mothers, the amateur detectives, and the fast-draw experts all be removed from television. Rather, it seems to us that the picture might be filled in with a few attractive examples of other kinds. For example, how about showing children the excitement of fighting modern problems other than murder—such problems as disease, scientific discovery and development, social problems, international relations, artistic success, and so forth. As Himmelweit, Oppenheim, and Vince pointed out, heroes who fight against such a problem as disease are generally depicted as figures out of history, dressed in period costume. We might add that heroes who fight on the frontiers of science are usually fantastic figures who drive space ships. And where are the heroes, men or women, who are making a contribution to good government, to business, or to good community life? Surely the talented television writers are capable of capturing these aspects of the modern scene.

Of course, this will require talent, freshness, originality. One small example: In one of the largest cities of this country, as we write this, children are seeing on television a series of animated cartoons made in the early 1940's. These films were made for wartime propaganda purposes. Shown now, twenty years later, they carry a message of racial prejudice and international hatred. They apparently come out of a stock pile purchased in bulk. What television needs to do for children can't be done out of stock piles!

The basic question remains: *Are these things really the responsibility of the television industry?*

We think they are, and that they are a particularly potent responsibility of an industry that controls so much of a child's life and such a valuable public resource as the electronic spectrum of television. We are not impressed with the excuses for not accepting such responsibilities. Let us take up those excuses:

1. *Television gives children what they want.*

Since when has this become a sufficient doctrine for adult responsibility? Children would doubtless eat a diet of candy and dessert, if we let them have from the beginning only what they want. Many of them would doubtless learn to like narcotics or hard liquor at an early age, if we made those things readily available. Sex out of wedlock would prove more popular if it were condoned and made easily available. One of the responsibilities of adults is to guide the tastes and values of children as they develop. To say that television should give children whatever they want is a thoroughly irresponsible and callous point of view.

2. *The responsibility is really with the parents. They should keep children from seeing programs too old for them, and they should ensure the children's mental health by providing a happy, secure home life.*

It is true that parents *share* the responsibility with broadcasters. But there is a limit on what parents can do about the situation. Most parents don't have the knowledge or skill to maintain robust mental health in children who, for one reason or other, are on the borderline of danger. Most parents don't have the time to give children all the home experiences they need to ensure these "happy, secure" relationships. Beleaguered with home duties and work responsibilities, parents are inclined to be grateful to television as a baby-sitter rather than to treat it as something that requires much of *their own* time if their children are to use it healthfully. And no parent can direct his child to a kind of television that doesn't exist, or expect that his child will use a very large proportion of his television time for a kind of program that is scarce, underfinanced, and placed at inconvenient hours.

3. *Television has to offer these kinds of programs for children because advertising sponsors demand large audiences.*

We sympathize with television broadcasters for the competitive pressure of the sponsor system. More than one broadcaster has told us that the sponsors and their agencies are "buying audiences"; they are concerned with "cost per thousand," not with quality or effect on viewers' personalities; and if he doesn't give it to them, his competitors will. Because of this competition, the networks also are forced to be tough-minded about program ratings—for example, even to discard some lower-rating and higher-quality programs because they influence the rating of programs next to them. It is necessary to maximize the drawing power of the schedule at the cost of experimentation with "quality." This undoubtedly represents a severe problem to commercial broadcasters. We consider that it also represents a short-sighted attitude which may produce immediate profits, but will ultimately result in harm to both sponsor and broadcaster.

However, if it is indeed said to be the case that the commercial sponsorship and competitive bidding of television permit the industry to

*Are the parents who are dissatisfied with what television offers their children doing everything possible about it?*

Parents seem not to realize their power with respect to television. Elsewhere the senior author of this book has tried to demolish the myth of "big television and little me." The television industry is indeed a big one, but it has relatively little feedback from its audiences and depends chiefly on program ratings, which are simply measures of size of audience. Our experience has been that the top men in television do not believe in a program policy built completely on size of audience, but rather feel that they must serve special interests as well as common-denominator interest, and that they must as a public service give the public some programs it needs to view in order to be good citizens of a democracy. Furthermore, our experience has been that these top men are often quite sensitive to outpourings of intelligent opinion from their audiences. In particular, they have often waited and listened for support when they have ventured to put on a new kind of children's program or an experiment in reality programming. At times like these, a letter to a network or station might determine whether the experiment continues.

Parents also have it in their power to make their opinions of programs felt through the advertisers who support these programs. A letter to an advertiser telling him intelligently and vigorously why his children's program is or is not satisfactory is a good tactic. Sponsors don't very often hear from their viewers. Even a few letters, therefore, may have considerable impact. For example, we remember a vice-president of a network reporting wryly that the sponsor of a news program wanted to change the program because he was "inundated with three complaining letters" from viewers! Writing helps. And if a person supports his letter with his buying, he has a one-two punch.

Parents have quite another way of expressing their opinions of television. In about forty-five communities in the United States, now, there are noncommercial educational stations, which, as we have mentioned, are entirely dependent on gifts and subscriptions for their support. These stations are dedicated to reality programming and to providing stimulating television experiences for adults and children. But they have for support of this policy less than one fortieth of the budget of the commercial stations. It stimulates the imagination to think what doors we might open to our children—indeed, to ourselves—if we had such a group of stations as well financed as the commercial stations, as readily able to acquire talent and equipment as the commercial stations, but devoted to realizing television's full potential as a reality medium rather than as a fantasy medium. The commercial stations are under great competitive pressure, which strongly restricts the programs they can offer children. The community stations are under no such pressure; but they are underfinanced and too little supported. At present, this is a challenge to every community that has an educational station. Are parents willing enough to support this kind of television idea to enable it to realize its potential effectiveness?

And finally, how about a spokesman for parents in regard to television? The broadcasters have a skilled and vigorous spokesman in the National Association of Broadcasters, and in the large networks and some of the station organizations. It would be interesting to have a kind of National Association of Parents of Television Viewers, although this would be unwieldy and impracticable. But suppose that by the support of a foundation, or the gifts of individuals, or both, it would be possible to establish an organization to speak for the public with respect to television. This might be a board of distinguished citizens, with a research staff to collect and report the opinions of parents and children, to observe and report on the nature of children's programs and to keep parents informed of new ventures in this field, to carry out or contract for research which needs doing on television and children. Such an organization could recommend policy to the government, and suggest good practice to the broadcasters. Such a board of citizens does not seem infeasible or unduly expensive. It would add a respected and influential voice to the debate on policy and responsibility.

## Questions to Schools

*Are schools doing everything possible to connect television to the intellectual growth of children?*

Schools can be of enormous help, it seems to us, in two ways. In the first place, they can direct children to the reality experiences of television and can reinforce the children's selection of those programs by talking about them in school. In the second place, they can make active use of commercial television in school. We are assuming that they *will* make active use of *instructional* television; what we are now suggesting is that they should consider commercial television also as a proper topic and resource. Anything to which children devote one-sixth of their waking hours has obvious importance for schools. If children are helped to know good books from poor ones, good music from poor music, good art from bad art, there is no reason why they should not be helped to develop some standards for television. How to read the newspaper (borrowing Edgar Dale's title) is a subject treated increasingly in schools; "how to view television" is just as important. Furthermore, television is a real resource for examples, assignments, and what the teachers call "enrichment." It seems to us all to the good to bring television into the real-life process of learning, to break down the barrier between passive fantasy experience and active use.

This, schools are particularly able to do. But parents have some responsibility for cooperating. It will do no good if the child is assigned to see "Hamlet" at an hour when the parents insist on watching "Peter Gunn." The schools must take the parents into their confidence and their planning when they undertake this use of television.

## Questions to Government

*What is the responsibility of government with regard to proper programming for children?* It has been argued that in our political system government should keep its hands off programs. On the other hand, it is argued that no agency except government is big enough to deal with the great mass media.

Our position is closer to the first than to the second of these. We prefer that the mass communicators should keep their own house clean, as an alternative to alarmed parents calling in the government to clean house. And although this does not preclude the possibility of government taking a part, we should feel more comfortable if it were a facilitative part rather than a restrictive or a punitive part. The question we should like to pose, therefore, would be:

*Is government doing everything possible to facilitate and encourage good programming for children?*

This question does not apply merely to one agency of government, or merely to the national government. All too frequently, critics of television have concentrated on the Federal Communications Commission, which clearly has the authority to do more than it has done to require licensees to live up to their promises about programming. But the responsibility is much wider than this. It extends to the Department of Health, Education, and Welfare, with its national Office of Education and its Children's Bureau, and through them to the state offices of education and welfare. Responsibility extends also to the Congress, to the bodies dealing with interstate commerce, and in some degree to other commissions and sections of departments.

The F.C.C. has made and kept reservations for noncommercial educational television, despite opposing pressure, and is to be commended for so doing. Is the Secretary of Health, Education, and Welfare doing all within his power to encourage better television for children? Is the United States Commissioner of Education, or the head of the Children's Bureau? Since the helpful and thought-provoking Kefauver Committee hearings, what has the Congress done toward this end?

The least that government could do, it seems to us, is to ensure that finances are made available to study the problems of effect and taste, family solidarity and mental health, as they underlie programming policy and public actions affecting television. Government might do more to ease the financial burden of establishing educational television. It may have to do more. But things at this level it can do without taking any control over programs or interfering in any way with things that, according to our political philosophy, are better handled by the media and the public. If the media and the public cannot solve the problems, then government will probably have to take more direct action.

## Questions to Researchers

*Should we not be undertaking some intensive but long-term studies of television in the lives of children?*

There are three main types of study by which researchers have tried to find out something about the effects of television.

One of these is the large-scale gross study, of which this volume and the Himmelweit-Oppenheim-Vince book are examples. A study of this kind is generally built along the lines of a survey, or a group of surveys, or a field experiment. It concerns itself with the large considerations of television behavior and the large patterns of television use. It deals with large samples of children. Its purpose is to contribute to a general framework for understanding the relationship of children to television, a framework into which more detailed results will fit.

A second type is the precise laboratory experiment, of which Maccoby [21], Siegel [29], and Albert [5] are samples. These typically deal with a short segment of the experience of fairly small samples of children. These children are presented with a carefully controlled stimulus, and their responses are carefully measured. Other stimuli and responses are carefully controlled or excluded. The results have the advantage of precision and replicability. Studies of this type are not very useful in studying summations of effect, or interactions between experiences, but they are extremely useful for furnishing insights into the process by which television has its "effect."

The large-scale study has the disadvantage of not being able to concentrate on the details of process or dynamics. The small laboratory experiment has the disadvantage of dealing with an isolated moment in the life of a child; it is not usually able to study the child over time, or to understand long-term effects. To do this well, a third kind of study is required. This is a long-term intensive study of a comparatively few children, in which the researchers become deeply enough acquainted with the children to understand in depth the results of experiments, the summations of effects, the interactions, the patterns of the growth and development. The scholarly literature contains no such long-term study of television and children.

It has seemed to us, as we approached the end of our own study, that the research now most needed is of this third type: extensive in time rather than in numbers or geography, intensive in treatment. The most worrisome effects, if they exist, are long-term effects. The process of effect is extremely complex, and cannot be well understood one variable at a time. We feel, therefore, that the situation calls for the kind of understanding and insight that come from knowing a few children very well, over time, and in interaction, rather than knowing a great many children only slightly, or a few children well but briefly.

We know the objections to long-term research. It requires a large commitment of time which not all researchers are willing to make in advance. It requires an assurance of continuity in financing and, if at all possible, in personnel. It requires, in this case, some interdisciplinary cooperation. Therefore, it is not something that one undertakes casually.

But it is of first importance, if we are to push steadily ahead in understanding the uses children make of television. We should like to see a ten-year project started now, with the possibility of lengthening it still further. We should hope that a child psychologist, a psychiatrist, a sociologist specializing in the family, and a specialist in communication research could be involved in the project. School cooperation v. '¹ be necessary, as would family cooperation. At least some of the sub,  should be together in school or play groups so that their interpersona. relationships might be related to their television and other behavior. We should expect that a series of small experiments would be built into the project, and the longer it continued and the better the children came to be understood, the more valuable the experiments would be. In particular, we should like to see a continued and more thorough study of children's learning from television, especially the learning of abilities; of developing patterns of taste in relation to television use; and of personality and behavior effects as the child grows older.

We should not have to wait ten years for the fruits of such a project. Interim products of the research would appear throughout the time. Research in other places would be designed to intersect this long-term project, so that results could be replicated, and the insights of the intensive study would be spread over the research world.

In other words, we feel that a major project of this kind would now advance our knowledge of the important questions in this field probably more than any other research activity. It would be of the utmost use to broadcasters, parents, schools, and counselors, and would have extremely interesting information on which to base a wise national policy for broadcasting in so far as that applies to children's television. It would be good for programs. It would be good for children.

A final word in summary of these suggestions: We are faced by a problem in cooperation and conservation. We have a resource in children, and a resource in television. We are concerned that television should strengthen, not debilitate, the human resource. This end can be accomplished most easily, most effectively, not by unilateral activity on the part of the television industry, or by parents, or schools, or churches, but rather by mobilizing all the chief forces in society which bear on the television-child relationship. It must be a shared effort to meet a shared responsibility. We must mobilize the talent and sense of public responsibility of broadcasters, the love and guidance and companionship of parents, guidance from schools, and yes, even the skills and interest of researchers. To the carrying out of this last responsibility, we hope this book will make some slight contribution.

# DAYDREAM IN A VACUUM TUBE

A PSYCHIATRIST'S COMMENT ON THE
EFFECTS OF TELEVISION[*]

*A memorandum written for this volume by*
LAWRENCE ZELIC FREEDMAN, M.D.
*Center for Advanced Study in the Behavioral Sciences*
*Stanford, California*

The daydreams of most children would make the fiercest television show seem tame; its most erotic productions would appear vague by comparison; the cupidity of its give-aways would be dwarfed by their massive acquisitiveness. But television is public; it is a shared experience and impinges on the visual and auditory senses with which these children are learning to distinguish between reality and fantasy.

Television, like daydreams, has been thought by some to be the idle effluvia of the serious business of life. Each supplies effective but harmless imagined gratifications in the face of realities' frustrations. But indulged in too deeply, either might become a harmful alternative to life and taken literally might mislead into pathology. We have come to regard both as potent refractors of the emotional forces within us and a powerful microscope into our personalities and the state of our society. This brief psychiatric inquiry concerns its impact on the psychic life and social behavior of juvenile televiewers.

The brilliant and doomed Orwell fantasied that in less than a quarter of a century a society could be created in which, through a monster audiovisual mass communication system, man could be molded into a controlled monolithic corpus. Aldous Huxley anticipated a world in which mass-indoctrinated man would be robbed of the diversity of his personal experience, his private hope and suffering. Conformity to the standards of mediocrity and constriction of creative striving can, others warn, smother the turbulent maverick genius of man.

[*] The preparation of these observations was assisted by the Foundations Fund for Research in Psychiatry.

Psychiatrists have raised grave questions concerning the pathogenic implications of prolonged watching of television with its associated surrender of personal, physical, and intellectual activity. They see passivity merging into autism, and predisposing to dependent, schizoid, and withdrawn personalities. Parents (often more relieved than concerned over their children's immobilization) resent the intensity of the bombardment of brutality glowering from our television screens. They fear that repetitive drama portraying criminality will stimulate delinquency.

Is television fostering habits of passivity and dependence, of conformity and schizoid symptoms in our children, and does it inculcate habits of violence and delinquency? And if it is doing so, to what degree and to how large a proportion of viewing children? The answers to these questions do not yet exist. There is, so far, no competent psychiatric study which demonstrates that schizoid symptomatology in children has increased since television became widespread; nor has any careful investigation linked the rise in juvenile delinquency to the content of television programs or the act of watching them. However, we are not justified in denying the thrust of either question. They have not yet been answered, but we may not assume that we would be pleased with the answers.

A general hypothesis that television is conducive to mental ill health and social delinquency includes a wide array of heterogeneous factors and diversified subjects. The American child televiewers range in age from two years to the late teens; they and their families differ in ethnic background, socioeconomic position, intelligence quotient, educational level, and geographical area. Television in the United States is itself a diverse and fluctuating stimulus.

The child's task of developing into an adult human being is psychologically far too complex to make it likely that any single stimulus pattern will predictably produce a particular behavioral response. The intricate meshing of psychic impulses and evolving defenses which characterize him must be studied in connection with what he is seeing and hearing. We must know the physiological predisposition of the developing child to activity or passivity; and how, within his intellectual limits, he imitates the language, behavior, and attitudes of his parents, teachers, siblings, and playmates, and incorporates elements of them into his own evolving personality; how an identity for himself emerges from the superimposed identifications of these significant persons, until finally he becomes a self-propelling personality—not an automaton. We must include in these observations the system of rewards and punishments which has characterized his environment, and the balance of self-approval and emotional freedom from self-denigration, guilt, and

shame. We need to learn whether the child has been reared in a relatively harmonious and loving atmosphere so that his own capacity to
emphasize—to feel with other human beings—has flourished. We must
investigate his capacity to repress, to put into unconsciousness, to deny
recognition, and to displace emotions, perceptions, and ideas which are
unacceptable to his total personality, so that he may integrate within
himself disparate and conflicting influences.

Upon the vitality and balance of these and similar psychic mechanisms—and not merely upon a content analysis of television productions
—will depend the influence of television upon him.

Stated briefly, we cannot evaluate the effect of television on a child
unless we know something of his personality and environment. Before
we can predict which responses any child will make, we must learn who
and what he is responding to. Does he identify with the hero or the
villain? Does he vicariously experience the violence of the gangster or
the virtue of the policeman? Is he reacting affectively and appercep-
tively to the feeling tone or cognitively to the story with its inevitable
triumph of good? Which is more important to him, the total drama or
the action which precedes the end? What is the significance to him of
the act of watching?

With these considerations in mind we might construct a hypotheti-
cal continuum of psychological factors to help us predict the probable
role of television in causing psychic pathology and precipitating delinquent behavior. Let us first isolate two factors which are generally con-
ceded to be true: first, that the average American child spends from
two to three hours a day watching television, and second, that he sees
much brutality and killing during those hours.

Clinical judgments concerning the psychiatric significance of the
*duration* of televiewing is meaningful only when we know how characteristic these viewing habits are when compared to others of his age,
social class, and community. However much we may deplore it as a
social value, individual psychopathology always involves significant deviation of overt behavior or subjective feeling and ideation. Only when
a child differs significantly from his peers, therefore, may we reasonably
suspect excessive viewing as being symptomatic of psychopathology.
When televiewing is, in fact, excessive by these criteria, it is reasonable
to assume that the behavior is symptomatic of intolerable stress in his
environment—whether conflicts in the home, frustrations at school, or
among his peers—or of brewing anxiety or emotional instability within
him.

More important than the duration of his televiewing, however, is its
emotional impact upon him. In general, we may hypothesize that the

average child in a reasonably stable environment does not confuse the "as if" of this pretend world with the real experiences of his personal and family relationships. Most youngsters find the immediate personal relationships more compelling and rewarding than the animated, pictorial substitutes. The defensive mechanisms of the child which we have listed serve as refractors and buffers, enabling him to be differentially responsive and to absorb with least effect brutal stimuli.

Allowing for differences in age and background, we might predict where the child will fall in this continuum on the basis of his mental health. The intensity and psychic significance of the child's response to television is the reciprocal of the satisfaction he gains in the milieu of his family, school, and friends. One would predict that the less intelligent, the most disturbed youngsters, and those having the poorest relationship with their family and peers would be most likely to immerse themselves in televiewing as escape and stimulus. Intelligent, relatively stable youngsters in reasonably harmonious homes would be comparatively unaffected by it. For children whose empathic capacities are unmarred, depersonalized substitute relationships are least rewarding and least likely to be imitated.

However, youngsters with schizoid personalities have persistent tendencies to avoid intimate relationships with other persons, to live deeply within themselves, and to lean heavily on daydreams and fantasies. Hostility, and often affection too, is hard for them to tolerate or to express. They therefore shut themselves away and are considered odd and unfriendly. If life deals too severely with them, they may deteriorate into schizophrenia. For such children, television provides a retreat from the unbearable stresses of relationships with friends and family and a vehicle for their fantasies. It is unlikely, however, that they are produced by television—even though its existence complements their psychic mosaic.

There are, also, younger viewers with hysterical and dissociative tendencies whose proclivity is for easy, and usually transitory, identification with their dramatic idols and a histrionic assumption of their habits and fantasied adventures. We may look to television for their models, but for the psychoneurotic predisposition we probably ought to look to their families.

Psychopathic youngsters, whose identifications with meaningful adult figures have been seriously impaired, whose self-censoring and self-governing mechanisms are defective, are likely to be shallow and transitory in their relations with others. Poised to rebel, unsure of their own image, distant in their relationships, they may use the television criminal as their model of rebellion and be precipitated and guided by him.

Psychotically disturbed children are confused in their identifications, and distressed by the violence of their impulses. For such youngsters, with aggressive impulses ready to erupt, the violence of television productions may provide the final stimulus. More frequently, they may be passively and completely absorbed, reacting inwardly, but physically quiescent.

An extreme of television suggestibility may, in rare instances, be found in certain forms of psychosis. For example, a schizophrenic patient followed immediately, exactly, and literally the recommendations of the characters in the play and of the advertisers. This extreme echolalia and echopraxia (repeating words and imitating movements) stands at the opposite end of the continuum from the mentally healthy child—even when that child consciously acts out the drama he views.

Even more difficult to evaluate than its impact on mental health and delinquency is the perhaps more important problem of its relation to our national values and national character. Television in the United States during this mid-twentieth century is inescapable; it is ubiquitous and it is democratic. An almost continual stream of identical audiovisual communications pours from a relatively few centers into all parts of the country, into all strata of society, and to virtually every age group over two. This social role of television transcends the psychiatric questions which I have discussed. But clarification of the more limited, clinical problems may sharpen the debate concerning its broad social implications. Conversely, a clearer articulation of our social values may give us the insights to distinguish between them and its allegedly individually deleterious effects. For example, most serious discussions concerning television today reflect the intellectual and aesthetic values of an educated and articulate minority who deplore its commercially motivated emphasis on entertainment aimed at the mass of marginally literate viewers. With this viewpoint I happen to agree, but the issues are confused unless a clear distinction is made between such ethical and cultural desiderata and the clear evidence that their absence causes mental and behavioral pathology. Major technological advances have always significantly altered the manner of living, certain values of life, and even the characters of the children and their descendants who grow up in its aegis.*

The challenge to us is threefold: (a) To sharpen the focus of our research, to study in depth and over time the effect of televiewing on the personalities of representative children as they develop in their en-

---

* So, when the automobile removed youngsters from the surveillance of their homes, we were concerned for their morals. Now television immobilizes them in the living room and we deplore their passivity.

vironment. This requires the collaboration of clinicians and behavioral scientists. (*b*) To evaluate whether television degrades the American ethos, or reflects it. Is television an amusement park distortion mirror reflecting a crazy caricature of ourselves—or is it a clear and accurate reflection of what we as a nation are and want to be? Finally, (*c*) we must respond pragmatically and effectively to the implications of the results of these studies and evaluations.

# APPENDIXES

# NOTES ON METHOD AND SAMPLE

We made eleven studies, beginning in early 1958.

## The San Francisco Study

This was the first of our studies, and it served to test many of the methods and instruments.

The idea of the study was approved by the city Superintendent of Schools, and the general plans of procedure were discussed and cleared by the assistant superintendents and supervisors concerned. The senior author met with a group of principals and teachers and explained the purpose and nature of the study. Cooperating supervisors were appointed from the staff of the school system— Mrs. Alice MacIntyre for the elementary schools, Mr. Lane deLara for the junior and senior high schools. Their help was invaluable. Finally, meetings of the cooperating teachers were convened, and detailed mimeographed instructions were distributed and discussed. This pattern of cooperation with and informing of the school system we found to be of immense help in speeding and smoothing the gathering of data, and in greater or less degree we used the same tactics in all the school systems where we worked.

Chief information from the first four grades in San Francisco was derived from a questionnaire which teachers gave pupils to take home to their parents. We headed this questionnaire:

To the parents of..............................:
We are trying to find out something about what our students read at home, what programs they hear and see, and what movies they go to. Won't you please answer these few questions, and send the pages back to school with your child, in the next day or two? What you tell us won't have any effect on your child's grades, but may help us to teach better.

YOUR CHILD'S TEACHER

Then followed a series of questions about the child's use of all the mass media, both amount of use and content selected. The parents were encouraged to observe their children, and to base their answers on averaged observations. There was an opportunity to say whether any of the child's media input especially worried or pleased the parents, and there was a question about playtime. Of these questionnaires 89.2 per cent were returned.

To check up on questionnaire answers, to find out something about the non-returns, and to provide information in greater detail on television and newspaper use, 50 children per grade were interviewed personally after school or at noon.

This was for the first four grades. Children in the fifth and sixth grades were given a diary to keep, and asked to fill in their leisure-time activities for the previous day, every morning at school, for one week. We were not well satisfied with these diaries, which seemed to be kept in greatly unequal quality. We decided that if we used diaries again we should have their filling out very carefully supervised and should make greater efforts to motivate the students to fill them out carefully.

In addition to the diary, the children in the fifth and sixth grades were given a set of questions intended to determine their "favorite" television programs, books, magazines, and so forth, and an opportunity to say as fully as possible what they thought of television, and what changes, if any, they would like to see made. These questions, and a few others, were printed on the diary form.

Teachers also devoted a period to administering certain additional questionnaires and tests which we supplied. Among these was a test of science knowledge (example: "A light year is a measure of which of these? Time? Speed? Distance? Power?"), a test of items about government in the news, a test of recognizing pictures of newsworthy persons from the worlds of public affairs and entertainment, and an opportunity to name as many as possible of comic strips or books, band leaders, singers, writers, composers, painters, and sculptors. There were also questions about what the child typically read in a newspaper, questions that required the placing of a prestige rating on the various media, and some value and aspiration questions. The usual demographic items were also asked.

The eighth-, tenth-, and twelfth-grade studies were made the following year. By this time we had given up the diary and depended entirely on a set of instruments administered by the teacher in approximately two periods. In these grades, our form was headed "A Confidential Report on Television, Radio, and the Other Mass Media, from (student's name)." After collecting the usual demography, we asked the children to remember back over the last few weeks and give us a good deal of information about their use of each of the media—time, content, and so forth. Then we led them through some general questions on their attitudes toward the media—the prestige they ascribed to the various media, the ones they would miss most, their favorite content on each of the media, and so forth. Then we asked them about how much they viewed educational television and what they thought of it. We gave them a set of questions to try to find out how much they used the media alone and how much with other persons, how much they talked about such media content as the news, and how often they did other things while using radio or television. We gave them a list of television programs and asked them to check the ones they had seen, and check *twice* the ones they especially liked. They were given the Guilford scale of introversion, and some questions about their experience with classroom television. Then we gave them the quiz on faces in the news, a set of questions intended to find how closely their aspirations corresponded to those of their peer group and their parents' aspirations for them, opportunities to name the singers, band leaders, rulers or prime ministers, writers, and so forth. We asked them whether what they saw on television helped them in school, whether after watching television they ever found school dull.

For a group of exceptional students, intelligence scores were supplied directly, and for the first six grades the school marks in all subjects were copied. These were handled so that the marks and IQ's were punched on IBM cards and destroyed, so that there would be no further opportunity to connect actual names with the records of intelligence and school performance. In all cases, teachers were asked to mark their students' questionnaires 1, 2, or 3, signifying respectively (on the basis of the teacher's knowledge of both IQ and class performance) whether a given student belonged in the top IQ group who could confidently be expected to do well in college, the great average IQ group, or the low IQ group whose mental ability was something of a handicap to him. Although there were exceptions, the low group usually included intelligence scores up to about 100, and the high group usually included IQ's over 115.

### The San Francisco "Whole Family" Study

These interviews, although at times hard to arrange, proved highly enjoyable both for interviewer and interviewees. The families seemed to enjoy talking over the mass media questions among themselves.

With all the family assembled, the interviewer began by recording names and ages, and then for each member of the family he recorded average television times for the last few weekdays and the last few Sundays. In each case, members of the family "checked up" on each other, and did not hesitate to challenge or correct such estimates. Thus what came out was the joint best estimate by the family for each member. Then the interviewer recorded programs that each member tried to hear regularly, and the frequency with which each member watched educational television. Here also there was checking and challenging back and forth. Then the interviewer took up a copy of the daily paper received in the home and marked with a special code the items that had been read by each member of the family. Rather than boring the interviewees, this proved interesting to them; they were apparently seeing for the first time how different their reading patterns were. The interviewer asked each member what part of the paper he would most miss. Then he asked from each member of the family the magazines he read regularly, the number of movies he had seen in the last month, the number of comic books the children read each month, the amount of radio listening, and then some questions about how much the person would trust newspaper news as compared to radio or TV news, and how much the news and other mass media materials were talked over in the family. He asked then which member of the family would miss each of the media most if he had to do without them for a long time.

After that, the children were excused, and the interviewer talked with the parents alone. He tried to find out how much and what kind of interaction relating to the media went on in the home, how the children's leisure time was usually divided, the ages at which the children had started using the various media, and a number of questions about the parents' attitudes toward the media, and the respects in which they considered the media helpful or unhelpful to their children. Finally, the necessary demographic facts were recorded. These interviews typically took from two to three hours.

## The Rocky Mountain Studies

Arrangements were initiated through the office of the local school district superintendent in each town. The superintendent arranged for a local person, usually a member of his staff, as liaison.

Explanations of the purpose and instruments of the study were mimeographed and distributed to all persons participating. In two of the towns, a field supervisor from Stanford University was present during the testing. An explanation session was held for those participating, with either the Stanford representative or the local person taking charge.

In three of the five towns, questionnaires were sent home to parents of first-grade children with a cover letter of explanation from the classroom teacher. In all cases, the teachers were able to obtain a high proportion of returns; for the three towns the returns were 83.5, 87.5, and 88.8 per cent.

This questionnaire asked the parent to estimate amount of exposure to the major mass media and also to tell at what approximate age the child first began to use each medium. Questions were also asked concerning whether the child imitated what he had seen on the screen, talked about news broadcasts, sang commercials, and so forth. Parents were asked if they thought the child was learning anything objectionable from the mass media, and if so, what. There were also questions about sleep and playtime, whether or not the child seemed bored with school, whether the child daydreamed a lot at home, and the child's job ambition. The occupation of the head of the household was also asked.

Most parents returning the questionnaire supplied all the requested information, although some failed to answer opinion questions.

First-grade children were given three knowledge tests. One was the Stanford-Binet oral vocabulary test. A second was a special five-word test prepared for this study for the purpose of gauging possible knowledge of words related to science, politics, and violence. These five words were: president, pistol, cancer, satellite, war. The third knowledge test was the Stanford-Binet picture identification card test, which was supplemented with two current drawings: an atom bomb explosion and a rocket. These two knowledge tests were administered individually to children either by their own classroom teacher or by a substitute teacher.

The picture identification test, which normally is not used beyond the kindergarten level, proved worthless for our purposes, as there was little spread in the distribution of scores: practically all the children made perfect scores—except for the atom bomb explosions. This was more often identified as "a tree with bird nests" than as an atom bomb, a fault more attributable to the artist than to the children.

In the sixth and tenth grades, the children were given self-administered questionnaires under the supervision of their regular classroom teacher. For the sixth-graders, two periods were reserved for this purpose; in the tenth grade, students were able to finish within one class period.

The questionnaire was in three parts.

Part 1 incorporated the media use question used in San Francisco. For two towns, which were expected to have low television penetration, television was omitted from the prestige and "medium missed most" question; also the television program check list was omitted.

Part 2 was a knowledge test, which was a somewhat modified version of that used in San Francisco. A seven-item science quiz was added, with more difficult questions (example: "How does a jet engine move an airplane?") and the question about naming rulers or prime ministers was changed to United States senators now in the Senate.

Part 3 was almost totally new. Questions were asked concerning hopes for the future, people and places the student desired to know, favorite singers and actresses, and a famous-places identification quiz. A series of questions were included which it was hoped might tap feelings of insecurity about the world in which the student lives: questions about possibility of war, estimate of the number of murders committed weekly in the United States, etc. There was a question on relative preference of popular vs. serious music, and whether or not school seems dull.

A series of questions were included to tap disagreement between child and his parents and peers concerning future aspirations. These dealt with job and educational aspirations, homework time, and person-to-be-like. The student was asked to give his own hope, what he thought was his parents' hope for him, and what he thought his close friends' hopes were. The question concerning personal example was dropped.

The indices used in San Francisco on conformity to peer group examples and appeal to peer group examples for personal support were included along with the questions concerning media selectivity and congruence of own and parents' media tastes.

Another addition, not used in San Francisco, were six four-item indices on aggression, selected from the Sears aggression indices.

After the questionnaires of each grade were gathered, the teacher was asked to mark the cover sheet with a 1, 2, or 3 as a rating of the child's mental ability as the teacher perceived it, the three divisions corresponding to those used in San Francisco.

Teachers were urged to contact the field supervisor or local liaison person in any case of unforeseen circumstances or problems.

In those towns where there was a field supervisor, he talked informally with teachers, sometimes individually, sometimes in groups, to ask the teachers' impressions as to the impact of television on the children, on the classroom, and on the community. Also, teachers were asked if they ever made use of television presentations for lesson preparation or as a part of lesson assignments.

## The Radiotown and Teletown Studies

The research design required two communities comparable in as many respects as possible, except that one had television reception and the other did not. In the spring of 1959, when the data were collected, there were very few pairs of communities of any reasonable size (say, over 2,000 population) in North

America which were not extremely atypical communities in other respects (e.g., isolated resort communities or company towns).

Radiotown is a not atypical Canadian community of some 5,000 population, different from many other Canadian communities mainly in the fact of its relative isolation (some 400 miles from a major metropolitan area) and in its lack of television. Its isolation is one of distance rather than terrain or transportation. It has excellent regular transportation connections with other Canadian cities by road, rail, and scheduled airline service. The nearest television to Radiotown was a small closed-circuit operation in a town about 100 miles away. The nearest broadcast television was a small station some 200 miles away—well beyond reception range.

Teletown is also a Canadian community of some 5,000 people. It is in the same Canadian province and hence has the same kind of school system and school curriculum. The industries in Teletown are comparable to the industries in Radiotown. Being within television reception distance of both a major Canadian city and the United States border, Teletown has television reception on several channels, including both the Canadian Broadcasting Corporation (CBC) and stations affiliated with United States networks.

Two years before the time of the study Teletown had one regular motion picture theater and one drive-in theater, the same as Radiotown. At the time of the study, both theaters were closed down. Townspeople attributed these closures to television. They still have access to movies shown in neighboring communities.

During the daytime hours Radiotown residents have clear reception on two radio stations—the local privately owned station and a CBC station. During the nighttime hours they have good radio reception from many radio stations all over North America. Teletown has clear radio reception from many radio stations, both Canadian and American, government-owned (CBC) and privately owned. Both communities have a local weekly newspaper and both have regular access to metropolitan daily newspapers, although the big-city papers arrive in Radiotown a day after the publication date.

All first-, sixth-, and tenth-grade students in schools within the town limits of Radiotown who were in attendance at school on the day the study was conducted were included in the Radiotown sample. In Teletown, all tenth-grade children and all the first- and sixth-grade children in about half of the elementary schools—all the urban and some of the rural schools—in the district were included. It was expected that by including some of the rural schools in the school district near a metropolitan area the sample of children would be more like the Radiotown sample, where the children are relatively isolated from large communities. School officials reported that there was not an unusual number of absentees at the time of the study. The study was conducted in both communities in the same week, at a time when both communities were having warm, dry spring weather.

All first-grade children in both communities were tested individually by their regular teachers on the oral vocabulary section of the 1933 standardization of the Stanford-Binet intelligence test, as in San Francisco and the Rocky Mountain towns. The teachers also tested the children on a special five-word vocabulary test of words likely to be heard on television, the same that had been used in the

Rocky Mountain towns. All first-grade teachers conducting this testing were met by a field supervisor from Stanford and given detailed instructions. Visits to the schools while the tests were being conducted indicated that instructions were being carried out correctly.

The first-grade teachers in both communities also gave two-page questionnaires to the first-grade children to take home to their parents, similar to the questionnaire used in the Rocky Mountain communities. Questionnaires were returned by 88.9 per cent of parents in Radiotown and by 85.5 per cent of parents in Teletown.

Sixth- and tenth-grade children in Teletown and Radiotown were given a questionnaire similar to the Rocky Mountain questionnaire. The questionnaire forms were filled in by the students in their regular classrooms during school time, under the supervision of their regular teachers. They gave assistance to students who had trouble understanding any of the questions, but emphasized that there were no right or wrong answers and that the information would not in any way influence their school grades. The field supervisor was available on the day the questionnaires were administered to answer any questions and to observe the data collection. The questionnaire forms took about an hour and a half for the sixth-grade children to complete and about an hour for the tenth-grade children to complete.

The school principals in each of the schools provided sufficient information to classify each student into one of three intelligence categories: high (Intelligence Quotient above 115), average (IQ 100–115), or low (IQ below 100).

*The Clifton Study*

This study was conducted with the cooperation of the school's parents club (which included the teaching staff). The general purpose and procedures were outlined at a meeting of this organization.

Check lists for five days, Sunday through Thursday, were prepared for all programs televised on the six channels in the primary reception zone of the community. For grades three to six, these were filled out by all children in each section under teachers' supervision. The children were instructed to check all programs which they had watched the preceding day and to indicate whether they had seen the entire program or only part of it. These check lists were given to the students early in the morning session.

In the kindergarten and grades one and two, volunteers from the parents club interviewed the children individually, reading the check list to the children and asking which programs they had watched and whether they saw all or only part of each program. Interviewers were cautioned in their training session to avoid overprompting of the children and thereby inflating viewing time. The children were also asked what time they had gone to bed the preceding evening. Interviewers remarked that children were better able to remember their television viewing than their bedtime, and that in many cases where bedtime was remembered, it was by association with their television viewing. Because of the additional time and labor required for the lower grades, only one section per grade was interviewed each day, except that on the first day of the study, when Sunday viewing was being recorded, two sections per grade were interviewed.

Preliminary tabulation of program selection and total viewing time was made by a committee of volunteer parents club members. The data and check sheets were then shipped to Stanford for further processing.

A Stanford staff member obtained additional information on each child from the school files. Included were: scores on the California Mental Maturity test (an intelligence measure), father's occupation, number of siblings, and the child's place in the birth order.

Shortly after the test week, children in grades three to six were given their annual sociometric questionnaire. Children in each section were asked to list their first, second, and third playmate choices, and were also asked if there was anyone with whom they would not play. The play choices were handled in a standard way: choices were given inverse values, and a score was computed for each child on the basis of the number of choices he received within the section. The rejections were ignored in this analysis, as few children filled in the blank.

### The Denver Study

The Denver study of 198 tenth-graders was conducted through the cooperation of the superintendent's staff, who selected the sample classes and acted as liaison officials.

A detailed cover letter with purpose and explanation was sent by Stanford for distribution to all participating teachers, along with copies of the questionnaire, which was disguised as one number of a continuing opinion study.

Included in the questionnaire was one question which it was hoped would directly measure the student's immediate or deferred gratification preference; this was the question concerning preference for obtaining a plain phonograph now or waiting six months and having a chance to get stereo.

A three-item index was used as an indirect gauge of immediate or deferred gratification patterns. The items did not meet Guttman scale criteria, but were highly correlated and so a total score was used as an index measure. There was a separate item concerned with perceived peer group agreement on index answers.

The questionnaire also asked the same media exposure questions used in the other cities, plus questions as to father's occupation and education.

The questionnaires were filled in by students during the class period and under supervision of their teacher. Afterwards, Stanford-Binet scores and sex designations were added to each child's questionnaire by the school staff.

### Data processing

During the three years of field work and analysis, a great many people worked on the various phases of this study. Without the diligent efforts of these people, the work could not have been accomplished.

Editors and coders were carefully trained within the Institute for Communication Research. Upon beginning each coding job, an effort was made to establish teams of coders for stages of the project. Members of the teams double-coded in the early phases until problems of agreement in interpretation and problems of unexpected codes were worked out.

In editing, one person with constant access to the study director handled each job. In this way ambiguous or doubtful answers were set into established patterns, and any idiosyncratic interpretation was held constant for each item.

All questionnaires and other source data from all of the studies were processed at the Stanford Institute for Communication Research. After editing and coding, the data were punched into IBM cards which were then machine-verified. Frequency distribution tables were produced on the IBM 101 electronic statistical machine.

The preliminary analysis was done by calculating percentages on each of the variables, within each town by grade and sex grouping. In further tables percentages were calculated by intelligence grouping. When a descriptive statistic of the frequency of occurrence or amount of time spent on any given behavior was appropriate, medians were calculated. When tests of differences between groups were appropriate, as in comparing Teletown with Radiotown, means were calculated, since means are a more stable measure of central tendency and permit more powerful tests of the statistical significance of obtained differences. Differences were tested by a critical ratio test of differences between means [83, p. 87], by $t$ test [83, p. 109], or by a critical ratio test of differences between proportions [83, p. 60], whichever was statistically appropriate. When testing differences in first-grade vocabulary scores between Teletown and Radiotown, with intelligence level controlled and with an interaction between intelligence and television predicted, an analysis of variance test was required. A two-way analysis of variance test correcting for disproportionate numbers of cases per cell was calculated, following the procedure outlined by Snedecor [89, pp. 289 ff.]. When tests of the significance of relationship between variables were appropriate, a chi-square test of significance was used. Any $p$ values reported in appendix tables where the nature of the test is not specified and not obvious from the context were obtained by chi-square test.

## San Francisco sample

School officials were asked to select a sample of elementary, junior high, and senior high schools which would supply a good cross section of the city's varied ethnic and social strata. Within this purposefully selected list of schools, classes were randomly selected for each grade studied, and the entire attendance of each class was included in the study.

For the family interviews, 350 residential addresses were selected at random from the San Francisco telephone directory. The requirement was that a family have one or more children under thirteen years of age and over one year old. A number of families did not meet this requirement; a few could not be reached; a few were uncooperative; and in a few cases a time could not be found, after a number of trials, when the whole family could be gotten together for an interview. The remaining 188 families were interviewed, each family as a group. The children were dismissed one by one as the interview moved out of the areas which concerned them.

## Rocky Mountain sample

The five towns were selected to give a wide range of media availability, both in terms of amount and length of availability. The towns were selected to be as similar as possible in terms of economic and demographic variables. Table I-1 in Appendix I summarizes the population and media characteristics of the towns.

On the basis of age trends found in San Francisco, it was decided to work with the first, sixth, and tenth grades. The first grade is the youngest group of children easily available. The sixth grade is at the high point of the media use curve. The tenth-grade members are well into adolescence, and are beginning to establish adult patterns of media use. The entire attendance of all classes within each grade in each town was included in the sample.

## Canadian sample

Radiotown was selected first, on the basis of having a population of at least 5,000 and no television reception available. Teletown was then selected on the basis of having matching economic and demographic structure with Radiotown, but having several television channels available.

Within towns, the same grades were used as in the Rocky Mountain towns, and again the entire attendance of all classes within the grades was included in the sample.

## Clifton sample

Another project was being done within a school in this suburban town, and it was possible to combine the work reported here with that project. The tested school is only one of several elementary schools in the community, which is approximately the same distance from San Francisco as Rocky 1 is from Denver. The school is in a strongly middle-class area, and the enrollment does not reflect a wide range of socioeconomic backgrounds.

For grades three through six, the entire attendance of each class within each grade was tested on all five days of the test week. Attendance varied somewhat from day to day. In the kindergarten and grades one and two, the children were individually interviewed, and only one class from each grade was used each day, except for the first day (Monday) when Sunday viewing was being measured. Scheduling of test classes for these grades from day to day was on a rotated basis.

## Denver sample

School officials were asked to supply a sample of 200 grade-ten students selected from the various city high schools so as to give a good representation of the city's entire tenth-grade population. A breakdown of the socioeconomic and intelligence measures suggests that the sample is biased in the direction of higher socioeconomic status and higher intelligence than average.

TABLE I-1. AVAILABILITY OF CERTAIN MEDIA IN
FIVE ROCKY MOUNTAIN TOWNS

| Town | Approximate Population | Television Saturation* | Television Availability | Radio Availability | Newspaper |
|------|------------------------|------------------------|-------------------------|--------------------|-----------|
| Rocky 1...... | 10,000 | 93% | Good reception of 5 Denver stations | 1 local station, plus Denver stations | Local daily |
| Rocky 2...... | 15,000 | 72% | 1 local station for 5 years | 3 local stations | 2 local dailies |
| Rocky 3...... | 10,000 | 51% | Cable service | 2 local stations | Local daily |
| Rocky 4...... | 2,000 | 44% | Fringe reception for several years | No local station | Local weekly |
| Rocky 5...... | 4,000 | 51% | Fringe reception for 1–2 years | 1 local station | Local daily |

* Television saturation means per cent of homes in area having television.

TABLE I-2. GRAND TOTALS FOR SAMPLES

| | San Francisco | Five Rocky Mt. Towns | Two Canadian Towns | Suburban Clifton | Denver | Total |
|------|------|------|------|------|------|------|
| Boys ............ | 1,353 | 849 | 458 | 185* | 118 | 2,963 |
| Girls ............ | 1,345 | 850 | 455 | 156* | 80 | 2,805 |
| Total: | | | | | | |
| Children ........ | 2,698 | 1,708 | 913 | 474* | 198 | 5,991 |
| Parents ......... | 1,405 | 284 | 269 | | | 1,958 |

* In the Clifton study, 133 very young children were not differentiated according to sex. They appear, therefore, in the over-all totals, but not in the totals of boys and of girls.

TABLE I-3. SAN FRANCISCO BASIC SAMPLE*
By Grade and Sex

| | 1st | 2d | 3d | 4th | 5th | 6th | 8th | 10th | 12th | Total |
|------|-----|-----|-----|-----|-----|-----|-----|------|------|-------|
| Boys ........... | 103 | 159 | 126 | 137 | 121 | 142 | 114 | 85 | 123 | 1,110 |
| Girls ........... | 107 | 158 | 114 | 126 | 131 | 120 | 105 | 116 | 109 | 1,086 |
| Total ......... | 210 | 317 | 240 | 263 | 252 | 262 | 219 | 201 | 232 | 2,196 |

* A total of 1,030 families filled out the parent questionnaire.

## TABLE I-4. SAN FRANCISCO FAMILY INTERVIEWS*

|  | K | 1st | 2d | 3d | 4th | 5th | 6th | Total |
|---|---|---|---|---|---|---|---|---|
| Boys .................... | 26 | 34 | 34 | 35 | 40 | 36 | 38 | 243 |
| Girls ................... | 27 | 39 | 31 | 36 | 47 | 38 | 41 | 259 |
| Total ................ | 53 | 73 | 65 | 71 | 87 | 74 | 79 | 502 |

* Parents: 187 fathers; 188 mothers; total: 375.

## TABLE I-5. ROCKY MOUNTAIN SAMPLE
### By Town, Grade, and Sex

|  |  | 1st | 6th | 10th | Total | Parents |
|---|---|---|---|---|---|---|
| Rocky 1 | Boys ............ | 53 | 80 | 105 | 238 |  |
|  | Girls ............ | 46 | 107 | 103 | 256 |  |
|  | Totals ........ | 99 | 187 | 208 | 494 | 99 |
| Rocky 2 | Boys ............ |  | 151 | 116 | 267 |  |
|  | Girls ............ |  | 131 | 132 | 263 |  |
|  | Total ......... |  | 282 | 248 | 530 |  |
| Rocky 3 | Boys ............ | 52 | 64 | 56 | 172 |  |
|  | Girls ............ | 58 | 58 | 74 | 190 |  |
|  | Total ......... | 110 | 122 | 130 | 362 | 110 |
| Rocky 4 | Boys ............ |  | 35 | 27 | 62 |  |
|  | Girls ............ |  | 28 | 23 | 51 |  |
|  | Total ......... |  | 63 | 50 | 113 |  |
| Rocky 5 | Boys ............ | 35 | 47 | 28 | 110 |  |
|  | Girls ............ | 40 | 27 | 32 | 99 |  |
|  | Total ......... | 75 | 74 | 60 | 209 | 75 |
| Total | Boys ............ | 140 | 377 | 332 | 849 |  |
|  | Girls ............ | 144 | 351 | 364 | 859 |  |
|  | Total ......... | 284 | 728 | 696 | 1,708 | 284 |

## TABLE I-6. CANADIAN SAMPLE
### By Town, Grade, and Sex

|  |  | 1st | 6th | 10th | Total | Parents |
|---|---|---|---|---|---|---|
| Teletown | Boys ........... | 91 | 91 | 86 | 268 |  |
|  | Girls ........... | 81 | 103 | 99 | 283 |  |
|  | Total ........ | 172 | 194 | 185 | 551 | 147 |
| Radiotown | Boys ........... | 71 | 49 | 70 | 190 |  |
|  | Girls ........... | 66 | 61 | 45 | 172 |  |
|  | Total ........ | 137 | 110 | 115 | 362 | 122 |
| Total | Boys ........... | 162 | 140 | 156 | 458 |  |
|  | Girls ........... | 147 | 164 | 144 | 455 |  |
|  | Total ........ | 309 | 304 | 300 | 913 | 269 |

TABLE I-7. CLIFTON SUBURBAN SAMPLE
By Grade and Sex

|  | K | 1st | 2d | 3d | 4th | 5th | 6th | Total |
|---|---|---|---|---|---|---|---|---|
| Boys ................... | * | * | * | 36 | 50 | 50 | 49 | |
| Girls .................... | | | | 44 | 34 | 39 | 39 | |
| Total ................ | 42 | 48 | 43 | 80 | 84 | 89 | 88 | 474 |

* Sex was not recorded for lower-grade children.

TABLE I-8. SAN FRANCISCO SAMPLE
By Grade, Sex, and Mental Ability

|  |  | Boys | Girls | Total |
|---|---|---|---|---|
| Eighth grade | High ................... | 17 | 26 | 43 |
| | Middle ................. | 64 | 59 | 123 |
| | Low ................... | 33 | 20 | 53 |
| Tenth grade | High ................... | 10 | 22 | 32 |
| | Middle ................ | 41 | 79 | 120 |
| | Low ................... | 34 | 15 | 49 |
| Twelfth grade | High ................... | 24 | 22 | 46 |
| | Middle ................. | 67 | 70 | 137 |
| | Low ................... | 32 | 17 | 49 |
| Total | .............................. | 322 | 330 | 652 |

TABLE I-9. ROCKY MOUNTAIN SAMPLE
By Town, Sex, Grade, and Mental Ability

| Mental Ability | Rocky 1 | Rocky 2 | Rocky 3 | Rocky 4 | Rocky 5 | Total |
|---|---|---|---|---|---|---|
| Sixth grade—boys: | | | | | | |
| High ............. | 22 | 45 | 16 | 8 | 12 | 103 |
| Middle ............. | 30 | 65 | 35 | 17 | 11 | 158 |
| Low ............... | 28 | 29 | 13 | 10 | 24 | 104 |
| Sixth grade—girls: | | | | | | |
| High ............. | 29 | 39 | 24 | 13 | 8 | 113 |
| Middle ............. | 50 | 64 | 27 | 8 | 13 | 162 |
| Low ............... | 28 | 17 | 7 | 7 | 6 | 65 |
| Tenth grade—boys: | | | | | | |
| High ............. | 16 | 29 | 12 | 6 | 6 | 69 |
| Middle ............. | 48 | 45 | 24 | 12 | 6 | 135 |
| Low ............... | 41 | 42 | 20 | 9 | 16 | 128 |
| Tenth grade—girls: | | | | | | |
| High ............. | 28 | 28 | 15 | 14 | 9 | 94 |
| Middle ............. | 56 | 79 | 33 | 7 | 16 | 191 |
| Low ............... | 19 | 22 | 26 | 2 | 7 | 76 |
| Total ............... | 395 | 504 | 252 | 113 | 134 | 1,398 |

TABLE I-10. CANADIAN SAMPLE
By Town, Sex, Grade, and Mental Ability

| Mental Ability | Teletown | | Radiotown | | Total | |
|---|---|---|---|---|---|---|
| | Boys | Girls | Boys | Girls | Boys | Girls |
| First grade: | | | | | | |
| High ............... | 11 | 18 | 7 | 14 | 18 | 32 |
| Middle .............. | 22 | 35 | 48 | 41 | 70 | 76 |
| Low ................ | 21 | 12 | 16 | 11 | 37 | 23 |
| Sixth grade: | | | | | | |
| High ............... | 32 | 41 | 4 | 10 | 36 | 51 |
| Middle ............. | 31 | 45 | 26 | 31 | 57 | 76 |
| Low ................ | 28 | 17 | 19 | 19 | 47 | 36 |
| Tenth grade: | | | | | | |
| High ............... | 9 | 19 | 22 | 17 | 31 | 36 |
| Middle ............. | 50 | 50 | 24 | 14 | 74 | 64 |
| Low ................ | 26 | 28 | 24 | 14 | 50 | 42 |
| Total ................ | 230 | 265 | 190 | 171 | 420 | 436 |
| | | 495 | | 361 | | 856 |

# TABLES ON THE COMING OF TELEVISION

▶ *These tables are referred to particularly in Chapter 2.*

TABLE II-1. THE EARLY GROWTH OF TELEVISION IN THE UNITED STATES
*(In per cent)*

|  | Sept. 1949 | Oct. 1950 | July 1951 | July 1952 | July 1953 |
|---|---|---|---|---|---|
| U.S. total .................. | 6 | 18 | 27 | 37 | 49 |
| By region: |  |  |  |  |  |
| Northeast .............. | 13 | 35 | 45 | 59 | 69 |
| South .................. | 1 | 4 | 13 | 17 | 30 |
| North central ............. | 4 | 15 | 27 | 39 | 50 |
| Mountain, southwest ........ | ? | 3 | 10 | 16 | 31 |
| Pacific ................. | 5 | 19 | 26 | 34 | 47 |
| By size of community: |  |  |  |  |  |
| Farm ................... | ? | 3 | 7 | 12 | 23 |
| Under 2,500 ............. | ? | 5 | 9 | 16 | 26 |
| 2,500–50,000 ............. | ? | 9 | 10 | 18 | 31 |
| 50,000–500,000 ........... | ? | 17 | 28 | 37 | 51 |
| 500,000 and over .......... | 14 | 40 | 53 | 69 | 77 |
| By education: |  |  |  |  |  |
| Grade school ............. | 4 | 16 | 23 | 31 | 43 |
| High school ............. | 7 | 22 | 34 | 45 | 57 |
| College ................ | 6 | 17 | 24 | 38 | 49 |
| By income: |  |  |  |  |  |
| Upper fourth ............. | 7 | 24 | 33 | 45 | 58 |
| Next fourth ............. | 7 | 19 | 32 | 41 | 55 |
| Next fourth ............. | 6 | 18 | 28 | 40 | 50 |
| Lowest fourth ............ | 3 | 12 | 18 | 23 | 32 |
| By age of children: |  |  |  |  |  |
| Number of children ........ | 4 | 13 | 21 | 29 | 37 |
| 5 years and under .......... | 7 | 23 | 36 | 48 | 54 |
| 6 to 12 years ............. | 7 | 22 | 35 | 46 | 56 |
| 13 to 20 years ............ | 6 | 18 | 28 | 39 | 49 |
| By size of family: |  |  |  |  |  |
| 1 and 2 members ........... | 4 | 12 | 19 | 28 | 38 |
| 3 members ............... | 6 | 18 | 30 | 41 | 52 |
| 4 and 5 members .......... | 7 | 22 | 35 | 45 | 58 |
| 6 and more members ....... | 6 | 19 | 27 | 39 | 53 |

Source: Market Research Corporation, quoted in Leo Bogart, *The Age of Television*, 2d ed. (New York: Ungar, 1958).

TABLE II-2. CHILDREN'S RADIO AND TELEVISION TIMES, 1950–51 AND 1959
*(In hours)*

| | 1950 Radio Time (No TV Available), Lyness, Des Moines | 1951 Television Time (Radio Available), Batty, Ann Arbor | 1959 Both TV and Radio San Francisco | |
|---|---|---|---|---|
| | | | Radio | Television |
| **Third grade:** | | **Second grade:** | | |
| Boys ......... 1.9* | | Boys ......... 2.4 | 0.9 | 2.2 |
| Girls ......... 1.7 | | Girls ......... 2.1 | 1.3 | 2.2 |
| **Fifth grade:** | | **Fourth grade:** | | |
| Boys ......... 3.4 | | Boys ......... 2.8 | 1.0 | 2.2 |
| Girls ......... 2.6 | | Girls ......... 2.8 | 1.2 | 2.3 |
| **Seventh grade:** | | **Sixth grade:** | | |
| Boys ......... 2.6 | | Boys ......... 3.7 | 1.0 | 2.5 |
| Girls ......... 3.2 | | Girls ......... 3.2 | 1.5 | 2.6 |
| **Ninth grade:** | | **Eighth grade:** | | |
| Boys ......... 2.4 | | Boys ......... 3.3 | 0.9 | 3.3 |
| Girls ......... 3.3 | | Girls ......... 3.3 | 1.8 | 3.2 |
| **Eleventh grade:** | | **Tenth grade:** | | |
| Boys ......... 2.4 | | Boys ......... 2.8 | 1.8 | 2.9 |
| Girls ......... 3.2 | | Girls ......... 2.7 | 2.3 | 2.9 |
| | | **Twelfth grade:** | | |
| | | Boys ......... 2.7 | 1.8 | 2.5 |
| | | Girls ......... 2.7 | 2.0 | 2.2 |

* These are approximate medians, computed from Lyness' published data. The other figures are from Tables IV-6 and VII-3.

# THE PROBLEM OF ESTIMATING
# VIEWING TIME

There are at least six common ways of estimating a child's viewing time. These are:

1. A general estimate by the parent—the parent is asked to remember some recent Sundays and give his best estimate of how much time the child spends viewing television on an average Sunday, for example.
2. A general estimate by the child—the child is asked to remember his television viewing on some recent Sundays and give his best estimate of how much time he spends viewing television on an average Sunday.
3. A supervised diary—for example, a diary kept at school, and filled in each morning under the supervision of the teacher.
4. An unsupervised diary—a diary kept at home and filled out by the child without supervision.
5. Aided recall—the child is given a list of the programs available on the preceeding day and asked to designate the ones he viewed.
6. Unaided recall—without the aid of a list of programs the child reports the television program he viewed on the previous day.

Unfortunately, these do not give identical results.

This is doubly unfortunate because one study will use one of these methods, another study a quite different method, and it will therefore be difficult to compare the results. For example, Maccoby [40] and the Videotown surveys [35] used parent estimates. Witty [45] depended on both child's and parent's estimates. Himmelweit, Oppenheim, and Vince [4] used children's own estimates and some supervised diaries. We have used four of the six methods in the course of our study—parent estimates in the case of very young children, children's estimates in the case of children in the sixth grade or beyond, aided recall in one study of elementary school children, and unsupervised diaries in the case of fifth and sixth grades in San Francisco. We also made use of an uncommon, and so far as we know a unique, method—an interview with an entire family, permitting the individuals to check up on each other's answers and arrive at time estimates which are approved by parents and siblings.

We are going to compare some of our results from these methods, in the hope that it will be useful information for future researchers and readers of television research.

In the course of our work in San Francisco, we made a very small study of different methods of recording viewing time. Using 30 fifth- and sixth-grade children (of whom 24 remained at the end of the exercise), we first asked each child for the best estimate he could give us of the time he spent watching television on an average Saturday and an average Sunday. Several weeks later, each child was given a diary to take home and fill in leisure-time activities for every day of the following week. During that week we made arrangements with an older brother or sister of the child, and in a few necessary cases with a parent, to record as accurately as possible the child's television time on the Saturday and Sunday of the week. Special pains were taken to keep the child from knowing he was under surveillance, but even so it is possible that some of them learned the secret. On Monday, we gave the child a list of the programs that had been on the air Saturday and Sunday, and asked him to tell us which ones he had seen, and whether he watched the whole program or a part of it. We asked each child whether he had viewed about the same as he usually did on Saturday and Sunday, or more or less. Five of them said the week end was not typical for them, for one reason or other—for example, a family auto trip or an illness that confined a child to his home. One child did not complete the diary through the week end. Thus we ended the study with 24 children, for each of whom we had four different measures of Saturday and Sunday viewing time.

These were the means for the different estimates, in hours:

|  | Time | sd |
|---|---|---|
| Unsupervised diary | 4.3 | .91 |
| Measured viewing time | 5.0 | .52 |
| Aided recall | 5.2 | .48 |
| Child's general estimate | 5.5 | .70 |

There appears to be more variation in the lowest and highest of these measures than in the others. We can assume that the unsupervised diary may be expected to give lower estimates than will the other methods. This agrees both with our observation and with our large sample results. We were much disappointed with the carelessness with which the children kept their diaries. Many of the children would admit, when asked about a particular program not recorded in the diary, that they had indeed seen the program but forgot to write it down. A few of them admitted that they had filled out the entire diary on the night before it was due. On the basis of this experience, we do not recommend the use of an unsupervised diary for fifth- and sixth-grade children, unless the researcher is able to instill much more motivation for accuracy than we were able to instill in the children.

The diaries also produced lower estimates in the large samples, as the following tabulation will illustrate (in hours per week):

|  | Unsupervised Diaries, San Francisco | | Whole Family Interviews, San Francisco | | Aided Recall, Clifton Suburb | |
|---|---|---|---|---|---|---|
|  | N | Hrs. | N | Hrs. | N | Hrs. |
| Fifth grade | 252 | 12.4 | 74 | 17.3 | 89 | 19.0 |
| Sixth grade | 262 | 14.1 | 79 | 18.2 | 88 | 19.0 |

In the first four grades, we can compare the aided recall used in the suburban

study with the results of the whole family interviews in San Francisco, and these
in turn with the estimates given by parents on questionnaires (in hours per
week):

| | Parents' Estimates, San Francisco | | Whole Family Interviews, San Francisco | | Aided Recall, Clifton Suburb | |
|---|---|---|---|---|---|---|
| | N | Hrs. | N | Hrs. | N | Hrs. |
| First grade ........ | 210 | 10.9 | 73 | 14.6 | 48 | 15.5 |
| Second grade ..... | 317 | 15.6 | 65 | 15.5 | 43 | 15.2 |
| Third grade ....... | 240 | 12.2 | 71 | 18.2 | 80 | 18.1 |
| Fourth grade ...... | 263 | 12.2 | 87 | 15.5 | 84 | 17.1 |

It therefore appears that parents' estimates of their children's viewing time
in the lower grades also give lower results than aided recall and whole family
interviews. Some of our cooperating teachers observed that many of the mothers
seemed rather ashamed of the amount of television their children saw, and
therefore probably underestimated when making a report. We have considerable
faith in the aided recall interviews, which were done most carefully in Clifton,
on the morning following the viewing day, with a complete list of programs as
a guide. We also have more faith in an estimate arrived at by a whole family,
checking back and forth, than in one parent's estimate. Therefore, we suggest
that any future researcher wishing to use parent estimates should endeavor to
get the parents to check up on the child's viewing, if possible with a list of programs; and, above all, to persuade the parent that there is no disgrace in reporting a large amount of viewing and that nothing bad will happen to the child
as a result of the report.

How does the child's own estimate compare with other types of estimate?
We have been very doubtful of the accuracy of a child's estimate earlier than
the sixth grade, but used it through the Rocky Mountain and Canadian sixth and
tenth grades, and the San Francisco eighth, tenth, and twelfth grades. We can,
therefore, compare a number of sixth- and tenth-grade estimates, in hours:

| | Sixth Grade | | Tenth Grade | |
|---|---|---|---|---|
| | N | Hrs. | N | Hrs. |
| Rocky Mountain samples: | | | | |
| 1 .................... | 187 | 23.1 | 208 | 17.1 |
| 2 .................... | 282 | 21.9 | 248 | 16.4 |
| 3 .................... | 122 | 22.5 | 130 | 20.9 |
| 4 .................... | 63 | 24.2 | 50 | 20.2 |
| 5 .................... | 74 | 23.4 | 60 | 22.1 |
| Teletown, Canada ......... | 194 | 20.5 | 185 | 11.6 |
| San Francisco ............ | 79 | 17.9* | 201 | 19.4 |
| Clifton (aided recall) ...... | 88 | 19.0 | | |

* Whole family estimate.

All the sixth-grade children's estimates are higher than the Clifton aided
recall estimates and the San Francisco whole family estimate. On the other hand,
the San Francisco children's estimates for the tenth grade are not out of line
with the other children's estimates. Does this mean that the children give high
estimates (at least in the sixth grade), or that the samples in the Rocky Mountain
states and in Canada are different from those in San Francisco and Clifton?

There is some reason for believing that much of the variation is really due to difference in the samples or the weather conditions.

In any case, these figures will serve to point out that different methods of recording children's viewing time give different results, and these differences must be kept in mind when comparing audience studies. We feel that the unsupervised diary tends to give a spuriously low estimate (unless the children are highly motivated), and that parents' estimates in the early grades may also be unduly low unless the parents are persuaded to record the time partly by observation and not to be fearful of reporting high figures. We have considerable faith in aided recall interviews, if made the day following, and in whole family interviews, although these are more costly. (We have used whole family estimates to represent the San Francisco sample from first through sixth grades.) A supervised diary should have the virtues of an aided recall interview, and an unaided recall interview might be expected to give a lower figure than one aided by a list of programs. Somewhere in the vicinity of the figures given by aided recall, supervised diary, and whole family interviews must be the most accurate figure. Such evidence as we have suggests that a child's own estimate tends to be high rather than low, but we have no reason to distrust these estimates seriously when they come from children in the sixth grade or higher.

The results of these several studies of viewing time are set forth in detail in Tables III-1 through III-6 for reference.

TABLE III-1. WHOLE FAMILY ESTIMATES OF SAN FRANCISCO
CHILDREN'S VIEWING TIME

Grades One to Six, by Sex

| Grade | | N | Median Estimate (*hours*) | | |
|---|---|---|---|---|---|
| | | | Weekdays | Sunday | Weekly Total° |
| First | M | 19 | 2.1 | 2.5 | 15.1 |
| | F | 18 | 1.9 | 2.6 | 14.0 |
| Second | M | 26 | 2.2 | 2.5 | 15.7 |
| | F | 28 | 2.1 | 2.8 | 15.4 |
| Third | M | 36 | 2.7 | 2.6 | 18.8 |
| | F | 25 | 2.4 | 2.9 | 17.3 |
| Fourth | M | 30 | 2.2 | 2.1 | 15.3 |
| | F | 22 | 2.2 | 2.6 | 15.8 |
| Fifth | M | 33 | 2.4 | 2.8 | 17.2 |
| | F | 25 | 1.9 | 2.3 | 13.7 |
| Sixth | M | 31 | 2.5 | 2.3 | 17.3 |
| | F | 19 | 2.6 | 2.6 | 18.2 |

° Weekly total is obtained by multiplying the weekday average by six and adding the Sunday time to the product.

TABLE III-2. AIDED RECALL ESTIMATES OF CLIFTON SUBURBAN
CHILDREN'S VIEWING TIME
Kindergarten, Grades One to Six

| | | Median Estimate (*hours*) | | |
|---|---|---|---|---|
| Grade | N° | Average of 4 Weekdays | Sunday | Weekly Total |
| Kindergarten ... (42–28)† | | 2.9 | 2.6 | 20.0 |
| First .......... (48–26)† | | 2.2 | 2.4 | 15.6 |
| Second ....... (32–21)† | | 2.1 | 2.6 | 15.2 |
| Third ......... (76–71) | | 2.4 | 3.7 | 18.1 |
| Fourth ........ (73–59) | | 2.2 | 3.9 | 17.1 |
| Fifth ......... (80–72) | | 2.5 | 4.0 | 19.0 |
| Sixth ......... (84–73) | | 2.5 | 3.9 | 18.9 |

° Attendance varied over the five days of the school week.
† Two sections were interviewed for Sunday viewing, only one section for the other four days.

TABLE III-3. WHOLE FAMILY ESTIMATES (SAN FRANCISCO) AND AIDED RECALL
ESTIMATES (CLIFTON) OF CHILDREN'S DAILY VIEWING TIME
Before Grade One (Median Estimates)

| | San Francisco | | Clifton | |
|---|---|---|---|---|
| | N | Hrs. | N | Hrs. |
| Age 3 ................... | 21 | .7 | | |
| Age 4 ................... | 29 | 1.4 | | |
| Age 5 (kindergarten) ..... | 34 | 2.2 | (42–28)° | 2.9 |

° Attendance on days on which the average time is based varied from day to day.

TABLE III-4. PARENTS' ESTIMATES OF CHILDREN'S VIEWING TIME
San Francisco, Grades One to Four; Rocky Mountain Towns
and Teletown, Canada, Grade One, by Sex

| | | | Median Estimate (*hours*) | | |
|---|---|---|---|---|---|
| | | N | Weekdays | Sunday | Weekly Total |
| San Francisco: | | | | | |
| First grade | M | 69 | 1.4 | 2.5 | 10.9 |
| | F | 79 | 1.4 | 2.5 | 10.9 |
| Second grade | M | 114 | 2.0 | 3.0 | 15.0 |
| | F | 108 | 2.2 | 3.1 | 16.3 |
| Third grade | M | 96 | 1.6 | 2.6 | 12.2 |
| | F | 84 | 1.6 | 2.6 | 12.2 |
| Fourth grade | M | 102 | 1.6 | 2.9 | 12.5 |
| | F | 100 | 1.5 | 2.9 | 11.9 |
| Rocky Mt. towns: | | | | | |
| First grade | M | 125 | 2.2 | 2.6 | 15.8 |
| | F | 126 | 2.2 | 2.6 | 15.8 |
| Teletown: | | | | | |
| First grade | M | 68 | 1.8 | 1.9 | 12.7 |
| | F | 46 | 1.6 | 1.9 | 11.5 |

TABLE III-5. UNSUPERVISED DIARY ESTIMATES OF CHILDREN'S VIEWING TIME,
SAN FRANCISCO
Grades Five to Six

| Grade | | N | Median Estimate (*hours*) | | |
|-------|---|---|----------|--------|--------------|
| | | | Weekdays | Sunday | Weekly Total |
| Fifth | M | 137 | 1.9 | 1.9 | 13.3 |
|       | F | 125 | 1.6 | 1.9 | 11.5 |
| Sixth | M | 142 | 1.9 | 2.1 | 13.5 |
|       | F | 120 | 2.1 | 2.2 | 14.8 |

TABLE III-6. CHILDREN'S OWN ESTIMATE OF VIEWING TIME, SAN FRANCISCO
Grades Eight, Ten, and Twelve

| Grade | | N | Median Estimate (*hours*) | | |
|-------|---|---|----------|--------|--------------|
| | | | Weekdays | Sunday | Weekly Total |
| Eighth | M | 114 | 3.2 | 3.6 | 22.8 |
|        | F | 105 | 3.2 | 3.2 | 22.4 |
| Tenth  | M | 85  | 2.8 | 3.5 | 20.3 |
|        | F | 116 | 2.8 | 3.4 | 20.2 |
| Twelfth | M | 123 | 2.5 | 2.8 | 17.8 |
|         | F | 109 | 2.1 | 3.1 | 15.7 |

# TABLES ON AMOUNT OF USE OF TELEVISION

▶ *These tables are referred to particularly in Chapter 3.*

TABLE IV-1. CUMULATIVE PERCENTAGE OF CHILDREN WHO HAVE BEGUN TO USE
GIVEN MEDIA BY GIVEN AGE (SAN FRANCISCO)

(N = 754)

| | | | | | | Books | | Newspapers | |
|---|---|---|---|---|---|---|---|---|---|
| Age | TV | Radio | Maga-zines | Comic Books | Movies | Read to Them | They Read | Read to Them | They Read |
| 2 | 14 | 11 | 3 | 1 | 1 | 38 | 0 | 0 | 0 |
| 3 | 37 | 20 | 11 | 6 | 8 | 58 | 0 | 0 | 0 |
| 4 | 65 | 27 | 20 | 17 | 21 | 72 | 2 | 4 | 0 |
| 5 | 82 | 40 | 33 | 35 | 39 | 74 | 9 | 9 | 0 |
| 6 | 91 | 47 | 41 | 50 | 60 | 75 | 40 | 12 | 9 |
| 7 | 94 | 53 | 53 | 61 | 70 | 75 | 73 | 12 | 44 |
| 8 | 95 | 62 | 59 | 68 | 76 | 75 | 86 | 12 | 59 |
| 9 | 96 | 65 | 62 | 70 | 77 | 75 | 89 | 12 | 71 |

TABLE IV-2. MEDIAN AGE OF CHILD AT BEGINNING OF MEDIA USE, BY EDUCATIONAL
LEVEL OF FATHER (SAN FRANCISCO FAMILY INTERVIEWS)

| Media | Father Did Not Finish High School (N = 61) | Father Finished High School (N = 61) | Father Had Some College (N = 40) |
|---|---|---|---|
| Television .................... | 3.3 | 3.4 | 2.8 |
| Radio ........................ | 3.6 | 4.4 | 3.4 |
| Movies ....................... | 5.4 | 4.9 | 4.7 |
| Magazines .................... | 4.8 | 5.2 | 4.2 |
| Books ........................ | 7.0 | 7.0 | 6.5 |
| Newspapers .................. | 7.6 | 7.8 | 6.9 |

TABLE IV-3. TYPES OF PROGRAMS WITH WHICH CHILDREN OF DIFFERENTLY EDUCATED
PARENTS BEGIN TO VIEW TELEVISION (SAN FRANCISCO)

(*In percentages*)

| Programs | Father Did Not Finish High School (N = 61) | Father Finished High School (N = 61) | Father Had Some College (N = 40) |
|---|---|---|---|
| Children's programs ............... | 76 | 86 | 84 |
| Westerns ........................ | 14 | 10 | 1 |
| Educational, science, etc. ........... | 0 | 0 | 6 |
| Other .......................... | 10 | 6 | 9 |

TABLE IV-4. ESTIMATES OF TELEVISION VIEWING TIME BEFORE FIRST GRADE
(SAN FRANCISCO, 1958, FAMILY ESTIMATES)*

| Age | N | Percentage Viewing Television | Average Weekday Amount of Viewing (*hours*) |
|---|---|---|---|
| 3 | 37 | 37 | .7 |
| 4 | 38 | 65 | 1.6 |
| 5 | 78 | 82 | 2.3 |

* The Clifton school questionnaires in 1960, with aided recall, studied a total of 42 kindergarten students. The average television viewing for four weekdays was 2.9 hours and on Sunday it was 2.6 hours.

TABLE IV-5. COMPARABLE TIME SERIES ON CHILDREN'S TELEVISION VIEWING
(*Hours per average day*)

| Grade | Sex | San Francisco 1957–58 (large city) | Batty, Ann Arbor 1951 (small city) | Witty, Evanston 1950 (large suburb) | Clifton 1960 (small suburb) |
|---|---|---|---|---|---|
| 2 | Boys ........... | 2.2 | 2.4 ⎫ | 3.0 | 2.2 |
|   | Girls .......... | 2.2 | 2.1 ⎬ |  |  |
| 4 | Boys ........... | 2.2 | 2.8 ⎫ | 3.3 | 2.4 |
|   | Girls .......... | 2.3 | 2.8 ⎬ |  |  |
| 6 | Boys ........... | 2.5 | 3.7 ⎫ | 3.7 | 2.7 |
|   | Girls .......... | 2.6 | 3.2 ⎬ |  |  |
| 8 | Boys ........... | 3.3 | 3.3 ⎫ | 2.7 |  |
|   | Girls .......... | 3.2 | 3.3 ⎬ |  |  |
| 10 | Boys ........... | 2.9 | 2.8 |  |  |
|   | Girls .......... | 2.9 | 2.7 |  |  |
| 12 | Boys ........... | 2.5 | 2.7 |  |  |
|   | Girls .......... | 2.2 | 2.7 |  |  |

TABLE IV-6. HOURS OF TELEVISION VIEWING IN SAN FRANCISCO
ON WEEKDAYS AND SUNDAY
By Grade and Sex

| | N | | Weekdays | | Sunday | | Total for Week | |
|---|---|---|---|---|---|---|---|---|
| Grade | Boys | Girls | Boys | Girls | Boys | Girls | Boys | Girls |
| 1 | 103 | 107 | 2.0 | 2.0 | 2.2 | 2.2 | 14.2 | 14.2 |
| 2 | 159 | 158 | 2.2 | 2.1 | 2.5 | 2.8 | 15.7 | 15.4 |
| 4 | 137 | 126 | 2.2 | 2.2 | 2.1 | 2.6 | 15.3 | 15.8 |
| 6 | 142 | 120 | 2.5 | 2.6 | 2.3 | 2.6 | 17.3 | 18.2 |
| 8 | 114 | 105 | 3.2 | 3.2 | 3.6 | 3.2 | 22.4 | 22.0 |
| 10 | 85 | 116 | 2.8 | 2.8 | 3.5 | 3.4 | 20.3 | 20.2 |
| 12 | 123 | 109 | 2.5 | 2.1 | 2.8 | 3.1 | 17.8 | 15.7 |

TABLE IV-7. HOURS OF TELEVISION VIEWING IN FIVE RELATIVELY ISOLATED
U.S. TOWNS ON WEEKDAYS AND SUNDAY
By Grade

| | | Sixth Grade | | | | Tenth Grade | | |
|---|---|---|---|---|---|---|---|---|
| | N | Weekdays | Sunday | Week | N | Weekdays | Sunday | Week |
| Rocky 1 ...... | 187 | 3.3 | 3.3 | 23.1 | 208 | 2.3 | 3.3 | 17.1 |
| Rocky 2 ...... | 282 | 3.4 | 3.8 | 24.2 | 248 | 2.9 | 2.8 | 20.2 |
| Rocky 3 ...... | 122 | 3.1 | 3.3 | 21.9 | 130 | 2.2 | 3.2 | 16.4 |
| Rocky 4 ...... | 63 | 3.2 | 3.3 | 22.5 | 50 | 3.0 | 2.9 | 20.9 |
| Rocky 5 ...... | 74 | 3.2 | 4.2 | 23.4 | 60 | 3.0 | 4.1 | 22.1 |

TABLE IV-8. HOURS OF TELEVISION VIEWING IN TELETOWN, CANADA,
ON WEEKDAYS AND SUNDAY
By Grade

| Grade | N | Weekdays | Sunday | Week |
|---|---|---|---|---|
| 6 | 194 | 2.9 | 3.1 | 20.5 |
| 10 | 185 | 1.6 | 2.0 | 11.6 |

TABLE IV-9. TIME SERIES ON HOURS SPENT PER WEEK ON TELEVISION, 1951–1959

| | 1951 | 1952 | 1953 | 1954 | 1955 | 1956 | 1957 | 1958 | 1959 |
|---|---|---|---|---|---|---|---|---|---|
| Cunningham and Walsh* | | | | | | | | | |
| Ages under 10 ..... | 9.1 | 8.6 | 8.5 | 7.7 | 11.0 | 7.3 | 7.6 | | |
| Ages 10–18 ....... | 12.3 | 11.6 | 11.7 | 10.8 | 12.7 | 9.6 | 9.2 | | |
| Witty† | | | | | | | | | |
| Elementary school.. | 19 | | 23 | | 24 | | 22 | 20 | 21 |
| High school ....... | 14 | | 17 | | 14 | | 12 | 13 | 21 |

* Five weekdays, evenings only. From "Videotown, 1948–57" (New York: Cunningham and Walsh, mimeo., 1958).
† Evanston and Chicago, seven-day week. From "School Children and Television" (distributed by the Television Information Office, mimeo., New York, 1960).

TABLE IV-10. CHILDREN'S DIVISION OF LEISURE TIME (SAN FRANCISCO)

|  | Ages 5–8 (N = 236) | | Ages 9–10 (N = 171) | | Ages 11–12 (N = 85) | |
|---|---|---|---|---|---|---|
|  | Time (minutes) | % of Total | Time (minutes) | % of Total | Time (minutes) | % of Total |
| Homework ........... | 24 | 5.8 | 57 | 11.5 | 88 | 15.8 |
| Play ................ | 240 | 51.9 | 210 | 42.3 | 182 | 32.6 |
| Television ........... | 128 | 27.7 | 130 | 26.2 | 150 | 26.9 |
| Other media .......... | 70 | 14.6 | 100 | 20.0 | 138 | 24.7 |
| Total leisure time..... | 462 | | 497 | | 550 | |
|  | (7 hrs. 42 min.) | | (8 hrs. 17 min.) | | (9 hrs. 18 min.) | |

TABLE IV-11. CHILDREN'S TELEVISION TIME BY DAY OF WEEK (CLIFTON)
(*In hours*)

| Grade | Sunday (N = 387) | Monday (N = 356) | Tuesday (N = 352) | Wednesday (N = 339) | Thursday (N = 349) |
|---|---|---|---|---|---|
| 1 | 2.4 | 3.2 | 1.7 | 2.1 | 2.2 |
| 2 | 2.6 | 2.0 | 1.7 | 2.5 | 2.2 |
| 3 | 3.7 | 2.7 | 2.6 | 2.2 | 1.8 |
| 4 | 3.9 | 2.6 | 2.1 | 2.2 | 2.0 |
| 5 | 4.0 | 3.2 | 2.2 | 2.4 | 2.1 |
| 6 | 3.9 | 2.9 | 2.4 | 2.5 | 2.3 |
| All grades | 3.5 | 2.8 | 2.2 | 2.4 | 2.1 |

TABLE IV-12. CHILDREN'S BEDTIME BY DAY OF WEEK (CLIFTON)

| Grade | N | Sunday | Monday | Tuesday | Wednesday | Thursday |
|---|---|---|---|---|---|---|
| K | 42 | 7:53 | 8:14 | 8:05 | 8:10 | 7:38 |
| 1 | 48 | 7:58 | 8:09 | 8:03 | 8:26 | 7:49 |
| 2 | 43 | 8:16 | 8:17 | 8:17 | 8:13 | 8:20 |
| 3 | 80 | 9:08 | 8:53 | 9:04 | 8:59 | 8:48 |
| 4 | 84 | 9:02 | 8:50 | 8:55 | 8:49 | 8:47 |
| 5 | 89 | 9:16 | 9:11 | 9:04 | 9:06 | 9:16 |
| 6 | 88 | 9:29 | 9:20 | 9:26 | 9:32 | 9:28 |

TABLE IV-13. PERCENTAGES OF CHILDREN VIEWING AT DIFFERENT HOURS ON SUNDAY (CLIFTON)

By Grade

| Time | K (N=42) | 1 (N=48) | 2 (N=43) | 3 (N=80) | 4 (N=84) | 5 (N=89) | 6 (N=88) |
|---|---|---|---|---|---|---|---|
| 7:00 A.M. | | | | 2.5 | | | |
| 7:30 | | | | 12.0 | | 2.1 | 5.1 |
| 8:00 | | | | 10.5 | 9.0 | 2.1 | 3.9 |
| 8:30 | | | | 6.7 | 7.5 | 7.9 | 5.1 |
| 9:00 | 58.3 | 54.2 | 39.5 | 42.5 | 58.2 | 30.2 | 28.2 |
| 9:30 | 47.2 | 54.2 | 34.9 | 46.6 | 52.2 | 32.9 | 32.1 |
| 10:00 | 41.7 | 39.6 | 23.2 | 38.6 | 37.3 | 26.3 | 25.6 |
| 10:30 | 33.3 | 42.2 | 16.3 | 25.3 | 47.8 | 27.6 | 28.2 |
| 11:00 | 30.6 | 25.0 | 7.0 | 30.6 | 43.3 | 22.4 | 24.4 |
| 11:30 | 8.3 | 4.2 | | 12.0 | 7.5 | 6.6 | 10.3 |
| 12:00 NOON | | 6.2 | 2.3 | 9.3 | 3.0 | 6.7 | 3.0 |
| 12:30 | | 4.2 | 2.3 | 5.3 | 4.5 | 9.2 | 3.9 |
| 1:00 | 16.7 | 4.2 | 9.3 | 12.0 | 7.5 | 10.5 | 12.8 |
| 1:30 | 19.4 | 2.1 | 16.3 | 16.0 | 11.9 | 14.5 | 15.4 |
| 2:00 | 8.3 | 6.2 | 9.3 | 18.7 | 7.5 | 19.7 | 16.7 |
| 2:30 | 11.1 | 8.3 | 9.3 | 18.7 | 10.4 | 19.7 | 12.8 |
| 3:00 | 25.0 | 10.4 | 9.3 | 18.7 | 20.9 | 23.7 | 23.1 |
| 3:30 | 22.2 | 4.2 | 9.3 | 17.3 | 23.9 | 26.3 | 26.9 |
| 4:00 | 13.9 | 10.4 | 7.0 | 30.6 | 22.4 | 25.0 | 28.2 |
| 4:30 | 19.4 | 8.3 | 2.3 | 26.6 | 23.9 | 19.7 | 26.9 |
| 5:00 | 30.6 | 27.1 | 16.3 | 34.6 | 32.8 | 28.9 | 35.9 |
| 5:30 | 22.2 | 25.0 | 4.6 | 29.3 | 23.9 | 25.0 | 33.3 |
| 6:00 | 8.3 | 12.5 | 9.3 | 29.3 | 37.3 | 32.9 | 44.9 |
| 6:30 | 8.3 | 6.2 | 9.3 | 28.0 | 31.3 | 32.9 | 44.9 |
| 7:00 | 61.1 | 68.7 | 65.1 | 57.6 | 71.6 | 53.9 | 64.1 |
| 7:30 | 33.3 | 37.5 | 58.1 | 60.0 | 61.6 | 59.2 | 69.2 |
| 8:00 | 16.7 | 31.2 | 32.6 | 44.0 | 53.7 | 48.7 | 75.6 |
| 8:30 | 5.6 | 10.4 | 9.3 | 33.3 | 38.8 | 46.0 | 61.5 |
| 9:00 | | 2.1 | 4.6 | 14.7 | 19.4 | 36.5 | 44.9 |
| 9:30 | | | | 12.0 | 1.5 | 21.0 | 16.7 |
| 10:00 | | | | 9.3 | 4.5 | 6.6 | 14.1 |
| 10:30 | | | | 4.0 | 3.0 | 1.3 | 5.1 |

TABLE IV-14. PERCENTAGE OF CHILDREN VIEWING AT DIFFERENT HOURS
ON WEEKDAYS (CLIFTON)
By Grade

| Time | K° (N=42) | 1 (N=48) | 2 (N=43) | 3 (N=80) | 4 (N=84) | 5 (N=89) | 6 (N=88) |
|---|---|---|---|---|---|---|---|
| 6:00 A.M. | | | | 1.7 | 0.7 | | 1.5 |
| 6:30 | | 0.9 | | 1.7 | 1.1 | 0.3 | 0.9 |
| 7:00 | 11.8 | 14.3 | 5.5 | 9.0 | 4.1 | 6.1 | 4.2 |
| 7:30 | 13.2 | 25.7 | 2.2 | 10.1 | 4.5 | 7.1 | 4.5 |
| 8:00 | 6.4 | 15.2 | 1.1 | 6.0 | 3.7 | 2.4 | 3.6 |
| 8:30 | 4.8 | 2.8 | | 4.0 | 2.2 | 1.7 | 1.8 |
| 9:00 | 27.4 | | | | | | |
| 9:30 | 53.1 | | | | | | |
| 10:00 | 59.6 | | | | | | |
| 10:30 | 29.0 | | | | | | |
| 11:00 | 14.5 | | | IN SCHOOL | | | |
| 11:30 | 16.1 | | | | | | |
| 12:00 NOON | 46.0 | | | | | | |
| 12:30 | 28.6 | | | | | | |
| 1:00 | 12.4 | | | | | | |
| 1:30 | 6.2 | | | | | | |
| 2:00 | 11.1 | | | | | | |
| 2:30 | 12.4 | 7.6 | 2.2 | 15.4 | | | |
| 3:00 | 13.6 | 13.3 | 6.6 | 16.1 | | | |
| 3:30 | 9.9 | 9.5 | 1.1 | 12.8 | 5.2 | 5.7 | 8.1 |
| 4:00 | 8.4 | 11.4 | 4.4 | 15.4 | 20.1 | 20.5 | 21.1 |
| 4:30 | 17.4 | 16.2 | 15.4 | 26.8 | 24.5 | 22.2 | 21.4 |
| 5:00 | 74.0 | 58.0 | 58.8 | 43.6 | 52.0 | 40.4 | 41.9 |
| 5:30 | 74.6 | 67.5 | 66.0 | 54.7 | 51.3 | 35.0 | 47.3 |
| 6:00 | 60.6 | 58.0 | 40.7 | 41.6 | 46.8 | 40.4 | 45.2 |
| 6:30 | 54.4 | 42.8 | 48.4 | 36.9 | 48.3 | 42.1 | 47.6 |
| 7:00 | 48.0 | 56.2 | 45.0 | 45.3 | 47.6 | 38.4 | 44.6 |
| 7:30 | 31.4 | 35.2 | 42.8 | 42.3 | 47.6 | 46.1 | 51.2 |
| 8:00 | 17.4 | 28.6 | 34.1 | 35.2 | 44.2 | 48.5 | 55.1 |
| 8:30 | 4.4 | 10.5 | 15.4 | 24.8 | 35.7 | 41.8 | 50.9 |
| 9:00 | 2.8 | 3.8 | 3.3 | 13.4 | 17.1 | 30.0 | 38.3 |
| 9:30 | 0.7 | 3.8 | 2.2 | 6.4 | 6.3 | 15.5 | 19.6 |
| 10:00 | 0.7 | 0.9 | 1.1 | 5.4 | 2.2 | 6.7 | 5.7 |
| 10:30 | | | | 2.4 | 0.7 | 4.0 | 3.0 |
| 11:00 | | | | 1.7 | 0.7 | 0.3 | 0.3 |

° Results for kindergarten watching between 9:00 A.M. and 2:30 P.M. are based on half the total population, since these children are on half-day session. Morning watching figures are a proportion of children who are in the afternoon kindergarten sections; afternoon figures are a proportion of those in the morning kindergarten sections.

TABLE IV-15. ESTIMATES OF CHILD'S MEDIAN DAILY TIME SPENT
ON TELEVISION

| Researcher | Place | Date | Method | N | Ages | Hours |
|---|---|---|---|---|---|---|
| Riley, Cantwell, Ruttiger | New Brunswick, N.J. | 1948 | Parent interviews | 106 87 | 6–12 13–19 | 3.1 2.6 |
| Lewis | | 1949 | Interviews, questionnaires | 1,700 | High sch. | 3.4 |
| Maccoby | Cambridge, Mass. | 1950–51 | Parent interviews | 622 | 4–17 | 2.4* 3.5† |
| Clark | | 1950–51 | Questionnaires | 750 | Grades 6, 7 | 3.7* |
| Besco | | 1952 | Questionnaires | 223 | Grades 10–12 | 2.7 |
| Sweetser | Boston | 1953 | Mother's estimate | 413 | 7–20 | 2.3* |
| Parker, others | New Haven | 1953 | Parent interviews | 650 | 4–15 | 1.9‡ |
| Dell Comics–Board of Education | Elmhurst, Ill. | 1954 | Questionnaires | 1,677 | Grades 4–8 | 3.7 |
| Himmelweit, Oppenheim, Vince | London, Portsmouth, Sunderland, Bristol, Norwich | 1955–56 | Questionnaires, diaries, program lists | 610 919 | 10–11 13–14 | 1.9 1.9 |
| *Television Age* | | 1957 | | | 6–11 12–17 | 2.0 2.0 |
| Cunningham, Walsh | "Videotown," Poughkeepsie, N.Y. | 1957 | Parent interviews | | –10 10–18 | 2.1 2.4 |
| Witty | Evanston, Chicago, other nearby towns | 1959 | Questionnaires, interviews | ca. 2,000 | Elem. sch. High sch. | 3.0 1.8 |

* Weekdays.          † Sunday.          ‡ Regular programs only.

TABLE IV-16. COMPARISON OF HOURS SPENT ON TELEVISION AND IN SCHOOL,
AGES 3–17 (SAN FRANCISCO)

| Age | School Time | | Television Time | |
|---|---|---|---|---|
| | Daily | Yearly* | Daily | Yearly† |
| 3 | 0 | 0 | .75 | 274 |
| 4 | 0 | 0 | 1.50 | 548 |
| 5 | 3 | 540 | 2.25 | 821 |
| 6–8 | 4.5 | 810 | 2.50 Weekdays / 3.00 Sunday | 936 |
| 9–11 | 5.5 | 990 | 2.50 Weekdays / 3.00 Sunday | 936 |
| 12–17 | 6.0 | 1,080 | 2.50 Weekdays / 3.00 Sunday | 936 |
| Total for ages 6–17‡ | | 11,880 | | 11,232 |
| Total for ages 5–17§ | | 12,420 | | 12,053 |
| Total for ages 3–17¶ | | 12,420 | | 12,875 |

* Yearly total figured on a basis of 180 school days per year.
† Yearly total figured by multiplying the weekly total by 52. These television times are conservative estimates based on tables in Appendix III.
‡ Total for school time arrived at by multiplying 810 hours by 3 (years); 990 by 3; 1,080 by 6. Total for television time arrived at by multiplying 936 hours by 12 (years).
§ Total for school time arrived at by adding 540 (for age 5) to previous figure. Total for television time arrived at by adding 821 (for fifth year) to previous total.
¶ Total for school time is identical with the previous total because of no school in the third or fourth year. Total for television time arrived at by adding 822 (for third and fourth years) to previous total.

TABLE IV-17. HOURS SPENT ON WEEKDAY TELEVISION, BY CHILDREN OF DIFFERENT
MENTAL ABILITIES AND GRADE
(San Francisco, Rocky Mountain Towns, Teletown, Canada)

| Mental Ability and Grade | N | Average Number of Hours | |
|---|---|---|---|
| | | Weekdays | Sunday |
| San Francisco | | | |
| Eighth grade: | | | |
| High | 43 | 1.9 | 2.3 |
| Middle | 123 | 3.5 | 3.8 |
| Low | 53 | 4.1 | 3.9 |
| Tenth grade: | | | |
| High | 32 | 2.2 | 2.0 |
| Middle | 120 | 3.0 | 3.8 |
| Low | 49 | 2.9 | 3.4 |
| Twelfth grade: | | | |
| High | 46 | 1.3 | 3.0 |
| Middle | 137 | 2.2 | 3.0 |
| Low | 49 | 2.9 | 3.0 |
| Rocky Mountain towns | | | |
| Sixth grade: | | | |
| High | 216 | 3.1 | 3.7 |
| Middle | 320 | 3.2 | 3.7 |
| Low | 169 | 4.0 | 3.9 |
| Tenth grade: | | | |
| High | 163 | 1.8 | 2.7 |
| Middle | 326 | 2.3 | 3.1 |
| Low | 204 | 3.0 | 3.6 |
| Teletown | | | |
| Sixth grade: | | | |
| High | 73 | 2.7 | 3.1 |
| Middle | 76 | 3.2 | 3.2 |
| Low | 45 | 3.5 | 3.9 |
| Tenth grade: | | | |
| High | 28 | 1.1 | 2.6 |
| Middle | 100 | 2.0 | 2.1 |
| Low | 54 | 2.2 | 3.0 |

TABLE IV-18. CHILDREN'S WEEKDAY VIEWING, BY FATHER'S SCHOOLING
(SAN FRANCISCO)

| Father | N | Ave. Viewing Time (hours) |
|---|---|---|
| Did not finish high school | 161 | 2.6 |
| Finished high school | 161 | 2.0 |
| Had at least some college | 140 | 1.6 |

TABLE IV-19. CHILDREN'S WEEKDAY VIEWING, BY FATHER'S OCCUPATION (SAN FRANCISCO)

| Father's Occupation | N | Children's Television Viewing | |
|---|---|---|---|
| | | Heavy (per cent) | Light (per cent) |
| White-collar .................... | 118 | 36 | 64 |
| Blue-collar ..................... | 164 | 66 | 34 |

TABLE IV-20. CHILDREN'S WEEKDAY VIEWING COMPARED TO PARENT'S VIEWING (SAN FRANCISCO)

| | N | Ave. Viewing Time (hours) |
|---|---|---|
| Father's television time in lowest quarter....... | 104 | 1.9 |
| Father's television time in highest quarter...... | 92 | 2.5 |
| Mother's television time in lowest quarter...... | 98 | 1.9 |
| Mother's television time in highest quarter..... | 103 | 2.4 |
| Both mother and father in lowest quarter....... | 59 | 1.6 |
| Both mother and father in highest quarter...... | 73 | 2.6 |

TABLE IV-21. CHILDREN'S VIEWING COMPARED TO VIEWING OF FATHER, MOTHER, AND SIBLINGS (SAN FRANCISCO)

| | N | Male Child Views (hours) | N | Female Child Views (hours) |
|---|---|---|---|---|
| If father views TV: | | | | |
| 0–1 hours | 32 | 1.84 | 30 | 1.33 |
| 1–2 | 25 | 1.90 | 15 | 1.77 |
| 2–3 | 14 | 1.93 | 23 | 2.15 |
| 3–4 | 9 | 2.72 | 4 | 2.50 |
| If mother views TV: | | | | |
| 0–1 hours | 32 | 2.52 | 29 | 1.28 |
| 1–2 | 23 | 1.93 | 21 | 1.98 |
| 2–3 | 19 | 2.34 | 19 | 2.08 |
| 3–4 | 10 | 2.10 | 13 | 2.19 |

| If older child views TV: | N | Younger Child Views (hours) |
|---|---|---|
| 0–1 hours | 7 | 1.2 |
| 1–2 | 39 | 1.8 |
| 2–3 | 32 | 2.5 |
| 3– | 9 | 2.9 |

APPENDIX V

# TABLES ON PROGRAM PREFERENCES

▶ *These tables are referred to particularly in Chapter 3.*

TABLE V-1. FAVORITE PROGRAMS FOR SAN FRANCISCO GRADES 1–6*

| Grade 1 (N = 210) | | Grade 2 (N = 317) | | Grade 3 (N = 240) | |
|---|---|---|---|---|---|
| Disneyland ........ | 11.7% | Disneyland ........ | 15.1% | Disneyland ........ | 10.9% |
| Cartoons ......... | 10.7 | Zorro ............. | 13.5 | Zorro ............ | 6.8 |
| Popeye .......... | 8.7 | Popeye .......... | 12.0 | Cartoons ......... | 6.8 |
| Zorro ............ | 7.8 | Cartoons ......... | 11.5 | Popeye .......... | 6.1 |
| Mickey Mouse Club | 6.7 | Lassie ........... | 8.1 | Mickey Mouse Club | 4.4 |
| Lassie ........... | 6.3 | Mickey Mouse Club | 8.0 | Lassie ........... | 3.7 |
| Captain Fortune .. | 4.5 | Rin Tin Tin ...... | 6.1 | Leave It to Beaver. | 3.6 |
| Westerns ........ | 3.8 | Cheyenne ........ | 4.4 | Circus Boy ....... | 3.3 |
| Rin Tin Tin ...... | 3.6 | Leave It to Beaver. | 4.2 | Amos and Andy ... | 3.1 |
| Leave It to Beaver. | 3.4 | Topper .......... | 3.9 | Cheyenne ........ | 2.9 |
| | — | Westerns ........ | 3.9 | | — |
| Total .......... | 67.2% | | — | Total .......... | 51.6% |
| Total mentions .. | 772 | Total .......... | 90.7% | Total mentions .. | 1,090 |
| | | Total mentions .. | 1,264 | | |

| Grade 4 (N = 263) | | Grade 5 (N = 252) | | Grade 6 (N = 262) | |
|---|---|---|---|---|---|
| Disneyland ........ | 11.1% | Disneyland ........ | 14.5% | Zorro ............. | 17.4% |
| Zorro ............ | 7.7 | Zorro ............ | 12.8 | Disneyland ........ | 16.4 |
| Cartoons ......... | 6.2 | Maverick ........ | 9.6 | Father Knows Best. | 8.2 |
| Popeye .......... | 4.4 | Leave It to Beaver. | 7.4 | Maverick ........ | 5.5 |
| Cheyenne ........ | 3.7 | Father Knows Best. | 4.3 | Topper .......... | 5.5 |
| Lassie ........... | 3.5 | Danny Thomas ... | 4.3 | American Bandstand | 5.5 |
| Rin Tin Tin ...... | 3.2 | American Bandstand | 4.3 | Leave It to Beaver. | 4.1 |
| Leave It to Beaver. | 3.0 | Amos and Andy ... | 3.2 | The Real McCoys.. | 4.1 |
| The Real McCoys.. | 3.0 | The Real McCoys.. | 3.2 | Cheyenne ........ | 4.1 |
| Danny Thomas ... | 2.8 | Fury ............ | 3.2 | Have Gun, Will | |
| Mickey Mouse Club | 2.8 | | — | Travel ......... | 2.7 |
| | — | Total .......... | 66.8% | Science Fiction ... | 2.7 |
| Total .......... | 51.4% | Total mentions .. | 188 | | — |
| Total mentions .. | 1,082 | | | Total .......... | 76.2% |
| | | | | Total mentions .. | 146 |

* The figures are percentages of total number of programs named in each grade. For grades one to four, the question was: "What, so far as you know, are your child's favorite programs? Name as many as five, if you can." For grades 5 and six: "If you had time to see just one television program a week, what program would you most like to see?"

TABLE V-2. FAVORITE PROGRAMS LISTED BY BOYS AND GIRLS OF GRADES
EIGHT, TEN, AND TWELVE (SAN FRANCISCO)*

### Grade 8

| Boys (N = 114) | | Girls (N = 105) | |
|---|---|---|---|
| Maverick | 15.9% | 77 Sunset Strip | 24.0% |
| 77 Sunset Strip | 11.1 | Dick Clark | 14.4 |
| Peter Gunn | 6.3 | Father Knows Best | 7.2 |
| Disneyland | 5.6 | Maverick | 5.6 |
| Father Knows Best | 4.8 | Perry Mason | 4.8 |
| Sea Hunt | 4.8 | The Real McCoys | 4.0 |
| Dick Clark | 3.2 | Danny Thomas | 4.0 |
| Nightmare | 3.2 | Disneyland | 2.4 |
| Steve Allen | 2.4 | Peter Gunn | 2.4 |
| Rifleman | 2.4 | | |
| Science Fiction Theater | 2.4 | Total | 68.8% |
| The Real McCoys | 2.4 | Total mentions | 125 |
| Total | 64.5% | | |
| Total mentions | 126 | | |

### Grade 10

| Boys (N = 85) | | Girls (N = 116) | |
|---|---|---|---|
| Maverick | 16.1% | 77 Sunset Strip | 25.8% |
| 77 Sunset Strip | 13.2 | Dick Clark | 17.9 |
| Peter Gunn | 7.4 | Father Knows Best | 7.9 |
| Sea Hunt | 5.9 | Maverick | 6.7 |
| Dick Clark | 44 | Wagon Train | 3.4 |
| Wagon Train | 2.9 | Movies on TV | 3.4 |
| Rifleman | 2.9 | Gunsmoke | 2.2 |
| Steve Allen | 2.9 | Cheyenne | 2.2 |
| Yancy Derringer | 2.9 | Ozzie and Harriet | 2.2 |
| | | Loretta Young | 2.2 |
| Total | 58.6% | | |
| Total mentions | 68 | Total | 73.9% |
| | | Total mentions | 89 |

### Grade 12

| Boys (N = 123) | | Girls (N = 109) | |
|---|---|---|---|
| Peter Gunn | 17.1% | 77 Sunset Strip | 15.2% |
| Maverick | 10.8 | Peter Gunn | 10.1 |
| 77 Sunset Strip | 8.1 | Maverick | 10.1 |
| Rifleman | 4.5 | Playhouse 90 | 6.1 |
| Science Fiction Theater | 4.5 | Father Knows Best | 5.1 |
| Steve Allen | 3.6 | Loretta Young | 4.0 |
| Dick Clark | 3.6 | Dick Clark | 4.0 |
| Danny Thomas | 2.7 | Steve Allen | 3.0 |
| Gunsmoke | 2.7 | Ozzie and Harriet | 3.0 |
| | | Bob Cummings | 3.0 |
| Total | 57.6% | | |
| Total mentions | 111 | Total | 63.6% |
| | | Total mentions | 99 |

* The question was: "If you had time to see just one television program a week, what program would you most like to see? The figures are percentages of total number of programs mentioned in each grade.

TABLE V-3. CATEGORIES OF FAVORITE PROGRAMS, IN ORDER OF PREFERENCE,
GRADES SIX AND TEN (SAN FRANCISCO, ROCKY MOUNTAIN TOWNS,
TELETOWN, CANADA)

|  | Sixth Grade | | Tenth Grade | |
|---|---|---|---|---|
|  | Boys | Girls | Boys | Girls |
| Rocky 1 | Western | Situation comedy | Western | Situation comedy |
|  | Adventure | Popular music | Adventure | Popular music |
|  | Mystery | Western | Situation comedy | Western |
|  | Situation comedy | Mystery | Variety-comedy | Mystery |
|  | Variety-comedy | Adventure | Mystery | Variety-comedy |
|  |  |  | Popular music |  |
| Rocky 2 | Western | Western | Western | Western |
|  | Adventure | Adventure | Mystery | Popular music |
|  | Variety-comedy | Popular music | Variety-comedy | Situation comedy |
|  | Mystery | Situation comedy | Adventure | Mystery |
|  | Situation comedy | Mystery |  | Variety-comedy |
| Rocky 3 | Western | Western | Western | Popular music |
|  | Adventure | Popular music | Situation comedy | Situation comedy |
|  | Variety-comedy | Situation comedy | Variety-comedy | Western |
|  | Mystery | Mystery | Mystery | Mystery |
|  | Situation comedy | Adventure | Adventure | Variety-comedy |
|  |  |  | Popular music |  |
| Rocky 4 | Western | Mystery | Western | Popular music |
|  | Adventure | Popular music | Adventure | Situation comedy |
|  | Mystery | Adventure | Mystery | Mystery |
|  | Variety-comedy | Western | Variety-comedy | Western |
|  | Situation comedy | Situation comedy | Popular music | Variety-comedy |
|  |  |  | Situation comedy |  |
| Rocky 5 | Western | Western | Western | Western |
|  | Adventure | Situation comedy | Mystery | Situation comedy |
|  | Variety-comedy | Mystery | Adventure | Variety comedy |
|  | Mystery | Adventure | Variety-comedy | Popular music |
|  | Situation comedy | Popular music |  | Mystery |
| San Francisco | Western | Situation comedy | Western | Popular music |
|  | Adventure | Popular music | Mystery | Situation comedy |
|  | Situation comedy | Western | Situation comedy | Mystery |
|  | Variety-comedy | Mystery | Variety-comedy | Western |
|  | Mystery | Adventure | Adventure | Variety-comedy |
|  |  |  | Popular music |  |
| Tele-town | Western | Children's | Western | Situation comedy |
|  | Children's | Situation comedy | Children's | Popular music |
|  | Situation comedy | Western | Situation comedy | Variety |
|  | Mystery |  | Mystery | Western |
|  |  |  | Popular music | Drama |
|  |  |  |  | Children's |

TABLE V-4. CATEGORIES OF FAVORITE PROGRAMS NAMED BY BOYS AND GIRLS
OF GRADES EIGHT, TEN, AND TWELVE (SAN FRANCISCO)*

(*In per cent*)

|  | N | Crime Mystery | Western | Popular Music | Situation Comedy | Other, or No Answer |
|---|---|---|---|---|---|---|
| Eighth grade: | | | | | | |
| Boys ........ | 114 | 29.8 | 24.6 | 4.4 | 11.4 | 29.8 |
| Girls ........ | 105 | 36.2 | 10.5 | 15.2 | 23.8 | 14.3 |
| Tenth grade: | | | | | | |
| Boys ........ | 85 | 28.3 | 27.1 | 5.9 | 8.2 | 31.5 |
| Girls ........ | 116 | 26.8 | 18.1 | 17.3 | 16.4 | 21.4 |
| Twelfth grade: | | | | | | |
| Boys ........ | 123 | 32.5 | 20.4 | 10.6 | 6.5 | 30.0 |
| Girls ........ | 109 | 40.3 | 14.7 | 13.8 | 18.3 | 12.9 |

* "If you had time to see just one program a week, what program would you most like to see?"

TABLE V-5. CHILDREN'S VIEWING OF TYPES OF PROGRAMS*
By Age
(*In per cent*)

|  | 6 and Under | 7–8 | 9–10 | 11–12 | 13–14 | 15–16 |
|---|---|---|---|---|---|---|
| Science fiction .............. | 9 | 17 | 15 | 14 | 11 | 7 |
| "Kid shows" ................ | 14 | 19 | 18 | 11 | 7 | 4 |
| Western .................... | 10 | 18 | 15 | 15 | 8 | 6 |
| Situation comedy ............ | 4 | 15 | 16 | 15 | 15 | 10 |
| Music ...................... | 2 | 7 | 5 | 5 | 6 | 9 |
| Comedy-variety .............. | 5 | 15 | 18 | 15 | 15 | 16 |
| Variety music ............... | 2 | 5 | 5 | 4 | 5 | 4 |
| Drama ..................... | 1 | 7 | 8 | 9 | 11 | 5 |
| Audience participation ........ | 3 | 5 | 8 | 5 | 7 | 5 |
| Daytime ................... | 4 | 5 | 4 | 3 | 4 | 3 |
| Mystery .................... | 1 | 5 | 6 | 6 | 8 | 4 |
| Average of all types ........ | 5 | 11 | 11 | 9 | 9 | 7 |

* Percentages are of children of a given age who viewed an average program of a given kind.
Source: American Research Bureau, 1954.

TABLE V-6. DIVISION OF CHILDREN'S VIEWING BETWEEN ADULT AND CHILDREN'S
PROGRAMS (CLIFTON)
(*In per cent*)

|  | First Grade (N = 98) | Sixth Grade (N = 88) |
|---|---|---|
| Percentage of viewing time devoted to: | | |
| Children's programs ..................... | 60 | 21 |
| Adult programs ......................... | 40 | 79 |
| Percentage of total programs: | | |
| Children's programs ..................... | 52 | 18 |
| Adult programs ......................... | 48 | 82 |

TABLE V-7. FAVORITE PROGRAM TYPES (SAN FRANCISCO, TELETOWN, CANADA, AND ENGLAND)

By Mental Ability and Grade

(*In per cent*)

| Mental Ability and Grade | N | Crime | Western | Popular Music | Situation Comedy |
|---|---|---|---|---|---|
| San Francisco | | | | | |
| Eighth grade: | | | | | |
| High .............. | 43 | 39.5 | 16.3 | 9.2 | 18.6 |
| Middle ............ | 123 | 20.9 | 13.8 | 12.2 | 20.3 |
| Low .............. | 53 | 32.1 | 28.3 | 3.8 | 9.4 |
| Tenth grade: | | | | | |
| High .............. | 32 | 40.6 | 16.2 | 12.5 | 16.0 |
| Middle ............ | 120 | 27.5 | 23.3 | 14.2 | 15.0 |
| Low .............. | 49 | 24.4 | 22.5 | 8.2 | 10.2 |
| Twelfth grade: | | | | | |
| High .............. | 46 | 17.3 | 26.0 | 13.1 | 15.2 |
| Middle ............ | 137 | 32.9 | 19.0 | 11.0 | 11.0 |
| Low .............. | 49 | 30.7 | 16.0 | 14.3 | 12.2 |
| Teletown | | | | | |
| Sixth grade: | | | | | |
| High .............. | 73 | 11.1 | 28.5 | 2.5 | 15.7 |
| Middle ............ | 76 | 3.3 | 27.2 | 4.4 | 17.7 |
| Low .............. | 45 | 1.8 | 33.7 | | 12.4 |
| Tenth grade: | | | | | |
| High .............. | 28 | | 28.8 | 2.7 | 35.1 |
| Middle ............ | 100 | 4.0 | 11.7 | 10.0 | 22.0 |
| Low .............. | 54 | 5.7 | 9.7 | 9.0 | 18.3 |
| England,* 13–14 years (comparable to ninth or tenth grade): | | | | | |
| High .............. | 180 | 28 | 3 | | |
| Middle ............ | 180 | 30 | 6 | | |
| Low .............. | 180 | 31 | 9 | | |

* Himmelweit, Oppenheim, and Vince, *Television and the Child* (London: Oxford, 1958). There may have been some differences between the programs which represented these categories in North America and in England.

TABLE V-8. REACTIONS TO 1958 ELECTION NIGHT COVERAGE (SAN FRANCISCO)*

By Mental Ability and Grade

(*In per cent*)

| Mental Ability and Grade | N | Not Seen | Seen but Not Particularly Liked | Seen and Particularly Liked |
|---|---|---|---|---|
| Eighth grade: | | | | |
| High ................. | 43 | 39.5 | 14.0 | 46.5 |
| Middle ................ | 123 | 67.5 | 4.1 | 28.4 |
| Low ................. | 53 | 79.2 | 1.9 | 18.9 |
| Tenth grade: | | | | |
| High ................. | 32 | 56.2 | 12.5 | 31.2 |
| Middle ................ | 120 | 64.2 | 5.8 | 30.0 |
| Low ................. | 49 | 65.3 | 10.2 | 24.5 |
| Twelfth grade: | | | | |
| High ................. | 46 | 30.4 | 8.7 | 60.9 |
| Middle ................ | 137 | 49.6 | 11.0 | 39.4 |
| Low ................. | 49 | 61.2 | 12.2 | 26.5 |

* Grades combined, $X^2 = 23.86$; with 2 *df*, $p = .001$.

TABLE V-9. FAVORITE PROGRAMS OF ELEMENTARY SCHOOL CHILDREN (SAN FRANCISCO)
By Socioeconomic Status of Family
(*In per cent*)

| | Lower Group (N = 289) | Higher Group (N = 305) |
|---|---|---|
| Western | 25 | 25 |
| Children's | 18 | 24 |
| Situation comedy | 18 | 18 |
| Adventure | 12 | 13 |
| Popular music and variety | 9 | 11 |
| Crime mystery | 9 | 4 |
| TV movies | 2 | 1 |
| Sports | 2 | 0 |
| Other | 5 | 4 |

TABLE V-10. POPULARITY OF TELEVISION PROGRAM TYPES AMONG TEEN-AGERS
By Socioeconomic Status of Family

| | Per Cent Who Watch Very Often, by Income Level | | |
|---|---|---|---|
| | Low | Medium | High |
| Plays | 55 | 54 | 53 |
| Sports | 48 | 40 | 38 |
| Mysteries | 63 | 55 | 49 |
| Family comedy | 62 | 61 | 54 |
| Quiz shows | 33 | 29 | 27 |
| Variety shows | 56 | 56 | 49 |
| Western movies | 39 | 27 | 25 |
| Opera | 8 | 10 | 13 |

Source: H. H. Remmers, R. E. Horton, and R. E. Mainer, *Attitudes of High School Students Towards Certain Aspects of Television* (Lafayette: Purdue Opinion Panel Report 36, 1953).

TABLE V-11. CHILDREN'S CHOICES OF PROGRAM TYPES CONTRASTED TO
PARENTAL CHOICES (SAN FRANCISCO)
(N children = 166)

| | Percentages of Children Viewing | | | Percentages of Children Viewing |
|---|---|---|---|---|
| CRIME PROGRAMS | | | WESTERN PROGRAMS | |
| If mother views: | | | If mother views: | |
| Many | 13 | | Many | 30 |
| Few | 1 | | Few | 22 |
| If father views: | | | If father views: | |
| Many | 15 | | Many | 31 |
| Few | 2 | | Few | 22 |

# TABLES ON WHAT THE CHILD THINKS OF TELEVISION

▶ *These tables are referred to particularly in Chapter 3.*

TABLE VI-1. PERCENTAGE OF CHILDREN WHO WOULD MOST MISS EACH OF THE MASS MEDIA (SAN FRANCISCO, THREE ROCKY MOUNTAIN TOWNS, TELETOWN, CANADA)*
By Grade and Sex

| | *N* | Book | Maga-zine | News-paper | Comic Book | Tele-vision | Radio | Movie |
|---|---|---|---|---|---|---|---|---|
| | | | SIXTH GRADE | | | | | |
| Rocky Mountain towns | | | | | | | | |
| Boys .......... | 191 | 13 | 1 | 9 | 4 | 50 | 10 | 10 |
| Girls .......... | 192 | 21 | 2 | 8 | 2 | 48 | 11 | 7 |
| Teletown | | | | | | | | |
| Boys .......... | 91 | 10 | 1 | 10 | 1 | 62 | 9 | 1 |
| Girls .......... | 103 | 20 | 0 | 9 | 3 | 53 | 12 | 3 |
| | | | EIGHTH GRADE | | | | | |
| San Francisco | | | | | | | | |
| Boys .......... | 114 | 6 | 4 | 5 | 3 | 71 | 4 | 3 |
| Girls .......... | 105 | 7 | 0 | 4 | 2 | 61 | 22 | 4 |
| | | | TENTH GRADE | | | | | |
| San Francisco | | | | | | | | |
| Boys .......... | 85 | 5 | 2 | 11 | 1 | 58 | 16 | 5 |
| Girls .......... | 116 | 6 | 1 | 3 | 1 | 45 | 39 | 3 |
| Rocky Mountain towns | | | | | | | | |
| Boys .......... | 189 | 9 | 4 | 16 | 1 | 38 | 23 | 5 |
| Girls .......... | 209 | 8 | 5 | 12 | 1 | 26 | 43 | 5 |
| Teletown | | | | | | | | |
| Boys .......... | 86 | 8 | 5 | 7 | 0 | 41 | 34 | 2 |
| Girls .......... | 99 | 12 | 6 | 12 | 0 | 22 | 44 | 2 |
| | | | TWELFTH GRADE | | | | | |
| San Francisco | | | | | | | | |
| Boys .......... | 123 | 5 | 2 | 20 | 0 | 32 | 32 | 4 |
| Girls .......... | 109 | 13 | 2 | 11 | 0 | 38 | 33 | 4 |

* "Suppose you had to do without any of the mass media for a long time. Which medium do you think you would miss most?" This question was not asked in the other two Rocky Mountain towns.

TABLE VI-2. PERCENTAGE OF CHILDREN WHO WOULD MOST MISS EACH OF THE
MASS MEDIA (SAN FRANCISCO, THREE ROCKY MOUNTAIN
TOWNS, TELETOWN, CANADA)*
By Mental Ability and Grade

| Mental Ability | N | Book | Maga-zine | News-paper | Comic Book | Tele-vision | Radio | Movies | No Answer |
|---|---|---|---|---|---|---|---|---|---|
| | | | SIXTH GRADE | | | | | | |
| Rocky Mountain towns | | | | | | | | | |
| High ....... | 111 | 29.1 | 1.8 | 7.9 | 2.3 | 44.0 | 8.3 | 5.6 | 0 |
| Middle ..... | 166 | 13.4 | 1.9 | 10.3 | 2.5 | 50.9 | 9.7 | 7.2 | 4.1 |
| Low ........ | 106 | 7.7 | 1.2 | 5.3 | 4.7 | 50.3 | 14.8 | 14.8 | 1.2 |
| Teletown, Canada | | | | | | | | | |
| High ....... | 73 | 15.1 | 0 | 13.7 | 1.4 | 53.4 | 13.7 | 1.4 | 1.4 |
| Middle ..... | 76 | 19.7 | 1.3 | 4.0 | 2.6 | 61.8 | 7.9 | 2.6 | 0 |
| Low ........ | 45 | 8.9 | 0 | 11.1 | 2.2 | 55.6 | 8.9 | 2.2 | 11.1 |
| | | | EIGHTH GRADE | | | | | | |
| San Francisco | | | | | | | | | |
| High ....... | 43 | 16.2 | 2.3 | 14.0 | 2.3 | 48.8 | 16.3 | 0 | 0 |
| Middle ..... | 123 | 4.1 | 0.8 | 3.2 | 0.8 | 68.3 | 14.6 | 4.9 | 4.9 |
| Low ........ | 53 | 3.8 | 5.7 | 0 | 5.7 | 79.2 | 3.8 | 0 | 1.9 |
| | | | TENTH GRADE | | | | | | |
| San Francisco | | | | | | | | | |
| High ....... | 32 | 12.5 | 0 | 6.2 | 0 | 53.1 | 25.0 | 0 | 3.1 |
| Middle ..... | 120 | 5.8 | 1.7 | 5.8 | 0.8 | 51.7 | 32.5 | 2.5 | 1.7 |
| Low ........ | 49 | 0 | 2.0 | 10.2 | 2.0 | 51.0 | 26.5 | 10.2 | 2.0 |
| Rocky Mountain towns | | | | | | | | | |
| High ....... | 86 | 9.8 | 7.4 | 25.8 | 0.6 | 22.7 | 28.2 | 4.3 | 1.2 |
| Middle ..... | 183 | 8.6 | 4.9 | 12.3 | 0.6 | 31.6 | 35.0 | 4.9 | 2.1 |
| Low ........ | 129 | 7.4 | 2.0 | 6.8 | 1.5 | 38.7 | 34.8 | 5.9 | 2.9 |
| Teletown | | | | | | | | | |
| High ....... | 28 | 21.4 | 7.1 | 17.9 | 0 | 17.9 | 28.6 | 7.1 | 0 |
| Middle ..... | 100 | 7.0 | 7.0 | 9.0 | 0 | 32.0 | 43.0 | 0 | 2.0 |
| Low ........ | 54 | 11.1 | 1.9 | 7.4 | 0 | 35.2 | 37.0 | 3.7 | 3.7 |
| | | | TWELFTH GRADE | | | | | | |
| San Francisco | | | | | | | | | |
| High ....... | 46 | 8.7 | 0 | 15.2 | 0 | 41.3 | 26.1 | 8.7 | 0 |
| Middle ..... | 137 | 11.7 | 2.0 | 15.3 | 0 | 34.3 | 34.3 | 2.9 | 2.2 |
| Low ........ | 49 | 4.1 | 2.0 | 18.4 | 0 | 32.6 | 34.6 | 2.0 | 6.3 |

* "Suppose you had to do without any of the mass media for a long time. Which medium do you
think you would miss most?" This question was not asked in the other two Rocky Mountain towns.

TABLE VI-3. PERCENTAGE OF PERSONS CHOOSING ONE MEDIUM ABOVE OTHERS

|  | Television | Radio | Newspaper | Movies | Magazines |
|---|---|---|---|---|---|
| **A. PERSONS IN FAMILY WHO WOULD MOST MISS EACH MEDIUM** * | | | | | |
| All equally ............... | 16 | 7 | 8 | 3 | |
| Children more ............ | 22 | 2 | 1 | 11 | |
| Only the children ......... | 16 | 3 | 0 | 12 | |
| Parents more ............. | 2 | 5 | 22 | 1 | |
| One parent .............. | 20 | 54 | 59 | 11 | |
| One child ................ | 16 | 13 | 1 | 18 | |
| Nobody ................. | 5 | 14 | 6 | 43 | |
| Can't decide ............. | 3 | 3 | 3 | 1 | |
| **B. PERSONS WHO WOULD KEEP ONE MEDIUM ABOVE OTHERS** † | | | | | |
| Fathers ................. | 40 | 12 | 38 | | 10 |
| Mothers ................. | 49 | 11 | 32 | | 8 |
| College-age youth ......... | 38 | 23 | 28 | | 11 |
| High school age ........... | 56 | 30 | 8 | | 6 |
| Younger children ......... | 91 | 2 | 5 | | 2 |

* San Francisco family interviews ($N = 188$ families).
† Results obtained by Dr. Reuben Mehling in 260 interviews in Indiana.

TABLE VI-4. MEMBERS OF FAMILY WHO WOULD MISS TELEVISION MOST,
RELATED TO EDUCATIONAL LEVEL OF FATHER (SAN FRANCISCO)
(*In per cent*)

|  | Father Did Not Finish High School ($N = 61$) | Father Finished High School ($N = 61$) | Father Had Some College or Finished College ($N = 40$) |
|---|---|---|---|
| All equally ................... | 21 | 15 | 10 |
| Children more than parents...... | 23 | 21 | 23 |
| Just children ................. | 13 | 18 | 18 |
| Just parents ................. | 3 | 0 | 0 |
| One parent only .............. | 24 | 23 | 19 |
| One child only ............... | 10 | 21 | 20 |
| None ...................... | 2 | 2 | 10 |
| No answer .................. | 4 | 0 | 4 |

TABLE VI-5. MEDIUM WHICH WOULD BE MOST MISSED BY CHILDREN IN
TOWN WITH TELEVISION AND TOWN WITHOUT TELEVISION
(*In per cent*)

|  | Teletown | Radiotown |
|---|---|---|
| Television | 47.2 | 3.3 |
| Radio | 26.3 | 54.1 |
| Movies | 2.0 | 16.7 |
| Comics | 0.8 | 7.2 |
| Book | 12.8 | 13.4 |
| Newspaper | 10.9 | 5.3 |

TABLE VI-6. MEDIUM WHICH CHILDREN THINK THEY WOULD MISS MOST
(ROCKY MOUNTAIN TOWNS)
By Sex, Grade, and Mental Ability
(*In per cent*)

| Mental Ability and Grade | N | Book | Maga-zine | News-paper | Comic Book | Tele-vision | Radio | Movies |
|---|---|---|---|---|---|---|---|---|
| | | | **BOYS** | | | | | |
| Sixth grade: | | | | | | | | |
| High | 83 | 19 | 0 | 16 | 0 | 44 | 19 | 0 |
| Middle | 130 | 6 | 3 | 3 | 3 | 77 | 3 | 3 |
| Low | 70 | 4 | 0 | 11 | 0 | 64 | 4 | 0 |
| Tenth grade: | | | | | | | | |
| High | 57 | 11 | 11 | 22 | 0 | 33 | 22 | 0 |
| Middle | 117 | 6 | 6 | 4 | 0 | 42 | 38 | 0 |
| Low | 103 | 12 | 0 | 8 | 0 | 42 | 27 | 8 |
| | | | **GIRLS** | | | | | |
| Sixth grade: | | | | | | | | |
| High | 92 | 12 | 0 | 12 | 2 | 61 | 10 | 2 |
| Middle | 141 | 29 | 0 | 4 | 2 | 51 | 11 | 2 |
| Low | 52 | 18 | 0 | 12 | 6 | 41 | 18 | 6 |
| Tenth grade: | | | | | | | | |
| High | 71 | 26 | 5 | 16 | 0 | 10 | 32 | 10 |
| Middle | 168 | 8 | 8 | 14 | 0 | 22 | 48 | 0 |
| Low | 87 | 11 | 4 | 7 | 0 | 29 | 46 | 0 |

TABLE VI-7. COMPARATIVE PRESTIGE OF THE MEDIA (SAN FRANCISCO, THREE ROCKY MOUNTAIN TOWNS, TELETOWN AND RADIOTOWN, CANADA)*

By Grade and Sex

| | N | Book | Maga-zine | News-paper | Comic Book | Tele-vision | Radio | Movies |
|---|---|---|---|---|---|---|---|---|
| | | | SIXTH GRADE | | | | | |
| Rocky Mountain towns | | | | | | | | |
| Boys ....... | 191 | 1.55 | .48 | .85 | .45 | 1.27 | .56 | .38 |
| Girls ....... | 192 | 1.91 | .59 | .95 | .27 | 1.09 | .79 | .28 |
| Teletown | | | | | | | | |
| Boys ....... | 91 | 1.47 | .35 | .78 | .33 | 1.05 | .62 | .47 |
| Girls ....... | 103 | 1.84 | .48 | .78 | .28 | 1.09 | .71 | .55 |
| Radiotown | | | | | | | | |
| Boys ....... | 49 | .82 | .43 | .90 | .74 | .49 | .70 | .96 |
| Girls ....... | 61 | 1.20 | .53 | .90 | .64 | .44 | 1.31 | .74 |
| | | | EIGHTH GRADE | | | | | |
| San Francisco | | | | | | | | |
| Boys ....... | 114 | 1.18 | .72 | .73 | .34 | .98 | .62 | .69 |
| Girls ....... | 105 | 1.05 | .66 | .39 | .19 | 1.19 | 1.45 | .65 |
| | | | TENTH GRADE | | | | | |
| San Francisco | | | | | | | | |
| Boys ....... | 85 | 1.08 | .50 | .50 | .15 | 1.18 | .92 | .55 |
| Girls ....... | 116 | .99 | .60 | .67 | .02 | .96 | 1.53 | .59 |
| Rocky Mountain Towns | | | | | | | | |
| Boys ....... | 189 | 1.44 | .88 | 1.00 | .09 | 1.07 | .89 | .44 |
| Girls ....... | 209 | 1.96 | .70 | .94 | .04 | .83 | 1.13 | .27 |
| Teletown | | | | | | | | |
| Boys ....... | 86 | .87 | .73 | .87 | .04 | 1.03 | 1.13 | .88 |
| Girls ....... | 99 | 1.32 | .69 | .93 | .00 | .65 | 1.35 | .68 |
| Radiotown | | | | | | | | |
| Boys ....... | 70 | 1.40 | .76 | .79 | .17 | .38 | 1.04 | 1.07 |
| Girls ....... | 45 | 1.75 | .40 | 1.31 | .02 | .25 | 1.36 | .55 |
| | | | TWELFTH GRADE | | | | | |
| San Francisco | | | | | | | | |
| Boys ....... | 123 | 1.30 | .64 | .91 | .05 | .80 | .80 | .47 |
| Girls ....... | 109 | 1.68 | .67 | .92 | .03 | .79 | .93 | .38 |

* Index is weighted for number of first, second, and third choices as to amount of prestige of each medium. The higher the figure, the higher the average perceived prestige. Range, 0 to 3.
The other two Rocky Mountain towns were not checked on comparative prestige.

TABLE VI-8. COMPARATIVE PRESTIGE OF THE MEDIA (SAN FRANCISCO, THREE ROCKY MOUNTAIN TOWNS, TELETOWN, CANADA)*

By Grade and Mental Ability

| Mental Ability | N | Book | Maga-zine | News-paper | Comic Book | Tele-vision | Radio | Movies |
|---|---|---|---|---|---|---|---|---|
| | | | SIXTH GRADE | | | | | |
| Rocky Mountain towns | | | | | | | | |
| High ....... | 111 | 2.07 | .84 | 1.07 | .29 | .82 | .57 | .31 |
| Middle ..... | 166 | 1.72 | .61 | 1.03 | .43 | .86 | .80 | .33 |
| Low ....... | 106 | 1.49 | .47 | .76 | .54 | 1.01 | .87 | .54 |
| Teletown | | | | | | | | |
| High ....... | 73 | 1.71 | .40 | .74 | .26 | .97 | .82 | .49 |
| Middle ..... | 76 | 1.71 | .39 | .64 | .45 | .97 | .65 | .59 |
| Low ....... | 45 | 1.20 | .23 | .80 | .40 | 1.47 | .66 | .33 |
| | | | EIGHTH GRADE | | | | | |
| San Francisco | | | | | | | | |
| High ....... | 43 | 2.16 | 1.19 | .71 | .00 | .48 | .83 | .50 |
| Middle ..... | 123 | .94 | .53 | .64 | .37 | 1.30 | 1.17 | .59 |
| Low ....... | 53 | .92 | .83 | .42 | .33 | 1.37 | 1.08 | .98 |
| | | | TENTH GRADE | | | | | |
| San Francisco | | | | | | | | |
| High ....... | 32 | 1.24 | .48 | .69 | .00 | 1.10 | 1.45 | .79 |
| Middle ..... | 120 | 1.12 | .55 | .89 | .10 | 1.12 | 1.12 | .57 |
| Low ....... | 49 | .91 | .71 | .64 | .06 | 1.11 | 1.22 | .60 |
| Rocky Mountain towns | | | | | | | | |
| High ....... | 86 | 2.28 | 1.02 | 1.19 | .03 | .57 | .50 | .21 |
| Middle ..... | 183 | 2.82 | .94 | 1.06 | .36 | .73 | 1.10 | .34 |
| Low ....... | 129 | 1.28 | .49 | .80 | .20 | .83 | 1.31 | .45 |
| Teletown | | | | | | | | |
| High ....... | 28 | 1.57 | .73 | .84 | .00 | .48 | .99 | .67 |
| Middle ..... | 100 | 1.00 | .65 | .83 | .01 | .74 | 1.15 | .64 |
| Low ....... | 54 | .72 | .52 | .86 | .03 | .71 | .96 | .41 |
| | | | TWELFTH GRADE | | | | | |
| San Francisco | | | | | | | | |
| High ....... | 46 | 2.07 | .73 | 1.04 | .00 | .84 | .86 | .39 |
| Middle ..... | 137 | 1.67 | .86 | 1.02 | .04 | .80 | .88 | .47 |
| Low ....... | 49 | 1.10 | .32 | .98 | .10 | 1.17 | 1.32 | .59 |

* Index obtained as in Table VI-7.
The other two Rocky Mountain towns were not checked on comparative prestige.

TABLE VI-9. ACCEPTANCE OF TELEVISION CONTENT (SAN FRANCISCO,
ROCKY MOUNTAIN TOWNS, AND TELETOWN, CANADA
By Grade and Sex
(*In per cent*)

| | | Application of Statement[*] | | | | | |
|---|---|---|---|---|---|---|---|
| | *N* | Applies Fully | Applies Pretty Well | Applies Fairly Well | Doesn't Much Apply | Doesn't Apply at All | No Answer |
| **SIXTH GRADE** | | | | | | | |
| Rocky Mountain towns | | | | | | | |
| Boys ............ | 377 | 16.4 | 17.8 | 25.8 | 18.5 | 18.3 | 3.2 |
| Girls ............ | 351 | 14.1 | 23.9 | 30.1 | 17.7 | 12.7 | 1.5 |
| Teletown | | | | | | | |
| Boys ............ | 91 | 15.4 | 11.0 | 22.0 | 19.8 | 25.3 | 6.6 |
| Girls ............ | 103 | 8.7 | 25.2 | 27.2 | 22.3 | 13.6 | 2.9 |
| **EIGHTH GRADE** | | | | | | | |
| San Francisco | | | | | | | |
| Boys ............ | 114 | 3.5 | 18.4 | 20.2 | 28.1 | 25.4 | 4.4 |
| Girls ............ | 105 | 8.6 | 7.6 | 34.3 | 24.8 | 20.0 | 4.8 |
| **TENTH GRADE** | | | | | | | |
| San Francisco | | | | | | | |
| Boys ............ | 85 | 3.5 | 7.1 | 14.1 | 30.6 | 32.9 | 11.8 |
| Girls ............ | 116 | 2.6 | 18.1 | 31.0 | 20.7 | 25.0 | 2.6 |
| Rocky Mountain towns | | | | | | | |
| Boys ............ | 332 | 2.7 | 14.8 | 24.4 | 25.6 | 23.2 | 9.3 |
| Girls ............ | 364 | 4.1 | 11.1 | 27.9 | 29.8 | 18.8 | 8.3 |
| Teletown | | | | | | | |
| Boys ............ | 86 | 3.5 | 8.1 | 14.0 | 32.6 | 40.7 | 1.2 |
| Girls ............ | 99 | 2.0 | 11.1 | 19.2 | 35.4 | 29.3 | 3.0 |
| **TWELFTH GRADE** | | | | | | | |
| San Francisco | | | | | | | |
| Boys ............ | 123 | 3.3 | 4.1 | 13.8 | 37.4 | 37.4 | 4.1 |
| Girls ............ | 109 | 4.6 | 13.8 | 18.3 | 27.5 | 33.9 | 1.8 |

[*] "I generally like anything I see on television."

TABLE VI-10. ACCEPTANCE OF TELEVISION CONTENT (SAN FRANCISCO,
ROCKY MOUNTAIN TOWNS, AND TELETOWN, CANADA)
By Grade and Mental Ability
(*In per cent*)

| Mental Ability | N | Application of Statement* | | | | | |
| --- | --- | --- | --- | --- | --- | --- | --- |
| | | Applies Fully | Applies Pretty Well | Applies Fairly Well | Doesn't Much Apply | Doesn't at All Apply | No Answer |
| **SIXTH GRADE** | | | | | | | |
| Rocky Mountain towns | | | | | | | |
| High | 216 | 6.9 | 21.3 | 31.9 | 19.0 | 19.4 | 1.4 |
| Middle | 320 | 17.2 | 21.9 | 25.9 | 18.1 | 14.7 | 2.2 |
| Low | 169 | 23.7 | 18.3 | 27.2 | 14.2 | 12.4 | 4.1 |
| Teletown | | | | | | | |
| High | 73 | 5.5 | 20.5 | 32.9 | 20.5 | 20.5 | 0.0 |
| Middle | 76 | 14.5 | 21.0 | 22.4 | 21.0 | 19.7 | 1.3 |
| Low | 45 | 17.8 | 11.1 | 15.6 | 22.2 | 15.6 | 17.8 |
| **EIGHTH GRADE** | | | | | | | |
| San Francisco | | | | | | | |
| High | 43 | 4.6 | 16.3 | 23.3 | 39.5 | 16.3 | 0.0 |
| Middle | 123 | 7.3 | 8.9 | 26.0 | 23.6 | 27.6 | 6.5 |
| Low | 53 | 3.8 | 20.8 | 32.1 | 22.6 | 17.0 | 3.8 |
| **TENTH GRADE** | | | | | | | |
| San Francisco | | | | | | | |
| High | 32 | 0.0 | 18.8 | 37.5 | 21.9 | 21.9 | 0.0 |
| Middle | 120 | 2.5 | 15.0 | 24.2 | 23.3 | 30.8 | 4.2 |
| Low | 49 | 6.1 | 6.1 | 14.3 | 30.6 | 26.5 | 16.3 |
| Rocky Mountain towns | | | | | | | |
| High | 163 | 1.8 | 9.2 | 25.8 | 31.3 | 24.5 | 7.4 |
| Middle | 326 | 3.7 | 11.6 | 25.4 | 29.1 | 20.2 | 9.8 |
| Low | 204 | 4.4 | 17.6 | 27.4 | 23.0 | 19.1 | 8.3 |
| Teletown | | | | | | | |
| High | 28 | 0.0 | 3.6 | 7.1 | 46.4 | 42.8 | 0.0 |
| Middle | 100 | 1.0 | 8.0 | 22.0 | 32.0 | 34.0 | 3.0 |
| Low | 54 | 5.6 | 16.7 | 13.0 | 31.5 | 31.5 | 1.8 |
| **TWELFTH GRADE** | | | | | | | |
| San Francisco | | | | | | | |
| High | 46 | 0.0 | 6.5 | 10.9 | 41.3 | 37.0 | 4.3 |
| Middle | 137 | 4.4 | 8.8 | 16.0 | 31.4 | 36.5 | 2.9 |
| Low | 49 | 6.1 | 10.2 | 20.4 | 28.6 | 32.6 | 2.0 |

* "I generally like anything I see on television."

TABLE VI-11. TRUST IN BROADCAST OR NEWSPAPER NEWS WHEN THEY
ARE CONTRADICTORY (SAN FRANCISCO, ROCKY MOUNTAIN
TOWNS, TELETOWN AND RADIOTOWN, CANADA)*

By Grade and Sex

(*In per cent*)

| | N | Broad-cast | News-paper | Unde-cided |
|---|---|---|---|---|
| **SIXTH GRADE** | | | | |
| Rocky Mountain towns | | | | |
| Boys .................... | 377 | 73.4 | 25.5 | 1.1 |
| Girls .................... | 351 | 76.8 | 22.9 | 0.3 |
| Teletown | | | | |
| Boys .................... | 91 | 59.3 | 39.6 | 1.1 |
| Girls .................... | 103 | 67.0 | 29.1 | 3.9 |
| Radiotown | | | | |
| Boys .................... | 49 | 61.2 | 30.6 | 8.3 |
| Girls .................... | 61 | 73.8 | 23.0 | 3.3 |
| **EIGHTH GRADE** | | | | |
| San Francisco | | | | |
| Boys .................... | 114 | 68.4 | 29.8 | 1.8 |
| Girls .................... | 105 | 76.2 | 19.0 | 4.8 |
| **TENTH GRADE** | | | | |
| San Francisco | | | | |
| Boys .................... | 85 | 54.1 | 41.2 | 4.7 |
| Girls .................... | 116 | 63.8 | 30.2 | 6.0 |
| Rocky Mountain towns | | | | |
| Boys .................... | 332 | 62.4 | 34.3 | 3.3 |
| Girls .................... | 364 | 75.6 | 23.3 | 1.1 |
| Teletown | | | | |
| Boys .................... | 86 | 66.3 | 32.6 | 1.2 |
| Girls .................... | 99 | 73.7 | 23.2 | 3.0 |
| Radiotown | | | | |
| Boys .................... | 70 | 67.1 | 31.4 | 1.4 |
| Girls .................... | 45 | 82.2 | 15.5 | 2.2 |
| **TWELFTH GRADE** | | | | |
| San Francisco | | | | |
| Boys .................... | 123 | 64.2 | 34.1 | 1.6 |
| Girls .................... | 109 | 67.0 | 27.5 | 5.5 |

* "If you heard a news item on television or radio, and read contradictory information in the
newspaper, which one would you be more likely to believe?"
In Radiotown, radio is the only broadcast medium available; elsewhere, both television and
radio.

TABLE VI-12. TRUST OF DIFFERENT MEMBERS OF FAMILY IN BROADCAST OR
NEWSPAPER NEWS WHEN THEY ARE CONTRADICTORY (SAN FRANCISCO
FAMILY INTERVIEWS)

(*In per cent*)

| | N | Broad-cast | News-paper | Neither | Uncer-tain | No Answer |
|---|---|---|---|---|---|---|
| Mother ................. | 188 | 35 | 35 | 11 | 14 | 5 |
| Father ................. | 187 | 29 | 37 | 11 | 4 | 19 |
| Children ............... | 502 | 28 | 15 | 4 | 13 | 38 |

# A CHILD'S USE OF MEDIA OTHER
# THAN TELEVISION

The relationship between use of the other mass media and television was discussed in Chapter 4, "What a Child Uses Television *For*." Information on children's attitudes toward the different media, and certain other details, are in Chapter 3, "How a Child Uses Television." However, our data include considerable information on use of each of the other mass media individually, information which was not pertinent to that chapter, but some of which we want to present in this appendix.

*Radio*

Although radio has found television a formidable competitor, it has nevertheless made a secure place for itself with children as (*a*) a music medium, and (*b*) a secondary medium to be enjoyed while the child is doing something else.

Radio is often the first medium with which the child comes into contact, but his first experiences are usually overhearing the program selections of a parent or sibling—his mother's soap operas or big sister's favorite disc jockey program.

In the early school years, the child listens to the radio, on the average, about an hour a day. This listening to a great extent is accompaniment to other activities: eating, reading, or playing. He does not, typically, give radio his whole attention in this period, as he does to television. Radio really becomes important for the child for the first time as he approaches the teen years, the years when popular music becomes important for him. There is a sharp rise in radio listening during the teens, and there is also a rise in the attention given it. Through the radio, the child maintains chief contact with many of his teen-age idols and keeps up on the current hit tunes. There is also a certain amount of listening to news and sports events on radio, but it is primarily a music medium during these years, and the disc jockey and popular singer are the chief personalities it introduces to children.

Because popular music is somewhat more important, and achieves its importance somewhat earlier, to girls than to boys, girls make more use of radio than do boys throughout all the school years. Girls are more avid music listeners. Boys tend, on the other hand, to hear more news and, of course, more sports than do girls. And there is a small, but loyal minority, chiefly boys, who are interested in radio as hi-fi and, in many of these cases, as a purveyor of serious

APPENDIX VII

music. This minority is especially interesting to us because it ordinarily requires an *active* as opposed to a passive interest; these youngsters learn to wire amplifiers and tuners, and often build this hobby into a lifework in engineering or natural science.

There is no apparent relationship between mental ability and amount of time devoted to radio listening. But high school children with lower IQ's in a number of cases seem to make more use of radio news. (By contrast, children with high IQ's make more use of the newspaper.) The reason for this may be that the more intelligent children prefer the more complete treatment of news in print, or that they prefer to give news their whole attention, rather than absorbing it, as they absorb most radio stimuli, while doing something else.

The teen-ager devotes more time to radio than to any other medium except television. Such an allocation of time would be impossible if radio use were not mostly simultaneous with other activities. Practically every child says that he habitually does something else while listening to the radio. This habit of using radio as a simultaneous medium grows stronger with age, and girls are more likely to engage in it than boys. The side activities are usually studying and reading. The high school student typically studies with a background of radio music, as one of these children told us, listening to the music with "half an ear." This division of attention—the eyes for studying, the ear (or half an ear) for entertainment—needs to be studied as a learning process.

Over half the teen-agers say they select a station and leave the receiver tuned there for hours, while the parade of disc jockeys and hit tunes continues. The proportion of girls tuning their sets this way is significantly larger than that of boys.

The general picture of radio use is one of a much greater passivity even than television viewing. Children turn on the receiver, open the textbooks, and let the disc jockey choose their background entertainment.

## Movies

Like radio, the movies were hard hit by the advent of television. But whereas radio has apparently rallied and found a solid place for itself as a purveyor of popular music and as a background for studying and reading, the movies have seemingly not found a new place for themselves.

This last statement needs qualification. There are so many movies now on television that children may well be seeing more movies now than they saw before television. But they are seeing fewer in the theater. Elementary school children in San Francisco now average little more than one movie a month in a theater. In the teen years, movie-going increases slowly until in the twelfth grade students are seeing, on the average, a little over two a month in San Francisco. The increase of movie-going in the teens is significantly larger for children of lower mental ability.

In addition to the rising frequency of movie theater attendance in the teens, the social use of movie-going changes as the child enters adolescence. Attendance *with parents* falls to 12 per cent in the eighth grade and 5 per cent in the tenth. On the other hand, the frequency of going to the movies *alone* also decreases from the eighth grade on. This is especially true in the case of boys, who have through the elementary years gone alone to movies much oftener than girls. Now the percentage of boys who go more often alone to movies declines almost to zero. Furthermore, tastes in films change around ages eleven to thirteen. As the animated cartoons were succeeded in favor by the Westerns, so now these are elbowed out of top position by the love pictures, and the horsy heroes are succeeded by the romantic lovers. This change happens more quickly with girls than with boys, as would be expected, inasmuch as girls are usually ahead of boys in the maturation process.

These changes may point to the niche that theater movies are carving for themselves against the hard competition of television. Movies are better *social* experience than is television. They provide a reason to go out socially, to meet one's peers, and to date. This is why the frequency of "going alone" or going with parents to the movies falls off so sharply in the teen years.

It is an open question whether television movies are contributing to the prestige of films. Children undoubtedly watch many of these pictures, but when they talk about them, they often mention that the pictures are out of date in costumes, customs, or language, that they are cut, or that they are full of commercials at awkward places. It would be interesting to know whether these free movies on television are doing harm to the prestige of movies because they are presented in an unfavorable manner and because they take away some of the excuse for going to movie theaters, or whether they are raising the prestige of the movies because they underline the superiority of the big theater screen to the tiny picture tube of the television set.

Whatever the true impact of televised motion pictures, it is clear that movies are no longer such a shining symbol for children as they once were.

*Books*

Books are the first mass medium with which most children become well acquainted. This is through the stories their parents read to them from books, and from the children's picture books which are now available even in the supermarket and drugstore. Story reading remains important to children until some time after they themselves learn to read. Then the child gradually substitutes the relatively easy books which he can read himself for the more difficult ones which must be read to him.

The amount of book reading increases from the first grade through the sixth. The average is between one and two books per month, not counting school texts. Supposedly, in-school reading is considerable, and in summer time it is assumed that out-of-school reading increases.

After the sixth grade, book reading during school months decreases. By the twelfth grade, the average is less than one book per month. Homework is more demanding, books are thicker.

For the first few years, boys seem to read more than girls. But beginning with the fifth or sixth grade, girls increase their book reading, and thereafter their average is higher than that of the boys.

Book reading goes by families. Families where the mother or father or both read heavily invariably have heavy readers among the children. Parents' education correlates strongly with book reading by children, and so does social class or status.

Children's intelligence also makes a difference. Brighter children read more books, and there is a small group constituting about 6 per cent of the brighter children, who from the eighth grade on read nine or more books a month. This subgroup helps to make up for some 30 per cent of the entire sample who said they had read *no* book outside of school in the past month.

What do they read? A bewildering number and diversity of books. Stories, of course, are what they chiefly select. Up to the sixth grade, books about everyday life, science, distant places and people, and other nonstory topics fill less than 15 per cent of their reading time. Biography and history begin to appear in the lists of titles by the third grade, and by the fifth or sixth grade, a few titles suggesting a hobby or vocational interest are found. In the high school years, one sees three patterns in addition to the apparently unpatterned diversity. One group, chiefly boys, is reading hobby books—automobiles, radio, mountain climbing, flying, and so on. Still another group, more girls than boys, is reading light romance—probably to the accompaniment of their disc jockeys on the radio. A third, very small group is reading in a voracious manner—taking half a dozen volumes from the library at a time, gulping down Dickens, Thomas Wolfe, Scott, and many others.

In children's lists of books read are many well-known titles that have given pleasure to earlier generations. In the fifth and sixth grades, for example, the most mentioned were almost entirely old favorites: *Black Beauty, Little Women, Wizard of Oz, Heidi, Huckleberry Finn, Tom Sawyer,* and *Treasure Island.* But even these great old favorites attracted only a tiny percentage of the votes for the book "most enjoyed during the past year." The significant feature of the data on book titles was the spread, rather than the concentration.

If one can guess at television's effect on book reading, one can point to the 40 per cent of the San Francisco teen-age sample who seem to read no books outside school during the school months. But in Teletown only 20 per cent of the tenth-grade children reported reading no books; in Radiotown 15 per cent reported reading no books. This, at least, can be said: the children's incidental remarks when we talked to them about books, the prestige ratings described in Chapter 3, and their willingness to recall titles and to name favorites, all suggest that children feel little, if any, less respect for books than did the children of an earlier generation.

*Magazines*

In the first year of school, less than half the children have any regular contact with magazines. Their acquaintance with magazines broadens as their reading skill increases. By the age of twelve, more than three-quarters of the children make some use of magazines, and by the time they are in the eighth grade, they are sampling at least three or four magazines a month, on the average. Throughout high school, the magazine audience grows larger (84 per cent in the eighth grade, 87 in the tenth, 92 in the twelfth), but they read, on the average, slightly fewer magazines each.

Brighter children tend to be somewhat heavier magazine readers than others.

We have found no significant relationships between parents' education and children's magazine reading, but have found a relationship between occupation and magazine reading. Magazine reading apparently increases with income.

Children typically begin their magazine reading with children's and picture magazines. They leaf through the picture journals before they read anything. In the early school years, a third of a child's magazine reading is likely to be in the children's magazines, a third in picture magazines, and the other third widely spread. As they grow older and learn their sex roles, boys tend to read more hobby, sports, and news magazines. Girls read more screen and confession magazines. A little later, when they become devotees of *Glamour, Mademoiselle,* and similar publications, they tend to read less in the pulps. Both sexes read a solid core of picture, general, news, and quality magazines.

Our results indicate that girls are somewhat more likely to select a particular story or article from a magazine than are boys, who are more likely to pick up a magazine and "just read."

## Comic books

Reading of comic books begins, typically, at a very early age. The child looks at the pictures in a comic book brought in by an older brother or sister. Often his parents read the comic strips in the newspaper to him. When he himself becomes old enough to read, the comics are the first newspaper content he selects. The purchase and reading of comic books is something he often learns as role behavior of older siblings or companions. If the child is typical, his comic reading increases until about the eighth grade, when it declines swiftly. The median number of comic books read each month by eighth-grade boys is about 4.5. By the twelfth grade, the figure has fallen to less than one a month.

There are large blocks of children in the early grades who read nine or more comic books monthly, but there are also sizable blocks of children who read no comic books.

Who are the heavy comic readers? Boys generally read more comic books than girls. Mental ability has little influence in the first six grades, but after that children of lower mental ability remain heavy comic readers, while higher-intelligence children read fewer comic books and finally cease reading them entirely. Heavy readers are more likely to be found in homes where parents have had only a high school education or less, and in lower-class rather than middle-class families. After the fifth or sixth grade, the heavy readers also tend to be heavy viewers of television and frequent movie-goers. Girls who read comics are more likely to read confession and screen magazines. In short, comic book reading falls into the patterns of media use discussed in Chapter 6.

## Newspapers

The newspaper is usually the last of the mass media to which the child is introduced. It is not until the age of seven that any substantial number of children read the newspaper, even a few times a month. A few children have the comic strips read to them as early as the age of four, and this is the usual method of introduction to this medium.

When children start to read the newspaper for themselves, the comics are usually their first content choice. Comic reading comes to its peak about the fourth grade, and rides on a gently falling plateau throughout the rest of the school years. The first signs of rounded readership of the newspaper are seen about the eighth grade. Before that, both boys and girls read the comics, boys read some sports, girls read some columns, and they sample the rest of the newspaper lightly.

The newspaper gets no great amount of *daily* use until about the seventh or eighth grade. At that stage, more girls than boys read the paper at least several times a week—the girls are ahead of boys in maturation. But an impressive increase in the proportion of boys regularly reading the newspaper has taken place by the tenth grade. About 90 per cent of boys in that grade say they read the paper regularly, compared with only 81 per cent of the girls. By the twelfth grade, there is little difference between the boys and girls.

Intellectual ability correlates positively with newspaper reading. Not only are the brighter students more likely to read the paper; they are also likely to begin earlier. There are also differences in content selection related to intelligence.

Indeed, just as it is possible (as described in Chapter 6) to establish typologies of media users, so it is possible to establish typologies of newspaper users. Some children apparently use the newspaper chiefly for entertainment, some strictly as a news source, and some (the majority) for both news and entertainment. The proportion of strictly entertainment users declines with age. Where a child fits into these typologies is highly correlated to which media-use typology he fits: entertainment users of the newspaper are generally fantasy users of the mass media at large; news users of the newspaper are generally reality users of the mass media. Low intelligence and low socioeconomic family background are both related to entertainment use of the newspaper. And the child who is in a state of conflict with his parents also is more likely than those without conflict to use the newspaper chiefly for entertainment.

TABLE VII-1. PERCENTAGE OF CHILDREN MAKING "FAIRLY REGULAR" USE OF MEDIA, IN GRADES ONE TO FOUR (SAN FRANCISCO)

| | N | TV | Radio | Movies | Comics | Maga-zines | Books | News-papers |
|---|---|---|---|---|---|---|---|---|
| First grade ........... | 210 | 95 | 45 | 41 | 47 | 21 | 66 | 47 |
| Second grade ......... | 317 | 96 | 53 | 60 | 55 | 29 | 74 | 62 |
| Third grade .......... | 240 | 93 | 62 | 77 | 76 | 42 | 70 | 93 |
| Fourth grade ......... | 263 | 97 | 63 | 83 | 60 | 39 | 71 | 97 |

TABLE VII-2. PERCENTAGE OF CHILDREN USING MEDIA ON ANY GIVEN DAY, IN GRADES FIVE AND SIX (SAN FRANCISCO)

| | N | TV | Radio | Movies | Comics | Maga-zines | Books | News-papers |
|---|---|---|---|---|---|---|---|---|
| Fifth grade ........... | 252 | 74 | 25 | 3 | 5 | 5 | 23 | 19 |
| Sixth grade ........... | 262 | 74 | 32 | 3 | 8 | 6 | 17 | 22 |

TABLE VII-3. MEDIAN HOURS SPENT BY CHILDREN LISTENING TO RADIO ON AVERAGE
SCHOOL DAY (SAN FRANCISCO, ROCKY MOUNTAIN TOWNS,
RADIOTOWN AND TELETOWN, CANADA)

By Grade and Sex

| | N | Second Grade | N | Fourth Grade | N | Sixth Grade | N | Eighth Grade | N | Tenth Grade | N | Twelfth Grade |
|---|---|---|---|---|---|---|---|---|---|---|---|---|
| **San Francisco** | | | | | | | | | | | | |
| Boys ....... | 159 | 0.9 | 137 | 1.0 | 142 | 1.0 | 114 | 0.9 | 85 | 1.8 | 123 | 1.8 |
| Girls ....... | 158 | 1.3 | 126 | 1.2 | 120 | 1.5 | 105 | 1.8 | 116 | 2.3 | 109 | 2.0 |
| **Rocky Mountain towns** | | | | | | | | | | | | |
| Boys ....... | | | | | 377 | 0.8 | | | 332 | 1.2 | | |
| Girls ....... | | | | | 351 | 1.0 | | | 364 | 2.0 | | |
| **Teletown** | | | | | | | | | | | | |
| Boys ....... | | | | | 91 | 0.8 | | | 86 | 1.2 | | |
| Girls ....... | | | | | 103 | 1.1 | | | 99 | 2.2 | | |
| **Radiotown** | | | | | | | | | | | | |
| Boys ....... | | | | | 49 | 3.0 | | | 70 | 2.8 | | |
| Girls ....... | | | | | 61 | 4.2 | | | 45 | 4.1 | | |

TABLE VII-4. MEDIAN HOURS SPENT BY CHILDREN LISTENING TO RADIO ON AVERAGE
SCHOOL DAY (SAN FRANCISCO, ROCKY MOUNTAIN TOWNS, TELETOWN, CANADA)

By Mental Ability and Grade

| Mental Ability | N | Sixth Grade | N | Eighth Grade | N | Tenth Grade | N | Twelfth Grade |
|---|---|---|---|---|---|---|---|---|
| **San Francisco** | | | | | | | | |
| High ....... | | | 43 | 1.3 | 32 | 1.9 | 46 | 1.8 |
| Middle ...... | | | 123 | 1.2 | 120 | 1.9 | 137 | 1.9 |
| Low ........ | | | 53 | 1.2 | 49 | 1.9 | 49 | 2.1 |
| **Rocky Mountain towns** | | | | | | | | |
| High ....... | 216 | 1.5 | | | 163 | 1.5 | | |
| Middle ...... | 320 | 0.9 | | | 326 | 1.5 | | |
| Low ........ | 169 | 0.7 | | | 204 | 1.9 | | |
| **Teletown** | | | | | | | | |
| High ....... | 73 | 0.9 | | | 28 | 1.9 | | |
| Middle ...... | 76 | 1.1 | | | 100 | 1.9 | | |
| Low ........ | 45 | 1.4 | | | 54 | 1.7 | | |

TABLE VII-5. PERCENTAGE OF CHILDREN LISTENING TO VARIOUS TYPES OF
RADIO PROGRAMS, BY GRADE AND SEX (SAN FRANCISCO)

| | N | Popular Music | News | Classical Music |
|---|---|---|---|---|
| **Eighth grade:** | | | | |
| Boys ............. | 114 | 70.2 | 28.0 | 5.2 |
| Girls ............. | 105 | 84.8 | 17.1 | 5.8 |
| **Tenth grade:** | | | | |
| Boys ............. | 85 | 81.1 | 20.2 | 9.4 |
| Girls ............. | 116 | 91.4 | 17.2 | 2.9 |
| **Twelfth grade:** | | | | |
| Boys ............. | 123 | 81.3 | 21.9 | 6.6 |
| Girls ............. | 109 | 84.4 | 16.5 | 9.2 |

TABLE VII-6. PERCENTAGE OF CHILDREN LISTENING TO RADIO NEWS (SAN FRANCISCO,
ROCKY MOUNTAIN TOWNS, TELETOWN AND RADIOTOWN, CANADA)
By Mental Ability and Grade

| Mental Ability | N | Sixth Grade | N | Eighth Grade | N | Tenth Grade | N | Twelfth Grade |
|---|---|---|---|---|---|---|---|---|
| **San Francisco** | | | | | | | | |
| High ....... | | | 43 | 18.6 | 32 | 15.6 | 46 | 19.6 |
| Middle ...... | | | 123 | 19.5 | 120 | 17.0 | 137 | 17.2 |
| Low ........ | | | 53 | 34.0 | 49 | 24.5 | 49 | 26.5 |
| **Rocky Mountain towns** | | | | | | | | |
| High ....... | 216 | 20.5 | | | 163 | 31.3 | | |
| Middle ...... | 320 | 19.1 | | | 326 | 21.2 | | |
| Low ........ | 169 | 14.8 | | | 204 | 20.1 | | |
| **Teletown** | | | | | | | | |
| High ....... | 73 | 29.6 | | | 28 | 25.0 | | |
| Middle ...... | 76 | 32.4 | | | 100 | 25.3 | | |
| Low ........ | 45 | 46.3 | | | 54 | 15.1 | | |
| **Radiotown** | | | | | | | | |
| High ....... | 14 | 38.5 | | | 39 | 46.2 | | |
| Middle ...... | 57 | 23.2 | | | 38 | 27.0 | | |
| Low ........ | 38 | 37.8 | | | 38 | 39.5 | | |

TABLE VII-7. PERCENTAGE OF CHILDREN WHO DO SOMETHING ELSE WHILE LISTENING
TO THE RADIO (SAN FRANCISCO, ROCKY MOUNTAIN TOWNS,
TELETOWN AND RADIOTOWN, CANADA)
By Grade and Sex

| | N | Often | Occa-sionally | Never | Not As-certained |
|---|---|---|---|---|---|
| | | SIXTH GRADE | | | |
| Rocky Mountain towns | | | | | |
| Boys ............ | 377 | 48.7 | 31.2 | 13.2 | 6.9 |
| Girls ............ | 351 | 56.4 | 31.9 | 7.7 | 4.0 |
| Teletown | | | | | |
| Boys ............ | 91 | 50.5 | 36.3 | 9.9 | 3.3 |
| Girls ............ | 103 | 59.2 | 33.0 | 3.9 | 3.9 |
| Radiotown | | | | | |
| Boys ............ | 49 | 44.9 | 36.7 | 14.3 | 4.1 |
| Girls ............ | 61 | 47.5 | 42.6 | 6.6 | 3.3 |
| | | EIGHTH GRADE | | | |
| San Francisco | | | | | |
| Boys ............ | 114 | 55.3 | 29.8 | 10.5 | 4.4 |
| Girls ............ | 105 | 74.3 | 21.0 | 1.9 | 2.9 |
| | | TENTH GRADE | | | |
| San Francisco | | | | | |
| Boys ............ | 85 | 58.8 | 35.3 | 3.5 | 2.4 |
| Girls ............ | 116 | 74.1 | 20.7 | 1.7 | 3.4 |
| Rocky Mountain towns | | | | | |
| Boys ............ | 332 | 63.3 | 28.9 | 5.7 | 2.1 |
| Girls ............ | 364 | 82.7 | 15.7 | 1.4 | 0.2 |
| Teletown | | | | | |
| Boys ............ | 86 | 58.1 | 33.7 | 5.8 | 2.3 |
| Girls ............ | 99 | 76.8 | 22.2 | | 1.0 |
| Radiotown | | | | | |
| Boys ............ | 70 | 55.7 | 38.6 | 5.7 | |
| Girls ............ | 45 | 66.7 | 31.1 | 2.2 | |
| | | TWELFTH GRADE | | | |
| San Francisco | | | | | |
| Boys ............ | 123 | 69.1 | 26.8 | 2.4 | 1.6 |
| Girls ............ | 109 | 73.4 | 21.1 | 0.9 | 4.6 |

TABLE VII-8. AMOUNT OF UNSELECTIVE RADIO LISTENING (SAN FRANCISCO)
By Grade and Sex

| | N | Application of Question[*] | | | | | |
|---|---|---|---|---|---|---|---|
| | | Applies Fully | Applies Pretty Much | Applies Fairly Well | Doesn't Apply Much | Doesn't Apply at All | No Answer |
| Eighth grade: | | | | | | | |
| Boys ........... | 114 | 30.7 | 20.2 | 15.8 | 12.3 | 17.5 | 3.5 |
| Girls ........... | 105 | 47.6 | 15.2 | 14.3 | 5.7 | 9.5 | 7.6 |
| Tenth grade: | | | | | | | |
| Boys ........... | 85 | 28.2 | 22.3 | 11.8 | 14.1 | 11.8 | 11.8 |
| Girls ........... | 116 | 45.7 | 14.7 | 12.1 | 15.5 | 8.6 | 3.4 |
| Twelfth grade: | | | | | | | |
| Boys ........... | 123 | 34.9 | 18.7 | 13.0 | 13.0 | 17.1 | 3.3 |
| Girls ........... | 109 | 39.4 | 27.5 | 11.9 | 11.9 | 7.3 | 1.8 |

[*] "Do you select a radio station and just leave the dial there for hours?"

TABLE VII-9. MEDIAN NUMBER OF MOVIES ATTENDED IN LAST MONTH (SAN FRANCISCO,
ROCKY MOUNTAIN TOWNS, TELETOWN AND RADIOTOWN, CANADA)
By Grade and Sex

| | N | San Francisco | N | Rocky Mountain Towns | N | Tele-town[*] | N | Radio-town |
|---|---|---|---|---|---|---|---|---|
| Sixth grade: | | | | | | | | |
| Boys ....... | | | 377 | 2.2 | 91 | 0.5 | 49 | 4.2 |
| Girls ....... | | | 351 | 2.2 | 103 | 0.4 | 61 | 4.4 |
| Eighth grade: | | | | | | | | |
| Boys ....... | 114 | 1.8 | | | | | | |
| Girls ....... | 105 | 1.7 | | | | | | |
| Tenth grade: | | | | | | | | |
| Boys ....... | 85 | 1.4 | 332 | 2.0 | 86 | 0.5 | 70 | 3.8 |
| Girls ....... | 116 | 1.4 | 364 | 2.4 | 99 | 1.2 | 45 | 4.1 |
| Twelfth grade: | | | | | | | | |
| Boys ....... | 123 | 1.2 | | | | | | |
| Girls ....... | 109 | 1.2 | | | | | | |

[*] There are no movie theaters in Teletown.

TABLE VII-10. MEDIAN NUMBER OF MOVIES ATTENDED IN LAST MONTH (SAN
FRANCISCO, ROCKY MOUNTAIN TOWNS, TELETOWN AND
RADIOTOWN, CANADA)

By Mental Ability and Grade

| Mental Ability | N | Sixth Grade | N | Eighth Grade | N | Tenth Grade | N | Twelfth Grade |
|---|---|---|---|---|---|---|---|---|
| San Francisco | | | | | | | | |
| High ....... | | | 43 | 1.6 | 32 | 1.6 | 46 | 2.2 |
| Middle ...... | | | 123 | 2.0 | 120 | 2.2 | 137 | 2.0 |
| Low ........ | | | 53 | 2.1 | 49 | 2.3 | 49 | 2.1 |
| Rocky Mountain towns | | | | | | | | |
| High ....... | 216 | 2.0 | | | 163 | 1.9 | | |
| Middle ...... | 320 | 2.1 | | | 326 | 2.2 | | |
| Low ........ | 169 | 2.5 | | | 204 | 2.4 | | |
| Teletown | | | | | | | | |
| High ....... | 73 | 0.4 | | | 28 | 0.5 | | |
| Middle ...... | 76 | 0.5 | | | 100 | 0.8 | | |
| Low ........ | 45 | 0.4 | | | 54 | 1.1 | | |
| Radiotown | | | | | | | | |
| High ....... | 14 | 3.5 | | | 39 | 3.9 | | |
| Middle ...... | 57 | 4.7 | | | 38 | 4.2 | | |
| Low ........ | 38 | 4.1 | | | 38 | 3.8 | | |

TABLE VII-11. ATTENDANCE AT MOVIES ALONE OR WITH OTHERS (SAN FRANCISCO, ROCKY MOUNTAIN TOWNS, TELETOWN\* AND RADIOTOWN, CANADA)

By Grade and Sex

| | N | Alone | With Someone | No Answer |
|---|---|---|---|---|
| **SIXTH GRADE** | | | | |
| Rocky Mountain towns | | | | |
| Boys ........... | 377 | 7.5% | 91.2% | 1.3% |
| Girls ........... | 351 | 5.9 | 90.1 | 5.0 |
| Teletown | | | | |
| Boys ........... | 91 | 5.5 | 79.1 | 15.4 |
| Girls ........... | 103 | 1.9 | 84.5 | 13.6 |
| Radiotown | | | | |
| Boys ........... | 49 | 18.4 | 79.6 | 2.0 |
| Girls ........... | 61 | 3.3 | 96.7 | 0 |
| **EIGHTH GRADE** | | | | |
| San Francisco | | | | |
| Boys ........... | 114 | 14.0 | 84.2 | 1.8 |
| Girls ........... | 105 | 1.9 | 95.2 | 2.9 |
| **TENTH GRADE** | | | | |
| San Francisco | | | | |
| Boys ........... | 85 | 7.1 | 91.7 | 1.2 |
| Girls ........... | 116 | 1.7 | 95.7 | 2.6 |
| Rocky Mountain towns | | | | |
| Boys ........... | 332 | 10.6 | 86.3 | 3.1 |
| Girls ........... | 364 | 2.7 | 93.4 | 3.9 |
| Teletown | | | | |
| Boys ........... | 86 | 0 | 87.2 | 12.8 |
| Girls ........... | 99 | 1.0 | 87.9 | 11.1 |
| Radiotown | | | | |
| Boys ........... | 70 | 10.0 | 82.9 | 7.1 |
| Girls ........... | 45 | 2.2 | 97.8 | 0 |
| **TWELFTH GRADE** | | | | |
| San Francisco | | | | |
| Boys ........... | 123 | 8.1 | 89.4 | 2.4 |
| Girls ........... | 109 | 0.9 | 96.3 | 2.8 |

\* There are no movie theaters in Teletown.

TABLE VII-12. ATTENDANCE AT MOVIES WITH OTHERS (SAN FRANCISCO, ROCKY MOUNTAIN TOWNS, TELETOWN* AND RADIOTOWN, CANADA)
By Grade and Sex

| | N | With Parents | With Someone of Own Age | Not Ascertained |
|---|---|---|---|---|
| | | SIXTH GRADE | | |
| Rocky Mountain towns | | | | |
| Boys .......... | 377 | 13.4% | 82.2% | 4.4% |
| Girls .......... | 351 | 17.9 | 77.1 | 5.0 |
| Teletown | | | | |
| Boys .......... | 91 | 41.8 | 45.1 | 13.2 |
| Girls .......... | 103 | 47.6 | 40.8 | 11.7 |
| Radiotown | | | | |
| Boys .......... | 49 | 10.2 | 87.8 | 2.0 |
| Girls .......... | 61 | 18.0 | 80.3 | 1.6 |
| | | EIGHTH GRADE | | |
| San Francisco | | | | |
| Boys .......... | 114 | 12.3 | 84.2 | 3.5 |
| Girls .......... | 105 | 12.4 | 83.8 | 3.8 |
| | | TENTH GRADE | | |
| San Francisco | | | | |
| Boys .......... | 85 | 4.7 | 89.4 | 5.9 |
| Girls .......... | 116 | 8.6 | 87.1 | 4.3 |
| Rocky Mountain towns | | | | |
| Boys .......... | 332 | 5.4 | 91.6 | 3.0 |
| Girls .......... | 364 | 4.4 | 90.6 | 5.0 |
| Teletown | | | | |
| Boys .......... | 86 | 8.1 | 79.1 | 12.8 |
| Girls .......... | 99 | 9.1 | 78.8 | 12.1 |
| Radiotown | | | | |
| Boys .......... | 70 | 11.4 | 84.3 | 4.3 |
| Girls .......... | 45 | 2.2 | 97.8 | 0.0 |
| | | TWELFTH GRADE | | |
| San Francisco | | | | |
| Boys .......... | 123 | 4.6 | 92.7 | 2.4 |
| Girls .......... | 109 | 7.3 | 89.9 | 2.8 |

* There are no movie theaters in Teletown.

TABLE VII-13. UNSELECTIVE CHOICE OF MOVIES (SAN FRANCISCO, ROCKY MOUNTAIN
TOWNS, TELETOWN AND RADIOTOWN, CANADA)
By Mental Ability and Grade

| Mental Ability | N | Application of Statement* | | |
|---|---|---|---|---|
| | | Doesn't Apply or Doesn't Much Apply | Applies at Least Fairly Well | No Answer |
| **SIXTH GRADE** | | | | |
| Rocky Mt. towns | | | | |
| High .......... | 216 | 68.8% | 29.8% | 1.4% |
| Middle ......... | 320 | 56.0 | 41.2 | 2.8 |
| Low .......... | 169 | 36.1 | 60.3 | 3.6 |
| Teletown | | | | |
| High .......... | 73 | 65.8 | 30.1 | 4.1 |
| Middle ......... | 76 | 57.9 | 34.2 | 7.9 |
| Low .......... | 45 | 37.8 | 48.9 | 13.3 |
| Radiotown | | | | |
| High .......... | 14 | 57.1 | 42.9 | |
| Middle ......... | 57 | 59.6 | 38.6 | 1.8 |
| Low .......... | 38 | 42.1 | 50.0 | 7.9 |
| **EIGHTH GRADE** | | | | |
| San Francisco | | | | |
| High .......... | 43 | 59.8 | 37.9 | 2.3 |
| Middle ......... | 123 | 55.3 | 34.9 | 9.8 |
| Low .......... | 53 | 56.6 | 34.9 | 7.5 |
| **TENTH GRADE** | | | | |
| San Francisco | | | | |
| High .......... | 32 | 78.2 | 21.8 | |
| Middle ......... | 120 | 64.2 | 31.8 | 5.0 |
| Low .......... | 49 | 28.6 | 53.6 | 18.4 |
| Rocky Mt. towns | | | | |
| High .......... | 163 | 55.2 | 37.4 | 7.4 |
| Middle ......... | 326 | 58.9 | 30.4 | 10.7 |
| Low .......... | 204 | 54.9 | 37.8 | 7.3 |
| Teletown | | | | |
| High .......... | 28 | 67.9 | 32.1 | |
| Middle ......... | 100 | 67.0 | 31.0 | 2.0 |
| Low .......... | 54 | 55.6 | 40.7 | 3.7 |
| Radiotown | | | | |
| High .......... | 39 | 79.5 | 15.4 | 5.1 |
| Middle ......... | 38 | 68.4 | 28.9 | 2.6 |
| Low .......... | 38 | 57.9 | 39.5 | 2.6 |
| **TWELFTH GRADE** | | | | |
| San Francisco | | | | |
| High .......... | 46 | 67.4 | 30.4 | 2.2 |
| Middle ......... | 137 | 52.6 | 45.7 | 3.7 |
| Low .......... | 49 | 40.8 | 57.2 | 2.0 |

* "Most movies appeal to me."

TABLE VII-14. MEDIAN NUMBER OF BOOKS READ MONTHLY DURING SCHOOL TERM
OUTSIDE SCHOOL (SAN FRANCISCO, ROCKY MOUNTAIN TOWNS,
TELETOWN AND RADIOTOWN, CANADA)
By Grade and Sex

| | N | Second Grade | N | Fourth Grade | N | Sixth Grade | N | Eighth Grade | N | Tenth Grade | N | Twelfth Grade |
|---|---|---|---|---|---|---|---|---|---|---|---|---|
| **San Francisco** | | | | | | | | | | | | |
| Boys ....... | 159 | 1.2 | 137 | 1.9 | 142 | 1.7 | 114 | 1.4 | 85 | 0.8 | 123 | 0.8 |
| Girls ....... | 158 | 1.0 | 126 | 1.6 | 120 | 2.5 | 105 | 1.7 | 116 | 1.1 | 109 | 0.9 |
| **Rocky Mountain towns** | | | | | | | | | | | | |
| Boys ....... | | | | | 377 | 2.3 | | | 332 | 1.7 | | |
| Girls ....... | | | | | 351 | 3.5 | | | 364 | 2.2 | | |
| **Teletown** | | | | | | | | | | | | |
| Boys ....... | | | | | 91 | 1.9 | | | 86 | 1.1 | | |
| Girls ....... | | | | | 103 | 3.0 | | | 99 | 2.7 | | |
| **Radiotown** | | | | | | | | | | | | |
| Boys ....... | | | | | 49 | 1.1 | | | 70 | 2.3 | | |
| Girls ....... | | | | | 61 | 2.5 | | | 45 | 3.3 | | |

TABLE VII-15. PERCENTAGE OF CHILDREN READING NO BOOKS IN LAST MONTH DURING
SCHOOL TERM OUTSIDE SCHOOL (SAN FRANCISCO, ROCKY MOUNTAIN
TOWNS, RADIOTOWN AND TELETOWN, CANADA)
By Grade and Sex

| | N | Sixth Grade | N | Eighth Grade | N | Tenth Grade | N | Twelfth Grade |
|---|---|---|---|---|---|---|---|---|
| **San Francisco** | | | | | | | | |
| Boys ........ | | | 114 | 34.2 | 85 | 41.2 | 123 | 41.4 |
| Girls ........ | | | 105 | 20.9 | 116 | 25.0 | 109 | 40.4 |
| **Rocky Mountain towns** | | | | | | | | |
| Boys ........ | 377 | 12.2 | | | 332 | 13.5 | | |
| Girls ........ | 351 | 6.9 | | | 364 | 9.5 | | |
| **Teletown** | | | | | | | | |
| Boys ........ | 91 | 15.4 | | | 86 | 25.6 | | |
| Girls ........ | 103 | 7.8 | | | 99 | 16.2 | | |
| **Radiotown** | | | | | | | | |
| Boys ........ | 49 | 18.3 | | | 70 | 20.0 | | |
| Girls ........ | 61 | 14.8 | | | 45 | 6.7 | | |

TABLE VII-16. MEDIAN NUMBER OF BOOKS READ MONTHLY (SAN FRANCISCO, ROCKY MOUNTAIN TOWNS, TELETOWN AND RADIOTOWN, CANADA)
By Mental Ability and Grade

| Mental Ability | N | Sixth Grade | N | Eighth Grade | N | Tenth Grade | N | Twelfth Grade |
|---|---|---|---|---|---|---|---|---|
| San Francisco | | | | | | | | |
| High ....... | | | 43 | 2.2 | 32 | 1.0 | 46 | 1.0 |
| Middle ...... | | | 123 | 1.2 | 120 | 0.9 | 137 | 0.8 |
| Low ........ | | | 53 | 1.1 | 49 | 0.9 | 49 | 0.8 |
| | | | | | | | | |
| Rocky Mountain towns | | | | | | | | |
| High ....... | 216 | 3.7 | | | 163 | 2.2 | | |
| Middle ...... | 320 | 2.6 | | | 326 | 1.8 | | |
| Low ........ | 169 | 2.3 | | | 204 | 1.8 | | |
| | | | | | | | | |
| Teletown | | | | | | | | |
| High ....... | 73 | 3.4 | | | 28 | 2.8 | | |
| Middle ...... | 76 | 2.9 | | | 100 | 1.7 | | |
| Low ........ | 45 | 2.2 | | | 54 | 1.7 | | |
| | | | | | | | | |
| Radiotown | | | | | | | | |
| High ....... | 14 | 3.0 | | | 39 | 3.8 | | |
| Middle ...... | 57 | 2.2 | | | 38 | 2.7 | | |
| Low ........ | 38 | 1.5 | | | 38 | 2.5 | | |

TABLE VII-17. READING OF BOOKS BY CHILDREN, AGED 6–10,
IN THE LAST SIX MONTHS (SAN FRANCISCO)

| | Mean Number of Books Read by Child | N |
|---|---|---|
| Mother read in last six months: | | |
| 4 or more books ...................... | 3.3 | 60 |
| 1–4 books ........................... | 2.3 | 98 |
| No books ........................... | 2.2 | 138 |
| Father's education: | | |
| High school or less ................... | 2.2 | 210 |
| Some college ....................... | 3.2 | 81 |
| Socioeconomic status of family: | | |
| Lower ............................ | 2.2 | 96 |
| Middle ............................ | 3.5 | 172 |

TABLE VII-18. PERCENTAGE OF CHILDREN WHO READ MAGAZINES DURING SCHOOL YEAR
(SAN FRANCISCO, ROCKY MOUNTAIN TOWNS, TELETOWN AND RADIOTOWN, CANADA)
By Grade and Sex

| | N | Sixth Grade | N | Eighth Grade | N | Tenth Grade | N | Twelfth Grade |
|---|---|---|---|---|---|---|---|---|
| San Francisco | | | | | | | | |
| Boys ........ | | | 114 | 78% | 85 | 88% | 123 | 92% |
| Girls ........ | | | 105 | 92 | 116 | 86 | 109 | 92 |
| Rocky Mountain towns | | | | | | | | |
| Boys ........ | 377 | 84% | | | 332 | 89 | | |
| Girls ........ | 351 | 87 | | | 364 | 88 | | |
| Teletown | | | | | | | | |
| Boys ........ | 91 | 82 | | | 86 | 86 | | |
| Girls ........ | 103 | 84 | | | 99 | 89 | | |
| Radiotown | | | | | | | | |
| Boys ........ | 49 | 74 | | | 70 | 93 | | |
| Girls ........ | 61 | 82 | | | 45 | 96 | | |

TABLE VII-19. MEDIAN NUMBER OF MAGAZINES READ PER MONTH DURING SCHOOL YEAR
(SAN FRANCISCO, ROCKY MOUNTAIN TOWNS, TELETOWN AND RADIOTOWN, CANADA)
By Grade and Sex

| | N | Sixth Grade | N | Eighth Grade | N | Tenth Grade | N | Twelfth Grade |
|---|---|---|---|---|---|---|---|---|
| San Francisco | | | | | | | | |
| Boys ........ | | | 114 | 3.7 | 85 | 4.7 | 123 | 2.2 |
| Girls ........ | | | 105 | 4.4 | 116 | 3.1 | 109 | 3.3 |
| Rocky Mountain towns | | | | | | | | |
| Boys ........ | 377 | 3.3 | | | 332 | 3.7 | | |
| Girls ........ | 351 | 3.6 | | | 364 | 3.6 | | |
| Teletown | | | | | | | | |
| Boys ........ | 91 | 2.3 | | | 86 | 2.8 | | |
| Girls ........ | 103 | 2.9 | | | 99 | 3.3 | | |
| Radiotown | | | | | | | | |
| Boys ........ | 49 | 1.5 | | | 70 | 5.0 | | |
| Girls ........ | 61 | 2.3 | | | 45 | 4.3 | | |

TABLE VII-20. MEDIAN NUMBER OF MAGAZINES READ MONTHLY (SAN FRANCISCO, ROCKY MOUNTAIN TOWNS, TELETOWN AND RADIOTOWN, CANADA)
By Mental Ability and Grade

| Mental Ability | N | Sixth Grade | N | Eighth Grade | N | Tenth Grade | N | Twelfth Grade |
|---|---|---|---|---|---|---|---|---|
| San Francisco | | | | | | | | |
| High ....... | | | 43 | 5.2 | 32 | 4.8 | 46 | 3.4 |
| Middle ...... | | | 123 | 2.2 | 120 | 4.1 | 137 | 3.7 |
| Low ........ | | | 53 | 4.7 | 49 | 3.7 | 49 | 2.0 |
| Rocky Mt. towns | | | | | | | | |
| High ....... | 216 | 4.0 | | | 163 | 4.2 | | |
| Middle ...... | 320 | 3.4 | | | 326 | 3.2 | | |
| Low ........ | 169 | 3.0 | | | 204 | 3.1 | | |
| Teletown | | | | | | | | |
| High ....... | 73 | 3.4 | | | 28 | 3.8 | | |
| Middle ...... | 76 | 1.7 | | | 100 | 3.1 | | |
| Low ........ | 45 | 2.1 | | | 54 | 2.2 | | |
| Radiotown | | | | | | | | |
| High ....... | 14 | 3.0 | | | 39 | 6.0 | | |
| Middle ...... | 57 | 2.3 | | | 38 | 3.9 | | |
| Low ........ | 38 | 1.6 | | | 38 | 3.6 | | |

TABLE VII-21. MOST PREFERRED CATEGORIES OF MAGAZINES (SAN FRANCISCO AND TELETOWN, CANADA)*
By Grade and Sex

| | N | Sex Role† | Picture and General | News | Film, Confession, Etc. | Quality | Other | Not Ascertained |
|---|---|---|---|---|---|---|---|---|
| | | | SIXTH GRADE | | | | | |
| Teletown | | | | | | | | |
| Boys ...... | 91 | 19.8 | 50.5 | 1.1 | 8.8 | | 6.6 | 13.2 |
| Girls ...... | 103 | 11.7 | 50.5 | 1.0 | 19.4 | | 1.0 | 16.5 |
| | | | EIGHTH GRADE | | | | | |
| San Francisco | | | | | | | | |
| Boys ...... | 114 | 31.6 | 25.3 | 1.8 | 7.0 | | 21.9 | 12.3 |
| Girls ...... | 105 | 26.7 | 21.9 | 1.9 | 23.8 | | 19.1 | 6.7 |
| | | | TENTH GRADE | | | | | |
| San Francisco | | | | | | | | |
| Boys ...... | 85 | 38.8 | 29.5 | 1.2 | 4.2 | | 15.7 | 10.6 |
| Girls ...... | 116 | 32.7 | 19.7 | 3.4 | 29.3 | 1.7 | 6.0 | 9.5 |
| Teletown | | | | | | | | |
| Boys ...... | 86 | 43.5 | 41.4 | 2.3 | 3.5 | | | 9.3 |
| Girls ...... | 99 | 14.1 | 48.4 | 1.0 | 30.3 | | 1.0 | 5.1 |
| | | | TWELFTH GRADE | | | | | |
| San Francisco | | | | | | | | |
| Boys ...... | 123 | 34.9 | 34.7 | 10.6 | 3.3 | 2.4 | 8.4 | 5.7 |
| Girls ...... | 109 | 23.9 | 45.8 | 4.6 | 11.9 | 3.7 | 5.5 | 4.6 |

* "If you could keep only one magazine, which would you select?"
† Hobbies and sports for boys; girls' and women's magazines for girls.

TABLE VII-22. MEDIAN NUMBER OF COMIC BOOKS READ MONTHLY (SAN FRANCISCO, ROCKY MOUNTAIN TOWNS, TELETOWN AND RADIOTOWN, CANADA)

By Grade and Sex

| | N | Second Grade | N | Fourth Grade | N | Sixth Grade | N | Eighth Grade | N | Tenth Grade | N | Twelfth Grade |
|---|---|---|---|---|---|---|---|---|---|---|---|---|
| San Francisco | | | | | | | | | | | | |
| Boys ........ | 159 | 1.1° | 137 | 2.6° | 142 | 3.3° | 114 | 4.5 | 85 | 3.0 | 123 | 0.9 |
| Girls ........ | 158 | 0.2° | 126 | 1.0° | 120 | 1.4° | 105 | 3.3 | 116 | 1.3 | 109 | 0.7 |
| Rocky Mountain towns | | | | | | | | | | | | |
| Boys ........ | | | | | 377 | 8.5 | | | 332 | 2.1 | | |
| Girls ........ | | | | | 351 | 4.7 | | | 364 | 0.5 | | |
| Teletown | | | | | | | | | | | | |
| Boys ........ | | | | | 91 | 5.0 | | | 86 | 0.1 | | |
| Girls ........ | | | | | 103 | 4.0 | | | 99 | 0.1 | | |
| Radiotown | | | | | | | | | | | | |
| Boys ........ | | | | | 49 | 10.5 | | | 70 | 10.0 | | |
| Girls ........ | | | | | 61 | 10.2 | | | 45 | 6.5 | | |

° These San Francisco figures may be slightly lower than they should be in comparison to the other towns, because any number of comics over nine was scored 9 in the first six San Francisco grades, whereas the full number was averaged in the totals for the other samples.

TABLE VII-23. MEDIAN NUMBER OF COMIC BOOKS READ MONTHLY (SAN FRANCISCO, ROCKY MOUNTAIN TOWNS, TELETOWN AND RADIOTOWN, CANADA)

By Mental Ability and Grade

| Mental Ability | N | Sixth Grade | N | Tenth Grade | N | Twelfth Grade |
|---|---|---|---|---|---|---|
| | | SAN FRANCISCO | | | | |
| High ....... | | | 32 | 2.5 | 46 | 0.3 |
| Middle ...... | | | 120 | 2.2 | 137 | 0.3 |
| Low ........ | | | 49 | 3.1 | 49 | 1.1 |
| | | ROCKY MOUNTAIN TOWNS | | | | |
| High ....... | 216 | 6.0 | 163 | 0.5 | | |
| Middle ...... | 320 | 7.0 | 326 | 1.0 | | |
| Low ........ | 169 | 7.9 | 204 | 2.4 | | |
| | | TELETOWN | | | | |
| High ....... | 73 | 5.0 | 28 | 0.4 | | |
| Middle ...... | 76 | 5.3 | 100 | 0.4 | | |
| Low ........ | 45 | 6.3 | 54 | 0.4 | | |

Per cent of children reading nine or more comic books monthly:

| | San Francisco | | Radiotown | | | | |
|---|---|---|---|---|---|---|---|
| | N | Eighth Grade | N | Sixth Grade | N | Tenth Grade |
|---|---|---|---|---|---|---|
| High ....... | 43 | 30% | 14 | 86% | 39 | 36% |
| Middle ...... | 123 | 25 | 57 | 93 | 38 | 55 |
| Low ......... | 53 | 24 | 38 | 89 | 38 | 67 |

TABLE VII-24. PERCENTAGE OF NONREADERS AND VERY HEAVY READERS OF
COMIC BOOKS (SAN FRANCISCO)
By Grade and Sex

| | N | No Comics | 9 or More per Month |
|---|---|---|---|
| Eighth grade: | | | |
| Boys ............... | 114 | 25.4% | 41.2% |
| Girls ............... | 105 | 26.7 | 34.3 |
| Tenth grade: | | | |
| Boys ............... | 85 | 24.7 | 29.4 |
| Girls ............... | 116 | 38.8 | 17.2 |
| Twelfth grade: | | | |
| Boys ............... | 123 | 54.4 | 13.0 |
| Girls ............... | 109 | 65.1 | 3.7 |

TABLE VII-25. FREQUENCY OF NEWSPAPER READING (SAN FRANCISCO, ROCKY
MOUNTAIN TOWNS, TELETOWN AND RADIOTOWN, CANADA)
By Grade and Sex

| | N | Every Day | Several Days a Week | One Day a Week | Seldom or Never | Not Ascertained |
|---|---|---|---|---|---|---|
| | | | SIXTH GRADE | | | |
| Rocky Mt. towns | | | | | | |
| Boys ......... | 377 | 50.7% | 25.2% | 11.5% | 10.7% | 1.9% |
| Girls ......... | 351 | 51.2 | 22.6 | 10.9 | 4.2 | |
| Teletown | | | | | | |
| Boys ......... | 91 | 46.2 | 18.7 | 16.5 | 16.5 | 2.2 |
| Girls ......... | 103 | 43.7 | 24.3 | 23.3 | 23.3 | |
| Radiotown | | | | | | |
| Boys ......... | 49 | 26.5 | 26.5 | 20.4 | 24.5 | 2.0 |
| Girls ......... | 61 | 39.3 | 36.1 | 14.8 | 9.8 | |
| | | | EIGHTH GRADE | | | |
| San Francisco | | | | | | |
| Boys ......... | 114 | 44.7 | 28.9 | 13.2 | 12.3 | 0.9 |
| Girls ......... | 105 | 50.5 | 30.5 | 8.6 | 9.5 | 1.0 |
| | | | TENTH GRADE | | | |
| San Francisco | | | | | | |
| Boys ......... | 85 | 62.3 | 28.2 | 5.9 | 2.4 | 1.2 |
| Girls ......... | 116 | 48.3 | 32.8 | 8.6 | 10.3 | |
| Rocky Mt. towns | | | | | | |
| Boys ......... | 332 | 68.1 | 27.9 | 5.1 | 9.4 | 0.6 |
| Girls ......... | 364 | 69.2 | 18.3 | 5.5 | 6.7 | 0.3 |
| Teletown | | | | | | |
| Boys ......... | 86 | 61.1 | 22.1 | 12.8 | 1.2 | 2.3 |
| Girls ......... | 99 | 52.5 | 26.3 | 16.2 | 16.2 | |
| Radiotown | | | | | | |
| Boys ......... | 70 | 44.3 | 35.7 | 18.6 | 1.4 | |
| Girls ......... | 45 | 42.2 | 33.3 | 17.8 | 6.7 | |
| | | | TWELFTH GRADE | | | |
| San Francisco | | | | | | |
| Boys ......... | 123 | 68.2 | 24.3 | 3.3 | 4.1 | |
| Girls ......... | 109 | 64.2 | 25.7 | 5.5 | 4.6 | |

TABLE VII-26. FREQUENCY OF NEWSPAPER READING (ROCKY MOUNTAIN TOWNS)
By Mental Ability and Grade

| Mental Ability and Grade | N | Every Day | Several Days a Week | One Day a Week | Seldom or Never | No Answer |
|---|---|---|---|---|---|---|
| Sixth grade: | | | | | | |
| High ........ | 216 | 63% | 25% | 7% | 5% | |
| Middle ....... | 320 | 51 | 28 | 11 | 8 | 2 |
| Low ......... | 169 | 34 | 24 | 18 | 21 | 3 |
| Tenth grade: | | | | | | |
| High ........ | 163 | 75 | 17 | 4 | 3 | |
| Middle ....... | 326 | 67 | 22 | 6 | 5 | |
| Low ......... | 204 | 62 | 22 | 6 | 10 | |

Sixth grade, $X^2 = 26.22$, $p < .001$, $df = 2$ (daily vs. other categories).
Tenth grade, $X^2 = 8.18$, $p < .02$, $df = 2$ (daily vs. other categories).

TABLE VII-27. CATEGORIES OF NEWSPAPER READING (ROCKY MOUNTAIN TOWNS)
By Grade

| | Sixth Grade (N = 52) | | | Tenth Grade (N = 62) | | |
|---|---|---|---|---|---|---|
| | Soft | Hard | Both | Soft | Hard | Both |
| Mental ability: | | | | | | |
| High .............. | 20.7% | 18.4% | 32.0% | 19.5% | 26.5% | 28.9% |
| Middle ............ | 48.4 | 44.6 | 44.7 | 38.2 | 39.7 | 47.3 |
| Low .............. | 29.6 | 32.3 | 19.0 | 42.3 | 32.5 | 23.2 |
| Occupational status: | | | | | | |
| White-collar ....... | 39.4 | 52.3 | 59.1 | 35.0 | 46.8 | 51.6 |
| Blue-collar ........ | 39.4 | 33.9 | 30.0 | 47.1 | 43.2 | 38.0 |
| Not classified ...... | 21.2 | 13.8 | 10.9 | 17.9 | 10.0 | 10.4 |
| High conflict with parents over aspirations for self .......... | 34.3 | 27.6 | 26.5 | 52.0 | 24.6 | 33.6 |

"Soft" category: those who read comic strips, columns, but no hard news. "Hard" category: those who read hard news and columns, but no comic strips. "Both" category: those who read all types of newspaper content.

TABLE VII-28. NEWSPAPER CONTENT READ (SAN FRANCISCO)
By Grade

| | Second Grade (N = 94) | Fourth Grade (N = 103) | Sixth Grade (N = 246) | Eighth Grade (N = 219) | Tenth Grade (N = 201) | Twelfth Grade (N = 232) |
|---|---|---|---|---|---|---|
| Comics .......... | 56% | 82% | 77% | 75% | 61% | 59% |
| Sports .......... | 3 | 25 | 27 | 34 | 42 | 45 |
| Society .......... | | 2 | 4 | 12 | 11 | 16 |
| Local news ...... | 6 | 8 | 12 | 54 | 58 | 76 |
| National news .... | 2 | 4 | 15 | 20 | 23 | 36 |
| Foreign news ..... | | 5 | 12 | 30 | 31 | 40 |
| Editorials ........ | | 8 | 10 | 10 | 13 | 22 |
| Columns ........ | 2 | 12 | 13 | 32 | 31 | 41 |

TABLE VII-29. PART OF NEWSPAPER CHILDREN WOULD MISS MOST
(SAN FRANCISCO AND TELETOWN, CANADA)
By Grade and Sex

| San Francisco | Eighth Grade | | Tenth Grade | | Twelfth Grade | |
|---|---|---|---|---|---|---|
| | Boys (N=114) | Girls (N=105) | Boys (N=85) | Girls (N=116) | Boys (N=123) | Girls (N=109) |
| Local news ....... | 3.5% | 8.6% | 16.5% | 17.2% | 11.4% | 21.1% |
| News about the national government | 0.9 | 1.0 | | 2.6 | 2.4 | 0.9 |
| News from a foreign country ........ | 3.5 | 2.9 | 4.7 | | 4.1 | 5.5 |
| Front page in general | 16.7 | 17.1 | 17.6 | 11.2 | 8.9 | 18.3 |
| Sports news ....... | 17.5 | 1.9 | 32.9 | 5.2 | 40.7 | 3.7 |
| Local society news.. | | | | 1.7 | | 4.6 |
| Editorials ......... | | | | 0.9 | | 2.8 |
| TV or radio program | 4.4 | 4.8 | 2.4 | 2.6 | 2.4 | |
| Columnist ........ | 0.9 | 14.3 | | 15.5 | 2.4 | 16.5 |
| Comics .......... | 43.9 | 45.7 | 23.5 | 35.3 | 18.7 | 18.3 |
| Something else .... | 7.9 | 3.8 | 2.4 | 7.8 | 8.1 | 5.5 |

| Teletown | Sixth Grade | | Tenth Grade | |
|---|---|---|---|---|
| | Boys (N=91) | Girls (N=103) | Boys (N=86) | Girls (N=99) |
| Local news ............... | 6.6% | 16.5% | 2.3% | 20.2% |
| News from a foreign country (other than the U.S.) ...... | 1.1 | | 5.8 | 3.0 |
| U.S. news ................. | | | 1.2 | |
| Sports news ............... | 9.9 | 1.9 | 24.4 | 3.0 |
| Editorials ................ | 1.1 | | 3.5 | 3.0 |
| TV or radio program ......... | 4.4 | 2.9 | 2.3 | 5.1 |
| Columnist ................ | | 1.0 | 1.2 | 6.1 |
| Comics .................. | 45.1 | 53.4 | 32.6 | 37.4 |
| Some advertising ............ | 2.2 | 1.9 | 5.8 | 1.0 |
| Something else ............. | 6.6 | 3.9 | 2.3 | 3.0 |
| No answer ................. | 23.1 | 18.4 | 18.6 | 18.2 |

Table VII-30. Frequency of Discussing the Day's News with Someone (San Francisco, Rocky Mountain Towns, Teletown and Radiotown, Canada)
By Grade and Sex

|  | N | Discuss Very Often | Not Discuss Often | Not Ascertained |
|---|---|---|---|---|
| | | SIXTH GRADE | | |
| Rocky Mountain towns | | | | |
| Boys .............. | 377 | 28.2% | 69.0% | 2.8% |
| Girls .............. | 351 | 33.4 | 66.0 | 0.6 |
| Teletown | | | | |
| Boys .............. | 91 | 28.6 | 68.1 | 3.3 |
| Girls .............. | 103 | 34.0 | 62.1 | 3.9 |
| Radiotown | | | | |
| Boys .............. | 49 | 10.2 | 87.7 | 2.0 |
| Girls .............. | 61 | 18.0 | 82.0 | |
| | | EIGHTH GRADE | | |
| San Francisco | | | | |
| Boys .............. | 114 | 37.7 | 61.4 | 0.9 |
| Girls .............. | 105 | 29.5 | 69.5 | 1.0 |
| | | TENTH GRADE | | |
| San Francisco | | | | |
| Boys .............. | 85 | 27.0 | 71.7 | 1.2 |
| Girls .............. | 116 | 41.4 | 56.0 | 2.6 |
| Rocky Mountain towns | | | | |
| Boys .............. | 332 | 31.3 | 67.2 | 1.5 |
| Girls .............. | 364 | 45.1 | 53.5 | 1.4 |
| Teletown | | | | |
| Boys .............. | 86 | 26.7 | 69.8 | 3.5 |
| Girls .............. | 99 | 43.3 | 55.6 | 1.0 |
| Radiotown | | | | |
| Boys .............. | 70 | 18.6 | 81.4 | |
| Girls .............. | 45 | 62.2 | 37.8 | |
| | | TWELFTH GRADE | | |
| San Francisco | | | | |
| Boys .............. | 123 | 38.2 | 60.2 | 1.6 |
| Girls .............. | 109 | 44.0 | 54.1 | 1.8 |

TABLE VII-31. PERSON WITH WHOM NEWS IS DISCUSSED (SAN FRANCISCO, ROCKY MOUNTAIN TOWNS, TELETOWN AND RADIOTOWN, CANADA)
By Grade and Sex

| | N | Your Parents | Someone Your Own Age | Someone Else | Not Ascertained |
|---|---|---|---|---|---|
| | | SIXTH GRADE | | | |
| Rocky Mt. towns | | | | | |
| Boys ........... | 377 | 38.9% | 36.2% | 16.7% | 8.2% |
| Girls ........... | 351 | 37.2 | 43.2 | 12.0 | 7.6 |
| Teletown | | | | | |
| Boys ........... | 91 | 30.8 | 42.9 | 16.5 | 9.9 |
| Girls ........... | 103 | 53.4 | 34.0 | 5.8 | 6.8 |
| Radiotown | | | | | |
| Boys ........... | 49 | 51.0 | 34.7 | 10.2 | 4.1 |
| Girls ........... | 61 | 49.2 | 36.1 | 13.1 | 1.6 |
| | | EIGHTH GRADE | | | |
| San Francisco | | | | | |
| Boys ........... | 114 | 30.7 | 43.9 | 2.6 | 22.8 |
| Girls ........... | 105 | 38.0 | 41.0 | 7.6 | 13.3 |
| | | TENTH GRADE | | | |
| San Francisco | | | | | |
| Boys ........... | 85 | 28.2 | 49.4 | 9.4 | 12.9 |
| Girls ........... | 116 | 33.6 | 44.0 | 10.3 | 12.1 |
| Rocky Mt. towns | | | | | |
| Boys ........... | 332 | 37.2 | 48.6 | 8.5 | 5.7 |
| Girls ........... | 364 | 37.1 | 49.9 | 7.8 | 5.2 |
| Teletown | | | | | |
| Boys ........... | 86 | 40.7 | 44.2 | 7.0 | 8.1 |
| Girls ........... | 99 | 49.5 | 34.3 | 4.0 | 12.1 |
| Radiotown | | | | | |
| Boys ........... | 70 | 40.7 | 42.9 | 10.0 | 5.7 |
| Girls ........... | 45 | 49.5 | 44.4 | 8.9 | 6.7 |
| | | TWELFTH GRADE | | | |
| San Francisco | | | | | |
| Boys ........... | 123 | 32.5 | 45.5 | 7.3 | 14.6 |
| Girls ........... | 109 | 34.9 | 42.2 | 10.1 | 12.8 |

TABLE VII-32. DISCUSSION OF NEWS WITHIN FAMILY (SAN FRANCISCO)
By Father's Educational Level
(*In per cent*)

| | Father Did Not Finish High School (N = 160) | Father Finished High School (N = 161) | Father Had Some College (N = 140) |
|---|---|---|---|
| Discuss news: | | | |
| Often ................... | 18 | 31 | 45 |
| Only very important news... | 33 | 43 | 17 |
| Rarely or not at all ........ | 47 | 23 | 38 |
| Not ascertained ........... | 2 | 3 | |

# TABLES ON WHAT A CHILD USES TELEVISION *FOR*

▶ *These tables are referred to particularly in Chapter 4.*

TABLE VIII-1. COMPARISON OF SOME LEISURE-TIME BEHAVIORS OF FIRST-GRADE CHILDREN IN TOWNS WITH AND WITHOUT TELEVISION

|  | Radiotown (N = 137) | Teletown (N = 172) |
|---|---|---|
| Bedtime .......................... | 8:02 | 8:13* |
| Hours of sleep ..................... | 10.81 | 10.64 |
| Age when movie-going began......... | 4.96 | 4.44* |
| Comic books read per month.......... | 4.32 | 1.86† |
| Hours of radio listening on school days.. | 1.29 | .69† |

* Differences significant at .01 level.  † Differences significant at .001 level.

TABLE VIII-2. VIEWING ALONE OR WITH OTHER PEOPLE (SAN FRANCISCO, ROCKY MOUNTAIN TOWNS, TELETOWN, CANADA)

| | N | More Often Alone | More Often with Other People | Not As-certained |
|---|---|---|---|---|
| **SIXTH GRADE** | | | | |
| Rocky Mountain towns | | | | |
| Boys .............. | 377 | 23.8% | 72.4% | 3.8% |
| Girls .............. | 351 | 16.1 | 81.2 | 2.7 |
| Teletown | | | | |
| Boys .............. | 91 | 11.0 | 85.7 | 3.3 |
| Girls .............. | 103 | 6.8 | 89.3 | 3.9 |
| **EIGHTH GRADE** | | | | |
| San Francisco | | | | |
| Boys .............. | 114 | 15.8 | 81.6 | 2.6 |
| Girls .............. | 105 | 17.1 | 80.0 | 2.9 |
| **TENTH GRADE** | | | | |
| San Francisco | | | | |
| Boys .............. | 85 | 23.5 | 72.9 | 3.5 |
| Girls .............. | 116 | 9.5 | 86.2 | 4.3 |
| Rocky Mountain towns | | | | |
| Boys .............. | 332 | 23.9 | 73.0 | 3.1 |
| Girls .............. | 364 | 24.4 | 74.0 | 1.6 |
| Teletown | | | | |
| Boys .............. | 86 | 7.0 | 83.7 | 9.3 |
| Girls .............. | 99 | 10.1 | 80.8 | 9.1 |
| **TWELFTH GRADE** | | | | |
| San Francisco | | | | |
| Boys .............. | 123 | 21.1 | 76.4 | 2.4 |
| Girls .............. | 109 | 11.0 | 86.2 | 2.8 |

TABLE VIII-3. PERSON WITH WHOM TELEVISION IS VIEWED (SAN FRANCISCO, ROCKY MOUNTAIN TOWNS, TELETOWN, CANADA)

By Grade and Sex

|  | N | Member of the Family | Someone outside the Family | No Answer |
|---|---|---|---|---|
| **SIXTH GRADE** | | | | |
| Rocky Mountain towns | | | | |
| Boys .............. | 377 | 80.3% | 15.9% | 3.8% |
| Girls .............. | 351 | 83.6 | 13.2 | 3.2 |
| Teletown | | | | |
| Boys .............. | 91 | 74.7 | 19.8 | 5.5 |
| Girls .............. | 103 | 75.7 | 20.4 | 3.9 |
| **EIGHTH GRADE** | | | | |
| San Francisco | | | | |
| Boys .............. | 114 | 82.5 | 14.0 | 3.5 |
| Girls .............. | 105 | 83.8 | 12.4 | 3.8 |
| **TENTH GRADE** | | | | |
| San Francisco | | | | |
| Boys .............. | 85 | 75.3 | 20.0 | 4.7 |
| Girls .............. | 116 | 77.6 | 15.5 | 7.0 |
| Rocky Mountain towns | | | | |
| Boys .............. | 332 | 69.5 | 26.0 | 4.5 |
| Girls .............. | 364 | 72.3 | 24.7 | 3.0 |
| Teletown | | | | |
| Boys .............. | 86 | 67.4 | 24.4 | 8.1 |
| Girls .............. | 99 | 63.6 | 26.3 | 10.1 |
| **TWELFTH GRADE** | | | | |
| San Francisco | | | | |
| Boys .............. | 123 | 72.4 | 23.6 | 4.1 |
| Girls .............. | 109 | 69.7 | 26.6 | 3.7 |

TABLE VIII-4. PERCENTAGE OF CHILDREN WHO VIEW TELEVISION MOST OFTEN WITH PARENTS (SAN FRANCISCO)

By Father's Educational Level

|  | Father Did Not Finish High School (N = 160) | Father Finished High School (N = 161) | Father Had Some College Work (N = 140) |
|---|---|---|---|
| More often view *with* parents | 83 | 70 | 70 |
| More often view *alone* ..... | 15 | 30 | 25 |
| Not ascertained .......... | 2 | 0 | 5 |

TABLE VIII-5. OTHER ACTIVITIES WHILE VIEWING TELEVISION (SAN FRANCISCO)
By Grade and Sex

|  | N | Often | Occasionally | Never | No Answer |
|---|---|---|---|---|---|
| **Eighth grade:** | | | | | |
| Boys ............ | 114 | 31.6% | 39.5% | 22.8% | 6.1% |
| Girls ............ | 105 | 38.0 | 44.8 | 14.3 | 2.9 |
| **Tenth grade:** | | | | | |
| Boys ............ | 85 | 23.5 | 44.7 | 24.7 | 7.1 |
| Girls ............ | 116 | 21.6 | 56.0 | 16.4 | 6.0 |
| **Twelfth grade:** | | | | | |
| Boys ............ | 123 | 22.8 | 46.3 | 26.8 | 4.1 |
| Girls ............ | 109 | 22.0 | 56.0 | 18.3 | 3.7 |

TABLE VIII-6. ACTIVITIES ENGAGED IN WHILE VIEWING TELEVISION AND WHILE
LISTENING TO RADIO (SAN FRANCISCO)
By Grade and Sex

|  | N | Study | Eat | Play Games | Read | Work | Dance | Something Else | No Answer |
|---|---|---|---|---|---|---|---|---|---|
| | | | | LISTENING TO RADIO | | | | | |
| **Sixth grade:** | | | | | | | | | |
| Boys ...... | 142 | 25.4% | 13.2% | 1.8% | 21.0% | 6.1% | 0.9% | 25.4% | 21.1% |
| Girls ...... | 120 | 51.4 | 10.5 | 1.0 | 21.0 | 30.5 | 9.5 | 18.0 | 5.7 |
| **Eighth grade:** | | | | | | | | | |
| Boys ...... | 114 | 40.0 | 5.9 | 2.4 | 27.0 | 14.1 | 3.5 | 17.6 | 12.9 |
| Girls ...... | 105 | 52.6 | 7.8 | 0 | 12.9 | 37.1 | 7.8 | 25.0 | 9.5 |
| **Tenth grade:** | | | | | | | | | |
| Boys ...... | 85 | 36.6 | 11.4 | 2.4 | 20.3 | 21.1 | 1.6 | 34.9 | 7.3 |
| Girls ...... | 116 | 43.0 | 3.7 | 14.7 | 48.6 | 22.8 | 24.8 | 10.0 | 7.3 |
| | | | | VIEWING TELEVISION | | | | | |
| **Sixth grade:** | | | | | | | | | |
| Boys ...... | 142 | 16.7 | 19.3 | 4.4 | 5.3 | 4.4 | 0 | 19.3 | 38.6 |
| Girls ...... | 120 | 31.4 | 24.8 | 1.0 | 10.5 | 13.3 | 1.9 | 21.9 | 17.1 |
| **Eighth grade:** | | | | | | | | | |
| Boys ...... | 114 | 16.5 | 28.2 | 1.2 | 7.1 | 3.5 | 1.2 | 12.9 | 38.8 |
| Girls ...... | 105 | 31.0 | 20.7 | 0.9 | 10.3 | 8.6 | 0.9 | 31.9 | 24.1 |
| **Tenth grade:** | | | | | | | | | |
| Boys ...... | 85 | 19.5 | 29.3 | 3.3 | 6.5 | 4.1 | 0.8 | 11.4 | 34.9 |
| Girls ...... | 116 | 25.7 | 13.8 | 0 | 10.1 | 18.3 | 0 | 33.9 | 22.0 |

TABLE VIII-7. COMMUNICATION BEHAVIOR BY CHILDREN IN TELETOWN
AND RADIOTOWN, CANADA

| | Grades | N | Mean | Per Cent | SD | CR |
|---|---|---|---|---|---|---|
| **Total hours of play:** | | | | | | |
| Teletown ........... | 1 | 138 | 2.92 | | .90 } | 4.98* |
| Radiotown .......... | 1 | 113 | 3.51 | | .96 } | |
| **Play with others, hours:** | | | | | | |
| Teletown ........... | 1 | 131 | 2.52 | | 1.07 } | 4.33* |
| Radiotown .......... | 1 | 114 | 3.13 | | 1.13 } | |

("About how many hours does the child use for play on a school day [not counting radio listening, and such activities]? How much of this play time would ordinarily be spent playing with other children?")

| | Grades | N | Mean | Per Cent | SD | CR |
|---|---|---|---|---|---|---|
| **Number of books read per month:** | | | | | | |
| Teletown ........... | 6, 10 | 364 | 3.18 | | 2.97 } | .88 |
| Radiotown .......... | 6, 10 | 214 | 3.41 | | 3.02 } | |

("How many books (*not* school books) have you read *in the last month?*")

| | Grades | N | Mean | Per Cent | SD | CR |
|---|---|---|---|---|---|---|
| **Children reading newspapers more than once a week:** | | | | | | |
| Teletown ........... | 6, 10 | 375 | | 74.4 } | | .57 |
| Radiotown .......... | 6, 10 | 224 | | 72.3 } | | |

("How often would you estimate that you read a newspaper? Just check one of these: Every day? — Several days a week? — One day a week? — Seldom or never? —")

| | Grades | N | Mean | Per Cent | SD | CR |
|---|---|---|---|---|---|---|
| **Number of magazines read per month:** | | | | | | |
| Teletown ........... | 6, 10 | 347 | 3.66 | | 2.83 } | 2.54† |
| Radiotown .......... | 6, 10 | 208 | 4.36 | | 3.42 } | |

("How many magazines have you read something in, *in the last month?*")

| | Grades | N | Mean | Per Cent | SD | CR |
|---|---|---|---|---|---|---|
| **Children reporting reading escape magazines (screen and confession, adventure and detective pulps)** | | | | | | |
| Teletown ........... | 6, 10 | 379 | | 20.3 } | | 3.69* |
| Radiotown .......... | 6, 10 | 225 | | 34.2 } | | |

("How many magazines have you read something in, *in the last month?* What magazines were they?")

| | Grades | N | Mean | Per Cent | SD | CR |
|---|---|---|---|---|---|---|
| **Number of hours per week reported spent on homework:** | | | | | | |
| Teletown ........... | 6, 10 | 354 | 5.32 | | 4.16 } | .78 |
| Radiotown .......... | 6, 10 | 213 | 5.61 | | 4.38 } | |

("About how many hours a week do you spend on homework?")

TABLE VIII-7 (*continued*)

| | Grades | N | Mean | Per Cent | SD | CR |
|---|---|---|---|---|---|---|
| **Number of comic books read per month:** | | | | | | |
| Teletown ........... | 6, 10 | 362 | 3.60 | | 3.89 } | 13.94* |
| Radiotown .......... | 6, 10 | 222 | 7.92 | | 3.47 } | |

("How many comic books would you estimate you have read *in the last month?*")

| | Grades | N | Mean | Per Cent | SD | CR |
|---|---|---|---|---|---|---|
| **Children reading 10 or more comic books per month:** | | | | | | |
| Teletown ........... | 6 | 187 | | 34.2 } | | 9.13* |
| Radiotown .......... | 6 | 109 | | 89.0 } | | |
| Teletown ........... | 10 | 175 | | 6.3 } | | 8.74* |
| Radiotown .......... | 10 | 113 | | 51.3 } | | |

("How many comic books would you estimate you have read *in the last month?*")

| | Grades | N | Mean | Per Cent | SD | CR |
|---|---|---|---|---|---|---|
| **Number of movies attended per month:** | | | | | | |
| Teletown ........... | 6, 10 | 369 | 1.15 | | 1.65 } | 17.36* |
| Radiotown .......... | 6, 10 | 217 | 3.07 | | 1.33 } | |

("How many times have you gone to the movies *in the last month?*")

| | Grades | N | Mean | Per Cent | SD | CR |
|---|---|---|---|---|---|---|
| **Number of hours spent listening to radio on an average school day:** | | | | | | |
| Teletown ........... | 6, 10 | 364 | 1.68 | | 1.32 } | 12.24* |
| Radiotown .......... | 6, 10 | 217 | 3.07 | | 1.33 } | |

("How much time would you estimate you spend listening to radio *on an average school day?*")

* Significant beyond .001 level.
† Significant beyond .05 level.

# TABLES ON LEARNING FROM TELEVISION

▶ *These tables are referred to particularly in Chapter 5.*

TABLE IX-1. MEAN GENERAL VOCABULARY SCORES FOR FIRST-GRADE CHILDREN
(TELETOWN AND RADIOTOWN, CANADA)
By Mental Ability

| Mental Ability | Teletown | | Radiotown | | S° | t |
|---|---|---|---|---|---|---|
| | N | Mean | N | Mean | | |
| High .............. | 29 | 9.10 | 21 | 8.19 | 1.78 | 1.78† |
| Middle ............ | 57 | 7.77 | 89 | 7.85 | 1.63 | |
| Low .............. | 33 | 7.52 | 27 | 6.33 | 1.48 | 3.11‡ |

° Unbiased estimate of standard deviation (within groups).
† Significant beyond the .10 level (.05 by one-tail test).
‡ Significant beyond the .01 level.

TABLE IX-2. RESULTS OF ANALYSIS OF VARIANCE CALCULATIONS FOR GENERAL
VOCABULARY SCORES FOR FIRST-GRADE CHILDREN (TELETOWN
AND RADIOTOWN, CANADA
By Mental Ability

| Source of Variation | Degrees of Freedom | Sum of Squares | Mean Square | F |
|---|---|---|---|---|
| Mental ability .............. | 2 | 59.98° | 29.99 | 11.36† |
| Television ................. | 1 | 22.05° | 22.05 | 8.35‡ |
| Interaction ................ | 2 | 21.43° | 10.71 | 4.06§ |
| Individuals within groups.... | 250 | 659.31 | 2.64 | |

° Corrected for disproportionate subclass frequencies.
† Significant beyond the .001 level.
‡ Significant beyond the .01 level.
§ Significant beyond the .05 level.

TABLE IX-3. MEAN SPECIAL VOCABULARY SCORES FOR FIRST-GRADE CHILDREN
(TELETOWN AND RADIOTOWN, CANADA)
By Mental Ability

| Mental Ability | Teletown | | Radiotown | | S* | t |
| | N | Mean | N | Mean | | |
|---|---|---|---|---|---|---|
| High .............. | 29 | 3.10 | 21 | 2.71 | 1.01 | 1.00 |
| Middle ............ | 57 | 2.68 | 89 | 2.52 | 1.11 | |
| Low .............. | 33 | 2.39 | 27 | 1.78 | 0.93 | 2.52† |

\* Unbiased estimate of standard deviation (within groups).
† Significant beyond the .05 level.

TABLE IX-4. ANALYSIS OF VARIANCE ON SPECIAL VOCABULARY SCORES FOR
FIRST-GRADE CHILDREN (TELETOWN AND RADIOTOWN, CANADA)
By Mental Ability

| Source of Variation | Degrees of Freedom | Sum of Squares | Mean Square | F |
|---|---|---|---|---|
| Mental ability ............. | 2 | | | |
| Television viewing ......... | 1 | 5.85* | 5.85* | 5.32† |
| Interaction ............... | 2 | 2.37* | 1.19 | |
| Individuals within groups.... | 250 | 276.06 | 1.10 | |

\* Corrected for disproportionate subclass frequencies.        † Significant beyond the .05 level.

TABLE IX-5. MEAN GENERAL VOCABULARY SCORES FOR FIRST-GRADE CHILDREN
(TELETOWN, CANADA)*
By Mental Ability and Television Viewing

| Mental Ability | Heavy Viewers | | Light Viewers | | S† | t |
| | N | Mean | N | Mean | | |
|---|---|---|---|---|---|---|
| High .............. | 13 | 9.69 | 16 | 8.63 | 1.89 | 1.50 |
| Middle ............ | 34 | 8.15 | 23 | 7.22 | 1.84 | 1.87 |
| Low .............. | 19 | 7.47 | 14 | 7.57 | 1.57 | |

\* Heavy viewing equals 1 hr. 15 min. or more per average school day by parents' report.
† Unbiased estimate of standard deviation (within groups).

TABLE IX-6. ANALYSIS OF VARIANCE ON GENERAL VOCABULARY SCORES FOR
FIRST-GRADE CHILDREN (TELETOWN, CANADA)
By Mental Ability and Television Viewing

| Source of Variation | Degrees of Freedom | Sum of Squares | Mean Square | F |
|---|---|---|---|---|
| Mental ability ............. | 2 | | | |
| Television viewing ......... | 1 | 13.21* | 13.21 | 4.15† |
| Interaction ............... | 2 | 6.80* | 3.40 | |
| Individuals within groups ... | 113 | 358.86 | 3.18 | |

\* Corrected for disproportionate subclass frequencies.        † Significant beyond the .05 level.

TABLE IX-7. MEAN SPECIAL VOCABULARY SCORES FOR FIRST-GRADE CHILDREN
(TELETOWN, CANADA)*

By Mental Ability and Television Viewing

| | Heavy Viewers | | Light Viewers | | | |
|---|---|---|---|---|---|---|
| Mental Ability | N | Mean | N | Mean | S† | t |
| High .............. | 13 | 3.53 | 16 | 2.75 | 0.95 | 2.23‡ |
| Middle ............. | 34 | 2.71 | 23 | 2.65 | 1.05 | |
| Low .............. | 19 | 2.68 | 14 | 2.00 | 0.95 | 2.03‡ |

* Heavy viewing equals 1 hr. 15 min. or more per average school day by parents' report.
† Unbiased estimate of standard deviation (within groups).
‡ Significant beyond .05 level.

TABLE IX-8. ANALYSIS OF VARIANCE ON SPECIAL VOCABULARY SCORES FOR
FIRST-GRADE CHILDREN (TELETOWN, CANADA)

By Mental Ability and Television Viewing

| Source of Variation | Degrees of Freedom | Sum of Squares | Mean Square | F |
|---|---|---|---|---|
| Mental ability .............. | 2 | | | |
| Television viewing ......... | 1 | 5.00* | 5.00 | 5.00† |
| Interaction ............... | 2 | 3.16* | 1.58 | |
| Individuals within groups.... | 113 | 112.61 | 1.00 | |

* Corrected for disproportionate subclass frequencies.
† Significant beyond the .05 level.

TABLE IX-9. DIRECTION OF DIFFERENCES BETWEEN TELETOWN AND RADIOTOWN
ON SIX INFORMATION MEASURES*

By Mental Ability and Grade

| | Sixth Grade | | | Tenth Grade | | |
|---|---|---|---|---|---|---|
| Information Test | Tele-town Scored Higher | Radio-town Scored Higher | Tied | Tele-town Scored Higher | Radio-town Scored Higher | Tied |
| Science quiz .................... | 0 | 2 | 1† | 0 | 3 | 0 |
| Naming of band leaders .......... | 0 | 3 | 0 | 1† | 2 | 0 |
| Naming of Canadian premiers..... | 0 | 3 | 0 | 3 | 0 | 0 |
| Naming of singers .............. | 0 | 3 | 0 | 0 | 2 | 1‡ |
| Naming of writers .............. | 0 | 3 | 0 | 2 | 1† | 0 |
| Identification of place names ...... | 0 | 3 | 0 | 3 | 0 | 0 |
| Total§ ..................... | 0 | 17 | 1 | 9 | 8 | 1 |

* Cell entries indicate the number of intelligence categories (from 0 to 3) in which the mean score is higher. The amount of difference in most cases is small, and Radiotown sixth-graders consistently outscore Teletown sixth-graders. There are three comparisons in each grade for each test—comparisons in the high, middle, and low mental ability groups.
† Low mental ability group.
‡ High mental ability group.
§ Sixth-grade difference significant beyond .001 level by sign test.

TABLE IX-10. DIRECTION OF DIFFERENCES BETWEEN HEAVY AND LIGHT TELEVISION VIEWERS ON FOUR INFORMATION MEASURES (SAN FRANCISCO, ROCKY MOUNTAIN TOWNS, AND TELETOWN, CANADA)*

| | Heavy TV Scored Higher | Light TV Scored Higher | Tied | Level of Significance† |
|---|---|---|---|---|
| **Naming of writers:** | | | | |
| San Francisco | 0 | 6 | 0 | |
| Teletown, Canada | 1‡ | 2 | 0 | |
| Rocky Mountain towns (combined) | 1‡ | 3 | 0 | |
| Total | 2 | 11 | 0 | .02 |
| **Naming of rulers or statesmen:** | | | | |
| San Francisco | 1§ | 5 | 0 | |
| Teletown, Canada | 0 | 3 | 0 | |
| Rocky Mountain towns (combined) | 0 | 2 | 2 | |
| Total | 1 | 10 | 2 | .003 |
| **Naming of singers:** | | | | |
| San Franicisco | 4 | 1‖ | 1 | |
| Teletown, Canada | 3 | 0 | 0 | |
| Rocky Mountain towns (combined) | 4 | 0 | 0 | |
| Total | 11 | 1 | 1 | .003 |
| **Naming of band leaders:** | | | | |
| San Francisco | 4 | 2‖, ¶ | 0 | |
| Teletown, Canada | 2 | 0 | 1 | |
| Rocky Mountain towns (combined) | 2 | 1¶ | 1 | |
| Total | 8 | 3 | 2 | .05 |

\* Cell entries indicate the number of ability groups for which the mean score is higher. The amount of difference in most cases is small. There are six groups in San Francisco, three grades (six, eight, and ten), each separated into high and low mental ability groups. There are three groups in Teletown, high and low ability in the sixth grade and low in the tenth grade (mean difference was not computed for high ability tenth-grade group since only four cases were high mental ability, high television in that sample). There are four groups in the combined Rocky Mountain sample (sixth and tenth grades by high and low mental ability).

† Level of significance tested by sign test.
‡ Low mental ability sixth grade.
§ High mental ability eighth grade.
‖ Low mental ability eighth grade.
¶ Low mental ability tenth grade.

TABLE IX-11. PERCEIVED HELPFULNESS OF CHILDREN'S TELEVISION VIEWING TO SCHOOL WORK (SAN FRANCISCO)*

By Grade and Sex

| | N | Yes | Neutral or Noncommittal | No | Not Ascertained |
|---|---|---|---|---|---|
| Eighth grade: | | | | | |
| Boys ............ | 114 | 43.0% | 0.9% | 43.9% | 12.3% |
| Girls ........... | 105 | 49.5 | 5.7 | 43.8 | 1.0 |
| Tenth grade: | | | | | |
| Boys ........... | 85 | 32.9 | 2.4 | 44.7 | 20.0 |
| Girls ........... | 116 | 46.6 | 2.6 | 38.8 | 12.1 |
| Twelfth grade: | | | | | |
| Boys ........... | 123 | 39.8 | 4.9 | 48.0 | 7.3 |
| Girls ........... | 109 | 33.0 | 3.7 | 52.3 | 11.0 |

* "Does what you see on television help you in school?"

TABLE IX-12. PERCEIVED HELPFULNESS OF CHILDREN'S TELEVISION VIEWING TO SCHOOL WORK (SAN FRANCISCO)*

By Grade and Mental Ability

| | N | Yes | No | Not Ascertained |
|---|---|---|---|---|
| Eighth grade: | | | | |
| High ............ | 43 | 74.4% | 23.2% | 2.3% |
| Middle ........... | 123 | 37.4 | 48.8 | 13.9 |
| Low ............. | 53 | 43.4 | 49.1 | 7.5 |
| Tenth grade: | | | | |
| High ............ | 32 | 46.9 | 37.5 | 15.6 |
| Middle ........... | 120 | 41.7 | 44.2 | 14.2 |
| Low ............. | 49 | 34.7 | 36.7 | 28.6 |
| Twelfth grade: | | | | |
| High ............ | 46 | 63.0 | 34.8 | 2.2 |
| Middle ........... | 137 | 29.9 | 53.3 | 16.8 |
| Low ............. | 49 | 30.6 | 55.1 | 14.2 |

* "Does what you see on television help you in school?"

TABLE IX-13. CHILDREN'S EXPERIENCE WITH INSTRUCTIONAL USE OF TELEVISION (SAN FRANCISCO)

By Grade and Sex

| | N | Have Had TV Class | Have Not Had TV Class | Not Ascertained |
|---|---|---|---|---|
| Eighth grade: | | | | |
| Boys ............. | 114 | 27.2% | 64.0% | 8.8% |
| Girls ............. | 105 | 34.3 | 58.1 | 7.6 |
| Tenth grade: | | | | |
| Boys ............. | 85 | 9.4 | 74.1 | 16.5 |
| Girls ............. | 116 | 9.5 | 81.9 | 8.6 |
| Twelfth grade: | | | | |
| Boys ............. | 123 | 7.3 | 77.2 | 15.4 |
| Girls ............. | 109 | 6.4 | 87.2 | 6.4 |

TABLE IX-14. FREQUENCY OF BOREDOM WITH SCHOOL AFTER TV AND RADIO
(SAN FRANCISCO, TELETOWN AND RADIOTOWN, CANADA)
By Grade and Sex

| | N | Sometimes Bored | Seldom or Never Bored | Not As-certained |
|---|---|---|---|---|
| | | SIXTH GRADE | | |
| Teletown | | | | |
| Boys ............. | 91 | 72.6% | 24.2% | 3.3% |
| Girls ............. | 103 | 62.2 | 35.9 | 1.9 |
| Radiotown | | | | |
| Boys ............. | 49 | 71.4 | 26.5 | 2.0 |
| Girls ............. | 61 | 77.1 | 19.7 | 3.3 |
| | | EIGHTH GRADE | | |
| San Francisco | | | | |
| Boys ............. | 114 | 56.1 | 34.2 | 9.6 |
| Girls ............. | 105 | 49.5 | 33.3 | 17.1 |
| | | TENTH GRADE | | |
| San Francisco | | | | |
| Boys ............. | 85 | 44.7 | 37.6 | 17.6 |
| Girls ............. | 116 | 49.1 | 44.0 | 7.0 |
| Teletown | | | | |
| Boys ............. | 86 | 75.6 | 24.5 | |
| Girls ............. | 99 | 80.9 | 18.2 | 1.0 |
| Radiotown | | | | |
| Boys ............. | 70 | 85.7 | 11.4 | 2.9 |
| Girls ............. | 45 | 93.4 | 6.6 | |
| | | TWELFTH GRADE | | |
| San Francisco | | | | |
| Boys ............. | 123 | 47.2 | 47.2 | 5.7 |
| Girls ............. | 109 | 34.9 | 61.5 | 3.7 |

TABLE IX-15. FREQUENCY OF BOREDOM WITH SCHOOL AFTER TV AND RADIO
(SAN FRANCISCO)
By Mental Ability and Grade

| | N | Sometimes Bored | Seldom or Never Bored | Not As-certained |
|---|---|---|---|---|
| Eighth grade: | | | | |
| High ............ | 43 | 25.6% | 55.8% | 18.6% |
| Middle ........... | 123 | 57.7 | 28.4 | 13.8 |
| Low ............. | 53 | 64.2 | 28.3 | 7.5 |
| Tenth grade: | | | | |
| High ............ | 32 | 43.8 | 40.6 | 15.6 |
| Middle ........... | 120 | 46.7 | 46.7 | 6.7 |
| Low ............. | 49 | 51.0 | 28.6 | 20.4 |
| Twelfth grade: | | | | |
| High ............ | 46 | 26.1 | 71.7 | 2.2 |
| Middle ........... | 137 | 46.0 | 50.4 | 3.7 |
| Low ............. | 49 | 42.8 | 46.9 | 10.2 |

TABLE IX-16. CHILDREN'S VIEWING OF EDUCATIONAL STATIONS
(SAN FRANCISCO AND ROCKY 1)
By Grade and Sex

| | N | Practically Every Day | Several Times a Week | One Day a Week | Occa-sionally— Less Than Weekly | Not at All | Not As-certained |
|---|---|---|---|---|---|---|---|
| **San Francisco** | | | | | | | |
| Sixth grade: | | | | | | | |
| Boys ......... | 142 | 2.0% | 8.5% | 10.9% | 16.5% | 61.1% | 1.0% |
| Girls ......... | 120 | 1.2 | 8.4 | 7.0 | 16.0 | 66.2 | 1.2 |
| Eighth grade: | | | | | | | |
| Boys ......... | 114 | 1.8 | 8.8 | 9.6 | 16.7 | 62.3 | 0.9 |
| Girls ......... | 105 | 1.0 | 8.6 | 5.7 | 17.1 | 65.7 | 1.9 |
| Tenth grade: | | | | | | | |
| Boys ......... | 85 | 1.2 | 4.7 | 5.9 | 14.1 | 72.9 | 1.2 |
| Girls ......... | 116 | 3.4 | 3.4 | 3.4 | 12.9 | 72.4 | 4.3 |
| Twelfth grade: | | | | | | | |
| Boys ......... | 123 | 0.8 | 4.1 | 13.0 | 21.1 | 59.3 | 1.6 |
| Girls ......... | 109 | 3.7 | 2.8 | 2.8 | 15.6 | 74.4 | 1.8 |
| **Rocky 1** | | | | | | | |
| Sixth grade: | | | | | | | |
| Boys ......... | 80 | 2.5 | 4.9 | 14.8 | 19.8 | 58.0 | 0 |
| Girls ......... | 107 | 0.9 | 4.7 | 14.0 | 9.3 | 69.1 | 1.9 |
| Tenth grade: | | | | | | | |
| Boys ......... | 105 | 0 | 0 | 6.7 | 18.1 | 73.3 | 1.9 |
| Girls ......... | 103 | 0 | 0 | 4.8 | 15.5 | 76.7 | 2.9 |

TABLE IX-17. VIEWING OF EDUCATIONAL TELEVISION (SAN FRANCISCO)*
By Children of Different Mental Abilities

| | N | Views ETV | Does Not View ETV | Not As-certained |
|---|---|---|---|---|
| **Eighth grade:** | | | | |
| High .............. | 43 | 63.5% | 46.5% | 0 |
| Middle ............. | 123 | 42.5 | 65.9 | 1.6 |
| Low .............. | 53 | 39.4 | 58.7 | 1.9 |
| **Tenth grade:** | | | | |
| High .............. | 32 | 43.8 | 56.2 | 0 |
| Middle ............. | 120 | 28.3 | 77.5 | 4.2 |
| Low .............. | 49 | 36.6 | 71.4 | 2.0 |
| **Twelfth grade:** | | | | |
| High .............. | 46 | 41.3 | 58.7 | 0 |
| Middle ............. | 137 | 29.9 | 67.9 | 2.2 |
| Low .............. | 49 | 30.7 | 67.3 | 2.0 |

* Difference between high and others significant, $p < .001$.

TABLE IX-18. PERCENTAGE OF CHILDREN VIEWING COMMUNITY EDUCATIONAL TELEVISION, RELATED TO VIEWING BY OTHER FAMILY MEMBERS*

| | 1 Hour or More per Week | Occasionally, But Less Than 1 Hour | Not at All |
|---|---|---|---|
| If father views ETV 1 hour or more per week..... | 46 | 38 | 16 |
| If father views ETV occasionally, but less than 1 hour per week ......................... | 16 | 73 | 10 |
| Not at all .................................. | 15 | 4 | 81 |
| If mother views ETV 1 hour or more per week.... | 48 | 26 | 26 |
| If mother views ETV occasionally, but less than 1 hour per week ......................... | 11 | 74 | 15 |
| Not at all .................................. | 14 | 0 | 86 |
| If older child views ETV 1 hour or more per week.. | 74 | 13 | 13 |
| If older child views ETV occasionally, but less than 1 hour per week ......................... | 5 | 87 | 4 |
| Not at all .................................. | 4 | 4 | 92 |

* 185 mothers, 182 fathers, 442 children.

# TABLES ON INTELLIGENCE AND SOCIAL NORMS

▶ *These tables are referred to particularly in Chapter 6.*

TABLE X-1. PER CENT OF STUDENTS IN FOUR MEDIA USE CATEGORIES (SAN FRANCISCO, FIVE ROCKY MOUNTAIN TOWNS, TELETOWN AND RADIOTOWN, CANADA)
By Grade

| | N | Low TV, Low Print | Pleasure-oriented, High TV, Low Print | Reality-Oriented, Low TV, High Print | High TV, High Print |
|---|---|---|---|---|---|
| San Francisco* | | | | | |
| Eighth grade ........ | 197 | 7.6% | 34.5% | 25.9% | 32.0% |
| Tenth grade ........ | 213 | 20.6 | 44.1 | 13.2 | 22.1 |
| Twelfth grade ....... | 183 | 31.1 | 17.5 | 27.9 | 23.5 |
| | | | | | |
| Rocky Mountain towns† | | | | | |
| Sixth grade ......... | 611 | 7.1 | 24.2 | 19.3 | 49.4 |
| Tenth grade ......... | 597 | 22.6 | 22.9 | 26.6 | 27.9 |
| | | | | | |
| Teletown, Canada‡ | | | | | |
| Sixth grade ......... | 191 | 15.7 | 23.0 | 25.7 | 35.6 |
| Tenth grade ........ | 181 | 32.6 | 18.8 | 34.8 | 13.8 |

| | N | Low Movies and Comics, Low Print | High Movies and Comics, Low Print | Low Movies and Comics, High Print | High Movies and Comics, High Print |
|---|---|---|---|---|---|
| Radiotown, Canada Sixth and tenth grades§ | 212 | 27.4% | 21.7% | 21.7% | 29.2% |

\* $X^2 = 64.95$, $p$ beyond .001, with $df = 6$.
† $X^2 = 94.26$, $p$ beyond .001, with $df = 3$.
‡ $X^2 = 31.84$, $p$ beyond .001, with $df = 3$.
§ Combined because of smallness of $N$.

TABLE X-2. RELATION OF MEDIA USE CATEGORIES TO USE OF VARIOUS MEDIA
(ROCKY MOUNTAIN TOWNS)*
By Grade

|  | Low TV, Low Print | Pleasure- oriented | Reality- oriented | High TV, High Print |
|---|---|---|---|---|
| **Sixth grade:** | | | | |
| Radio, median minutes daily... | 32 | 41 | 43 | 61 |
| Comic books, monthly median. | 5.8 | 5.4 | 4.4 | 7.1 |
| Movies, monthly median ..... | 2.4 | 1.9 | 1.8 | 2.4 |
| Newspapers,† per cent reading daily ................... | 44 | 36 | 57 | 56 |
|  | (N = 43) | (N = 148) | (N = 118) | (N = 302) |
| **Tenth grade:** | | | | |
| Radio, median minutes daily... | 98 | 73 | 107 | 96 |
| Comic books,‡ monthly median | 0.4 | 1.7 | 0.4 | 2.0 |
| Movies,§ monthly median .... | 1.8 | 2.1 | 2.0 | 2.8 |
| Newspapers,‖ per cent reading daily ................... | 67 | 61 | 81 | 70 |
|  | (N = 135) | (N = 137) | (N = 159) | (N = 166) |

* Significance tests apply *within* grades.
† $X^2 = 19.17, p = .001, df = 3.$
‡ $X^2 = 33.56, p = .001, df = 3.$
§ $X^2 = 9.41, p = .01, df = 3.$
‖ $X^2 = 15.18, p = .01, df = 3.$

TABLE X-3. PERCENTAGES OF CHILDREN IN MEDIA USE CATEGORIES SELECTING
VARIOUS NEWSPAPER CONTENT (ROCKY MOUNTAIN TOWNS)
By Grade
(*In per cent*)

|  | Low TV, Low Print | Pleasure- oriented | Reality- oriented | High TV, High Print |
|---|---|---|---|---|
| **Sixth grade:** | | | | |
| Local news ................ | 30.2 | 34.5 | 58.5 | 54.0 |
| Foreign news ............... | 25.6 | 28.4 | 46.6 | 38.1 |
| News of national government.. | 20.9 | 18.9 | 29.7 | 28.5 |
| Editorials .................. | 9.3 | 9.5 | 11.9 | 12.6 |
| Comics ................... | 83.7 | 83.1 | 90.7 | 88.4 |
|  | (N = 43) | (N = 148) | (N = 118) | (N = 302) |
| **Tenth grade:** | | | | |
| Local news ................ | 71.1 | 55.5 | 88.0 | 72.9 |
| Foreign news ............... | 19.3 | 18.2 | 42.8 | 31.9 |
| News of national government.. | 17.8 | 16.1 | 40.2 | 37.3 |
| Editorials ................. | 15.6 | 8.8 | 22.0 | 13.9 |
| Comics ................... | 81.5 | 83.9 | 83.0 | 89.8 |
|  | (N = 135) | (N = 137) | (N = 159) | (N = 166) |

TABLE X-4. PERCENTAGES OF CHILDREN IN MEDIA USE CATEGORIES READING
VARIOUS TYPES OF MAGAZINES (ROCKY MOUNTAIN TOWNS)

By Grade

(*In per cent*)

|  | Low TV, Low Print | Pleasure-oriented | Reality-oriented | High TV, High Print |
|---|---|---|---|---|
| **Sixth grade:** | | | | |
| Pulps | 7.0 | 8.1 | 8.5 | 13.9 |
| Sports, hobby | 34.7 | 39.0 | 49.2 | 49.3 |
| General | 58.2 | 55.4 | 70.3 | 76.2 |
| News | 27.9 | 27.7 | 39.8 | 36.4 |
| Quality | 2.3 | 4.7 | 6.8 | 4.5 |
| Weighted average (higher score, higher quality) | 4.35 | 4.71 | 5.58 | 5.40 |
| | (N = 43) | (N = 148) | (N = 118) | (N = 302) |
| **Tenth grade:** | | | | |
| Pulps | 13.3 | 24.1 | 15.1 | 19.9 |
| Sports, hobby | 40.7 | 33.6 | 39.9 | 41.6 |
| General | 66.7 | 58.4 | 87.4 | 81.9 |
| News | 27.4 | 21.9 | 45.9 | 42.8 |
| Quality | 5.2 | 3.6 | 11.3 | 3.0 |
| Weighted average (higher score, higher quality) | 4.68 | 4.11 | 6.01 | 4.99 |
| | (N = 135) | (N = 137) | (N = 159) | (N = 166) |

TABLE X-5. VIEWING OF NEWS AND PUBLIC AFFAIRS PROGRAMS ON TELEVISION
(ROCKY MOUNTAIN TOWNS)

By Media Use Categories and by Grade

|  | Low TV, Low Print | Pleasure-oriented | Reality-oriented | High TV, High Print |
|---|---|---|---|---|
| **Sixth grade:** | | | | |
| Average number of news and public affairs programs checked as watched | 1.35 | 1.62 | 1.53 | 1.90 |
| | (N = 43) | (N = 148) | (N = 118) | (N = 302) |
| **Tenth grade:** | | | | |
| Average number of news and public affairs programs checked as watched | 1.61 | 1.67 | 1.99 | 1.93 |
| | (N = 135) | (N = 137) | (N = 159) | (N = 166) |

TABLE X-6. MEDIA WHICH WOULD BE MISSED MOST BY CHILDREN IN DIFFERENT
MEDIA USE CATEGORIES (ROCKY MOUNTAIN TOWNS)
By Grade
(*In per cent*)

|  | Low TV, Low Print | Pleasure-oriented | Reality-oriented | High TV, High Print |
|---|---|---|---|---|
| **Sixth grade:** | | | | |
| Books ..................... | 3.2 | 3.6 | 24.8 | 13.8 |
| Magazines ................. | | 0.9 | 1.1 | 0.4 |
| Newspaper ................ | 19.4 | 4.5 | 5.6 | 2.2 |
| Comic books .............. | | 1.8 | 1.1 | 1.8 |
| Television ................ | 67.8 | 81.3 | 54.0 | 72.0 |
| Radio ..................... | 3.2 | 5.4 | 9.0 | 5.3 |
| Movies ................... | 3.2 | 0.9 | 3.4 | 2.7 |
| No answer ................ | 3.2 | 1.8 | 1.1 | 1.8 |
| | (*N* = 43) | (*N* = 148) | (*N* = 118) | (*N* = 302) |
| **Tenth grade:** | | | | |
| Books ..................... | 2.0 | 4.0 | 9.7 | 9.9 |
| Magazines ................. | 2.0 | 1.0 | 5.7 | 3.8 |
| Newspaper ................ | 12.9 | 4.0 | 22.0 | 12.9 |
| Comic books .............. | 1.0 | 1.0 | 0.8 | |
| Television ................ | 33.6 | 69.0 | 21.2 | 50.0 |
| Radio ..................... | 42.6 | 16.0 | 36.5 | 20.4 |
| Movies ................... | 1.0 | 4.0 | 4.1 | 3.0 |
| No answer ................ | 4.9 | 1.0 | | |
| | (*N* = 135) | (*N* = 137) | (*N* = 159) | (*N* = 166) |

TABLE X-7. EXPOSURE TO EDUCATIONAL TELEVISION BY CHILDREN IN DIFFERENT
MEDIA USE CATEGORIES (ROCKY MOUNTAIN TOWNS)*
(*In per cent*)

|  | Low TV, Low Print (*N* = 178) | Pleasure-oriented (*N* = 285) | Reality-oriented (*N* = 277) | High TV, High Print (*N* = 468) |
|---|---|---|---|---|
| Never watch ETV........... | 82 | 85 | 62 | 64 |
| Sometimes watch ETV....... | 18 | 15 | 38 | 36 |

* $X^2 = 17.43, p = .001, df = 3.$

TABLE X-8. KNOWLEDGE SCORES BY CHILDREN IN DIFFERENT MEDIA USE CATEGORIES
(ROCKY MOUNTAIN TOWNS)
By Grade

| | Sixth Grade | | | | Tenth Grade | | | |
|---|---|---|---|---|---|---|---|---|
| | LoPr LoTV (N = 43) | LoPr HiTV (N = 148) | HiPr LoTV (N = 118) | HiPr HiTV (N = 302) | LoPr LoTV (N = 135) | LoPr HiTV (N = 137) | HiPr LoTV (N = 159) | HiPr HiTV (N = 166) |
| *Average score on:* | | | | | | | | |
| Science quiz ......... | 1.58 | 1.35 | 1.52 | 1.64 | 1.92 | 1.76 | 2.19 | 2.11 |
| Place identification* ... | 1.24 | 1.21 | 1.40 | 1.65 | 1.96 | 1.91 | 3.13 | 2.57 |
| Senators named† ...... | 0.09 | 0.12 | 0.13 | 0.28 | 0.58 | 0.36 | 1.08 | 0.78 |
| Writers named‡ ...... | 0.42 | 0.34 | 0.76 | 0.59 | 1.03 | 0.85 | 2.37 | 1.32 |
| Jazz band leaders named | 0.40 | 0.47 | 0.58 | 0.69 | 2.53 | 1.71 | 2.83 | 2.66 |
| Singers named ........ | 4.02 | 5.06 | 4.80 | 5.23 | 6.89 | 6.44 | 7.35 | 7.14 |
| Top ten songs ........ | 3.07 | 3.16 | 3.43 | 3.56 | 4.78 | 4.26 | 4.45 | 4.49 |
| Picture quiz§ ......... | 2.79 | 3.15 | 3.23 | 3.45 | 5.12 | 5.03 | 5.87 | 5.76 |
| *Picture identification:* | | | | | | | | |
| Identified more public affairs than entertainment pictures ...... | 4.7% | 11.5% | 19.5% | 17.9% | 22.2% | 23.4% | 26.4% | 23.5% |
| Equal .............. | 9.3 | 14.2 | 11.9 | 14.9 | 22.2 | 19.7 | 25.8 | 18.7 |
| Identified more entertainment than public affairs pictures ...... | 79.1 | 73.0 | 65.3 | 65.5 | 55.6 | 54.7 | 47.8 | 57.2 |
| None correct ......... | 6.9 | 1.3 | 3.3 | 1.7 | | 2.2 | | 0.6 |

* Tenth grade, $X^2 = 26.10$, $p < .001$, $df = 3$.
† Tenth grade, $X^2 = 11.62$, $p < .001$, $df = 3$.
‡ Tenth grade, $X^2 = 25.14$, $p < .001$, $df = 3$.
§ Tenth grade, $X^2 = 16.01$, $p < .001$, $df = 2$ (two high-print categories combined).


TABLE X-9. RELATION OF MEDIA USE CATEGORIES TO SEX
(ROCKY MOUNTAIN TOWNS)
By Grade

| | N | Low TV, Low Print | Pleasure-oriented | Reality-oriented | High TV, High Print |
|---|---|---|---|---|---|
| Sixth grade: | | | | | |
| Boys ........... | 314 | 10.2% | 27.1% | 16.2% | 46.5% |
| Girls ........... | 297 | 3.7 | 21.2 | 22.6 | 52.5 |
| Tenth grade: | | | | | |
| Boys ........... | 288 | 22.9 | 26.0 | 23.3 | 27.8 |
| Girls ........... | 309 | 22.3 | 20.1 | 29.8 | 27.8 |

Table X-10. Relation of Media Use Categories to Intelligence (San Francisco, Rocky Mountain Towns, Teletown and Radiotown, Canada)*

By Grade

| Mental Ability | N | Low TV, Low Print | Pleasure-oriented | Reality-oriented | High TV, High Print |
|---|---|---|---|---|---|
| **San Francisco** | | | | | |
| Eighth grade: | | | | | |
| High ........ | 43 | 14.0% | 9.3% | 55.8% | 20.9% |
| Middle ....... | 113 | 6.2 | 41.6 | 17.7 | 34.5 |
| Low ......... | 41 | 4.9 | 41.5 | 17.1 | 36.5 |
| Tenth grade: | | | | | |
| High ........ | 32 | 21.9 | 37.5 | 25.0 | 15.6 |
| Middle ....... | 131 | 20.6 | 45.0 | 13.0 | 21.4 |
| Low ......... | 50 | 10.0 | 46.0 | 6.0 | 28.0 |
| Twelfth grade: | | | | | |
| High ........ | 39 | 38.5 | 7.7 | 30.8 | 23.0 |
| Middle ....... | 108 | 28.5 | 17.6 | 33.3 | 10.4 |
| Low ......... | 36 | 30.6 | 28.8 | 8.3 | 33.3 |
| **Rocky Mountain towns** | | | | | |
| Sixth grade: | | | | | |
| High ........ | 188 | 3.2 | 14.4 | 22.9 | 59.6 |
| Middle ....... | 267 | 8.2 | 25.5 | 19.1 | 47.2 |
| Low ......... | 137 | 8.0 | 34.3 | 16.1 | 41.6 |
| Tenth grade: | | | | | |
| High ........ | 142 | 25.4 | 9.2 | 44.4 | 21.1 |
| Middle ....... | 281 | 23.5 | 21.4 | 25.3 | 29.9 |
| Low ......... | 171 | 18.7 | 36.8 | 14.6 | 29.8 |
| **Teletown** | | | | | |
| Sixth grade: | | | | | |
| High ........ | 73 | 12.3 | 17.9 | 34.2 | 35.6 |
| Middle ....... | 75 | 18.7 | 22.7 | 24.0 | 34.6 |
| Low ......... | 43 | 16.3 | 32.6 | 13.9 | 37.2 |
| Tenth grade: | | | | | |
| High ........ | 28 | 21.4 | 10.7 | 64.3 | 3.6 |
| Middle ....... | 98 | 31.6 | 18.3 | 33.8 | 16.2 |
| Low ......... | 52 | 38.5 | 25.0 | 21.1 | 15.4 |
| **Radiotown** | | | | | |
| Sixth and tenth grades: | | | | | |
| High ........ | 53 | 22.6 | 9.4 | 32.1 | 35.9 |
| Middle ....... | 90 | 23.3 | 27.8 | 20.0 | 28.9 |
| Low ......... | 69 | 36.2 | 23.3 | 15.9 | 24.6 |

* San Francisco grades combined, $X^2 = 40.3339$, $p$ beyond .001, with $df = 6$.
Rocky Mountain towns, grades combined, $X^2 = 74.65$, $p$ beyond .001, with $df = 6$.
Teletown, Canada, sixth grade, n.s.; tenth grade, $X^2 = 15.58$, $p = .02$, with $df = 6$.
Radiotown, Canada, grades combined, $X^2 = 19.38$, $p = .01$, $df = 6$.

TABLE X-11. RELATION OF MEDIA USE CATEGORIES TO SOCIOECONOMIC STATUS
(ROCKY MOUNTAIN TOWNS)*

By Grade

| Socioeconomic Status | N | Low TV, Low Print | Pleasure-oriented | Reality-oriented | High TV, High Print |
|---|---|---|---|---|---|
| Sixth grade: | | | | | |
| Highest ........ | 155 | 8.3% | 17.1% | 22.7% | 51.9% |
| High .......... | 154 | 6.6 | 25.7 | 17.1 | 50.7 |
| Low ........... | 154 | 7.2 | 24.7 | 18.7 | 49.4 |
| Lowest ........ | 149 | 3.3 | 40.0 | 23.3 | 33.3 |
| Tenth grade: | | | | | |
| Highest ........ | 148 | 21.3 | 8.3 | 43.5 | 26.9 |
| High .......... | 149 | 26.5 | 19.9 | 26.0 | 27.6 |
| Low ........... | 150 | 18.8 | 27.5 | 24.8 | 28.9 |
| Lowest ........ | 150 | 26.8 | 31.7 | 14.6 | 26.8 |

* Grades combined, $X^2 = 34.07$, $p = .001$, $df = 9$.

TABLE X-12. RELATION OF MEDIA USE CATEGORIES TO EDUCATIONAL GOALS*
(ROCKY MOUNTAIN TOWNS)

By Grade

(*In per cent*)

| Educational Goals | Low TV, Low Print ($N = 178$) | Pleasure-oriented ($N = 285$) | Reality-oriented ($N = 277$) | High TV, High Print ($N = 468$) |
|---|---|---|---|---|
| Will only finish high school or less | 21.7 | 28.8 | 14.8 | 18.0 |
| Some college ................. | 14.0 | 9.1 | 12.1 | 8.6 |
| Finish college ................ | 48.8 | 38.9 | 60.4 | 52.1 |
| Not ascertained .............. | 15.5 | 22.1 | 12.6 | 21.3 |

* $X^2 = 22.79$, $p < .001$, $df = 6$.
Compare also these figures:

| Average weekly homework time...... | 7.8 hrs. | 6.0 hrs. | 7.32 hrs. | 5.8 hrs. |
|---|---|---|---|---|

TABLE X-13. RELATION OF MEDIA USE CATEGORIES TO DISCUSSING THE NEWS
WITH OTHERS (ROCKY MOUNTAIN TOWNS)*

By Grade

(*In per cent*)

| Discussing the News | Low TV, Low Print | Pleasure-oriented | Reality-oriented | High TV, High Print |
|---|---|---|---|---|
| Sixth grade: | | | | |
| Yes ...................... | 25.6 | 22.3 | 37.3 | 35.4 |
| No ...................... | 72.1 | 76.4 | 61.0 | 64.2 |
| No answer ................ | 2.3 | 1.7 | 1.7 | 0.3 |
| | ($N = 43$) | ($N = 148$) | ($N = 118$) | ($N = 302$) |
| Tenth grade: | | | | |
| Yes ...................... | 36.3 | 30.7 | 52.8 | 38.0 |
| No ...................... | 63.0 | 68.6 | 45.3 | 60.2 |
| No answer ................ | 0.7 | 0.7 | 1.9 | 1.8 |
| | ($N = 135$) | ($N = 137$) | ($N = 159$) | ($N = 166$) |

* Sixth grade, $X^2 = 14.23$, $p = .01$, $df = 3$.
Tenth grade, $X^2 = 18.74$, $p = .001$, $df = 3$.

TABLE X-14. RELATION OF MEDIA USE CATEGORIES TO FINDING SCHOOL DULL
(ROCKY MOUNTAIN TOWNS)*
By Grade
(In per cent)

| Find School Dull | Low TV, Low Print | Pleasure-oriented | Reality-oriented | High TV, High Print |
|---|---|---|---|---|
| Sixth grade: | | | | |
| Very often ................ | 16.3 | 14.9 | 13.6 | 13.4 |
| Often .................... | 14.0 | 8.1 | 8.5 | 12.1 |
| Sometimes ................ | 35.0 | 52.7 | 47.4 | 44.1 |
| Not very often ............. | 20.7 | 14.2 | 18.6 | 22.3 |
| Never .................... | 14.0 | 8.8 | 10.9 | 7.2 |
| | (N = 43) | (N = 149) | (N = 118) | (N = 302) |
| Tenth grade: | | | | |
| Very often ................ | 17.7 | 23.1 | 11.9 | 15.1 |
| Often .................... | 17.1 | 16.7 | 13.2 | 18.1 |
| Sometimes ................ | 42.2 | 49.6 | 44.6 | 47.6 |
| Not very often ............. | 16.3 | 8.1 | 22.6 | 10.4 |
| Never .................... | 5.2 | | 6.3 | 5.4 |
| | (N = 135) | (N = 137) | (N = 159) | (N = 166) |

* Sixth grade, n.s.; tenth grade, $X^2 = 23.8$, $p = .001$, $df = 6$.


TABLE X-15. PERCENTAGE OF CHILDREN IN FOUR MEDIA USE CATEGORIES WHO SCORE
ABOVE AND BELOW THE MEDIAN ON AN INDEX OF "FUTURE"
ORIENTATION (DENVER)*

| | N | Low | High |
|---|---|---|---|
| Media use category: | | | |
| Low TV, low print ............ | 72 | 40.3% | 59.7% |
| High TV, low print ............ | 58 | 69.0 | 31.0 |
| Low TV, high print ............ | 36 | 16.7 | 83.3 |
| High TV, high print ........... | 32 | 40.6 | 59.4 |

* $X^2 = 26.08$, $df = 3$, $p < .001$.


TABLE X-16. MEAN SCORES ON AN INDEX OF "FUTURE" ORIENTATION BY TENTH-GRADE
CHILDREN OF DIFFERING SOCIOECONOMIC STATUS (DENVER)

| | N | Mean | SD |
|---|---|---|---|
| Socioeconomic status: | | | |
| High ...................... | 87 | 12.1* | 2.29 |
| Middle .................... | 61 | 11.7 | 2.58 |
| Low ...................... | 35 | 11.3* | 2.86 |

* Difference between high and low is significant at the .06 level by one-tail test ($CR = 1.54$).

TABLE X-17. Responses to "The Best Way to Live Is to Enjoy Today and Not Think about Tomorrow" Related to Four Media Use Categories for Tenth-Grade Students, Holding Socioeconomic Status Constant (Denver)

| | Low TV Low Print | High TV Low Print | Low TV High Print | High TV High Print |
|---|---|---|---|---|
| High SES ($N = 87$)* | | | | |
| Disagree ............... | 23 | 5 | 22 | 6 |
| Agree .................. | 10 | 11 | 5 | 5 |
| Middle SES ($N = 61$) | | | | |
| Disagree ............... | 7 | 13 | 10 | 5 |
| Agree .................. | 7 | 11 | 3 | 5 |
| Low SES ($N = 35$) | | | | |
| Disagree ............... | 2 | 7 | 6 | 4 |
| Agree .................. | 6 | 5 | 2 | 3 |

* Relationship between response to question and media use categories is significant at the .01 level in the high socioeconomic status group. ($X^2 = 11.9$, $df = 3$.)

# TABLES ON INTERPERSONAL RELATIONSHIPS*

▶ *These tables are referred to particularly in Chapter 7.*

TABLE XI-1. MEAN SCORES ON SIX AGGRESSION INDICES BY CHILDREN IN DIFFERENT
MEDIA USE CATEGORIES
By Grade

| | Sixth Grade° | | | | Tenth Grade† | | | |
|---|---|---|---|---|---|---|---|---|
| | LoPr LoTV ($N =$ 43) | LoPr HiTV ($N =$ 148) | HiPr LoTV ($N =$ 118) | HiPr HiTV ($N =$ 302) | LoPr LoTV ($N =$ 135) | LoPr HiTV ($N =$ 137) | HiPr LoTV ($N =$ 159) | HiPr HiTV ($N =$ 166) |
| Aggression anxiety ...... | 10.13 | 10.43 | 10.82 | 10.72 | 10.95 | 10.33 | 11.25 | 10.53 |
| Attenuated aggression ... | 8.98 | 9.85 | 9.68 | 9.97 | 9.50 | 10.24 | 9.44 | 9.20 |
| Projective aggression ... | 8.18 | 8.00 | 7.76 | 7.73 | 7.44 | 7.76 | 6.88 | 7.37 |
| Self-aggression . | 8.38 | 8.22 | 8.38 | 8.32 | 7.42 | 7.40 | 7.50 | 7.04 |
| Prosocial aggression ... | 10.40 | 10.26 | 10.16 | 10.38 | 9.27 | 9.05 | 9.16 | 9.63 |
| Antisocial aggression ... | 7.13 | 7.41 | 6.63 | 6.53 | 6.16 | 6.84 | 5.44 | 5.98 |

° N.S.
† Aggression anxiety, $X^2 = 18.23$, $p = .01$, $df = 6$.
Antisocial aggression, $X^2 = 17.84$, $p = .01$, $df = 6$.

TABLE XI-2. MEAN AGGRESSION SCORES FOR CHILDREN OF HIGHEST SOCIOECONOMIC
STATUS, FANTASY-ORIENTED VS. OTHERS
By Grade

| | Sixth Grade | | Tenth Grade | |
|---|---|---|---|---|
| | Fantasy-oriented ($N = 31$) | All Others ($N = 179$) | Fantasy-oriented ($N = 9$) | All Others ($N = 110$) |
| Aggression anxiety ......... | 9.82 | 10.51 | 11.25 | 11.36 |
| Attenuated aggression ...... | 9.43 | 9.46 | 9.25 | 9.33 |
| Projective aggression ....... | 7.40 | 7.00 | 8.36 | 6.74 |
| Self-aggression ............ | 7.76 | 8.15 | 7.00 | 7.54 |
| Prosocial aggression ........ | 9.35 | 10.30 | 9.25 | 9.78 |
| Antisocial aggression ........ | 6.80 | 6.04 | 7.00 | 5.39 |

* All tables except XI-12 are for five Rocky Mountain towns.

TABLE XI-3. AMOUNT OF CONFLICT STEMMING FROM CHILDREN OF HIGH SOCIO-
ECONOMIC STATUS HAVING LOWER ASPIRATIONS THAN THEIR
PARENTS HAVE FOR THEM

By Media Orientation and Grade

(*In per cent*)

| | Sixth Grade | | Tenth Grade | |
|---|---|---|---|---|
| | Fantasy-oriented (N = 31) | All Others (N = 179) | Fantasy-oriented (N = 9) | All Others (N = 110) |
| **A. CASES IN WHICH PARENTS' ASPIRATIONS ARE HIGHER** | | | | |
| No conflict ............. | 48.4 | 52.8 | 22.2 | 40.9 |
| Light conflict ........... | 25.8 | 32.9 | 22.2 | 29.1 |
| Moderate conflict ....... | 19.4 | 10.6 | 44.4 | 24.5 |
| Heavy conflict .......... | 3.2 | 3.1 | | 2.7 |
| N.A. .................. | 3.2 | 0.6 | 11.1 | 2.7 |
| **B. CASES IN WHICH PARENTS' ASPIRATIONS ARE LOWER** | | | | |
| No conflict ............. | 83.9 | 93.3 | 77.8 | 87.3 |
| Light conflict ........... | 6.5 | 3.4 | 11.1 | 6.4 |
| Moderate conflict ....... | 6.5 | 2.8 | | 3.6 |
| N.A. .................. | 3.2 | 0.6 | 11.1 | 2.7 |

TABLE XI-4. AMOUNT OF CONFLICT STEMMING FROM CHILDREN OF HIGH SOCIO-
ECONOMIC STATUS HAVING HIGHER ASPIRATIONS THAN
THEIR PEERS HAVE

By Media Orientation and Grade

(*In per cent*)

| | Sixth Grade | | Tenth Grade | |
|---|---|---|---|---|
| | Fantasy-oriented) (N = 31) | All Others (N = 179) | Fantasy-oriented (N = 9) | All Others (N = 110) |
| **A. CASES IN WHICH PEERS' ASPIRATIONS ARE HIGHER** | | | | |
| No conflict ............. | 74.0 | 77.0 | 44.4 | 73.6 |
| Light conflict ........... | 10.0 | 14.0 | 22.2 | 13.6 |
| Moderate conflict ....... | 6.0 | 6.0 | 11.1 | 8.2 |
| Heavy conflict .......... | 6.0 | 2.0 | | |
| N.A. .................. | 3.0 | 2.0 | 22.2 | 4.5 |
| **B. CASES IN WHICH PEERS' ASPIRATIONS ARE LOWER** | | | | |
| No conflict ............. | 61.0 | 67.0 | 33.0 | 61.0 |
| Light conflict ........... | 19.0 | 21.0 | 22.0 | 17.0 |
| Moderate conflict ....... | 16.0 | 9.0 | 11.0 | 15.0 |
| Heavy conflict .......... | | 1.0 | 11.0 | 2.0 |
| N.A. .................. | 3.0 | 2.0 | 22.0 | 5.0 |

TABLE XI-5. PERCENTAGE OF CHILDREN HAVING CONFLICT STEMMING
FROM LOWER ASPIRATIONS THAN PARENTS OR PEERS[*]
By Media Use Categories

| | N | High Parent High Peer Conflict | High Parent Low Peer Conflict | Low Parent High Peer Conflict | Low Parent Low Peer Conflict |
|---|---|---|---|---|---|
| Low print, low TV .... | 164 | 5.4% | 22.6% | 9.8% | 62.2% |
| Pleasure-oriented ..... | 251 | 12.7 | 24.3 | 9.2 | 53.8 |
| Reality-oriented ...... | 261 | 5.0 | 22.6 | 6.1 | 66.3 |
| High print, high TV ... | 423 | 6.9 | 22.2 | 7.3 | 63.6 |

[*] $X^2 = 18.75$, $p = .025$ (one-tail test), $df = 9$.

TABLE XI-6. AMOUNT OF CONFLICT STEMMING FROM CHILDREN HAVING
LOWER ASPIRATIONS THAN THEIR PARENTS HAVE FOR THEM
By Grade, Sex, and Mental Ability

| | N | No Conflict | Light Conflict | Moderate Conflict | Heavy Conflict |
|---|---|---|---|---|---|
| | | GRADE[*] | | | |
| Sixth ............ | 712 | 45.2% | 26.7% | 20.8% | 7.3% |
| Tenth ............ | 626 | 36.3 | 27.6 | 26.2 | 9.9 |
| | | SEX[†] | | | |
| Boys ............ | 685 | 35.5 | 27.4 | 26.7 | 10.4 |
| Girls ............ | 563 | 46.9 | 26.8 | 19.7 | 6.6 |
| | | MENTAL ABILITY[‡] | | | |
| High ............ | 374 | 57.2 | 24.3 | 15.0 | 3.5 |
| Middle ............ | 610 | 39.8 | 28.0 | 23.4 | 8.7 |
| Low ............ | 327 | 26.0 | 28.1 | 31.5 | 14.4 |

[*] $X^2 = 13.88$, $p = .01$, $df = 3$.
[†] $X^2 = 23.19$, $p = .001$, $df = 3$.
[‡] $X^2 = 86.10$, $p = .001$, $df = 6$.

TABLE XI-7. RELATION OF MEDIA EXPOSURE TO CONFLICT STEMMING FROM CHILD
HAVING LOWER ASPIRATIONS FOR SELF THAN PARENTS

|  | Heavy Conflict ($N = 114$) | Moderate Conflict ($N = 312$) | Light Conflict ($N = 363$) | No Conflict ($N = 549$) |
|---|---|---|---|---|
| MEDIA USE* | | | | |
| School day TV time (minutes)... | 186.84 | 166.8 | 174.1 | 158.6 |
| School day radio time (minutes). | 102.43 | 79.8 | 86.9 | 77.5 |
| Average number of movies monthly .................. | 3.12 | 2.81 | 2.91 | 2.45 |
| Average number of comic books monthly .................. | 4.11 | 4.28 | 4.33 | 4.02 |
| Average number of magazines monthly .................. | 3.79 | 4.11 | 4.13 | 4.30 |
| Average number of books monthly | 2.60 | 3.13 | 2.84 | 3.20 |
| NEWSPAPER READING† | | | | |
| Daily ....................... | 57.0% | 59.8% | 57.1% | 61.6% |
| Several times weekly ........... | 28.1 | 26.4 | 22.4 | 21.9 |
| Once a week ................. | 7.9 | 8.0 | 9.3 | 7.7 |
| Seldom .................... | 5.3 | 5.5 | 9.9 | 8.6 |
| TYPES OF MAGAZINES READ‡ | | | | |
| Pulps, confession ............. | 14.9% | 13.5% | 12.2% | 11.5% |
| Sports, hobby, special interest.... | 33.3 | 44.9 | 45.8 | 38.8 |
| General ..................... | 54.4 | 72.5 | 62.2 | 74.5 |
| News ....................... | 28.1 | 35.5 | 29.8 | 37.3 |
| Quality .................... | 1.8 | 4.4 | 5.8 | 6.7 |
| N.A. ....................... | 19.3 | 8.3 | 14.1 | 8.7 |

* TV, $X^2 = 18.27$, $p = .005$, $df = 6$. Radio, $X^2 = 10.33$, $p = .10$, $df = 6$. Movies, $X^2 = 13.98$, $p = .025$, $df = 6$. Comic books, no significant difference. Magazines, $X^2 = 6.05$, $p = .025$, $df = 3$. Books, $X^2 = 8.77$, $p = .025$, $df = 3$. (All one-tail tests.)
† No significant difference.
‡ Choices were not exclusive so that children could name more than one type. Sports, hobby, special interest, $X^2 = 8.87$, $p = .05$, $df = 3$. General, $X^2 = 29.09$, $p = .001$, $df = 3$. News, $X^2 = 7.87$, $p = .05$, $df = 3$.


TABLE XI-8. MEAN SCORES ON AGGRESSION INDICES BY AMOUNT OF CONFLICT
STEMMING FROM CHILD HAVING LOWER ASPIRATIONS FOR
SELF THAN PARENTS*

|  | Heavy Conflict ($N = 114$) | Moderate Conflict ($N = 312$) | Light Conflict ($N = 363$) | No Conflict ($N = 549$) |
|---|---|---|---|---|
| Aggression anxiety ......... | 9.87 | 10.37 | 10.69 | 10.96 |
| Attenuated aggression ...... | 9.73 | 9.56 | 9.63 | 9.40 |
| Projective aggression ....... | 7.97 | 7.85 | 7.43 | 7.37 |
| Self-aggression ............ | 7.93 | 8.22 | 7.86 | 7.49 |
| Prosocial aggression ........ | 9.59 | 9.58 | 9.84 | 10.11 |
| Antisocial aggression ....... | 8.05 | 7.07 | 6.19 | 6.11 |

* Aggression anxiety, $X^2 = 24.39$, $p. = .001$, $df = 6$. Attenuated aggression, n.s. Projective aggression, $X^2 = 6.18$, $p. = .05$, $df = 2$(dicho. no,lt vs. mod,hi). Self-aggression, $X^2 = 16.31$, $p = .02$, $df = 6$. Prosocial aggression, $X^2 = 6.60$, $p = .05$, $df = 2$(dicho. no,lt vs. mod,hi). Antisocial aggression, $X^2 = 50.82$, $p = .001$, $df = 6$.

TABLE XI-9. CHILDREN'S ANTISOCIAL AGGRESSION SCORES RELATED TO AMOUNT OF
CONFLICT STEMMING FROM CHILD HAVING LOWER ASPIRATIONS THAN
PARENTS AND/OR PEERS*
(*In per cent*)

|  | High Parent High Peer Conflict ($N = 98$) | High Parent Low Peer Conflict ($N = 210$) | Low Parent High Peer Conflict ($N = 27$) | Low Parent Low Peer Conflict ($N = 414$) |
|---|---|---|---|---|
| Antisocial aggression score: |  |  |  |  |
| High ...................... | 69.4 | 52.6 | 48.1 | 43.2 |
| Low ...................... | 30.6 | 47.4 | 51.9 | 56.8 |

\* $X^2 = 22.20, p = .001, df = 3.$

TABLE XI-10. CONFLICT BETWEEN CHILDREN'S ASPIRATIONS AND PARENTS' AND PEERS'
ASPIRATIONS, WHEN CHILDREN'S ASPIRATIONS ARE LOWER

|  | $N$ | Per Cent of Children Having High Antisocial Aggression Scores | | |
|---|---|---|---|---|
|  |  | High Parent High Peer Conflict | High Parent Low Peer Conflict | Low Parent Low Peer Conflict |
| A. DIFFERENT SOCIOECONOMIC CATEGORIES* | | | | |
| Highest ............ | 169 | 77.8% | 45.6% | 36.8% |
| High ............. | 197 | 76.9 | 53.6 | 39.1 |
| Low .............. | 198 | 51.5 | 47.1 | 49.2 |
| Lowest ............ | 66 | 75.0 | 70.4 | 63.0 |
| B. DIFFERENT MENTAL ABILITIES† | | | | |
| High ............. | 205 | 55.5 | 40.4 | 30.9 |
| Middle ............ | 326 | 67.4 | 42.7 | 49.5 |
| Low .............. | 166 | 75.6 | 69.7 | 59.4 |

\* $N$'s in some cells are too small to permit testing by $X^2$. "High SES" group, $X^2 = 11.67, p = .01, df = 2.$ "Low SES" group, n.s.
† High, n.s. Middle, $X^2 = 7.60, p = .05, df = 2.$ Low, n.s.

TABLE XI-11. RELATION OF ANTISOCIAL AGGRESSION SCORES TO MEDIA USE
CATEGORIES, BY PARENT/PEER CONFLICT*
(*In per cent*)

|  | High Parent High Peer | | High Parent Low Peer | | Low Parent Low Peer | |
|---|---|---|---|---|---|---|
|  | Low Agg. Score ($N = 30$) | High Agg. Score ($N = 68$) | Low Agg. Score ($N = 99$) | High Agg. Score ($N = 111$) | Low Agg. Score ($N = 235$) | High Agg. Score ($N = 179$) |
| Low TV, low print.... | 18.2 | 9.8 | 15.2 | 13.5 | 8.9 | 13.1 |
| High TV, low print... | 36.4 | 33.4 | 15.2 | 27.0 | 15.8 | 22.1 |
| Low TV, high print... | 27.2 | 11.8 | 29.2 | 18.8 | 31.7 | 26.2 |
| High TV, high print... | 18.2 | 45.0 | 40.4 | 39.7 | 43.6 | 38.6 |

\* We cannot test reality-oriented vs. pleasure-oriented in the high-high conflict array as the $N$'s are too small; in the high-low, the effect of aggression is significant, $X^2$ being 5.14, $p = .025$, one-tail test. Testing just high television vs. low television, we find that the interaction of aggression and conflict is significant for the high-high array ($X^2 = 3.28, p = .05$, one-tail test) and for the high-low array ($X^2 = 5.72, p = .01$, one-tail test), but not for the low-low array.

TABLE XI-12. Mean Scores on Three Measures of Aggression (Radiotown and Teletown, Canada)[*]

By Grade and Sex

| | Antisocial Aggression | | | Prosocial Aggression | | | Aggression Anxiety | | |
|---|---|---|---|---|---|---|---|---|---|
| | N | Mean | SD | N | Mean | SD | N | Mean | SD |
| **TELETOWN** | | | | | | | | | |
| Sixth-grade boys .... | 80 | 5.49[a] | 3.02 | 82 | 5.58[i] | 2.87 | 83 | 4.90 | 2.76 |
| Sixth-grade girls .... | 97 | 4.42[b] | 3.16 | 95 | 5.94[j] | 2.40 | 97 | 6.27[q] | 2.57 |
| Tenth-grade boys ... | 86 | 5.15[c] | 2.94 | 85 | 3.73[k] | 2.27 | 84 | 4.61 | 2.48 |
| Tenth-grade girls ... | 97 | 2.91[d] | 2.84 | 96 | 4.11[l] | 2.29 | 97 | 6.09 | 2.37 |
| **RADIOTOWN** | | | | | | | | | |
| Sixth-grade boys .... | 47 | 6.49[e] | 2.50 | 46 | 5.63[m] | 2.44 | 48 | 4.67 | 2.34 |
| Sixth-grade girls .... | 61 | 6.20[f] | 2.99 | 59 | 5.51[n] | 2.50 | 61 | 5.03[r] | 2.56 |
| Tenth-grade boys ... | 64 | 5.22[g] | 2.97 | 59 | 3.98[o] | 2.46 | 61 | 4.75 | 2.11 |
| Tenth-grade girls ... | 44 | 3.32[h] | 2.83 | 42 | 4.36[p] | 2.29 | 43 | 6.21[s] | 2.41 |

[*] Significance of differences between means:

Between a and b, <.05

Between a and e, <.05

Between b and d, <.05

Between b and f, <.01

Between i and k, <.01

Between j and l, <.01

Between m and o, <.01

Between n and p, <.05

Between q and r, <.05

Between r and s, <.05

# ANNOTATED BIBLIOGRAPHY

# ANNOTATED BIBLIOGRAPHY

STUDIES OF CHILDREN AND TELEVISION

*General studies*

1. Belson, W. A. "Television and the family" (mimeo.). London: British Broadcasting Corporation, 1959

   This is a careful study, done in 1955 and 1956, by means of self-completion questionnaires and diaries filled out by large matched groups of television viewers and nonviewers in London, Birmingham, and Wakefield, England. The scores of viewers and nonviewers were corrected by a regression technique. This is a novel method of matching, and probably a good one, although the method makes it impossible for the experimenter to test the significance of observed differences.

   Belson found a series of slight differences apparently related to television. Television brings the family together at home a little longer and oftener in the evenings. It tends to reduce both home-centered and family activity, but only slightly. Little was found to suggest that the effect of television in keeping the family together at home will disappear with time. On the other hand, television's effect on family and home-centered activity seems to be temporary only, and to disappear as the receiving set becomes more familiar.

   Very small changes were found in the total amount of time spent at home by children and young people, though there were considerable redistributions of this time. In general, it seems to increase the time *after* 6:00 P.M. that young people fourteen to twenty-two spend at home, and to increase the time *before* 6:00 P.M. that children under fourteen spend at home.

   Belson found great variation in all these effects with seasonal and regional conditions, and felt that these variations ruled out any sweeping generalizations about the effect of television on family life.

2. Bogart, Leo. The age of television. 2d ed. New York: Ungar, 1958.

   This is a useful summary look at the coming of television to the United States. There are many interesting tables, particularly concerning television's audiences. The data in the second edition carry to about 1957. A chapter on television and children summarizes some of the research studies and a number of the criticisms, pro and con.

3. Harris, Dale B. Children and television. Urbana: National Association of Educational Broadcasters, 1959.

   A useful, extensively annotated bibliography, heavy on opinion and advice articles, and on early surveys.

4. Himmelweit, Hilde, A. N. Oppenheim, and Pamela Vince. Television and the child. Published for the Nuffield Foundation. London: Oxford, 1958.

This is a careful, thoughtful, and important study, and the most extensive examination of television in the lives of children at least until the present book.

The research was done in England in 1955 and 1956. The main sample surveyed consisted of 946 thirteen- and fourteen-year-olds and 908 ten- and eleven-year-olds. Half of each group were viewers of television; half were not. The groups were carefully matched for age, sex, IQ, and social class. The main sample came from London, Bristol, Portsmouth, and Sunderland. In addition to these, 376 children in Norwich were interviewed before and after their families acquired television. There were also smaller substudies, such as a content analysis of commercial programs and questions to teachers.

The main findings can perhaps most easily be summarized in terms of the questions these authors ask early in their book:

*Who are the early viewers?* The people with strongest need for ready-made entertainment.

*How many hours per week do children view television?* Viewers in both age groups watched eleven to thirteen hours a week, more time than they put on any other leisure activity.

*What factors reduce interest in and time spent on viewing?* Lower viewing goes with high intelligence, with an active life, and with parental example in that direction.

*Do the children watch many programs designed for adults?* Yes, many.

*What kinds of programs do children like best?* Three-quarters of the votes were for adult programs, particularly crime thrillers. Adult political programs, documentaries, and discussions held little appeal. Even the most popular program, however, was mentioned by no more than one-third of the children.

*Can children's tastes be developed by seeing programs which are not, on the whole, popular with children?* When only one channel was available, it was observed that children viewed and came to like programs they ordinarily would not have selected.

*How is taste affected by access (in Great Britain) to a second channel?* Programs with educational value or programs produced especially for children are most likely to suffer.

*What constitutes television's appeal for children?* Easy availability . . . value as time filler . . . the satisfaction of being in the know . . . security and reassurance through familiar themes and formats . . . change, excitement, suspense . . . escape . . . identification . . . warm and friendly personalities.

*To what extent is the child's outlook colored by what he sees on television?* The values of television make an impact if they are presented in dramatic form, if they touch on ideas or values for which the child is emotionally ready, and if the child cannot turn for information on the same points to parents and friends.

*What frightens children on television?* Realistic rather than stylized violence; fictional events in horror or space programs. Viewing in the dark or alone makes fright more likely.

*What types of aggression prove most disturbing to children?* Guns least, and daggers and sharp instruments most. Danger to animals like Lassie.

*Do these programs make children aggressive?* No evidence was found that they did; but, on the other hand, there was no evidence of beneficial result.

*Does television improve a child's general knowledge?* A net gain was found only for the younger, duller viewers.

*How does television affect children's schoolwork?* Brighter children tended to fall behind comparable children who were nonviewers.

*What is the effect of television on leisure?* Younger viewers reduced cinema-going, and all children listened less to radio after television came. Book reading was less at first, then returned to the expected level. Entertaining at home increases with television, but casual companionship somewhat decreases.

*What is the effect on family life?* It keeps members of the family at home more, but really does not bind them together.

*Does television make children passive?* The authors found no evidence that it does.

*Does television make children more enterprising, or stimulate them to make things, enter competitions, visit places of interest, or develop new hobbies?* On the whole, they conclude, it does not.

*What is the effect of television on night rest and eyesight?* Bedtime is, on the average, about twenty minutes later in television homes, but the television children turn out the light more quickly and play less in bed. Defective eyesight was no more frequent among viewers than nonviewers.

*What type of child becomes a television addict?* The authors treat addiction simply as heavy viewing. The chief correlates are lower intelligence, insecurity, maladjustment, and inadequate contacts and friendships.

*Studies of process and effect*

5. Albert, Robert S. "The role of the mass media and the effect of aggressive film content upon children's aggressive responses and identification choices," *Genet. Psychol. Monogr.*, 55 (1957), 221–85.

A total of 220 eight- to ten-year-old children were shown three versions of a Western film: one in which the hero won the conventional victory, one in which the villain won and went unpunished, and one which ended before the conflict was decided and before anybody could be punished. Children who saw the first treatment significantly reduced their aggressiveness, and so also did those who saw the third treatment. Those who saw the treatment in which the villain won showed on the average no change: those initially high on aggression decreased their aggression, and those who had been low on aggression became more aggressive. Younger children and children with low IQs were more affected by all treatments.

6. Bailyn, Lotte. "Mass media and children: a study of exposure habits and cognitive effects," *Psych. Monogr.*, 73 (1959), 1–48.

A detailed analysis of the media habits of about 600 fifth- and sixth-grade children, related to social and psychological characteristics. Significant correlations were found between viewing of television, movies, and comic books, justifying the grouping of these media together as a cluster of "pictorial media." Boys expose themselves to the pictorial media more than girls, Catholics more than Protestants, children of blue-collar families more than children of white-collar families, and children of low mental ability more than children of high mental ability. Parental restrictions on media use also account for much of the variability. Girls who are over-achievers (school grades better than would be expected from intelligence scores) are less exposed to the pictorial media than girls who are under-achievers. Having personal problems was not related to exposure to the pictorial media, but those with more problems listened to less radio and read fewer books. A combination of having many personal problems and being rated high on rebellious independence was related to increased use of pictorial media. Regarding content of media use, the author found that boys who are rebelliously independent, get spanked, are not restricted on exposure time, and have low intelligence scores are more likely to prefer "aggressive hero" type of content.

7. Becker, Samuel, and Glenn Joseph Wolfe. "Can adults predict children's interest in a television program?" in Schramm, ed., The impact of television. Urbana: University of Illinois Press, 1960.

Twenty-nine fifth-grade students and twenty preschool children (four or five years old) in Iowa were shown educational television programs. Their curves of interest in these programs were also predicted by a group of elementary schoolteachers (in the case of the fifth-graders) and a group of experts in childhood education from the University of Iowa staff and a group of mothers of preschool children (in the case of the young children). It was found that trained adults could make a fairly satisfactory prediction of what would interest fifth-graders, but that neither the professionals nor the mothers could very satisfactorily predict what would interest the preschool children. Unfortunately, there was no validation for the technique of measuring the "true" interest of the children in the film. This was done by advanced students who observed their overt reactions continuously throughout the film.

8. Brodbeck, A. J. "The mass-media as a socializing agency" (mimeo.). Paper read to American Psychological Association Symposium on Children and the Mass-Media, San Francisco, 1955.

This is a highly stimulating paper, which raises more questions than it answers, and refers to some tantalizing unpublished research. The author says that "the really formidable questions about the mass-media, and indeed about any socializing agency, begin when one attempts to discover and state the exact conditions under which the message succeeds or fails to take hold, quite independently of its usefulness." Like the authors of the present volume, he thinks of television viewing as a problem-solving activity for children. The fantasy experiences may, therefore, be helpful or harmful, depending on conditions rather than on some sort of "essential nature" that resides inherently in all forms of fantasy. He reports the results of an experiment in which aggressive feeling and drive rose markedly after exposure to a comic book story in which the villain was not punished, but standards of right and wrong did not change at all. In another experiment, a stereotyped cowboy film proved to have considerable impact on younger children, but very little on older children. This he explained in terms of the children's familiarity with the type of plot. Contrasting the orthodox version of this Western film with an edited version in which the hero did not win although he was still morally right, the author suggests that "when aggression is socially successful in fantasy, it tends to remove inhibitions of aggression in real life; when punished in fantasy, it tends to be inhibited in real life." He suggests a number of ways in which this process of "effect" needs study. Among them are such galvanometer, pneumograph, and pulse studies as Lasswell in the 1930's made of patients in therapy; and analysis of the way social roles are depicted in films and comic books.

9. Duggan, E. P. "Children at the television set," *Times Ed. Sup.*, 2112:1165, November 11, 1955.

Study of children in an English boys' school (reported by *Times* correspondent) found that nonviewers of television consistently placed higher on school exams, but were reported to have scored lower on a test of general knowledge.

10. Dunham, F. "Effect of television on school achievement of children," *Sch. Life*, 34 (1952), 88–89.

Survey of nearly 1,000 sixth- and seventh-graders in Cincinnati, Ohio. Found no over-all significant difference in school achievement between children with and without television.

11. Emery, F. E., and David Martin. Psychological effects of the Western film—a study in television viewing. Melbourne: Department of Audio-Visual Aids, University of Melbourne, 1957.

This is the first of a series of studies of the effect of television drama on children undertaken at the University of Melbourne. Showing Western films to small samples of children in Melbourne, and collecting evidence including responses to the Rosenzweig Picture Frustration Test, before and after, the investigators thought they detected evidence of "perceptual defence" against possible shock from such a film. They were unable to duplicate the Feshbach effect in which fantasy is hypothesized to be able to release aggressive impulses and thus reduce the general level of aggression. In general, the investigators felt that the "happy" conclusion, and identification with a hero who seemed more dynamic and effective after the film, probably dissipated much of the anxiety resulting from the film's "stress-laden" themes.

12. Evans, C. C. "Television for the preschool child," *Elem. Engl.*, 32 (1955), 541–42.

Observing reactions of forty kindergarten and twenty-two nursery school children to educational television programs, the author concluded that the most notable effect was on their vocabulary. This finding should be compared with our results in the first grades of Teletown and Radiotown.

13. Feshbach, S. "The drive reducing function of fantasy behavior," *J. Abnorm. Soc. Psychol.*, 50 (1952), 3–12.

An experimental study with undergraduate subjects testing the hypothesis that subjects who were severely insulted and given the opportunity to express aggression in fantasy would show less aggression than subjects similarly insulted but not given the same opportunity for fantasy reduction of aggression. Thematic apperception test pictures were used as a vehicle for fantasy. The "insult-fantasy" group showed significantly less aggression than the "insult-non-fantasy" group. There was more aggression in the fantasies of the "insult-fantasy" group than the "non-insult-fantasy" group. In the "insult-fantasy" group there was a significant negative correlation between fantasy aggression and later expression of aggression toward the experimenter.

14. Geiger, Kent, and Robert Sokol. "Social norms in television watching," *Amer. J. Soc.*, 65 (1959), 174–81.

An analysis of survey data collected from 519 respondents in the Boston area in 1956. The authors found that for all social classes the image of the "television fan" was of a person of low socioeconomic status. They discuss television watching as predominantly entertainment seeking and suggest that it is more congruous with "the value given to immediate gratification in the lower or working class than with the time orientation and ideal of deferred gratification of the middle class." They suggest as working hypotheses: "(1) behavior involving gratification but subject to cultural taboos is likely to lead to addiction; (2) there is a taboo against television-viewing in the middle class but not in the working class; (3) television addicts would therefore be found predominantly among middle-class persons who are constant viewers."

They present data relating enthusiasm for television to perceived characteristics of the television fan. Among the middle-class members of the sample, particularly middle-class men, those who were more enthusiastic about television were more likely than lower-class people to perceive TV fans as being like their own reference groups. Middle-class people who were less enthusiastic about television were less likely than lower-class people to perceive television fans as being like their own reference groups. The observed findings may well be an example of the tendency of an individual, in the face of social norms, to think in such fashion as to minimize his own awareness of his deviant behavior and to dwell on those portions of his behavior which conform to the norms. The fact that this kind of misperception is found more among the better-educated middle-class respondents than among the less well-educated (working class) respondents is taken as indication of the operation of a middle-class taboo against television viewing.

15. Greenstein, Jack. "Effects of television upon elementary school grades," *Journ. Educ. Res.*, 48 (1954), 161–76.

No evidence that school performance of TV-viewers among sixty-seven sixth-grade children in elementary school was adversely affected by viewing. Over-all viewing times averaged between three and four hours.

16. Haines, William H. "Juvenile delinquency and television," *Journ. Soc. Ther.*, 1 (1955), 192–98.

Interviews with 100 teen-age prisoners in Chicago jail, concerning their judgments as to whether television, movies, radio, and pornographic literature played any part in their turning to crime, led to the conclusion that "TV, pornography, and movies play a distinct role in the creation of anti-social behavior in susceptible teen-agers."

17. Lazarsfeld, Paul F., and Robert K. Merton. "Mass communication, popular taste, and organized social action," in W. Schramm, ed., Mass communications, 2d ed. Urbana: University of Illinois Press, 1960.

A theoretical discussion of the social functions and effects of the mass media in general. The authors discuss a "status conferral function'" of the mass media, mass media as enforcers of social norms, and what they call the "narcotizing dysfunction" of the mass media. They discuss the implications of the structure and ownership of the media and conclude ". . . the very conditions which make for the maximum effectiveness of the mass media of communication operate toward maintenance of the going social and cultural structure rather than toward its change."

18. Maccoby, Eleanor E. "Why do children watch television?" *Pub. Opin. Quart.*, 18 (1954), 239–44.

Interviews with 379 mothers of five- and six-year-olds in the Boston area furnished material on child-training practices and estimates of children's television-viewing habits. The extent of a child's interest in television was studied as a symptom of a need for vicarious satisfaction through fantasy when the child is frustrated in his efforts to obtain satisfaction in real life. She found that in the upper-middle class, children who are highly frustrated in their current home life (subject to many restrictions and not treated permissively or warmly) spend more time viewing television than comparable children not so frustrated. In the upper-lower class, no relationship between frustration and television viewing was found. The differences between the classes was interpreted as meaning that in the upper-lower class, where the parents themselves spend a good deal of time watching television, there is more positive motivation for a child to watch television, so that a child will be drawn to it even in the absence of frustration because it is a dominant activity of the family circle. In the upper-middle class, the effects of frustration may be seen more clearly, because, in the absence of frustration, the child is drawn away from television.

19. Maccoby, Eleanor E., H. Levin, and B. M. Selya. "The effect of emotional arousal on the retention of aggressive and non-aggressive movie content" (abstract), *Amer. Psychologist,* 10 (1955), 359.

A report of findings that children who are frustrated just prior to seeing a movie remember more of the aggressive content of the film than children not so frustrated. An attempted replication [20] did not produce the same results, however.

20. Maccoby, Eleanor E., H. Levin, and B. M. Selya. "The effects of emotional arousal on the retention of film content: a failure to replicate," *J. Abnorm. Soc. Psychol.,* 53 (1956), 373–74.

An earlier study of public school children in the Boston area [19] found that when children were frustrated prior to viewing a movie they tended to remember more of the aggressive content of the film than a control group not so frustrated. The 1956 study repeated the same design with 190 fifth- and sixth-grade children in an upstate New York area. Children were frustrated in a spelling contest (experimental group were given ninth-grade words to spell in a contest with their control group classmates who were given fourth-grade words) and then shown a Dead End Kids film with much aggressive content. Measures taken a week later showed no significant differences between the experimental and the control group in recall of aggressive film content.

21. Maccoby, Eleanor E., and W. C. Wilson. "Identification and observational learning from films," *J. Abnorm. Soc. Psychol.*, 55 (1957), 76–87.

An experimental study in which seventh-grade children were shown a movie and tested a week later on their knowledge of the content of the movie. They found that a child identifies with the like-sexed leading character and with the character whose social class corresponds with the viewer's aspired social class (rather than with his membership class). Viewers tend to remember somewhat better the actions and words of the character with whom they identify, but the advantage in learning does not apply equally to all the actions of the viewer's chosen character. Both choice of character with whom to identify and the "need relevance" of that character's actions were important. Boys remember aggressive content better than girls, provided its agent is the boy hero. Girls remember boy-girl interactive content better than boys whenever the girl heroine is the agent of the action.

22. Maccoby, Eleanor E., W. C. Wilson, and R. V. Burton. "Differential movie-viewing behavior of male and female viewers," *J. Pers.*, 26 (1958), 259–67.

An experimental study in which the eye movements of forty-eight college-aged subjects (twenty-four men, twenty-four women) were observed as they watched scenes of movies in which the hero and heroine were on the screen together with no subsidiary characters. Presuming same-sex identifications, the investigators asked, "Do viewers concentrate their attention primarily upon the character who is for them, the subject (ego) of the drama or upon the other person (alter) with whom the viewer's identification is interacting?" Men spent more time, relative to women, watching the hero, and female viewers spent more time looking at the heroine.

23. Parker, Edwin B. "The functions of television for children." Ph.D. dissertation, Stanford University, 1960.

Parallels Chapter 4 and part of Chapter 5 in the present book. Discussion of adoption of television from the point of view of cultural change. Presents tables showing positive relationships among print media—books, newspapers, magazines—and showing positive relationships among fantasy media—comic books, television, movies.

24. Pearlin, L. I. "Social and personal stress and escape television viewing," *Pub. Opin. Quart.*, 23 (1959), 255–59.

Interviews with 736 television owners in a southern industrial city permitted classification of respondents according to amount of stress and according to whether they were "escape viewers" or "reality viewers." A statistically significant positive relationship was found between escape viewing and high stress.

25. Riley, Matilda W., and John W. Riley, Jr. "A sociological approach to communication research," in Schramm, ed., The process and effects of mass communication. Urbana: University of Illinois Press, 1954.

Survey of 400 children in the eastern United States shows that radio and television programs characterized by violence, action, and aggression, "and including Westerns, mysteries, crime, horror, and other such adventure themes," are more popular with nonmembers of peer groups (children who have few friends) "who presumably are in a social position which is most likely to provoke feelings of hostility and aggression." Among older children who ordinarily have lost much of their liking for programs of action and violence, this liking remains strongest among children who are most frustrated in wanting to belong to and be accepted by the peer group. For the nonmember of the peer group, the content of these programs "may form a fantasy world into which he may escape from a real world in which the standards seem impossibly high." For nonmembers, for example, adventure-type programs seem to be sheer escape; for members, they are more apt to be liked because they have social utility.

26. Schramm, Wilbur. "Television in the life of the child—implications for the school," in *New teaching aids for the American classroom*. Stanford: Institution for Communication Research, 1960.

Drawing on some of the early findings of the present research project, the author points out some of the implications of home television to the schoolteacher: a child who gets a faster start with vocabulary and general knowledge about environment; a child who has a kind of "immature maturity" so far as adult subject matter is concerned; a child who early knows how to learn from television and films; a child who needs help and direction in finding the more intellectually rewarding parts of television and in developing program tastes; and a child who may expect high standards of performance from classroom performers as well as from his television performers.

27. Schramm, Wilbur, Jack Lyle, and Edwin B. Parker. Learning from television. Chicago: Public Communication (University of Chicago), 1960.

Parallels material in Chapter 5 of the present volume.

28. Scott, L. F. "Television and school achievement," *Phi Delta Kappan*, 38 (1956), 25–28.

A sample of 456 sixth- and seventh-grade California children was studied in 1954. Heavy viewers of television were compared with light viewers, with the finding that light viewers scored significantly better on achievement tests in arithmetic and reading and on total achievement. Heavy viewers were from lower socioeconomic status families and had lower intelligence quotients than light viewers.

29. Siegel, Alberta E. "Film-mediated fantasy aggression and strength of aggressive drive," *Child Developm.*, 27 (1955), 365–78.

An experimental study of twenty-four nursery school children, each serving as his own control, designed to test the hypotheses that both aggression and aggressive anxiety and guilt are lower after seeing a film with much aggressive content. Results were opposite to those predicted but the differences were not statistically significant.

30. Siegel, Alberta E. "The influence of violence in the mass media upon children's role expectations," *Child Developm.*, 29 (1958), 35–56.

An experimental study in which two groups of second-grade children were exposed to different radio presentations of the role of taxi driver. The programs given to the experimental group depicted an aggressive driver and those given to the control group depicted a nonaggressive driver. A story completion test, given later, contained two situations involving a taxi driver, one story similar to a story heard in the radio presentation and one unlike any radio presentation. The experimental group attributed more aggression to the taxi driver than did the control group, but only in the story situation similar to the radio presentation.

31. Thompson, R. J. Television crime-drama. Melbourne: Department of Audio-Visual Aids, University of Melbourne, 1959.

Two crime dramas were shown to forty-eight intermediate (high school) students in Melbourne. Photographs taken during the viewing indicated a building-up of tension during the picture. Projective responses to picture tests obtained before and after the showing indicated that, after the showing, subjects were more likely to regard women as passive but women's goals as more idealistic, and that the "general buoyancy level" of the subjects—meaning "the expectation of a happy outcome for all parties"—dropped very distinctly. The investigator conjectured that there may possibly be "evidence here of some sort of natural safeguard operating to protect the typical adolescent crime-drama audience from stress effects." He found in his data "no evidence that viewing a crime film provoked any criminal or psychopathic tendencies in the great majority of viewers . . . If there is some risk to children viewing this type of programme constantly, it would appear to lie rather in the direction of the acquisition of certain relatively stereotyped and insensitivized reactions . . ." He had, of course, no time series of experiments or observations on which to test this.

*Studies of viewing patterns*

32. Abrams, Mark. "Child audiences for television in Great Britain," *Journ. Quart.*, 33 (1956), 35–41.

A survey of 1,500 children, eight to fifteen years old, in Great Britain. Shows that these children typically prefer adult to children's programs. Greatest effect of television seems to be a reduction in radio listening; finds little evidence of effect on movie-going, reading of comics, or club membership. Middle-class children give highest preference to reading books. Working-class children much prefer television and are more likely than middle-class children to watch adult programs.

33. Battin, T. G. "The use of the diary and survey method involving the questionnaire-interview technique to determine the impact of television on school children in regard to viewing habits and formal and informal education." Ph.D. thesis, University of Michigan, 1952. (*Dissertation Abstr.*, 12 [1952], 343; and *Sp. Monogr.*, 20 [1953], 135.)

Children in Ann Arbor, Michigan, who had had TV for six months or longer were given seven-day diaries to record all televiewing for a week. Those in grades four to twelve who returned diaries were interviewed. Reported average weekly television viewing time of 18.5 hours in grades one to six and 21 hours weekly in grades seven to twelve.

34. Clark, W. J. Of children and television. Cincinnati, Ohio: Xavier University, 1951.

Questionnaires administered to 750 sixth- and seventh-grade children in 1950–51. Reported 3.7 hours as average weekday viewing time

35. Cunningham and Walsh. "Videotown, 1948–57" (mimeo.). New York: Cunningham and Walsh, 1958.

Every year beginning in 1948, the advertising firm of Cunningham and Walsh has surveyed the use of television in New Brunswick, New Jersey, which it has called Videotown. In 1948 only 1 per cent of the homes had television; now 92.7 per cent have it. Average daily hours of viewing per home increased until 1955, when it fell slightly, and has slowly decreased since. In 1957 it was 3.21 hours per home per day. Long-time television owners watch their sets a little longer than more recent television owners. In 1957, about three-fourths of children under ten viewed on any one evening. When they do view, it is for a little over 2 hours, on the average. Teen-agers who watch average about 2 hours 23 minutes. Social and gregarious activities have been increasing slightly with the decline in television time. Movie attendance, very much reduced by the coming of television, was in 1957 at the low level of the first TV years. Magazine reading is also considerably reduced. Radio listening, cut from 60 per cent of families to 5 per cent in TV homes in 1951, has slightly increased each year since. Of all the media, only the newspaper has never shown any reduction in reading time because of television. A footnote to television's effect on family life is that fewer young children and many fewer teen-agers were watching television while they ate in 1957 than several years before.

36. Evry, Hal. "TV murder causes bad dreams," Film World, 8 (1952), 247.

Teachers interviewed 2,000 six-year-olds in private and parochial schools. More than half said they dreamed about television programs they watched, and a quarter of those said their dreams were bad. Of children with television in their homes, 59 per cent said they are sometimes frightened by programs they see. Sixty-two per cent of children in TV homes would rather watch TV than play outside, whereas 88 per cent of children in radio-only homes would rather play outside than listen to radio.

37. Fager, J., and R. Smith. "New views on television," Nat. Parent Teach., 46 (1951), 39–40.

Survey of parents in upper-middle-class suburb. A little over half thought television had not affected parent-child relationship; a little less than half thought it had. Less than 3 per cent thought television had harmed their children's school work; 20 per cent thought it had helped. Eighty-six per cent reported it had not lessened interest in activities such as scouting, dramatics, and music lessons, and most of them reported that sleeping and eating habits and emotional behavior were unchanged.

38. Fine, B. J., and N. Maccoby. "Television and family life" (mimeo.). Boston: Boston University School of Public Relations and Communications, 1952.

A replication of the Maccoby study [40] using an older group of children in two New England communities, comparing television with nontelevision adolescents. They found that adolescents watch less television than younger children. They found no difference in viewing patterns between children who had had a television set for six months and those who had had a set for two years.

39. Lewis, P. "Tv and teen-agers," *Educational Screen*, 28 (1949), 159–61.

Questionnaires administered to 1,700 high school students in 1949. Reports an average viewing time of 3.4 hours per day.

40. Maccoby, Eleanor E. "Television: its impact on school children," *Pub. Opin. Quart.*, 15 (1951), 421–44.

A study of 622 children in the Boston area in 1950 and 1951, half with television and half without, matched with respect to age, sex, and socioeconomic status. It found that TV increased the total amount of time which family members spend together, but cut into the amount of non-TV joint family activity. Increased family contact brought about by TV is not social except in the sense of being in the same room with other people. Television cuts into both outdoor and indoor playing time and into the amount of time a child spends helping with household tasks. The study found that children are substituting TV for radio, movies, and reading to a significant extent.

41. Parker, Everett. Parents, children, and television. New York: Information Service of National Council of Churches, 1954.

Includes summary of survey of 3,559 homes in New Haven, Connecticut. In these, 69 per cent of parents generally approved of children's programs as they are, and 26 per cent generally disapproved of them. Among the best-educated parents and the parents of young children, however, there was a greater percentage of disapproval, but still not a majority.

42. Riley, J. M., F. V. Cantwell, and Katherine Ruthiger. "Some observations on the social effects of TV," *Pub. Opin. Quart.*, 13 (1949), 223–34.

All 278 homes in an Eastern industrial city and 278 non-TV homes interviewed in 1948. Activities of 1,100 TV persons and 1,027 persons in the control sample were studied. They found that children spend 3 hours 7 minutes daily with TV and that teen-agers spend 2 hours 33 minutes daily with TV. Of the teen-age group, 59 per cent of the TV children and 61 per cent of the non-TV children participated in sports; 37 per cent of the TV and 20 per cent of the non-TV children attended sports events.

43. Scott, L. "Social attitudes of children revealed by responses to television programs," *Calif. Journ. Elem. Educ.*, 22 (1954), 176–79.

A total of 478 California school children completed questionnaires on attitudes toward law enforcement. Of these, 60 per cent thought it was all right to use dishonesty in law enforcement; 12 per cent thought sheriffs today are dishonest (as compared to 43 per cent who thought television sheriffs were dishonest); 79 per cent felt that law enforcement officers mistreat Western bad men on television; and 33 per cent thought cowboys today carry guns like their TV counterparts. Effect on attitudes toward law enforcement seemed to be more pronounced in lower socioeconomic groups.

44. Seagoe, M. V. "Children's television habits and preferences," *Quart. Film, Radio, Television*, 6 (1952), 143–52.

Reports reduction in radio listening and motion picture attendance as a result of television. Says older children watch television with increasing frequency, at least to age twelve. Low socioeconomic status is positively related to amount of television viewing.

45. Witty, Paul A. "School children and television. Summary of the results of ten yearly studies of children's television viewing in the Chicago metropolitan area" (mimeo.). Presented at the annual meeting of the American Association for the Advancement of Science, Chicago, December 29, 1959. Distributed by the Television Information Office, New York, 1960.

This is a summary of Professor Witty's annual questionnaire surveys of Chicago area school children. Most of the original reports have been published in the form of articles in *Elementary English*. Sample sizes are not specified in this summary report, except the total as "approximately 2,000." These are the amounts of viewing he has found in hours per week, 1951 to 1959:

|  | 1951 | 1953 | 1955 | 1957 | 1959 |
|---|---|---|---|---|---|
| Elementary school pupils ........... | 19 | 23 | 24 | 22 | 21 |
| High school pupils ............... | 14 | 17 | 14 | 12 | 12 |

His surveys show that favorite programs change somewhat from year to year. From 1952 through 1954, however, "I Love Lucy" was the favorite program of both elementary and high school children. Then "Disneyland" was the favorite of elementary school children for three years, to be succeeded by "Zorro" in 1958, and that in turn by a crime mystery in 1959. Since 1954, the favorite programs of his high school students have been two comedians, two Westerns, and "baseball and sports."

In his studies, he reports, "excessive viewing of television seems to be associated with somewhat lower academic attainment. In an early investigation the average time devoted to TV by pupils in the upper fourth on standardized tests was 21 hours per week, while the average lower fourth was about 26 hours. Similar results were obtained again in 1957." It should be pointed out that this does not control for IQ or age.

*Professional comment*

46. Foundation for Character Education. Television for children. Boston: The Foundation (about 1958).

Analysis and advice to parents and broadcasters written by a panel of well-known scholars, broadcasters, and educators: Thomas Carskadon, Rudy Bretz, George Crothers, Ralph Garry, Robert Goldenson, Dale Harris, Paul Homme, Eleanor Maccoby, Paul Reed, Robert Lewis Shayon, and I. Keith Tyler. They sum up the probable effects of television on children thus:

Little or no effect on eyesight and health, achievement in school, or reading of books and library usage.

Considerable effect on time spent watching, keeping some children off streets, reducing amount of sleep, reducing play with other children.

Unknown effects on character development, moral behavior, fears, aggression, behavior patterns.

47. Glynn, Eugene David. "Television and the American character—a psychiatrist looks at television," in William Y. Elliott. Television's impact on American culture. East Lansing: Michigan State University Press, 1956.

Dr. Glynn, a psychiatrist, views television with considerable alarm. Calling upon analogies from neurotic and psychotic cases, he concludes that "the chief effect of television is passivity and dependence in multiple shapes and forms." He notes also "the claim . . . that aggression is not so much inhibited by television as displaced." Another thing that worries him is the great stimulation of television's fantasy. He wonders, "what will be the result of such constant stimulation from such early ages? . . . Will reality match up to the television fantasies this generation has been nursed on? These children are in a peculiar position; experience is exhausted in advance . . . When the experience itself comes, it is watered down, for it has already been half lived, but never truly felt." He recommends that educational television find the ways of stimulating its viewers to meaningful activity. "With this orientation," he says, "television can overcome the dangers pointed out."

48. Logan, C. S. "What our children see," *Inst. for Educ. by Radio Yearbook*, 1950, pp. 170–74.

Reports answers to questions by 314 pediatricians, sociologists, neuropsychiatrists, and psychologists. Ninety per cent of these felt that television crime programs have in some way a detrimental psychological effect on children, and 81 per cent said they contributed to children's delinquency or antisocial behavior. Extent and process of contribution not specified.

49. Maccoby, Eleanor E. "Testimony before the Subcommittee to investigate juvenile delinquency, of the Committee on the Judiciary, United States Senate, Eighty-fourth Congress," *S. Res. 62.* April 1955. Washington, D.C.: United States Government Printing Office, 1955.

Discussion of research results presented elsewhere [18] and reprinted here. The author says there is no doubt that children learn from television (e.g., what to wear at a nightclub, how to act at a wedding), and she proceeds to discuss conditions under which aggressive content might be learned and levels of aggression affected by television content. She questions the effectiveness of discharge of aggressive feelings by viewing violent activity on television. "Presumably, if he reenters a frustrating situation when the TV situation is over, he can be made angry again and will be just as ready for . . . [real-life] aggression as he ever was before." She further says, "I expect when we do the research that we will find that aggressive feelings are sometimes increased rather than reduced by aggressive scenes on television or in the movies."

50. Meerlo, J. A. M. "Television addiction and reactive apathy," *Journ. Nerv. and Mental Diseases*, 120 (1954), 290–91.

Psychiatrist's report of a girl who became addicted to television and became unable, until treated, to distinguish between the world of television fantasy and the real world.

51. Pool, I. de Sola. "Free discussion and public taste," *Pub. Opin. Quart.*, 24 (1960), 19–23.

Testimony presented at public hearings held by the Federal Communications Commission on December 11, 1959, urging the FCC to engage in extensive research in the behavioral sciences. He discusses the Himmelweit [4] finding that children came to like "good cultural programs" which they watched because they had no alternative, although they would not have chosen the program if they had had a choice. He says, "If the situation is reciprocal, then we may guess that at times when only poor programming is available on the air people will watch it for lack of something better to do, and in so doing they may develop bad taste habits. If the Himmelweit finding can be generalized, then when there is a choice of program levels people will pick programs at their own level, and the presence of a poor program among those available will do little or no harm, for it will not be chosen by viewers whom it would change."

52. Shayon, Robert Lewis. Television and our children. New York: Longmans, Green, 1951.

An informed and moderate look at the probable effects and possible gains of television, by a television producer and critic.

### RELATED STUDIES OF CHILDREN AND OTHER MEDIA

53. Allwood, Martin S. The impact of the comics on a European country. Mullsjo: Institutet fyra Samhallsforskning (Institute for Social Research), 1956. (Short English version published as a pamphlet.)

Questionnaires were completed by 649 persons in Sweden, 74 per cent of them eighteen years of age or younger. Thirty-two per cent never read comic strips in newspapers and 72 per cent never read comic books. Manual workers and their children are more interested in comics than are white-collar workers and their children. Heavy movie-goers are more likely to be comic book readers. Among male readers, "Phantom" was the favorite comic, with "Tarzan" second; among female readers, "Blondie" was first, with "Phantom" second.

Concerning effects, Allwood says: "The effect of comics . . . is peripheral to the personality. The security or insecurity of the personality depends on quite different things, and above all on the kind of human relations it has developed in the home, with father, mother, brothers and sisters . . ."

54. Charters, W. W. Motion pictures and youth: a summary. New York: Macmillan, 1933.

This is the summary of the Payne Fund studies of children and motion pictures. The volumes it summarizes are the following, all published in New York, by Macmillan, in 1933:

Holaday, P. W., and George D. Stoddard. Getting ideas from the movies.
Peterson, Ruth C., and L. L. Thurstone. Motion pictures and the social attitudes of children.
Shuttleworth, Frank K., and Mark A. May. The social conduct and attitude of movie fans.
Dysinger, W. S., and Christian A. Ruckmick. The emotional responses of children to the motion picture situation.
Peters, Charles C. Motion pictures and standards of morality.
Renshaw, Samuel, Vernon L. Miller, and Dorothy Marquis. Children's sleep.

Blumer, Herbert. Movies and conduct.
Dale, Edgar. The content of motion pictures.
Dale, Edgar. Children's attendance at motion pictures.
Blumer, Herbert, and Philip Hauser. Movies, delinquency, and crime.
Cressey, Paul G., and Frederick M. Thrasher. Boys, movies, and city streets.
Dale, Edgar. How to appreciate motion pictures.

This is a rich series of studies, to which a short summary will not do justice. They represent the best-staffed and best-financed research approach to the questions of childrens' relation to films.

Children from five to eight years old, in the early 1930's, averaged .42 movies a week; children from eight to nineteen averaged .99 movies per week. (This is almost exactly what we found them averaging just before the coming of television.)

At that time in the 1930's, 29.6 per cent of all movie themes were love, 27.4 per cent crime, and 15 per cent sex.

These investigators found that children remembered a very great deal from theater movies. They concluded that an eight- or nine-year-old child will catch three out of five of the items a superior adult will catch, an eleven- or twelve-year-old child will catch three out of four, and a fifteen- or sixteen-year-old will catch nine out of ten. They found the retention curves of this information to be unusually high. Action is remembered best, they said, "when it concerned sports, general conversation, crime, and fighting, when it had a high emotional tonus, and when it occurred in a familiar type of setting such as home, school, or tenement . . . It was understood least when it concerned unfamiliar activities such as bootlegging and business, when it had practically no emotional tonus, and when it occurred in surroundings of an unfamiliar and interesting type such as cafe and frontier." In summary, they said, the amount of information children gain from movies is "tremendously high."

They found, furthermore, that attitudes were often significantly changed by motion pictures. Even though one picture related to a social issue might not significantly change an attitude, the effect is cumulative, and successive exposure to pictures of this type will usually make for an attitude change.

Working with galvanometer and pneumo-cardiograph, they found that movies induced considerable emotional reaction, even when that was not detectable by visual observation of face or movements. In the six- to 12-year-olds, the greatest emotional effect came from scenes of danger and conflict. In these years, erotic scenes had the least effect. Erotic material stirred emotions most with sixteen-year-olds. They caution, however, that there are great individual differences in these respects. They report that 93 per cent of children have been frightened by movies at some time, and that some children lose sleep as a result of movies.

Movies have an influence on children, they hypothesized, chiefly by "taking possession" emotionally of them. This can be avoided by developing "adult discount" or "emotional detachment"—that is, by learning to look at the movie as a story or a play, rather than as the real thing.

Attempting to relate movies to behavior, they concluded that movies do indeed influence children's action, notably the form of their play. They found that a group of delinquents went to the movies more often than a group of nondelinquents, but stopped short of blaming delinquency on the movies. Rather, they pointed out, the causes of such behavior are complex. Movies are only one strand in the experience that goes into delinquency. The influence of movies cannot easily be generalized, they said. It is "specific for a given child and a given movie. The same picture may influence different children in distinctly opposite directions."

55. Lyness, Paul I. "The place of the mass media in the lives of boys and girls," *Journ. Quart.*, 29 (1952), 43–54.

A total of 1,418 children in grades three, five, seven, nine, and eleven in Des Moines, Iowa, were questioned about their media behavior in 1951, prior to the introduction of television in the area. Figures on radio listening and on newspaper, magazine, book, and comic reading are presented. Radio was found to be the one medium children would keep if they had to give up all but one. Radio was picked by children as their favorite source for news and was considered more reliable than newspapers.

56. Schramm, Wilbur, Jack Lyle, and Edwin B. Parker. "Patterns in children's reading of newspapers," *Journ. Quart.*, 37 (1960), 35–40.

Drawing on material from the present study, the authors describe the beginnings of newspaper use (the newspaper is the last of the media to come into real use by children) and the development of a pattern of reading many parts of the paper. Comic reading comes to its height about the fourth grade, thereafter decreases. There is very little general reading of the paper before the sixth grade, and no great amount of daily reading until the eighth grade. During the teen years, however, the newspaper comes to be more read and much more highly valued, especially by the brighter children.

57. Wolfe, Katherine M., and Marjorie Fiske. "Why they read the comics," in Lazarsfeld and Stanton, eds., Communication Research, 1948–49. New York: Harper, 1949.

Basing their conclusions on interviews with children of different ages, the authors say that for normal children comic reading is a means of ego-strengthening, and therefore satisfies real developmental needs. For insecure, maladjusted children, on the other hand, the comics become a substitute for what they do not find in life. Superman becomes a father-figure. The comics provide "an authority and power which settles the more difficult or ultimate issues, enables these children to perform their daily tasks without too much anxiety." These children, therefore, also satisfy an emotional need with comics, but they do not readily outgrow the need. The normal child learns to stand on his feet, and comics become of little importance for him. But for the maladjusted child "the religion of comics is not easily given up, for the child is frightened and no new religion beckons."

58. Zajonc, Robert. "Some effects of the 'space' serials," *Publ. Opin. Quart.*, 18, No. 4 (1954), 367–74.

Two groups of children (thirty-two and forty-five in number) ten to fourteen years old were allowed to listen to different versions of a radio "space" program, in one of which the hero was a power-oriented character, and in the other an affiliation-oriented character. There was also a control group, given the questions but no radio program. Each of the groups said overwhelmingly it would wish to be like the successful character, regardless of the methods used in the program to make him successful. The vote was not quite so unanimous for the power hero as for the cooperative one. Furthermore, the children who saw the power hero also saw the attribute of power as significantly more attractive than did the other group, and they expressed a significantly greater approval of power-based attitudes. Zajonc warns that these changes may not be permanent, but there seems to be reason to believe that, at least in cases like this one, children seem to admire and copy "what works."

### SUMMARIES OF RESEARCH ON INSTRUCTIONAL TELEVISION

59. Allen, William H. "Audio-visual communication research," prepared for the Encyclopedia of educational research, 3d ed., and reproduced in advance (mimeo.) by System Development Corporation, Santa Monica, California, 1959.

This study consists of 343 unannotated titles, and 58 pages of discussion, four and one-half pages directly on instructional television. In general, these pages report evidence on the effectiveness of television as a method of teaching, but they record less clear evidence on the attitudes of students toward it. The commentary is especially useful in that it considers all the audiovisual devices.

60. Carpenter, C. R. "Approaches to promising areas of research in the field of instructional television," in *New teaching aids for the American classroom.* Stanford: Institute for Communication Research, 1960.

Before suggesting needed research, Carpenter sums up the state of research on instructional television by answering eight questions:

1. Can teaching by television be done? "Unequivocally yes."
2. How can it be done? "In a great variety of ways," which he proceeds to specify. One is "with all grades and classes."
3. What are the effects of teaching by television as compared to a wide range of comparable conventional arrangements? "Generally 'no significant differences' have been found. The differences plus or minus from this generalization are not worth arguing about."
4. What are the economy and cost of facilities factors? A good deal of this information is at hand.
5. Does the arrangement of having the "best" teachers instruct over television improve the quality of teaching? "Generally yes," but even superior teachers need special help and preparation for television.
6. Can television be used to provide instruction to students who might not otherwise be taught? Yes, especially to rural students.
7. Can television be used to provide appropriate educational programs for dispersed adult populations including professional groups? Yes, this has been demonstrated most impressively.
8. Can television be used to consolidate and combine educational resources of a section, state, or region? This, too, has been successfully demonstrated.

A list of thirty-six selected titles accompanies the article.

61. Coffin, T. E. "Television's impact on society," *Amer. Psychologist,* 10 (1955), 630–41.

A review of research, discussing and comparing evidence on the impact of TV on society in various ways, including effects on family and social activities, on children, school achievement, leisure activities, and home behavior.

62. Finn, J. D. "Television and education: a review of research," *AV Communication Rev.,* 1 (1953), 106–26.

A carefully detailed summary and review of the research literature on television prior to 1953.

63. Hoban, C. F., and E. B. Van Ormer. Instructional film research, 1918–1950. Special Devices Center Human Engineering Project 20-E-4. Port Washington, N.Y.: Special Devices Center (U.S. Army), 1951.

Useful gathering of hypotheses and summaries of research from studies of teaching film, through 1949. Many of these results are applicable to instructional television.

64. Kumata, Hideya. "Ten years of instructional television research," in Schramm, ed., The impact of educational television. Urbana: University of Illinois Press, 1960.

This article is an updating of Kumata's earlier summary, *An Inventory of Instructional Television Research* (Ann Arbor: Educational Television and Radio Center, 1956). This article lists 121 research titles and summarizes the state of knowledge. Kumata's general conclusions:

1. The mode of presentation, TV or face-to face, apparently has little effect on how much knowledge is retained by the audience.

2. Motivation, however, is a prime variable in determining how much is retained. Voluntary classes usually learn more than captive audiences.

3. Adequate and skillful preparation of subject matter, and integration into a teaching process, are prime factors. This may be one reason why superiority of TV is reported more often at elementary than at higher levels.

4. Television seems to affect different intelligence levels differently, but the pattern is not quite understood as yet.

5. Interaction is an important factor. If a television audience has talk-back facilities, that serves as at least a partial substitute for face-to-face interaction.

6. Attitudes toward TV are not related to amount of learning, but are related to the student's likelihood of taking another class by TV.

## OTHER SOURCES

65. Banay, R. S. "Testimony before the Subcommittee to investigate juvenile delinquency, of the Committee on the Judiciary, United States Senate, Eighty-fourth Congress." *S. Res. 62.* April 1955. Washington, D.C.: United States Government Printing Office, 1955.

66. Barrow, Lionel C., Jr., and Bruce H. Westley. "Intelligence and the effectiveness of radio and television," *Audio-Visual Communication Review,* 7, No. 3 (Summer, 1959), 193–208.

67. British Broadcasting Corporation. Minors—an enquiry into the interests, listening and viewing, and availability of the 5–20 year old population of the United Kingdom. BBC Audience Research Report, 1954.

68. *Daedalus* (Proceedings, Journal of the American Academy of Arts and Sciences), 89, No. 2 (Spring, 1960). Special number of "Mass Culture and Mass Media."

69. Geiger, Kent, and Robert Sokol. "Educational television in Boston," in Schramm, ed., The impact of educational television. Urbana: University of Illinois, 1960.

70. Gorer, Geoffrey, "Television in our lives," The Sunday *Times* (London), April 13–May 4, 1958.

71. Graham, S. "Cultural compatibility in the adoption of television," *Social Forces*, 33 (1954), 166–70.

A sample of 150 heads of households, stratified by socioeconomic class, was drawn from the New Haven, Connecticut, area to test the following hypothesis: "The more closely the behavior demanded for use of the innovation is compatible with the structure of the culture prior to its introduction, the greater are the chances of its acceptance." Accepters of television were found to be more likely than rejecters to be people of low education, low income, who read no nonfiction books and who spent more time than rejecters listening to radio and attending movies. Rejecters of television were more likely to engage in active kinds of recreation and to belong to more voluntary organizations. It was concluded that when the recreation behavior employed without television is compatible with the kind of behavior associated with television, acceptance is most apt to take place.

72. Hovland, Carl I. "Effects of the mass media of communication," in G. Lindzey, ed., Handbook of social psychology. Cambridge: Addison Wesley, 1954.

73. Hovland, Carl I., Irving L. Janis, and Harold H. Kelley. Communication and Persuasion. New Haven: Yale, 1953.

74. Hyman, H. H. "The value systems of different classes: a social psychological contribution to the analysis of stratification," in Bendix and Lipset, eds., Class, status, and power. Glencoe: Free Press, 1953.

75. Klapper, Joseph. The effects of mass communication. Glencoe: The Free Press, 1960.

76. Klapper, Joseph. "The effects of mass communication" (mimeo.), 1959.

77. Lazarsfeld, Paul F. Radio and the printed page. New York: Duell, Sloan, and Pearce, 1940.

78. Lazarsfeld, Paul F., and Patricia Kendall. Radio listening in America. New York: Pentice Hall, 1948.

79. Lazarsfeld, Paul F., and Frank Stanton. Communications research, 1948–49. New York, 1949.

80. Lazarsfeld, Paul F., and Frank Stanton. Radio research, 1941. New York: Duell, Sloan, and Pearce, 1941.

81. Lazarsfeld, Paul F., and Frank Stanton. Radio research, 1942–43. New York: Duell, Sloan, and Pearce, 1944.

82. Maccoby, Eleanor E. "Role-taking in childhood and its consequences for social learning," *Child Development*, 30 (1959), 239–52.

83. McNemar, Q. Psychological statistics. 2d ed. New York: Wiley, 1955.

84. Mehling, Reuben. Quoted in Poynter McEvoy. "Media habit survey of Indiana homes," *Journalism Quarterly*, 36 (Winter 1959), 63–64.

85. Purdue Opinion Panel. Four years of New York television, 1951–1954. Urbana, Illinois: National Association of Educational Broadcasters, 1954.
    (See also other monitoring studies published by NAEB, and chiefly under the direction of Dallas Smythe. These include Los Angeles, Chicago, and New Haven, as well as three previous New York studies.)

86. Remmers, H. H., R. E. Horton, and R. E. Mainer. Attitudes of high school students towards certain aspects of television. Lafayette: Purdue Opinion Panel Report 36, 1953.

87. Riley, M. W., and S. Flowerman. "Group relations as a variable in communication research," *Amer. Sociol. Rev.*, 16 (1951), 174–80.

88. Siepmann, C. A. Radio, television, and society. New York: Oxford, 1950.

89. Snedecor, G. W. *Statistical Methods*. 4th ed. Ames, Iowa: Iowa State College Press, 1946.

90. Stuckrath, F., and G. Schottmayer. Psychologie des Film-Erlebens in Kindheit und Jugend. Hamburg: Verlag der Schropp'schen Lehrmittelanstalt, 1955.

91. "Television and the eyes" (unsigned), *Vision*, 6 (1952), 9–11.

# INDEX OF NAMES

# GENERAL INDEX

Addiction, does television cause? 167–68

"Adult discount," 133 ⨭

Adult life, picture of; too early knowledge, 4; in children's television hours, 140; is television's picture inaccurate? 155

Adult programs, children's viewing of, 42–45, 231

Adventure programs, 137–39, 230–31, and *passim*

Advertising, parents' opinions of, 56 ⨭

Age: and amount of viewing, 30 ff.; and program taste, 45; and prestige of media, 51 ff.; and effects, 144 ff.; and beginnings of media use, table, 219

Aggression: and television behavior, 120 ff.; aggression anxiety, projective aggression, attenuated aggression, self-aggression, prosocial aggression, antisocial aggression, tests of, 120 ff.; relation to fantasy seeking, 121 ff.; relation to parent-child conflict, 128–29; when does television reduce? 131–34; "critical mass" of, 133–34; and passivity, 158–61; and interpersonal relationships, 289 ff.

Amount of viewing, 169–70; in early months of television, 14–15; in Teletown, 17–18; how measure? 29; individual differences in, 29–30; at different ages, 30 ff.; by day and hour, 31 ff.; heavy viewers, 32–35; and mental ability, 34–35, 79–82; related to social norms, 98 ff.; "high users," "low users," 99 ff.; related to conflict, 118 ff.; problem of estimating 213 ff.; tables, 219 ff.; by types, 231–33; and reality or fantasy seeking, 280 ff.

Anxiety, when does television cause? 148–49. *See also* Aggression

Aspirations: educational, 113, 123–24; difference between children's and parents', 124 ff., 289 ff.; occupational, 125

Attitudes toward television, 48 ff., 170; "missing" the media, 48–50, 234–37; trust in television, 50–52; effect of scandals on, ⨭

51; prestige of television, 51–53; prestige of other media, 53, 238–39; changes children would like, 54–55; changes parents would like, 55–56; and mental ability, 82, 235, 237, 239, 241; tables, 234 ff.

Bedtime: effect of television on, 14–15, 17, 147–48; Radiotown and Teletown compared, 73; in suburb, 223

Beginning of television use, 17, 24 ff., 219–20

Behavioral effects, *see* Effects

Bibliography, 295 ff.

Books: beginning of children's use of, 24 ff.; amount of use of, 35–37; related to parents, 47; children's attitudes toward, 51 ff.; Radiotown and Teletown compared, 71; children's present use of, 244–45, tables, 248 ff.; and reality or fantasy seeking, 280 ff.

Broadcasters, responsibilities of, 175 ff.; violence in programs, 176–77; challenge in program, 177–78; picture of adult life, 178–79 ⨭

Brutality, *see* Violence

California mental maturity test, *see* Methodology

Canada studies, 9, 15 ff., 201–3, 206–8. *See also* Radiotown; Teletown

Cartoon programs, 37 ff., 137, 230–33

Center for Advanced Study in the Behavioral Sciences, vii

Centers scale, 106

Changes desired in television, *see* Attitudes toward television

Children's programs, 43–45. *See also* Program preferences ⨭

Clifton study, 9, 203–4, 206–7, 209

Cognitive effects, *see* Effects

Comedy, *see* Program preferences

Comic books, 18; amount of use of, 35–37;